Scoring the Rorschach

Seven Validated Systems

The LEA Series in Personality and Clinical Psychology
Irving B. Weiner, Editor

Bornstein/Masling (Eds.) • *Scoring the Rorschach: Seven Validated Systems*
Calhoun/Tedeschi • *Facilitating Posttraumatic Growth: A Clinician's Guide*
Dana (Ed.) • *Handbook of Cross-Cultural and Multicultural Personality Assessment*
Eisen/Quas/Goodman (Eds.) • *Memory and Suggestibility in the Forensic Interview*
Exner (Ed.) • *Issues and Methods in Rorschach Research*
Frederick/McNeal • *Inner Strengths: Contemporary Psychotherapy and Hypnosis for Ego-Strengthening*
Gacono (Ed.) • *The Clinical and Forensic Assessment of Psychopathy: A Practitioner's Guide*
Gacono/Meloy • *The Rorschach Assessment of Aggressive and Psychopathic Personalities*
Ganellen • *Integrating the Rorschach and the MMPI-2 in Personality Assessment*
Goodman/Rudorfer/Maser (Eds.) • *Obsessive-Compulsive Disorder: Contemporary Issues in Treatment*
Hall/Bernieri (Eds.) • *Interpersonal Sensitivity: Theory and Measurement*
Handler/Hilsenroth (Eds.) • *Teaching and Learning Personality Assessment*
Hy/Loevinger • *Measuring Ego Development, Second Edition*
Kelly • *The Assessment of Object Relations Phenomena in Adolescents: TAT and Rorschach Measures*
Kelly • *The Psychological Assessment of Abused and Traumatized Children*
Kohnstamm/Halverson/Mervielde/Havill (Eds.) • *Parental Descriptions of Child Personality: Developmental Antecedents of the Big Five?*
Loevinger (Ed.) • *Technical Foundations for Measuring Ego Development: The Washington University Sentence Completion Test*
McCallum/Piper (Eds.) • *Psychological Mindedness: A Contemporary Understanding*
Meloy/Acklin/Gacono/Murray/Peterson (Eds.) • *Contemporary Rorschach Interpretation*
Needleman • *Cognitive Case Conceptualization: A Guidebook for Practitioners*
Nielsen/Johnson/Albert Ellis Institute • *Counseling and Psychotherapy With Religious Persons: A Rational Emotive Behavior Therapy Approach*
Nolen-Hoeksema/Larson • *Coping With Loss*
Rosowsky/Abrams/Zwieg (Eds.) • *Personality Disorders in the Elderly: Emerging Issues in Diagnosis and Treatment*
Sarason/Pierce/Sarason (Eds.) • *Cognitive Interference: Theories, Methods, and Findings*
Silverstein • *Self Psychology and Diagnostic Assessment: Identifying Selfobject Functions Through Psychological Testing*
Taylor (Ed.) • *Anxiety Sensitivity: Theory, Research, and Treatment of the Fear of Anxiety*
Tedeschi/Park/Calhoun (Eds.) • *Posttraumatic Growth: Positive Changes in the Aftermath of Crisis*
Van Hasselt/Hersen (Eds.) • *Handbook of Psychological Treatment Protocols for Children and Adolescents*
Weiner • *Principles of Rorschach Interpretation*
Wong/Fry (Eds.) • *The Human Quest for Meaning: A Handbook of Psychological Research and Clinical Applications*
Zillmer/Harrower/Ritzler/Archer • *The Quest for the Nazi Personality: A Psychological Investigation of Nazi War Criminals*

Scoring the Rorschach

Seven Validated Systems

Edited by

Robert F. Bornstein
Gettysburg College

Joseph M. Masling
State University of New York at Buffalo

LAWRENCE ERLBAUM ASSOCIATES, PUBLISHERS
2005 Mahwah, New Jersey London

Lawrence Erlbaum Associates, Inc., Publishers
10 Industrial Avenue
Mahwah, New Jersey 07430
www.erlbaum.com

Cover design by Kathryn Houghtaling Lacey

Library of Congress Cataloging-in-Publication Data

Scoring the Rorschach : seven validated systems / [edited by] Robert F. Bornstein, Joseph M. Masling.
p. cm.
Includes bibliographical references and index.
ISBN 0-8058-4734-0 (cloth : alk. paper)
1. Rorschach Test. I. Bornstein, Robert F. II. Masling, Joseph M.
BF698.8.R5S36 2005
155.2'842—dc22 2004053321
CIP

Books published by Lawrence Erlbaum Associates are printed on acid-free paper, and their bindings are chosen for strength and durability.

Printed in the United States of America
10 9 8 7 6 5 4 3 2 1

To Seymour Fisher and Philip Holzman,
valued friends and colleagues,
whose pioneering work has inspired
generations of clinicians

Contents

About the Contributors

Robert F. Bornstein received his PhD in clinical psychology from the State University of New York at Buffalo in 1986, and is Professor of Psychology at Gettysburg College. He has written numerous articles on personality assessment, personality disorders, and unconscious mental processes. Dr. Bornstein wrote *The Dependent Personality* (Guilford Press, 1993), coauthored (with Mary Languirand) *When Someone You Love Needs Nursing Home Care* (Newmarket Press, 2001), and *Healthy Dependency* (Newmarket Press, 2003), coedited (with Thane Pittman) *Perception Without Awareness: Cognitive, Clinical, and Social Perspectives* (Guilford Press, 1992), and coedited (with Joseph Masling) six volumes of the *Empirical Studies of Psychoanalytic Theories* book series (APA). Dr. Bornstein's research has been funded by grants from the National Institutes of Mental Health and the National Science Foundation, and he received the Society for Personality Assessment's 1995, 1999, and 2003 Awards for Distinguished Contributions to the Personality Assessment Literature.

Joseph M. Masling is Emeritus Professor of Psychology at the State University of New York at Buffalo. He has written numerous articles on interpersonal and situational variables influencing projective tests, and has published widely on the empirical study of psychoanalytic concepts. Dr. Masling edited the first three volumes of the *Empirical Studies of Psychoanalytic Theories* book series (APA, 1983, 1986, 1990); coedited with Robert F. Bornstein an additional six volumes, *Psychoanalytic Perspectives on Developmental Psychology* (APA, 1996), *Empirical Studies of the Therapeutic Hour* (APA, 1998), *Empirical Perspectives on the Psychoanalytic Unconscious* (APA, 1998), and *The Psychodynamics of Gender and Gender Role* (APA, 2002); and coedited with Paul R. Duberstein one volume in the series, *Psychodynamic Perspectives on Sickness and Health* (APA, 2000).

Dr. Masling received the Society for Personality Assessment's 1997 Bruno Klopfer Award for Lifetime Achievement in Personality Assessment.

John S. Auerbach, PhD, is a staff psychologist and Coordinator of the Post-Traumatic Stress Program at the James H. Quillen Veterans Affairs Medical Center in Mountain Home, Tennessee. He is a professor of psychiatry and Behavioral Sciences in the James H. Quillen College of Medicine at East Tennessee State University and a research affiliate in Psychiatry at the Yale University School of Medicine. He is also in private practice in Johnson City, Tennessee. He is an honorary member of the American Psychoanalytic Association, and he serves on the editorial board of *Psychoanalytic Psychology*. With Kenneth Levy and Carrie Schaffer, he is coeditor of *Relatedness, Self-Definition, and Mental Representation: Essays in Honor of Sidney J. Blatt*, to be published by Brunner-Routledge in 2004. In addition to post-traumatic stress disorder, his interests include projective testing, borderline disorders, narcissism, and the relationships among intersubjectivity, representational processes, and the development of the self.

Sidney J. Blatt, PhD, Professor of Psychiatry and Psychology at Yale University, is also Chief of the Psychology Section, Department of Psychiatry, Yale University School of Medicine. He is a graduate and member of the faculty of the Western New England Psychoanalytic Institute. His primary interests are in the development of mental representations, their differential impairment in various forms of psychopathology (especially schizophrenia and depression), and their change in the therapeutic process. His most recent book, *Experiences of Depression: Theoretical, Clinical, and Research perspectives*, was published in 2004 by the American Psychological Association.

Amanda Jill Clemence is completing a postdoctoral fellowship at Pennsylvania Hospital, University of Pennsylvania Health System, in Philadelphia. Dr. Clemence earned her PhD in clinical psychology from the University of Tennessee. She has published several works on the use of projective assessment with clinical populations and is currently conducting research exploring the use of therapeutic assessment with cancer patients and their families. Additional research interests include the investigation of the effectiveness of group psychotherapy in addressing the psychosocial adjustment of breast cancer patients.

Leonard Handler, PhD, is Professor of Psychology and Associate Director of the clinical training program at the University of Tennessee. President of the Society for Personality Assessment, a Diplomate of the American Board of Assessment Psychology, and a Fellow of the American Psychological Association, he has lectured and published nationally and internationally on personality assessment, psychotherapy, and other related areas. He is also the coeditor of *Teaching and Learning Personality Assessment* (Lawrence Erlbaum Associates, 1998).

Robert R. Holt was educated at Princeton and Harvard, and worked in survey research before being trained in diagnostic testing by David Rapaport. He left Topeka, where he was Chief Psychologist at the Menninger Foundation, to direct the Research Center for Mental Health at New York University in 1953, and was made professor in 1958. Before his retirement in 1989, Dr. Holt received the Great Teacher award, was founding director of the Program on Peace and Global Policy Studies, and held a Research Career Award from NIMH for 26 years. He was President of the Division of Clinical Psychology (APA Division 12) from 1961 to 1962, received the Society for Personality Assessment's Great Man Award (now the Bruno Klopfer Award) in 1969, and received the Division 12 Award for Distinguished Contributions to Clinical Psychology in 1974. Dr. Holt is the author or editor of seventeen books and about 250 other publications.

Philip S. Holzman was the Esther and Sidney R. Rabb Professor of Psychology, Emeritus, at Harvard University. Before moving to Harvard he was a professor in the Departments of Psychiatry and Behavioral Science at the University of Chicago. He published many research articles on the psychophysiology and genetics of schizophrenia as well as on contemporary issues in psychoanalysis. He received his clinical training at the Menninger Foundation under David Rapaport and received psychoanalytic training at the Topeka Institute of Psychoanalysis.

Mary Hollis Johnston received her PhD from the Committee on Human Development at the University of Chicago in 1975. She is currently a clinical psychologist in private practice in Chicago, Illinois. She is also a faculty member in the Department of Psychiatry at the University of Chicago and a training analyst at the Center for Psychoanalytic Study, where she specializes in the assessment and treatment of children and adults with psychotic conditions.

Paul M. Lerner, PhD, ABPP, is in the private practice of psychoanalysis, psychotherapy, and psychological testing in Camden, Maine. He is also a consultant to several teams in the National Hockey League. A past president of the Society for Personality Assessment, he was the 1996 recipient of the Society's Bruno Klopfer Award for distinguished contributions to personality assessment. He has authored two books and coedited numerous others on the Rorschach, and has written numerous articles on psychoanalytic theory, therapy, and the Rorschach. His 1991 book *Psychoanalytic Theory and the Rorschach* (Atlantic Press) received an award from the Menninger Foundation.

Deborah L. Levy received her PhD in 1976 from the Department of Psychology at the University of Chicago. She received clinical training at New York Hospital-Cornell Medical Center and at the Menninger Foundation. She is codirector of the Psychology Research Laboratory at McLean Hospital, the teaching hospital of the Harvard Medical School, where she is an associate professor in the Department of Psychiatry. She has published widely on psychophysiological studies of schizophrenia as well as on the Thought Disorder index, which she has used in research studies and in clinical practice.

Kenneth N. Levy is an assistant professor in the Department of Psychology at the Pennsylvania State University. He is also an adjunct assistant professor of psychology in psychiatry in the Department of Psychiatry at the Joan and Sanford I. Weill Medical College of Cornell University. He conducts research on child and adult attachment, affect regulation, borderline personality disorder, and psychotherapy process and outcome. He also maintains a private practice in State College, PA.

Kevin B. Meehan, who earned a BA in psychology from New York University and an MA from John Jay College, City University of New York, is currently a doctoral candidate in clinical psychology at City College and the Graduate School and University Center, City University of New York. His research interests include the development of mental representations, language, and affect regulation in childhood, and the impact of impairment in these lines of development on personality and character structure across the lifespan.

Richard M. O'Neill, PhD, is an associate professor in psychiatry and behavioral sciences at the State University of New York Upstate Medical University. Like Fisher and Cleveland (Dover, 1968), he is interested in how the psychological boundaries of individuals and groups can be enhanced to improve functioning. He finds Agazarian's theory of living human systems and Systems-Centered Therapy intriguing and potentially fruitful frameworks for conceptualizing, investigating, and intervening.

Foreword

Rorschach assessment generates three sources of information about the personality characteristics of respondents. *Structural* features of Rorschach responses provide representative indications of how people are likely to think, feel, and act. Such representation occurs, for example, when a high XA% indicates generally accurate perception of people and events, when a high Lambda indicates a narrowly focused and uncomplicated way of attending to experience, and when introversiveness indicates a preference for deliberation and contemplation as opposed to an action-oriented approach to solving problems.

Thematic features of Rorschach responses contain symbolic clues to underlying attitudes and concerns that are likely to influence how people interpret and react to situations. Such symbolization occurs, for example, when an image of "someone hurt and bleeding" suggests possible morbid preoccupation with vulnerability to being harmed, when "eyes looking out from behind a bush" suggests possible hypervigilant preoccupation with being under the scrutiny of others, and when "two people leaning against each other" suggests possible yearnings for mutually cooperative and dependent interpersonal relationships.

Behavioral features of how respondents handle the testing situation and interact with the examiner exemplify their customary manner of dealing with task-oriented and interpersonal situations. Such behavioral manifestations occur, for example, when saying "I don't think I'm doing very well on this test" identifies self-critical attitudes and negative expectations of success, and when repetitively addressing the examiner as "doctor," "sir," or "ma'am" identifies a deferential stance toward persons in authority.

Each of these Rorschach sources of information is most likely to serve useful purposes, and to be validated for these purposes, when it is quantified into reliably coded scales. The emergence of the Comprehensive System (CS) for the Rorschach Inkblot Method (RIM), by virtue of providing numerous quantitative scales in the context of a standard format for administration and coding, contributed substantially to strengthening the psychometric foundations of Rorschach assessment and expanding its areas of application. Separately from the development of the CS, and in some instances preceding it, other sound and useful scales for quantifying structural and thematic Rorschach data have also emerged in the hands of skilled clinicians and researchers. In this edited volume, Robert Bornstein and Joseph Masling present state-of-the-art reviews of seven such coding systems.

The editors begin their book with an overview chapter in which they discuss the evolution of the RIM, issues concerning validation and use of the instrument, and guidelines for future Rorschach research and practice. In the course of this informative chapter, Masling and Bornstein call special attention to the importance of distinguishing between the RIM as an assessment method and the CS as one approach to working with the data that Rorschach administrations generate. While acknowledging the value of the CS and the widespread reliance of Rorschach clinicians on it, they urge readers to keep in mind that the RIM and the CS are not synonymous and that valuable approaches to scoring and interpreting Rorschach responses exist outside of the CS.

In five of the seven chapters that follow the editors' introduction, Rorschach scoring systems are reviewed in part by their original author(s): Philip Holzman on the Thought Disorder index, in collaboration with Deborah Levy and Mary Hollis Johnston; Sidney Blatt on the Concept of the Object scale, in collaboration with Kenneth Levy, Kevin Meehan, and John Auerbach; Bornstein and Masling on the Rorschach Oral Dependency scale; Robert Holt on Primary Process scales; and Paul Lerner on Rorschach Defense scales. The other two chapters concern Klopfer's Rorschach Prognostic Rating scale, reviewed by Leonard Handler and Amanda Jill Clemence, and Fisher and Cleveland's Rorschach Boundary and Barrier-Penetration scoring, reviewed by Richard O'Neill.

Each of these seven chapters describes the conceptual underpinnings of the particular system and delineates guidelines for its scoring and interpretation. This information has previously been scattered in diverse sources, many of which are not readily available. This Bornstein and Masling volume now allows clinicians and researchers to access in one source the essential elements of understanding and applying these seven approaches to Rorschach data. Each chapter also includes a current literature review, with special attention to research findings relevant to the reliability and validity of the system being discussed. Assessment psychologists and Rorschach students and scholars in particular will appreciate the contribution the editors and contributors have made in preparing this fine volume.

—Irving B. Weiner

Preface

This book was born of controversy. For nearly a decade, the pages of psychology's leading assessment journals have been filled with articles criticizing the Rorschach inkblot method (RIM), sometimes in blunt—even scathing—terms. Each critical article has brought forth a response from RIM proponents; in many cases these rebuttals have been as strongly worded as the critiques that prompted them.

Psychologists on both sides of this debate have made many valid points regarding the strengths and limitations of the RIM, but as the dialogue evolved an unfortunate event occurred: Although many of the disagreements center on one particular RIM scoring method—Exner's Comprehensive System (CS)—this fact has become lost in the ongoing exchange. To many Rorschach critics, the CS has come to symbolize the RIM, and at times these two distinct entities are discussed as if they were one and the same. As a result, many clinicians and clinical researchers have lost sight of the fact that there are other useful RIM scoring systems in use today. Some of these systems have yielded compelling findings, and have the potential to enhance use of the RIM in clinical and research settings. Before this can occur, psychologists and other mental health professionals must recognize the value of these alternative RIM scoring systems in assessing personality and psychopathology.

Given these considerations, we believe the time has come for an edited volume focusing on non-CS RIM scoring and interpretation. That is the purpose of this book. By providing detailed reviews of well-validated alternative RIM systems, the chapters in this volume encourage continued growth and refinement of these interpretive frameworks, and facilitate constructive dialogue and collaboration among RIM researchers with different backgrounds and interests.

This volume has not only noteworthy clinical and empirical implications, but important policy implications as well. During the past decade the debates between RIM proponents and critics, which began in journals such as *Psychological Science, Psychological Assessment, Journal of Personality Assessment*, and *Journal of Clinical Psychology*, have spilled over into journals outside the mental health field, and even into the popular press. Proposals by RIM opponents include a severe restriction on reimbursement for projective testing in clinical settings, because these critics believe evidence supporting the concurrent and predictive validity of projective measures is weak. Some critics would also ban RIM use in the courts because they contend the RIM fails to meet Daubert criteria for admissibility.

Make no mistake: These critiques influence the broader professional community for the same reason they have resonated within the mental health community. RIM opponents have focused largely on global, impressionistic use of the Rorschach, and on limitations in the CS. In the minds of many attorneys, judges, medical policy makers, and members of the media, problems with the CS (in particular) have been taken as evidence that the RIM (in general) is flawed. We hope this book will make explicit the fact that RIM research is broader than critics admit, with first-rate research being carried out on a variety of scoring and interpretive systems.

The chapters in this volume span a range of topics and issues—mental representations and psychological defenses, personality traits and thought disorder, body boundaries and psychotherapy potential. Some scoring methods focus exclusively on thematic content in Rorschach responses; others integrate thematic and structural data. Some of these systems are designed specifically for clinical populations; others are used in community samples as well. Despite their diversity, these RIM methods share a common quality: They have been validated extensively in laboratory and clinical settings so that the empirical underpinnings of each system are strong and compelling.

To set the stage for chapters reviewing specific RIM systems, chapter 1 opens with the editors' overview of RIM scoring and interpretation. The evolution of the Rorschach method is discussed, as are issues related to methodology, validation, and clinical use. Suggestions for strengthening the empirical foundation of the RIM are offered to set the stage for continued growth during the coming years.

Chapters 2 and 3 describe RIM scoring systems with extensive clinical applications. In chapter 2 Leonard Handler and Amanda Jill Clemence review research on the Rorschach Prognostic Rating scale, an index of psychotherapy potential that has been tested extensively in recent years using traditional research methods and meta-analytic techniques. In chapter 3 Philip Holzman, Deborah Levy, and Mary Hollis Johnston describe Holzman's Thought Disorder index. As this chapter illustrates, a well-constructed RIM scale is capable not only of generating compelling validity data, but also of bridging the gap between clinical research and findings in other areas of psychology, including cognitive neuroscience.

Chapters 4 and 5 describe RIM scoring methods that have been validated extensively (and used frequently) on community as well as clinical samples. In chapter 3 Kenneth Levy, Kevin Meehan, John Auerbach, and Sidney Blatt discuss the concept of the object in the Rorschach. Since this scoring method was first developed by Blatt and his colleagues in the mid-1970s it has been updated and refined considerably, illustrating the responsiveness of RIM researchers to theoretical changes and accumulating evidence. In chapter 4 Robert Bornstein and Joseph Masling describe the development and validation of the Rorschach Oral Dependency scale, which has been used in more than sixty published studies during the past 35 years. Research using this measure underscores the importance of distinguishing personality data based on self-reports from those derived from measures (like the Rorschach) that circumvent many self-presentation effects.

The final three chapters describe RIM scoring methods that assess internal mental processes which have clear implications for psychological assessment and treatment. In chapter 6 Richard O'Neill discusses Seymour Fisher's Barrier-Penetration scoring system, a method of quantifying concerns regarding body boundary and body integrity, and linking these scores to other dimensions of personality and psychopathology. In chapter 7 Robert Holt discusses his approach to assessing primary process thought on the Rorschach. Holt's groundbreaking research is important not only because of its theoretical and empirical contributions, but also because of its broader impact on assessment psychology: Holt's work is a model for other RIM researchers who seek to quantify elusive psychological constructs.

In chapter 8, the book's closing chapter, Paul Lerner reviews research on the Rorschach assessment of defense, a topic particularly amenable to measurement via the RIM. Lerner's review makes a compelling case that when these types of "hidden" constructs are assessed, the RIM is not merely a substitute for more traditional measures, but taps a unique dimension of functioning that cannot be uncovered via self-report tests.

We are indebted to these authors—leading figures in Rorschach research—for contributing compelling and cogent reviews. We would also like to thank several people who contributed to this volume in important ways; without them the book could not have been written. We are grateful to Susan Milmoe, who supported this project from its inception and helped turn an idea into reality. We are indebted to Irving Weiner for his confidence and encouragement, and for providing a Foreword that underscores the importance of empirical research on the RIM. We would like to thank Kristen Depken for her help in organizing our efforts and staying one step ahead of us on each detail. Finally, we would like to thank Larry Erlbaum. His longstanding commitment to the Rorschach has helped generations of clinicians to realize the potential of this valuable clinical and research tool.

1

Scoring the Rorschach: Retrospect and Prospect

Joseph M. Masling
SUNY-Buffalo

Robert F. Bornstein
Gettysburg College

To communicate with Mars, converse with spirits,
To report the behaviour of the sea monster,
Describe the horoscope, haruspicate or scry,
Observe disease in signatures, evoke
Biographies from the wrinkles of the palm
And tragedy from fingers, riddle the inevitable
With playing cards, fiddle with pentagrams
Or barbituric acids or dissect
The recurrent image into pre-conscious terrors—
To explore the womb, or tomb or dreams; all these are usual
Pastimes and drugs, and features of the press;
And always will be, some of them especially
When there is distress of nations and perplexity
Whether on the shores of Asia, or in the Edgware Road.
Men's curiosity searches past and future
And clings to that dimension ...
—Eliot (1943, p. 27)

In the beginning was the test. The fear of the unknown, the need to reduce ambiguity, and the desire to predict the future are as old as humanity. For the Romans the preferred medium for divination was bird entrails. The *haruspex*, the entrails reader, in the ritual of auspicium would examine the innards of a fowl to see what the Fates had in store.[1]

[1]From *auspicium* comes the word auspicious, a rosy forecast.

The haruspex relied considerably on form and color, as with inkblots, though the material examined was liver rather than cardboard cards. Skill in liver reading was so important that Cicero wrote a treatise, "De Divinatione," on the subject. Before risking their armies to danger, the Greeks consulted the oracle to decide where and when it was safe to wage war.

Though widely used, poultry were not the only media used to decipher the unknown in the early days of testing. Reading tea leaves (tasseography) was an ancient attempt to foretell the future and to this day there are those who practice this form of prophecy; several web sites give information and advice on tasseography. Even the Old Testament reports several instances of requests for divination. In I Samuel 28:3–19, Saul asks a medium to raise Samuel from the dead so Samuel can predict the outcome of a battle. (Saul was probably unhappy with the medium's prediction: He was to be killed.)

Questionnaires and behavioral measures also have long histories. More than 4,000 years ago, Chinese officials developed a series of tests to predict success in civil servant positions (Kaplan & Saccuzzo, 2001). The Summarians, too, invented a psychological test, constructing a word-association technique to help diagnose those plagued by devils: "They would pronounce a list of stimulus words and watch reactions. When the patient became agitated, they would note the word and relate it to the devil which was bothering him" (Barclay, 1991, p. 196).

Tests of various sorts are efforts by which societies attempt to match their members' talents with group needs. Not every citizen has the aptitude necessary to become expert in farming, pearl diving, carpentry, or nursing, and the proper test, properly used, can help with this task. In the United States the history of psychology and the history of psychological testing are inextricably intertwined. From efforts during the first World War to create an easily administered, easily scored intelligence test, to the considerably more sophisticated current attempts to assess human skills, traits, and psychiatric disorders, psychologists have been involved in test construction, administration, and interpretation. For many members of the community, psychologists are people who use psychological tests.

THE RORSCHACH INKBLOT METHOD AS A PROVIDER OF ANSWERS

It was inevitable that as assessment became more widespread, both the public and psychologists would hold unrealistic expectations for psychological tests, the public because it needed to believe that psychological science could provide answers to its problems, and psychologists because they needed to believe that their recommendations about the fate of others were based on scientific evidence. It is a daunting responsibility to determine which job candidate should be hired, whether someone can benefit from psychotherapy (and if so what type), whether it is safe to discharge a psychiatric patient from the hospital, or whether a defendant was legally insane at the time of a crime. Those who make such decisions have a strong motive to believe in the integrity of their data and their ability to interpret those data.

Many psychological tests developed a strong following during the height of the mid-twentieth-century psychometric movement, but the Rorschach Inkblot Method (RIM) was held by some to be a uniquely powerful means for revealing the psyche—a sort of psychological X-ray that enabled the psychologist to peer inside the mind just as a radiologist peers inside the body (Frank, 1939). In 1942, Lewis declared that the Rorschach method:

> reveals the basic organization of the personality structure, including the fundamental affective and cognitive features of mental life .... [It is] remarkably effective in estimating the intellectual status of an individual; in revealing the richness or poverty of his psychic experience; in making known his present mood .... In psychiatry, the validity of the method as a diagnostic instrument has been established. It points the way to new understanding of mental disorders. (p. ix)

Two decades later, Schachtel (1966) asserted that the Rorschach test offered "the first major contribution to the problem of perception and personality, which, in the past twenty or thirty years, has become one of the foremost issues in psychology" (p. 1).

These optimistic statements, however well intentioned, were born of hope and faith, not replicated empirical results. Their unabashed optimism helped produce a backlash against the RIM that continues to this day (see Wood, Nezworski, Lilienfeld, & Garb, 2003).

The quasi-formlessness of the Rorschach inkblots compels respondents to provide interpretations based on their prior experiences, associations, personal histories, and culture. In its most basic form, the projective hypothesis held that "we reveal ourselves in the way we deal with unstructured stimuli" (Korchin, 1976, p. 126). However, the many meanings of projection (see Juni, 1980, for a useful discussion) make this concept unreliable as a descriptor of those assessment methods that bear its name. A lively controversy over the extent to which projection can be said to underlie responses to inkblots was recently developed by Hibbard (2003); as usual, proponents and critics of the Rorschach method have diametrically opposing views on the subject.

A MORE CAREFUL EXAMINATION OF THE RIM

In due time, academic psychologists began to investigate empirically the claims made by Rorschach proponents (see Masling, 2002). As might be expected, the training and professional affiliations of the investigators influenced the methods they chose and the results they reported. Thus, when Levy and Orr (1959) examined 168 Rorschach validity studies published between 1951 and 1955, they found systematic differences in methodology and outcome as a function of the researchers' professional affiliation. Academic psychologists investigated construct validity far more often than criterion validity (73 studies vs. 35), whereas nonacademic researchers' experimenters had a more even balance (28 construct validity studies vs. 32 criterion validity studies).

Professional affiliation also moderated the outcome (as well as the content) of RIM investigations in Levy and Orr's (1959) survey: Academic psychologists who studied construct validity found positive results more frequently than negative ones by about a 2-to-l ratio, but when they studied criterion validity the ratio of significant to nonsignificant results was 1 to 2. In contrast, positive and negative results obtained by the nonacademic psychologists were about evenly divided for construct and criterion validity studies. Clearly, those on each side of the issue came to this question showing the effects of particular training programs, institutional loyalties, and theoretical preferences.

When the reliability and validity limitations of the Rorschach method were made known, disillusion replaced the prior unrealistic expectations. The earlier claim that the Rorschach test could do everything was replaced in some circles by the conclusion that it could do little or nothing (see Bornstein, 2001, for a discussion of this shift). Some critics believed that Rorschach interpretation, though less messy, was no more scientific than bird hepatoscopy. Jensen (1965) summarized this disparaging attitude toward the Rorschach method quite directly:

> It seems not unreasonable to recommend that the Rorschach be altogether abandoned in clinical practice .... Meanwhile, the rate of scientific progress in clinical psychology might well be measured by the speed and thoroughness with which it gets over the Rorschach. (p. 509)

More recently, Garb (1999) recommended a moratorium on the use of the Rorschach test in clinical and forensic settings.

Jensen's (1965) conclusion continues to be widely cited by RIM critics, but because that statement was made 40 years ago a good deal of creative, methodologically solid research has been conducted, demonstrating that, properly used, the RIM can be employed validly (as the other chapters in this volume illustrate). A number of scholars (e.g., Hiller, Rosenthal, Bornstein, Berry, & Brunell-Neuleib, 1999; Meyer et al., 2001), have also documented acceptable levels of reliability and validity in Rorschach studies.

Nevertheless, critics continue to maintain that the RIM has unacceptable validity and minimal utility (Garb, 1999; Lilienfeld, Fowler, & Lohr, 2003; Lilienfeld, Wood, & Garb, 2000; Lohr, Fowler, & Lilienfeld, 2002; Wood, Lilienfeld, Garb, & Nezworski, 2000). Naturally, those who use the Rorschach method have found these criticisms unfounded (Hiller et al., 1999; Meyer et al., 2001; Weiner, Spielberger, & Abeles, 2002, 2003). The conflicting positions of scholars on each side of this controversy is reminiscent of an observation made over 70 years ago by Bertrand Russell: "Every man, wherever he goes, is encompassed by a cloud of comforting convictions, which move with him like flies on a summer day" (1928, p. 28).

These arguments persist in part because psychologists on each side cite different data; when common findings are discussed, they tend to be interpreted differently by RIM proponents and critics. A particularly telling recent example of selective citation may be found in Wood et al.'s (2003) volume, which describes in detail many of the flaws and limitations in past and current RIM research. Although Wood et al. raised a number of important issues regarding problems with the RIM, they ignored a vast literature documenting the efficacy of the empirically validated RIM scoring systems described in this volume. Thus, Fisher and Cleveland's (1958) Barrier-Penetration (BP) index was never mentioned, even though BP studies have been conducted in at least fifteen countries, and Fisher's (1986) volume includes 175 citations of published BP investigations. The 130-plus published studies involving Holt's (1978) Primary Process (pripro) scoring system were also ignored. Clearly the RIM has been wonderfully heuristic, a quality valued by empirically oriented psychologists; however, this feature was not given much weight either in the Wood et al. volume or in earlier criticisms of the RIM.

Not surprisingly given such selective citation, projective tests, particularly the Rorschach, continue to get a drubbing in Psychology 101 texts. One popular book declared that "projective tests tend to have problems of reliability and validity .... The validity of projective tests is also low" (Bootzin, Bower, Crocker, & Hall, 1991, p. 511). Another made a similar claim: "The validity and reliability [of the Rorschach and TAT] have been questioned .... Perhaps as a result, their use has declined since the 1970s" (Morris, 1996, p. 479). This theme is repeated by Huffman, Vernoy, and Vernoy (1994), who reported that "the reliability and validity of the Rorschach are low" (p. 501).

These statements suggest that skepticism regarding the RIM has become the accepted position within mainstream scientific psychology. What is worse, this skepticism is being passed on to the next generation of psychologists (and consumers of psychology) even before they graduate from college.

THE RIM AND THE COMPREHENSIVE SYSTEM

The reliability and validity of seven RIM scoring methods are documented in the following chapters of this volume. These reviews suggest a plausible interpretation for much of the animosity of RIM critics: Rather than reviewing the breadth of research on the RIM, many contemporary critics have chosen to equate the test with one widely used interpretive method, Exner's (1993, 2000) Comprehensive System (CS). The same error has been made by textbook authors, who draw sweeping (and inaccurate) conclusions regarding the RIM by focusing exclusively on research examining the CS.

The psychological literature contains many instances where Exner's (1993, 2000) CS is called the "Rorschach test" (see, e.g., Garb, 1999; Lilienfeld et al., 2003). Such a synecdoche—confusing a class with one of its members—wrongly implies that the CS and the Rorschach test are synonymous. As the chapters in the present volume demonstrate, the CS is only one of a series of methods for scoring responses to the Rorschach blots (see also Masling, 2002). The RIM is really a family of scoring systems, and statements made about one member of this family do not always apply to others.[2]

THE CHALLENGES OF INTERPRETING RESPONSES TO INKBLOTS: SOURCES OF ERROR AND BIAS

The observation that ambiguous stimuli can be seen in many different ways is centuries old. Consider the famous scene in *Hamlet*, wherein the title character toys with Polonius (act 3, scene 2, lines 376–382):

> *Hamlet*: Do you see yonder cloud that's almost in shape of a camel?
>
> *Polonius*: By the mass, and 'tis like a camel, indeed.
>
> *Hamlet*: Methinks it is like a weasel.
>
> *Polonius*: It is backed like a weasel.
>
> *Hamlet*: Or like a whale?
>
> *Polonius*: Very like a whale.

Systematic use of inkblots to capture personality traits did not begin until the early twentieth century, when Hermann Rorschach, after 10 years of experimentation, published his set in 1921, only 1 year before

---

[2]By design, this volume did not include a chapter describing the CS or the extensive research it has generated. For all its virtues, the CS has attracted a good deal of criticism, much of it harsh and not all merited. The strengths and limitations of the CS deserve separate discussion; numerous books and articles have addressed this issue in detail.

his death at age 38. Although Alfred Binet suggested using inkblots as a personality measure in 1894, he did not pursue this idea. The Rorschach blots were introduced in the United States by a psychiatrist, David Levy, some years after scholars in Spain, Russia, and Japan had shown interest in the blots (Weiner & Greene, in press). The first publication in English on the Rorschach blots was written by Beck in 1930; Beck also wrote the first American dissertation (1932) based on the RIM (Kaplan & Saccuzzo, 2001). Beck's (1944) manual on Rorschach administration and interpretation was widely used in many clinical psychology training programs, even though his norms for determining the adequacy of the form quality of a response were primitive by today's standards.

In the absence of any well-defined, objective manual for working with responses to inkblots, the first generations of clinicians who used the test were perforce compelled to rely on their own experiences and intuitions, the suggestions of their supervisors, and what they could glean from the writings of Rorschach experts, combining all these in some informal amalgam. Learning to assemble and interpret the hundreds of bits of information available in any Rorschach protocol is extremely difficult because, for most neophyte clinicians, objective feedback regarding the validity of their conclusions is rarely available. Thus, inexperienced examiners often have only one criterion to satisfy: their instructor's evaluation of their test reports. This sort of apprenticeship system is how generations of psychologists learned to administer, score, and interpret responses to the Rorschach blots.

Writing an accurate Rorschach report is made even more difficult because humans inundated with more information than they can process—as in a Rorschach testing situation—commit systematic errors in constructing meaningful gestalts. The literature documenting errors in complex human judgments is impressive (see, e.g., Garb, 1998). Moreover, scientists fall prey to these errors as readily as do laypersons: Mahoney and DeMonbreun (1977) demonstrated that a group of scientists (including psychologists), when asked to form a hypothesis to explain a set of data, tended to ask questions to confirm their hunches, avoiding the opportunity to disconfirm. Evidently, people seek to retain their favored hypotheses rather than looking for alternative explanations that might fit the data better; doctoral training does not inoculate against this tendency.

The late George Kelly used to tell his students that when psychologists have data that disconfirm their hypothesis, they retain the hypothesis and discard the data. Experimental evidence now confirms his pithy observation.

Hypotheses need not be formalized to bias our thinking: Implicit hypotheses also guide perception, thought, and behavior. For example, clinicians insensitive to a possible history of sexual or physical assault may not routinely ask about it, yet evidence reveals that many patients do not acknowledge such assaults unless they are questioned directly (Briere & Zaidi, 1989; Cascardi, Mueser, DeGiralmo, & Murrin, 1996; Jacobson, Koehler, & Jones-Brown, 1987). Applying a psychiatric label to people creates a set of expectations that alter consequent interpretations of their behavior. Thus, Rosenhan's classic (1973) study showed that, once admitted to a psychiatric hospital, confederates are perceived as dysfunctional even when they behave normally. In setting after setting the same pattern emerges: Expectation often trumps veridical perception, even in experts.

Not surprisingly, then, an examiner's expectations can influence the responses of a test subject. Masling (1965) led one group of novice graduate students to believe that competent Rorschach examiners obtained more human than animal responses from their subjects; a second group of students was told the opposite—that competent examiners obtained more animal than human responses. The results supported the importance of the examiners' indoctrination: The ratio of animal to human responses varied as a function of what the examiners hoped to obtain, though tape recordings of the testing sessions revealed no hint of verbal coaching by the examiner (see Masling, 1960, for an extensive discussion of situational influences on RIM responses).

Even after RIM data are collected, interpretive biases intrude. One such bias arises from the illusory correlation described by Chapman (1967) and Chapman and Chapman (1969). Here the clinician, on the basis of preexisting beliefs, perceives a relationship between two variables (e.g., homosexuality and buttock responses on the Rorschach, white-space responses and contrariness, detailed drawings of the eye on the draw-a-person test and paranoia) where none exists. The problem is compounded because the illusory correlation, once formed, can conceal from the clinician a more accurate association (e.g., homosexuality and the report of monsters and part-human, part-animal responses; see Masling, 1998).

The clinician's theoretical positions may have biasing effects as well. Thus, those with psychodynamic beliefs tend to look within a patient to explain behavior, often overlooking situational causes; psychologists who favor cognitive and behavioral theories are less sensitive to intrapsychic factors while focusing on external variables (Garb, 1998). Situational and interpersonal variables such as examiner and subject gender, social class, race, and the quality of the examiner-subject relationship have all been shown to influence subjects' test responses and the meaning clinicians impose on them (Masling 1960, 1966).

Once the Rorschach protocol has been scored and interpreted, the examiner's report should ideally describe the mental status of test subjects, identify and clarify the subjective psychological processes that motivate them, and predict the subjects' behavior in the immediate future. This is a daunting challenge, to be sure, and many RIM examiners—consciously or unconsciously—opt to take a safer approach: They make statements so general that their accuracy is impossible to assess. Consider, for example, Beck's (1944, p. 245) interpretation: "The record points to a central anxiety that must be deeply distressing. The heavy blacks of the test create for her a disintegrating situation." A more recent description was given by Acklin, Wright, and Bruhn (1997, p. 462): "Most of her control and defensive scores, which reflect defensive operations in the face of drive-laden ideation, are based on remoteness operations (shift of the percept to other contexts): avoidance based on displacement." Propositions like this might well be correct, but they are difficult to quantify and their behavioral referents are not obvious.

Poorly defined constructs in Rorschach write-ups are not the only obstacles in attaining satisfactory reliability and validity. Rorschach reports frequently contain statements with high probability of occurrence (e.g., "The energy with which he is investing in containing his emotions leaves him vulnerable to stimulus overload and disorganized behavior when under stress" [Carstairs, 1997, p. 186]; "We may conclude that her thinking, although quite intact, is quite vulnerable to disruption" [Smith, 1997, p. 196]). Test interpretations like this create what has been called the "Barnum effect": Many trite, nonspecific statements about human behavior seem profound and ring true (Forer, 1949; Ulrich, Stachnik, & Stainton, 1963).[3]

OBJECTIVE VERSUS INTUITIVE METHODS OF SCORING AND INTERPRETING RIM RESPONSES

Given these sources of error and bias, it is not surprising that assessments of reliability and validity of the RIM, scored and interpreted impressionistically, do not always meet scientific standards. However, if responses are scored objectively by following the rules outlined in a formal manual, many sources of error are avoided, thereby increasing reliability and validity. Thus, when Levine and Spivak (1964) summarized research utilizing their Rorschach Index of Repressive Style, their method yielded retest reliabilities ranging from .74 to .92 and considerable validity in predicting a variety of psychiatric phenomena. Similar encouraging results have emerged for the RIM scoring methods described in this book.

When clinicians and researchers restrict their interpretation of a response to the guidelines in a carefully developed scoring manual, the

---

[3]To be fair, many MMPI reports are similarly vague, and contain statements with high base rates. This is especially true of computer-generated MMPI reports.

unique contributions of the clinician, both favorable and unfavorable, are curtailed. Therein lies the objective method's strengths: These methods do not eliminate clinical intuition, but transfer it to where it does the most good—deriving testable hypotheses, then methodically comparing them against external criteria until valid measures are found.

The superiority of the actuarial method over the intuitive has been demonstrated in a wide variety of situations, including card playing, weather forecasting, and locating underground oil. There is nothing mysterious or arcane about the actuarial method: Various predictors are systematically tested for their efficacy, and those that work are retained whereas those that do not are abandoned. Ultimately, a set of variables that predict the criterion can usually be found. Compare this process with the global use of the Rorschach responses, a method that does not allow for rigorous cross-checking between score and criterion. Holt (1978, p. 120) summarized this difference well:

> There is no magic in clinical intuition that enables a clinician to predict a criterion about which he knows little, from data the relation of which to the criterion he has not studied, and to do so better than an actuarial formula based on just such prior study of predictor-criterion relations. In retrospect, it seems absurd to have expected that it could have been done.

Arguments for and against the statistical (i.e., objective) versus the clinical (i.e., intuitive) manner of scoring and interpreting Rorschach responses were described by Meehl (1954), Gough (1962), Sawyer (1966), Holt (1978), and Marchese (1992), among others. By and large, those who scored the Rorschach objectively published their results; those who interpreted Rorschach responses intuitively did not. It is regrettable that few clinicians have published evidence documenting the accuracy of an intuitive interpretation of a Rorschach protocol, though clinical lore is filled with anecdotes describing impressive feats of clinical interpretation.

Cronbach (1970) referred to one such example. Another instance arose when Sacuzzo, a self-described Rorschach skeptic, was supervised during his internship by Marguerite Hertz, a Rorschach expert (Kaplan & Saccuzzo, 2001, p. 451):

> When his turn came to present a Rorschach, he used the protocol of a patient he had been seeing in psychotherapy for several months. He knew this patient very well and fully expected Hertz to make errors in her interpretation. He was surprised, however, when Hertz was able to describe this patient after reading only the first four or five responses and examining the quantitative summary of the various scoring categories and ratios. Within 25 minutes, Hertz told him not only what he already knew but also things he hadn't seen but were obviously true once pointed out. This

experience was most unsettling. Having started with a strong bias against the Rorschach, he could not dismiss what Hertz had done.

RIM SCORING AND ASSESSMENT TRAINING

Over the years, the demonstrated lack of reliability and validity when RIM scores are interpreted impressionistically led many academic psychologists to deemphasize training in projective testing. Where once almost all doctoral programs in clinical psychology offered training in the administration, scoring, and interpretation of projective tests, there has been a recent turn against these methods. Despite this, most clinical facilities continue to use psychological assessment (though not always Rorschach testing) in their work with patients. When Kinder (1994) examined the "Position Openings" section of the *APA Monitor*, he discovered that 64% of the openings in mental health centers and private practices required applicants to be qualified for psychodiagnostic work, but not one of the academic positions was designated for faculty members to teach assessment procedures. A survey (Piotrowski & Zelewski, 1993) of thirteen Psy.D. and sixty-seven PhD programs revealed that 51% of them offered either no course in projective methods or only a partial course, 39% offered one course in projectives, and 10% offered more than one. Moreover, the directors of clinical training were almost unanimous (96%) in predicting that interest in projective tests would either decline or remain constant; only 4% thought such interest was likely to increase.

There appears to be a disconnection between the training offered to doctoral candidates in clinical psychology and the skills clinical service agencies require of their staff members. Good psychological work-ups are required by mental health agencies and psychologists are expected to be competent at this. The lack of demonstrated scientific evidence of the merits of projective tests, used impressionistically, does not diminish the need for a thorough personality evaluation of an agency's clients. Clinics and clinicians need to know the nature of their clients' disorders and whether they are amenable to either psychological or pharmacological treatment. The Minnesota Multiphasic Personality Index (MMPI) and other self-report tests, for all their psychometric merit, do not describe the psychodynamic characteristics of patients. Neither clinic nor patient can be expected to go away and not return until better tests are developed. Until a perfect assessment method is available, most humans will prefer a road map that is only partially correct to no road map at all. Empirically driven RIM scoring systems such as those described in this volume help close the gap between the intuitive use of the Rorschach and the as yet unachieved perfect method.

RIM DATA IN CONTEXT: PROJECTIVE METHODS VERSUS SELF-REPORTS

As confidence in projective methods declined, interest in self-reports grew. It is easy to understand the appeal of self-reports: There is an obvious link between the question asked and the criterion assessed (which in the vast majority of studies is simply another form of self-report; see Bornstein, 2003). Asking depressed people if they are sad requires far fewer assumptions than inferring depression from reaction times, productivity, vista, and texture responses to inkblots. Self-reports also have the considerable advantage of requiring less time to administer, score, and interpret—no mean considerations for a clinical agency. The possibility of computer scoring and interpretation adds to their appeal. When researchers validate a questionnaire measure of depression by determining whether it predicts the number of depressive symptoms reported by a patient, it is hardly surprising (and hardly impressive) that strong results are obtained: Those who report a particular trait or experience when answering questions on paper will probably acknowledge the same trait or experience when asked the same questions verbally an hour or two later.

Tests with high face validity have an additional limitation: Their items are aimed so directly at the criterion that their purpose can be detected and responses easily faked. Although it is easy to ask respondents directly if they are angry, law abiding, hallucinatory, or friendly, there is no reason to assume that all are willing or able to answer truthfully. Even if most respondents respond honestly, some deliberately lie, some try to answer truthfully but are self-deceived, some will confess to almost anything, some are confused by the question, and some are so unmotivated that they did not bother to read it. There is far more complexity (and ambiguity) in self-reports than meets the eye.[4]

These problems have been well documented. Shedler, Mayman, and Manis (1993), for example, provided evidence that a significant number of people provide false-positive reports of their mental health. Bornstein, Rossner, Hill, and Stepanian (1994) demonstrated that responses to self-report measures of dependency are more easily faked than responses to inkblots. Bornstein's (1995) meta-analysis found that, although women produced higher scores than men on self-report measures of dependency (presumably because men do not like to acknowledge dependency needs), women and men did not differ on a Rorschach measure of dependency. Critics of the Rorschach method seldom dis-

---

[4]Some objective test items are unintentionally ambiguous. One of our experimental participants once vigorously complained about the question "I loved my father" because if he answered "yes" it meant he no longer loved him.

cuss these limitations of self-report tests, evidently holding stricter standards for the former than the latter.

It should be evident that both self-report and projective measures of personality have assets and limitations. Rather than demonize either method, as is sometimes done, a more sensible position—one that stays closer to the data—is to acknowledge the particular assets and liabilities of each and to use the procedures selectively, where they can contribute the greatest amount of information.[5]

ASSESSING THE VALIDITY OF TEST SCORES VIA EXTERNAL CRITERIA

Given the errors of measurement inherent in all psychological assessment procedures, their ability to predict a wide variety of behaviors over fairly long periods speaks well of their virtues. Table 1.1, taken from a larger set of three tables and 259 validity coefficients provided by Meyer et al. (2001), shows some representative results documenting the ability of objective and projective measures to predict various dimensions of behavior. To provide perspective we have also included data regarding links between several nonpsychological variables and salient external criteria. The data in Table 1.1 offer no support whatsoever for the assertion that self-report tests outperform projective tests.

Scrutiny of Table 1.1 confirms that psychological test data compare favorably with such well-established medical practices as using aspirin to reduce heart attacks ($r = .02$) and chemotherapy to prolong life after breast cancer ($r = .03$). The correlation of .05 between MMPI scores and subsequent cancer within 20 years and the correlation of .07 between the Rorschach Interaction scale score and subsequent occurrence of cancer within 30 years seem trivial until they are compared with the .02 correlation describing the relationship between aspirin and heart attacks. More impressive still are correlations of .44 between the Rorschach Prognostic Rating scale and psychotherapy outcome, and .37 between projective measures of dependency and observed dependent behavior.

Meyer et al. (2001, pp. 133–134), commenting on their results, noted:

> These findings highlight how challenging it is to consistently achieve uncorrected univariate correlations that are much above .30 … psychologists generally should be pleased when they can attain replicated univariate correlations among independently measured constructs that approximate the magnitude seen for gender and weight ($r = .26$) … or elevation above sea level and daily temperature ($r = .34$).

[5]George Kelly (quoted in Barclay, 1991) put it well: "When the subject is asked to guess what the examiner is thinking, we call it an objective test; when the examiner tries to guess what the subject is thinking, we call it a projective device" (p. 195).

TABLE 1.1

Selected Examples of Relationships Between Predictor and Criterion: Adult Participants

Predictor and Criterion	*r*	*N*
Correlational studies		
Aspirin and reduced risk of death by heart attack	.02	22,071
Chemotherapy and surviving breast cancer	.03	9,069
General batting skill as a Major League baseball player and hit success on a given estimate at bat	.06	—
Coronary artery bypass surgery for stable heart disease and survival at 5 years	.08	2,649
Combat exposure in Vietnam and subsequent PTSD within 18 years	.11	2,490
Validity of job employment interviews for predicting job success	.20	25,244
Psychotherapy and subsequent well-being	.32	(K = 375)
Meta-analytic studies		
MMPI depression profile and subsequent cancer within 20 years	.05	2,018
Rorschach Interaction Scale scores and subsequent cancer within 30 years	.07	1,027
General intelligence and success in military pilot training	.13	15,403
Graduate Record Exam Verbal or Quantitative scores and subsequent graduate GPA in psychology	.15	963
Self-reported dependency test scores and physical illness	.21	1,034
TAT scores of achievement motivation and spontaneous achievement behavior	.22	(K = 82)
Self-reported dependency test scores and dependent behavior	.26	3,013
Incremental contribution of Rorschach Prognostic Rating scales scores over IQ to predict psychotherapy outcome	.36	290
Rorschach Prognostic Rating scale scores and subsequent psychotherapy outcome	.44	783
Projective dependency test scores and dependent behavior	.37	1,808
MMPI scale scores and average ability to detect depressive or psychotic disorders	.37	927

Predictor and Criterion	*r*	*N*
Cross-method convergent associations		
Self-report versus significant other: Attentional problems and impulsivity	.22	202
Self-report versus clinician: DSM Axis II personality disorder characteristics	.33	2,778
Self-report versus clinician: DSM Axis I disorders	.34	5,990
Self-report versus TAT: Achievement motivation	.09	2,785
Self-report versus TAT: Problem solving	.13	199
Self-report versus Rorschach: Emotional distress, psychosis, and interpersonal wariness	.04	689
Self-report versus observed behavior: Attitudes	.32	15,624

Note. Data are from Meyer et al. (2001). *N* = total number of participants; *K* = number of studies used to derive corresponding effect size.

Meyer et al.'s (2001) conclusions were made in the report of a blue-ribbon panel appointed by the American Psychological Association's Board of Professional Affairs; this report is the most comprehensive, thorough evaluation ever made of psychological testing and assessment. Beyond their general statement regarding the utility of psychological test data, three of the report's observations are germane in the present context.

Even Within a Category, Test Validities Vary Considerably

Meyer et al. (2001, p. 135) noted that "both psychological and medical tests have varying degrees of validity, ranging from tests that are essentially uninformative for a given criterion ... to tests that are strongly predictive of appropriate criteria."

Medical Tests in General Do Not Outperform Psychological Tests

As Meyer et al. (2001, p. 135) observed:

> Validity coefficients for many psychological tests are indistinguishable from those observed for many medical tests ... the validity coefficients found for psychological tests frequently exceed the coefficients found for many ... medical and psychological interventions.

The Validity Coefficients of Projective Tests Are Comparable to Those of Self-Report Tests

Their results led Meyer et al. (2001, p. 135) to conclude:

> [Our] review does not reveal uniformly superior or uniformly inferior methods of psychological assessment. Despite the perceptions held by some, assessments with the Rorschach and TAT do not produce consistently lower validity coefficients than alternative personality tests ... all produce a range of validity coefficients that vary largely as a function of the criterion under consideration.

One other aspect of the Meyer et al. (2001) data warrants comment. The correlations reported in the "Cross-Method Convergent Association" section (items 19–25) show that, although self-reports frequently overlap a number of assessment methods to a statistically significant degree, they account for little of the variance. This observation is consistent with prior research (Bornstein, 1995; McClelland, Koestner, & Weinberger, 1989) that had already established the lack of a strong relationship between objective and projective assessment of the same trait or need state. When this fact is added to Meyer et al.'s (2001) conclusion that neither the objective nor the projective method has demonstrated superiority over the other, it is evident that the two measures essentially examine different phenomena (see Bornstein, 2002, for a detailed discussion of this issue).

These observations imply that some behaviors are better assessed with a projective measure, others with a self-report test. McClelland (1980) demonstrated that a Thematic Apperception Test (TAT) protocol scored objectively for particular motives can predict some behavior over the long term more accurately than self-reports. For example, the TAT scored for power motives predicted management skills over a 16-year period (McClelland & Boyatzis, 1982) and also predicted blood pressure in undergraduates over 20 years (McClelland, 1979). A physiological measure, dopamine release in subjects who had just viewed a romantic movie, was more successfully predicted by affiliation scores on the TAT than by objective test responses (McClelland, Patel, Stier, & Brown, 1987). The TAT stories of 30-year-olds scored for intimacy were significantly related to marital satisfaction 17 years later (McAdams & Vaillant, 1982). Objective test scores did much less well in assessing several of those variables.

In contrast, self-reports are most valid when the test is administered close to the time the criterion is sampled. Ajzen and Fishbein (1970), who reviewed this literature, concluded that for objective tests "the longer the time interval between the statement of intention and the actual behavior, the lower the correlation between intent and behavior will be" (p. 469). Not surprisingly, self-reports of achievement needs predicted short-term yielding behavior better than a TAT measure of achievement (deCharms, Morrison, Reitman, & McClelland, 1955). Self-reports of dependency predicted direct (but not indirect) help seeking in an in vivo study of college students who completed diary records over 4 weeks; projective dependency scores predicted indirect (but not direct) help seeking (Bornstein, 1998).

The implicit motives assessed by projective measures and the self-attributed motives tapped by objective measures clearly function differently in organizing and sustaining behavior (Bornstein, 2002). Objective tests reflect cognitive responses from those willing and capable of self-disclosing to a stranger. Projective measures tap underlying needs and concerns, and the person's reflexive, habitual manner of organizing and responding to ambiguous stimuli.

Tests that assume goal-directed, continuing, sustained motivation, even in differing situations, should be able to predict a considerable variety of behaviors over long periods of time. Consider the impressive range of behaviors predicted by the scoring methods described in this book: creativity, cognitive skills in children, ego strength, psychological effects of separation, psychiatric rehospitalization rates, interpersonal yielding, participation in psychological experiments, utilization of health services, accuracy of interpersonal perception, delay in seeking medical help, ability to tolerate pain, response to stress, changes following psychotherapy, various physical and psychological disorders, physiological arousal in social isolation, and success in various types of training programs. Given the caveats outlined earlier about its use, and recognizing the need for improved research methods and outcome measures in RIM research, we believe the evidence is clear: The RIM constitutes a unique, heuristic means for studying the human condition—a method that yields insight and information no other personality assessment tool can provide.

WHERE DO WE GO FROM HERE?

For more than 80 years the RIM has played a major role in psychological assessment. From the beginning, the RIM was controversial—admired by some, denigrated by others—and these strong attitudes show no sign of softening. Although RIM critics have called for a moratorium on use of the test in applied settings, this is not likely to happen anytime soon, nor should it. Although many optimistic assertions regarding the Rorschach method are unjustified, the hundreds of published, well-designed empirical studies are proof that the test can be used reliably and validly. The task for clinicians—RIM proponents and skeptics alike—is to separate the valid from the invalid, fact from hyperbole, and determine what the instrument can and cannot do.

The chapters in this volume describe seven well-designed RIM scoring procedures. The findings they report provide a basis for rigorous, balanced assessment of the RIM. This solid foundation is not sufficient, however; more research is needed to clarify important issues. Some principles that can help guide RIM research during the first decades of the twenty-first century follow.

Submit RIM Studies for Peer Review

Unfortunately, many investigations cited in this book have not been published in refereed journals, depriving scholars of the chance to examine the work themselves. For example, just over half of the 300-plus BP studies cited by Fisher (1986) were published. Similar difficulties pervade the CS database (see Wood et al., 2003). This rate of publication is unacceptably low and suggests that some investigators engage in research only because it is required and not because they believe that all clinical theories and hypotheses should be put to empirical test. Their studies, if published, would aid the attempt to make the RIM more scientifically respectable. Whether there are more unpublished studies of the RIM than the MMPI is unknown, as is the overall base rate of unpublished studies in psychology. Perhaps the social contract between students and thesis advisors should routinely include an explicit agreement that a journal article suitable for submission for publication be submitted to their MA or PhD committees along with the thesis itself.

Choose Appropriate Outcome Criteria

Recent critiques of the RIM have focused on the modest correlations of RIM scores with self-reports of personality and pathology (e.g., Lilienfeld et al., 2000). These criticisms are invalid. Because RIM scores reflect implicit (i.e., underlying, unconscious) need states whereas self-reports assess self-attributed (i.e., conscious, openly acknowledged) need states, scores on projective and self-report tests should be modestly intercorrelated. In fact, these modest intercorrelations represent evidence supporting the discriminant validity of the RIM (see Bornstein, 2001). RIM proponents and critics alike must distinguish outcome measures that are expected to show strong correlations with RIM scores from outcome measures that should show more modest correlations.

Analyze Data for Gender Effects

In the past, many studies using projective tests either used participants of one gender and then generalized to both or combined data across gender without first determining whether this was appropriate. Furthermore, there has been a tendency, at least in psychoanalytic research, for male experimenters to study men more frequently than women (Masling, Bornstein, Fishman, & Davila, 2002). There is no reason not to examine the data for gender effects and every reason to do so.

Focus on Process as Well as Outcome

Recent advances in intelligence research have not come from studies examining group differences in IQ or the predictive validity of intelligence tests, but from investigations of the psychological and neurological processes that occur as people respond to intelligence test items (see Sternberg & Lautrey, 2003). Such studies explain not only how people differ in intelligence, but why—they help identify variables that account for these differences. The same logic holds for RIM studies: Exploration of the processes that occur when a person responds to inkblots—and comparison of these processes with those that occur when responding to questionnaire items—is vital in understanding the factors that underlie individual and situational variations in RIM scores.

Focus on Normative Data in Those Contexts Wherein It Is Most Meaningful

Clinical and forensic use of the CS has been severely criticized for flaws in published norms (e.g., Garb, 1999). Because any diagnosis or conclusion about deviancy rests on differences from norms, deficient norms may indeed result in inappropriate recommendations. However, if the RIM is not used to label someone in a clinical or forensic context (e.g., as psychotic, dangerous, or neurologically impaired), but is used instead to investigate the dynamics of a particular group (e.g., alcoholics, arthritic persons, creative artists), norms are less central. Most of the research reported in this book is of the latter kind—investigations of a particular nosological group or as a measure of change from pre- to posttreatment. The adequacy of normative data here becomes less important.

Use Idiographic Material for Training, and Nomothetic Data for Test Validation

Case material is invaluable in clinical training and in illustrating the practical uses (and limitations) of personality assessment tools. However, such material has little value in validating test scores or demonstrating the utility of the instrument. Nomothetic data, in contrast, cannot teach a person how to administer or score a Rorschach, nor can they illustrate the power of the test to illuminate aspects of personality that other instruments cannot. However, these are the only data that can provide compelling evidence regarding the construct validity of the RIM.

Articulate the Theoretical Underpinnings of Every RIM Scoring Method

Without exception, all the scoring methods described in this book originate at least in part from psychodynamic formulations. In some form or another, the concepts of needs, motives, defenses, symbolic representations, compromises, and object relations can be found in these scoring schemes. If the purpose of investigation is to form or test hypotheses about what is going on inside someone's head, there is no substitute for a projective test. Even some scores on the CS, though ostensibly atheoretical at the time they were developed, have subsequently been associated with psychodynamic constructs (Viglione, Brager, & Haller, 1991).

Do Not Confuse a Single Scoring Method With the Test Itself

Without question, the CS has played—and will continue to play—a central role in Rorschach testing and research. Exner's (1993, 2000) work helped the RIM regain credence following decades of disuse and sometimes misuse. This book documents the range of valid and useful RIM scoring systems beyond the CS. In their research and clinical work Rorschach critics and supporters must distinguish findings based on the CS from those derived from other scoring and interpretive systems (Masling, 2002).

Hold Self-Report Tests to the Same Standards as Projective Tests

No psychological assessment tools are perfect; all have flaws. As noted in this chapter, RIM critics have focused almost exclusively on limitations in the RIM, ignoring some equally important problems in self-report tests. To provide a more balanced and accurate picture of the current state of psychological testing, those who review assessment tools should hold all instruments to the same high standards. A complete description of personality and interpersonal functioning can best be obtained by combining and contrasting the results of different assessment tools. For this to occur, the strengths and limitations of all psychological tests—objective and projective, interview and behavioral—are given consistent, balanced, and unbiased evaluations.

REFERENCES

Acklin, M. W., Wright, D. E., & Bruhn, A. R. (1997). He-she-it: The construction and destruction of an illusory identity. In J. R. Meloy, M. W. Acklin, C. B. Gacono, J. F. Murray, & C. A. Peterson (Eds.), *Contemporary Rorschach interpretation* (pp. 453–467). Mahwah, NJ: Lawrence Erlbaum Associates.

Ajzen, I., & Fishbein, M. (1970). The prediction of behavior from attitudinal and normative variables. *Journal of Experimental Social Psychology, 6,* 466–487.

Barclay, J. A. (1991). *Psychological assessment: A theory and systems approach* (7th ed.). Malabar, FL: Krieger Publishing.

Beck, S. J. (1930). Personality diagnosis by means of the Rorschach test. *American Journal of Orthopsychiatry, 1,* 81–88.

Beck, S. J. (1944). *Rorschach's test: Basic processes.* New York: Grune & Stratton.

Bootzin, R. R., Bower, G. H., Crocker, J., & Hall, E. (1991). *Psychology today: An introduction* (7th ed.). New York: McGraw-Hill.

Bornstein, R. F. (1995). Sex differences in objective and projective dependency tests: A meta-analytic review. *Psychological Assessment, 2,* 319–331.

Bornstein, R. F. (1998). Implicit and self-attributed dependency strivings: Differential relationships to laboratory and field measures of help-seeking. *Journal of Personality and Social Psychology, 75,* 778–787.

Bornstein, R. F. (2001). Clinical utility of the Rorschach Inkblot Method: Reframing the debate. *Journal of Personality Assessment, 77,* 39–47.

Bornstein, R. F. (2002). A process dissociation approach to objective-projective test score interrelationships. *Journal of Personality Assessment, 78,* 47–68.

Bornstein, R. F. (2003). Behaviorally referenced experimentation and symptom validation: A paradigm for 21st century personality disorder research. *Journal of Personality Disorders, 17,* 1–18.

Bornstein, R. F., Rossner, S. C., Hill, E. J., & Stepanian, M. L. (1994). Face validity and fakability of objective and projective measures of dependency. *Journal of Personality Assessment, 63,* 363–368.

Briere, J., & Zaidi, L. Y. (1989). Sexual abuse histories and sequelae in female psychiatric emergency room patients. *American Journal of Psychiatry, 146,* 1602–1606.

Carstairs, K. S. (1997). The skull as a symbol of death in one man's Rorschach. In I. B. Weiner (Ed.), *Rorschachiana XXII: Yearbook of the International Rorschach Society* (pp. 179–197). Seattle: Hogrefe & Huber.

Cascardi, M., Mueser, K. T., DeGiralmo, J., & Murrin, M. (1996). Physical aggression against psychiatric inpatients by family members and partners. *Psychiatric Services, 47,* 531–533.

Chapman, L. J. (1967). Illusory correlation in observational report. *Journal of Verbal Learning and Verbal Behavior, 6,* 151–155.

Chapman, L. J., & Chapman, J. P. (1969). Illusory correlation as an obstacle to the use of valid psychodiagnostic signs. *Journal of Abnormal Psychology, 74,* 271–280.

Cronbach, L. J. (1970). *Essentials of psychological testing* (3rd ed.). New York: Harper & Row.

deCharms, R., Morrison, H. W., Reitman, W. R., & McClelland, D. C. (1955). Behavioral correlates of directly and indirectly measured achievement motive. In D. C. McClelland (Ed.), *Studies in motivation* (pp. 414–423). New York: Appleton-Century-Crofts.

Eliot, T. S. (1943). *Four quartets.* New York: Harcourt, Brace.

Exner, J. E. (1993). *The Rorschach: A comprehensive system: Vol. l. Basic foundations* (3rd ed.). New York: Wiley.
Exner, J. E. (2000). *A primer for Rorschach interpretation.* Asheville, NC: Rorschach Workshops.
Fisher, S. (1986). *Development and structure of the body image.* Hillsdale, NJ: Lawrence Erlbaum Associates.
Fisher, S., & Cleveland, S. E. (1958). *Body image and personality.* New York: Van Nostrand.
Forer, B. R. (1949). The fallacy of personal validation: A classroom demonstration of gullibility. *Journal of Abnormal and Social Psychology, 44,* 118–123.
Frank, L. K. (1939). Projective methods for the study of personality. *Journal of Psychology, 8,* 389–413.
Garb, H. N. (1998). *Studying the clinician: Judgment research and psychological assessment.* Washington, DC: American Psychological Association.
Garb, H. N. (1999). Call for a moratorium on the use of the Rorschach Inkblot Test in clinical and forensic settings. *Assessment, 6,* 433–448.
Gough, H. G. (1962). Clinical versus statistical prediction in psychology. In L. Postman (Ed.), *Psychology in the making: Histories of selected research problems* (pp. 526–584). New York: Knopf.
Hibbard, S. (2003). A critique of Lilienfeld et al.'s (2000) "The scientific status of projective techniques." *Journal of Personality Assessment, 80,* 260–271.
Hiller, J. B., Rosenthal, R., Bornstein, R. F., Berry, D. T. R., & Brunell-Neuleib, S. (1999). A comparative meta-analysis of Rorschach and MMPI validity. *Psychological Assessment, 11,* 278–296.
Holt, R. R. (1978). *Methods in clinical psychology: Vol. 2. Predictions and research.* New York: Plenum Press.
Huffman, K., Vernoy, M., & Vernoy, J. (1994). *Psychology in action* (3rd ed.). New York: Wiley.
Jacobson, A., Koehler, J. E., & Jones-Brown, C. (1987). The failure of routine assessment to detect histories of assault experienced by psychiatric patients. *Hospitals and Community Psychiatry, 38,* 386–389.
Jensen, A. R. (1965). A review of the literature. In O. K. Buros (Ed.), *The sixth mental measurements yearbook* (pp. 501–509). Highland Park, NJ: Gryphon.
Juni, S. (1980). Classical projection: A critique of experimental methodologies. *Genetic Psychology Monographs, 101,* 119–146.
Kaplan, R. M., & Saccuzzo, D. P. (2001). *Psychological testing: Principles, applications, and issues* (5th ed.). Belmont, CA: Wadsworth/Thompson.
Kinder, B. N. (1994). Where the action is in personality assessment. *Journal of Personality Assessment, 62,* 585–588.
Korchin, S. J. (1976). *Modern clinical psychology.* New York: Basic Books.
Levine, M., & Spivack, G. (1964). *The Rorschach index of repressive style.* Springfield, IL: Charles Thomas.
Levy, L. H., & Orr, T. B. (1959). The social psychology of Rorschach validity research. *Journal of Abnormal and Clinical Psychology, 58,* 79–83.
Lewis, N. D. L. (1942). Introduction. In B. Klopfer (Ed.), *The Rorschach technique* (pp. ix–x). Yonkers-on-Hudson, NY: World Book.
Lilienfeld, S. O., Fowler, K. A., & Lohr, J. M. (2003). And the band played on: Science, pseudoscience, and the Rorschach Inkblot Method. *The Clinical Psychologist, 56,* 6–9.
Lilienfeld, S. O., Wood, J. M., & Garb, H. N. (2000). The scientific status of projective techniques. *Psychological Science in the Public Interest, 1,* 27–66.

Lohr, J. M., Fowler, K. A., & Lilienfeld, S. O. (2002). The dissemination and promotion of pseudoscience in clinical psychology: The challenge to legitimate clinical science. *The Clinical Psychologist, 55,* 4–10.
Mahoney, M. J., & DeMonbreun, B. G. (1977). Psychology of the scientist. *Cognitive Therapy and Research, 1,* 229–238.
Marchese, M. C. (1992). Clinical versus actuarial prediction: A review of the literature. *Perceptual and Motor Skills, 75,* 583–594.
Masling, J. M. (1960). The influence of situational and interpersonal variables in projective testing. *Psychological Bulletin, 57,* 65–85.
Masling, J. M. (1965). Differential indoctrination of examiners and Rorschach responses. *Journal of Consulting Psychology, 29,* 198–201.
Masling, J. M. (1966). Role-related behavior of the subject and psychologist and its effect upon psychological data. In D. Levine (Ed.), *Nebraska Symposium on Motivation* (pp. 67–104). Lincoln: University of Nebraska Press.
Masling, J. M. (1998). Interpersonal and actuarial dimensions of projective testing. In L. Handler & M. Hilsenroth (Eds.), *Teaching and learning personality assessment* (pp. 119–136). Mahwah, NJ: Lawrence Erlbaum Associates.
Masling, J. M. (2002). How do I score three: Let me count the ways (or some methods of categorizing Rorschach responses). *Journal of Personality Assessment, 79,* 399–421.
Masling, J. M., Bornstein, R. F., Fishman, I., & Davila, J. (2002). Can Freud explain women as well as men? A meta-analytic review of gender differences in psychoanalytic research. *Psychoanalytic Psychology, 19,* 328–347.
McAdams, D. P., & Vaillant, G. E. (1982). Intimacy, motivation and psychosocial adjustment: A longitudinal study. *Journal of Personality Assessment, 46,* 586–593.
McClelland, D. C. (1979). Inhibited power motivation and high blood pressure in men. *Journal of Abnormal Psychology, 88,* 182–190.
McClelland, D. C. (1980). Motive disposition: The merits of operant and respondent measures. In L. Wheeler (Ed.), *Review of personality and social psychology* (Vol. 1, pp. 10–41). Beverly Hills, CA: Sage.
McClelland, D. C., & Boyatzis, R. E. (1982). The leadership motive pattern and long-term success in management. *Journal of Applied Psychology, 67,* 737–743.
McClelland, D. C., Koestner, R., & Weinberger, J. (1989). How do self-attributed and implicit motives differ? *Psychological Review, 96,* 690–702.
McClelland, D. C., Patel, V., Stier, D., & Brown, D. (1987). The relationship of affiliative motive to dopamine release. *Motivation and Emotion, 11,* 51–66.
Meehl, P. E. (1954). *Clinical versus statistical prediction.* Minneapolis: University of Minnesota Press.
Meyer, G. J., Finn, S. E., Eyde, L. D., Kay, G. G., Moreland, K. L., Dies, R. R., Eisman, E. J., Kubiszyn, T. W., & Reed, G. M. (2001). Psychological testing and psychological assessment: A review of evidence and issues. *American Psychologist, 56,* 128–165.
Morris, E. G. (1996). *Psychology: An introduction* (9th ed.). Upper Saddle River, NJ: Prentice-Hall.
Piotrowski, C., & Zalewski, C. (1993). Training in psychodiagnostic testing in APA-approved PsyD and PhD clinical psychology programs. *Journal of Personality Assessment, 61,* 394–405.
Rosenhan, D. (1973). On being sane in insane places. *Science, 179,* 250–258.
Russell, B. (1928). *Skeptical essays.* New York: Norton.
Sawyer, J. (1966). Measurement and prediction, clinical and statistical. *Psychological Bulletin, 66,* 178–200.

Schachtel, E. G. (1966). *Experiential foundations of Rorschach's test.* New York: Basic Books.
Shedler, J., Mayman, M., & Manis, M. (1993). The illusion of mental health. *American Psychologist, 48,* 117–131.
Smith, B. L. (1997). White bird: Flight from the terror of empty space. In J. R. Meloy, M. W. Acklin, C. B. Gacono, J. F. Murray, & C. A. Peterson (Eds.), *Contemporary Rorschach interpretation* (pp. 191–209). Mahwah, NJ: Lawrence Erlbaum Associates.
Sternberg, R. J., & Lautrey, J. (Eds.). (2003). *Models of intelligence: International perspectives.* Washington, DC: American Psychological Association.
Ulrich, R. E., Stachnik, T. J., & Stainton, N. R. (1963). Student acceptance of generalized personality interpretations. *Psychological Reports, 13,* 831–834.
Viglione, D. J., Brager, R., & Haller, N. (1991). Psychoanalytic interpretation of the Rorschach: Do we have better hieroglyphics? *Journal of Personality Assessment, 57,* 1–9.
Weiner, I. B., & Greene, R. L. (in press). *Handbook of personality assessment.* Hoboken, NJ: Wiley.
Weiner, I. B., Spielberger, C. D., & Abeles, N. (2002). Scientific psychology and the Rorschach Inkblot Method. *The Clinical Psychologist, 55,* 7–12.
Weiner, I. B., Spielberger, C. D., & Abeles, N. (2003). Once more around the park: Correcting misinformation about Rorschach assessment. *The Clinical Psychologist, 56,* 6–9.
Wood, J. M., Lilienfeld, S. O, Garb, H. N., & Nezworski, M. T. (2000). The Rorschach test in clinical diagnosis: A critical review, with a backward look at Garfield (1947). *Journal of Clinical Psychology, 56,* 395–430.
Wood, J. M., Nezworski, M. T., Lilienfeld, S. O., & Garb, H. N. (2003). *What's wrong with the Rorschach?* San Francisco: Jossey-Bass.

2

The Rorschach Prognostic Rating Scale

Leonard Handler
University of Tennessee

Amanda Jill Clemence
Pennsylvania Hospital and University of Pennsylvania Medical School

The usefulness of a well-validated scale to predict a patient's success in psychotherapy or a student's success in a training situation is obvious. A great deal of time, money, and effort are wasted when, despite doing one's best, a patient makes little or no progress, or when candidates fail in their training efforts. In addition, many patients drop out of psychotherapy prematurely; it is often said that the median number of sessions for patients in an agency is between five and eight (Bergin & Garfield, 1994). Dropout rates as high as 80 to 90% have been reported (Bergin & Garfield; Owen & Kohutek, 1981). Many valuable resources are wasted in these efforts. Although many early researchers grappled with the prediction of success or failure in treatment or in training (e.g., Harris & Christiansen, 1946; Kotkov & Meadow, 1953; Lipton, Tamarin, & Lotesta, 1951; Piotrowski, 1941; Piotrowski & Lewis, 1952; Pollins, 1951; Rogers, Knauss, & Hammond, 1951), none of their approaches, typically using merely the sum of individual "good" or "bad" signs, were conceptually driven. In addition, few studies produced results that consistently identified individual Rorschach variables that could be cross-validated in subsequent studies. Meyer and Handler (1997) noted, "There has been relatively little theorizing about Rorschach constructs that should predict various kinds of outcomes" and, as with all personality measures, there has been little replication in the Rorschach literature from one study to the next, with the result that the literature contains "an extensive list of potential predictor-criterion relations to consider" (p. 1). The Rorschach literature contains many exploratory studies that use a large array of variables, along with small sample sizes "to generate completely empirical predictive equations—equations for who will drop out of therapy, for who will improve in therapy, and so on" (Meyer & Handler, pp. 1–2). Many of these equations fail to work out in later studies. Therefore, it is difficult to summarize the literature concerning the effectiveness of the Rorschach as a prognostic instrument.

Fortunately, a little-known scale in the literature, the Rorschach Prognostic Rating Scale (RPRS), was constructed with the eventual goal of predicting accurately those patients who would be successful and those who would not be successful in psychotherapy. Bruno Klopfer, an early conceptualizer, theoretician, and teacher of the Rorschach, along with his associates, developed the RPRS (Klopfer, Kirkner, Wisham, & Baker, 1951) in an attempt to predict a patient's response to psychotherapy. However, this complex scale is much more than an attempt to predict how well a patient will do in psychotherapy. The components of the scale were said to measure ego strength, primarily aspects of reality testing, emotional integration, self-realization, and mastery of reality situations (Klopfer, Ainsworth, Klopfer, & Holt, 1954).

Although Klopfer wanted, eventually, to measure present ego strength separately from potential ego strength, the scale as it is presently constructed assesses both present and potential ego strength combined. Whereas available ego strength was said to be tied to the patient's "general adjustment status or diagnostic level of functioning" (Klopfer et al., 1954, p. 689) the other aspect of the test, potential ego strength, was theorized to become mobilized during the course of psychotherapy. This second factor, Meyer and Handler (1997) indicated, "reflected 'therapeutic promise' or the ability to make treatment gains, *regardless of diagnosis or general functioning capacity*" (p. 3, emphasis added). Klopfer et al. (1954) indicated that there are a number of patients who have more unused ego strength than the severity of their disorder would suggest: "We have all encountered patients who show a favorable discrepancy between the diagnostic 'label' attached to them and their ability to profit from psychotherapy. These are the patients who will show the greatest relative improvement in therapy. The difficulty, of course, has been in identifying such patients" (p. 689).

The RPRS was presented by Klopfer et al. (1951, 1954) as a work in progress, for use by colleagues in experimental work concerning the selection of therapy patients. Although the RPRS has not been frequently used or subjected to research since its presentation in 1951, researchers have suggested that it should be more broadly conceived as a scale that can also measure the potential ability of people in the helping professions to function well in their respective settings. As we show in a later discussion of the available research, several studies focused on the helping professions of nursing and teaching.

The complexity of the RPRS may be seen from an examination of its scoring components. (The scale is reproduced in the appendix.) For example, Human Movement (*M*) is scored for amount of movement present—whether the percept reflects movement that increases or decreases living space, movement described as "merely alive" (e.g., sleeping, sitting), movement described spontaneously, movement that appears in an intermediate step (e.g., a picture of a person walking), or movement mentioned only in the Inquiry. The implication is that those patients who use movement to increase their living space would probably make better progress in psychotherapy, compared with those patients whose living space is decreased or who are depicted as "merely alive," because the first condition is given a rating of 1, the second a rating of ½, and the third, 0.

The RPRS also measures one other aspect of the *M* response: whether it reflects "real people" in the patient's (subject's) immediate cultural milieu, or a culturally distant real person, such as a culturally popular fantasy figure, a figure that is concealed by clothing or other equipment, or, more extreme, an unusual fantasy figure or a culturally or historically distant figure. In addition, credit is taken off for each *M*– response, thus incorporating an aspect of reality testing in the *M* score. The best *M* score is given for an accurately perceived response that increases the amount of living space, is seen spontaneously, and reflects real people in the patient's immediate milieu. The theoretical implication of these scores focuses on individuals' deep-seated feelings about themselves with respect to their ability to be motivated. Individuals with predominantly compliant or "merely alive" *M* responses are said to be dependent on more assertive people in order to initiate behavior and organize their activities in an active, productive manner. "The stronger the compliant and non-assertive nature of the personality, the less chance the individual has to influence his own behavior along the direction of whatever self-role he has conceived" (Rockberger, 1953, pp. 94–95). Rockberger continued: "An important goal in psychotherapeutic endeavors is to help bring about a self-initiating, self-directing individual. If the need to lean and depend upon others, including the therapist, is strong, then the goal of independence becomes a relatively difficult task" (p. 95).

It appears that with *M*, as well as the other variables, Klopfer et al. (1954) used a great deal of clinical acumen in their construction of the RPRS. There are many subtle nuances built into this scale, as can be seen in the actual RPRS scoring system. Responses in each area considered (*M*, Animal Movement [*FM*], Inanimate Movement [*m*], Shading [*c*, *K*, *k*], Color [*FC*, *CF*, *C*], Form Level (*F*+) and the Final (Total) Prognostic Scale Score) are weighted, "empirically determined on the basis of clinical judgment and [have] frequently been revised" (Klopfer et al., 1951, p.

428). Thus, the scale uses a configural approach; not only are the number of components taken into consideration, but many qualitative aspects of each component are also considered and quantified. In addition, the RPRS procedure is not summative, but rather, it considers the interrelatedness of the elements. Thus, for example, *FM* scores are given a smaller total weight if the raw scores are twice that of *M* responses.

The second part of the scoring system is devoted to *FM* responses, with essentially the same approach as in scoring for *M*. The *m* responses are scored somewhat similarly. The first aspect of measurement concerns whether natural forces, such as an explosion or a rocket, are perceived as operating counter to gravity, or as responding to gravity (e.g., falling), and the inclusion of abstract forces expressed in the percept. Credit is given, for example, if an expression is projected onto an inanimate object, or if the inanimate movement deals with repulsion or attraction, but no credit is given for movement due to dissipation (e.g., melting ice cream).

Shading responses are scored using differential weightings, with credit given for texture responses in which form predominates (*Fc*) and that are warm, soft, or transparent, and for shading (form predominant) that is seen as depth, or vista (*FK*). Less credit is given when the texture seen is hard or cold (form predominant), and credit is taken off for shading in which a three-dimensional percept is seen in two dimensions (*Fk*), such as when x-ray and topographical map responses are given, when texture is seen as not form dominant, when the form-dominant texture response is a minus, when vista responses are a minus, or when the form-dominant texture response is seen as a diseased organ. Credit is also taken off if in the entire record there is shading evasion or shading insensitivity.

Thus, with shading responses, those that are described as warm, soft, or transparent are given one point, whereas those that are described as cold or hard are scored as 0, based on the clinical observation that softer shading responses are given by those subjects who view interpersonal contacts as quite positive, a necessary prerequisite for building a positive therapeutic relationship. Similarly, a texture response in a percept that is described as a diseased organ is given a score of –1, indicating a very negative experience of interpersonal relationships. Similar subtle details exist for C and form ratings. For example, *FC* is given more weight than *CF*, and color without form C) is given a negative weight. A number of color responses usually considered as detracting from present adjustment level (e.g., color description) are given low positive weightings, primarily because they are said to indicate potential ego strength.

FC color responses are given the best score (1 point) and less credit is given (½ point) for *CF* responses that are explosive or passive, for Color

Denial, for color used symbolically in a euphoric manner, and for unscorable color remarks that express discomfort. No credit (0) is given for forced use of color and for *F/C* and *C/F* responses. Symbolic use of color as dysphoric, color seen in a diseased organ, and explosive *CF* responses given with no affect earn a score of –½ , whereas *FC* responses, *CF* responses, color name responses (*Cn*), pure *C* responses, and color used in a contaminated response are all scored as –1.

The last variable scored is Form Level. In Klopfer's (1954) system, Form Level is rated on a scale ranging from +5.0 to –2.0, in half steps (.5). A basal rating for the percept is given, and then credit is either added or subtracted "for each constructive specification or for a successful organization and subtracting a credit (.5) for a specification or organization that weakens the match of concept to blot" (p. 219). The average Form Level rating of the entire record is then used as a weighted score, except when there are any "weakening" specifications in the record, as when a .5 credit is subtracted.

Klopfer et al. (1954) used a number of terms in the scale that may be unfamiliar to some readers. *Shading evasion* is defined as: (a) using the shading stimuli on the heavily shaded cards but not in the most usual and most conspicuously shaded areas (e.g., calling the bottom center of Card IV an "animal skin" instead of the rest of the card, or giving a shading-determined response to the top center *D* in Card VI rather than to the large lower area); (b) giving a usual response to the shaded areas, such as an "animal skin" or "fur-bearing animal," and justifying the response in the Inquiry by pointing to the ragged or fuzzy edge rather than emphasizing the texture of the blot; (c) using the common shading areas but with vague shading responses of content, suggesting avoidance of direct contact sensations (e.g., in Card IV, "about the only thing I could see would be maybe something under water" (Klopfer, 1954, p. 346). The hypothesis is that shading evasion indicates "reluctance to accept one's need for affection, with the emphasis on repressive mechanisms rather than conscious denial, stemming from early experiences of rejection and deprivation, resulting in difficulties in forming satisfactory object relations, although not to the extent of the severe impairment shown by shading insensitivity" (p. 347).

Shading insensitivity is defined as follows: There is no reference to shading in either the performance proper or in the Inquiry, with minimal use of the concepts that subjects usually connect with the shading stimuli (clouds, animal skins, and the like). Klopfer et al. (1954) stated:

> Even the insensitive subject may respond "animal skin" to Card VI, however, because of the shape of the blot. In testing the limits he either may not understand the most explicit explanation of the possible use of shading stimuli or may show very little interest in it, without any marked re-

> sistance to the idea. In any case, he will not be able to apply the principle of shading differences to another card because he is not sensitive to such differences. (p. 347)

Shading insensitivity is said by Klopfer et al. the most seriously disturbed pattern of response to shading. The hypothesis is that it indicates "such an early and severe deprivation experience that the need for stable dependent and affectional relationships either has never been properly mobilized or developed, or it has been severely repressed; in either case the capacity for any deep or meaningful object relations has been seriously impaired" (p. 347). Shading denial is scored when, in the Inquiry, the subject or patient will go to any length to avoid mentioning the usual shading stimuli.

Forced color use ($F \leftrightarrow C$) is used when the actual color of the blot is not the natural color of the object seen (e.g., two red seals on Card II). The subject is said to make an effort to rationalize or reconcile the color of the blot area with the object seen. *Arbitrary use of color* (*F/C, C/F*) is defined as the use of color in a colorless way, to demark subdivisions of an object of definite form; any color would serve to demarcate the area(s), such as the arbitrary use of colors to demarcate various countries on a map. *Symbolic use of color* (*Csym*) is defined as the use of color symbolically, as, for example, standing for an abstract idea, such as evil, youth, or gaiety. *Color naming* (*Cn*) is scored when the response to color on a card is merely to name the various colors on the card, where this is the only response given to the card, and does not merely indicate a description of the card. The patient or subject must indicate that the *Cn* response is an adequate response to the card. *Color contamination* is scored when color is used as a determinant in a contaminated response (e.g., grass bear, in Card IX) and the subject or patient offers such a response in a serious manner. (See the appendix for the complete RPRS.)

INTERRATER RELIABILITY

Ten previous studies using the RPRS reported interrater reliability statistics (Adams & Cooper, 1962; Clemence, 2003; Edinger & Weiss, 1974; Endicott & Endicott, 1964; Hathaway, 1982; Newmark, Finkelstein, & Frerking, 1974; Newmark, Hetzel, Walker, Holstein, & Finklestein, 1973; Newmark, Konanc, Simpson, Boren, & Prillaman, 1979; Sheehan, Frederick, Rosevear, & Spiegelman, 1954; Williams, Monder, & Rychlak, 1967). Of those, reliabilities ranged from .79 (Newmark et al., 1974) to .95 (Hathaway, 1982) for the entire scale. Other investigators reported "good" to "excellent" levels of agreement, ranging from 71% to 88% (Sheehan et al., 1954) and from .93 to 1.00 (Adams & Cooper) among rater pairs for the calculation of individual variables resulting in the Total

Prognostic Score. The only study to report interrater reliability for individual subscales to date is the one by Clemence. Intraclass correlation coefficients ranged from .51 (*m*) to .84 (Form Level). Interrater reliability for the Total Prognostic Score was .85. All scores were in the good to excellent range except *m*, which was considered fair at .51 (Fleiss, 1981).

PREDICTIVE VALIDITY

The first studies concerning the RPRS were published in 1953, but research on the scale died down as the Comprehensive System gained popularity. With the more frequent use of the Exner Comprehensive System, fewer and fewer clinicians scored the Rorschach using the Klopfer system. It is also difficult to translate the nuances of the RPRS into the Comprehensive System. However, there has been a renewed interest in the RPRS more recently (e.g., Clemence, 2003; Meyer, 2000; Meyer & Handler, 1997, 2000).

Adult Outpatient Samples

In one of the first published validation studies of the RPRS, Mindess (1953) investigated the ability of the RPRS to predict level of adjustment and improvement in therapy. The sample was made up of 80 patients seeking treatment at a California clinic. Patients carried a wide range of diagnoses, from psychotic to neurotic levels of symptomatology. Rorschachs were administered at the beginning of treatment. Level of adjustment, measured using an 11-point scale ranging from 5 ("problems can be handled without help") to –5 ("can be considered completely psychotic"), were assigned by therapists retrospectively for their patients' level of adjustment at the beginning of treatment and after at least 6 months of therapy. The RPRS was found to be highly correlated with therapist-rated level of adjustment for the entire sample ($r = .81$). RPRS scores of ten psychotic patients were found to have the highest correlations with adjustment at six months. Therefore, these patients were removed from the analysis and the correlation was recalculated, resulting in a slightly smaller correlation ($r = .66$).

Kirkner, Wisham, and Giedt (1953) utilized case histories from 40 patients consecutively admitted for treatment at a VA hospital. Pretreatment Rorschachs were scored using the RPRS, and outcome data were derived by reviewing the closure notes for each patient and rating the participants into categories of improved or unimproved according to their success in achieving their individual goals of psychotherapy. The mean RPRS score for the total sample was 5.77. The phi coefficient between the RPRS score and patient improvement was .67 (chi-square level of confidence < .01).

Sheehan et al. (1954) examined 35 stutterers in combined speech therapy and psychotherapy, conducted both individually and in a group format. The goal was to increase stutterers' capacity for tolerating anxiety. RPRS Total Prognostic Scores in this study differentiated those who demonstrated improvement in psychotherapy from those who showed little to no improvement, as measured by therapist ratings. Mean RPRS scores were 7.24 for the most improved group and 4.67 for the least improved ($p < .01$). The RPRS also discriminated between those who remained in treatment and those who left treatment prematurely ($p < .01$).

Cartwright (1958) utilized a sample consisting of 13 individuals participating in client-centered therapy at a university counseling center to examine the ability of the RPRS to predict patient progress. Improvement was measured using a dichotomous success score based on a cutoff point of a 9-point therapist rating scale. Pretreatment RPRS scores were related to therapist-rated improvement with a tau of .52 ($p = .03$).

In an investigation of patients seeking treatment at a university-based counseling center, Schulman (1963) administered the Rorschach to 20 male patients prior to beginning therapy. At the termination of therapy, the Hunt-Kogan Movement scale (Hunt & Kogan, 1950) was used as a measure of progress in therapy. Treatment for this sample averaged 28 sessions. A small, nonsignificant correlation was found (rho = .32) in the examination of the relationship between "movement" and RPRS scores.

Endicott and Endicott (1964) investigated the ability of the RPRS to predict improvement in a group of untreated individuals. They examined pretreatment RPRS scores of 40 individuals assigned to a waitlist condition, along with 21 individuals involved in once-weekly psychodynamically oriented outpatient therapy. After approximately 6 months in both conditions, participants were rated for level of improvement according to the criteria described in the Evaluation of Improvement scale (Miles, Barrabee, & Finesinger, 1951). For the untreated waitlist group, the initial RPRS scores were significantly correlated with improvement ($r = .38$; $p < .05$). Correlations were higher among the treated group ($r = .43$; $p < .05$). No significant correlation was found between improvement and Barron's Ego Strength scale (Barron, 1953) on the Minnesota Multiphasic Personality Inventory (MMPI), indicating that in this study the RPRS predicted patient improvement better than the Barron scale in both treated and untreated samples.

Newmark et al. (1973) also used the MMPI along with the Rorschach in their investigation of 27 participants exhibiting neurotic-level symptoms (predominantly depression and anxiety) being treated with behavior modification techniques. The average number of sessions for this sample was 18.3; all patients in the study had terminated therapy on the mutual decision of patient and therapist. Each participant completed a Rorschach and an MMPI prior to treatment and following termination. Outcome measures included MMPI difference scores for initial and termination protocols, therapist ratings of behavior change, and researcher ratings of improvement based on interviews. The RPRS significantly differentiated improved from unimproved groups (point-biserial $r = .41$, $t = 2.2$, $p < .05$); none of the MMPI scales, including Barron's Ego Strength scale, was significantly correlated with patient improvement.

Newmark et al. (1974), in a continuation of the previous study, used participants from the Newmark et al. (1973) study as a comparison group, with a second group consisting of 26 patients participating in rational emotive therapy. The RPRS again differentiated improved from unimproved patients (point-biserial $r = .48$, $p < .05$).

Fiske, Cartwright, and Kirtner (1964) and Luborsky, Mintz, and Christoph (1979) conducted exploratory investigations of the ability of numerous research measures to predict change in psychotherapy. In the Fiske et al. study, participants were 93 individuals in client-centered psychotherapy at a university counseling center in Chicago. Therapy improvement was rated by patients, therapists, and researchers. The Rorschach was administered to 42 of the participants in the sample, and their RPRS scores were negatively and nonsignificantly correlated with all ratings of improvement, ranging from –.06 (client self-evaluation) to –.23 (TAT Adequacy score). Interestingly, this is the only RPRS study reporting a negative correlation with improvement. In fact, none of the predictor variables in this study was consistently positively and significantly related to measures of improvement in this sample.

The Fiske et al. (1964) data were reanalyzed by Luborsky et al. (1979), who conducted a similar study as part of the Penn Psychotherapy Project. In the Luborsky et al. analysis, outcome was measured by patient, therapist, and researcher ratings of benefits as well as by calculation of residual gain during treatment. Using these modified computations RPRS scores from the Fiske et al. study were again negatively correlated with outcome measures at –.13 (residual gain) and –.28 (rated benefits). Luborsky et al. also used the RPRS in their investigation of 73 university counseling center patients receiving psychoanalytic psychotherapy. The results indicated that RPRS scores in their sample were positively correlated, but were not significant ($r = .16$, residual gain; $r = .15$, rated benefits).

In a sample consisting of 46 VA outpatients, Bloom (1956) separated participants into groups based on their level of productivity on the Rorschach and on their response to treatment. The author identified "underproductive Rorschachs," defined as protocols with 10 or fewer responses and at least one rejection, and "normally productive Rorschachs," or Rorschachs that contained at least 30 responses and no rejections. Bloom found that, when patients generated Rorschach protocols considered normally productive, the RPRS differentiated those patients who demonstrated a good treatment history from those with a poor treatment history ($p = .02$). The RPRS failed to discriminate poor treatment responders from good treatment responders in the underproductive group. These findings indicate that care should be taken when interpreting the RPRS with Rorschach protocols of 10 or fewer responses when one or more rejections is present.

Providing further evidence for the validity of the RPRS is Lundin and Schpoont's (1953) longitudinal case study. The authors presented the results of six Rorschachs from a patient, administered across the course of 28 months (100 sessions) of psychotherapy. Prior to starting therapy, the patient had a Total Score of –.95. After only eight therapy sessions the patient's RPRS score increased to 2.92. After 39 sessions, the patient's RPRS score increased to 3.54 and again to 6.53 after a total of 44 sessions. The authors described changes in the patient's behavior during therapy to this point that included a decrease in hostility, an increase in self-sufficiency, and an increase in interests outside of therapy. After making significant gains in therapy (reduction of symptoms, success in love and work), the patient cut back on therapy and then stopped therapy in agreement with the therapist. Six months later, the patient returned to therapy after a rupture in her love relationship and an increase in symptoms. The patient's Rorschach after returning to therapy (session 90) demonstrated a score of 4.69 and the final RPRS score was 3.01 (99 sessions). The authors suggested that the second RPRS score (2.92) more accurately reflected the patient's ego strength than did the initial pretherapy score (–.95), given later therapy gains. Thus, they conjectured that a Rorschach completed after beginning therapy may tap into the potential for change "in relation to the therapist" (p. 297), as opposed to pretherapy scores that attempt to assess potential for change independent of the therapeutic relationship. The authors made an interesting argument for the importance of assessing future therapy gains within the context of the patient-therapist relationship, given that not all patient-therapist relationships are the same and thus may not provide the same benefit for each patient. Furthermore, the authors concluded that the RPRS was able to accurately predict therapy gains and that with this case it appeared to tap "unused ego strength" per Klopfer et al.'s (1954) formulation.

Adult Inpatient Samples

Only three previously published studies have examined the RPRS in relation to outcome with adult inpatient populations. Filmer-Bennett (1955) used the RPRS as an instrument for understanding the nuances involved in intuitive clinical judgments of ego strength and prognosis. Outcome was measured by determining patient status 2 years on average following discharge from the hospital; patient improvement was defined as "a continuously satisfactory vocational and social adjustment after leaving the hospital" (p. 331). Using pretreatment Rorschachs, the RPRS differentiated improved versus nonimproved patients in 4 of 11 matched pairs. However, the author used a subjective and unvalidated method for separating patients into groups, based on the original model put forth by Klopfer et al. (1951). These categories have no empirical basis and were presented as "tentative" delineations by Klopfer et al.

Seidel (1960) examined the relationship between RPRS scores and therapy outcome by comparing the recovery and discharge status of 63 Caucasian male inpatients diagnosed with schizophrenia. The RPRS Total Prognostic Score significantly correlated with recovery status after 3 years of treatment at $r = .40$ ($p < .01$); higher RPRS scores at the beginning of treatment were related to improvement in therapy as long as 3 years after the initial testing.

Newmark et al. (1979) addressed methodological shortcomings of previous research investigating the RPRS by using more stringent, standardized methods of diagnosis. Participants were 98 male and female schizophrenic inpatients admitted for their first hospitalization; none had had previous psychiatric treatment. Treatment included psychotropic medication, structured therapeutic milieu, group therapy, family therapy, and insight-oriented psychotherapy conducted five times per week. Improvement was defined as evidence of remitted thought disorder on at least one of the three outcome scales. The results revealed that improved patients scored significantly higher on the RPRS scale than did those patients identified as unimproved (point biserial $r = .37$, $p < .05$ for females; point biserial $r = .40$, $p < .02$ for males).

Dissertations

Two additional studies of the effectiveness of the RPRS come from doctoral dissertations, one by Rockberger (1953), and one by Clemence (2003). Rockberger tested 36 veterans (13 schizophrenics and 23 "psychoneurotics") who had received individual outpatient therapy for at least 6 months, and who had at least average IQ scores. Each of these subjects had been administered a Rorschach before beginning therapy. The correlation between number of months in therapy and improvement status ($r = .21$) was not significant, nor was the correlation between age and improvement status. Therapists were asked to rate the improvement of their patients using a 4-point scale consisting of 32 variables. In addition, they were also asked to rate their patient(s) as either "improved" or "unimproved." Using a random selection of 24 patients, Rockberger obtained a highly significant correlation (.58, $p > .01$) between the RPRS score and the results of the scale of improvement. None of the subjects with RPRS scores from 0 to 9 improved, in contrast to subjects with scores from 10 to 31, all of whom were rated as improved. The correlation between the RPRS rating and the yes-no ratings of improvement was .70, significant at the .001 level. Rockberger also found that the RPRS cut across diagnostic lines, with some schizophrenics as well as some neurotics achieving high RPRS scores and some in both groups achieving low scores, even though there was a significant correlation between RPRS scores and diagnosis. There was no difference in the intelligence level, age, or education of the improved and unimproved subjects.

Recent studies (Clemence, 2003; Clemence et al., 2003) investigated the ability of the RPRS to predict treatment success and to examine predictions concerning success in anaclitic and introjective patients (Blatt & Shichman, 1983). Participants in the study were 90 seriously disturbed individuals seeking treatment at the Austen-Riggs Center, an intensive, long-term inpatient facility, the same patients studied by Blatt and Ford and described in their book, *Therapeutic Change: An Object Relations Perspective* (1994). Treatment was provided following a psychodynamic model, with patients receiving intensive psychotherapy several times per week. These individuals were quite ill and required a very long hospitalization with over 2 years of inpatient treatment, on average. For the purposes of the study, Rorschach protocols from admission and after 1 year of treatment (averaging 15 months after admission) were scored using the RPRS. The second testing occurred close to the midpoint of treatment and almost a year prior to discharge on average, making this an investigation of progress during treatment as opposed to an examination of outcome of long-term inpatient psychotherapy.

For all participants, Total Prognostic scores on the RPRS at Time 1 demonstrated a mean score of 3.35, with a standard deviation of 3.44. Total RPRS scores at Time 1 ranged from –4.63 to 10.17, demonstrating a wide range of scores for the sample on admission. This range of Total Prognostic Scores suggests that, even though this is a sample of seriously disturbed psychotic, depressed, and character-disordered patients, the RPRS is able to detect a wide array of available and potential ego functioning present despite the severity of diagnosis. This is consistent with Klopfer's (1954) formulation of the scale in that he intended it to be useful in detecting potential ego strength in those patients who might benefit from treatment despite their diagnostic label.

Consistent with previous research, the RPRS prognostic scores in this study significantly predicted symptom scores at 15 months into treatment, with higher admission prognostic scores correlating significantly with fewer reported symptoms after approximately 1 year of treatment. Regression coefficients were significant for both the neurotic ($\beta = -.30, F = 8.43, p < .005$) and psychotic ($\beta = -.21, F = 4.10, p < .05$) symptoms on the Strauss-Harder Case Record Rating Scale (Strauss & Harder, 1981), but low correlations were found with measures of flattened affect, labile affect, and bizarre behavior. Therefore, the RPRS may be most useful when used to predict the reduction of symptoms such as depression, anxiety, hallucinations, and delusions during treatment, but less useful in reflecting the level of disorganized or odd behavior and flattened or labile affect.

An exploratory investigation of the ability of the subscales to predict neurotic and psychotic symptoms at 15 months revealed that *C* and *FM* successfully predicted neurotic symptoms, whereas *M* neared significance as a predictor of psychotic symptoms. The *C* scale is purported to assess individuals' emotional responsiveness, with higher scores reflecting capacity for emotional integration, potential efficacy in responding to emotional situations in their environment, and intensity of emotional experience. In this sample, higher scores on the *C* scale were correlated with fewer neurotic symptoms at 15 months into treatment. This result makes intuitive sense given that the neurotic symptoms assessed were primarily related to expression and management of emotion (e.g., depression, anxiety, obsessions, etc.), suggesting that the *C* scale may be reliably measuring what it is purported to measure, providing further evidence for the construct validity of this subscale.

Likewise, the *M* scale predicted psychotic symptoms, with a significance level of .10. *M* scores in the Klopfer system are said to reflect the individual's "inner stability," and low scores reflect a higher level of preoccupation with inner experiences to the degree that external reality situations are neglected and social relationships suffer. Conversely, higher scores indicate an ability to integrate external reality and internal fantasy in such a way that empathy and self-realization are fostered (Klopfer et al., 1954). Again, this finding makes intuitive sense because the symptoms measured by the Strauss-Harder Psychotic scale include a variety of delusions, hallucinations, depersonalization, and derealization. These symptoms certainly reflect an overreliance on internal fantasy material to the detriment of external reality and the ability to relate to others. This finding further supports the construct validity of this subscale to measure what it is theorized to measure.

An examination of changes in RPRS scores over time demonstrated distinct changes in RPRS scores in the total group of patients from Time 1 to Time 2, with main effect differences for Form Level, *FM*, and the Total Prognostic score. The Total Prognostic scores decreased significantly from the initial assessment to Time 2 ($F = 4.10, p \leq .05$) with a significant decrease in the Form Level scores ($F = 7.71, p \leq .01$). The main effect difference for *FM* ($F = 5.70, p \leq .05$) was in the positive direction, with this subscale demonstrating a significant increase from admission to 15 months on average for this sample.

Form Level was conceptualized by Klopfer et al. (1954) as a measure of reality testing. They theorized that difficulties with reality testing would be reflected in the Rorschach via distortions in the use of form data supplied by the blot. One could then speculate that Form Level decreases in this sample suggest the emergence of more primary process material stimulated by intensive psychodynamic psychotherapy. Such changes could reflect a loosening of a rigid thinking style that may allow the patient to demonstrate improvement in cognitive flexibility within the context of the therapy, and in addition, may reflect the further emergence of the projection of internal needs on the surrounding environment, as facilitated by the emphasis on transference in the therapeutic interaction via intensive psychotherapy. In addition, these patients were being studied at a point midway through treatment; at 15 months into treatment, patients with this level of initial psychopathology may still have a way to go before achieving the full benefits of psychotherapy.

Although the Total Prognostic scores tended to decrease, the *FM* subscale scores demonstrated significant improvement across patients from admission to 15 months. Klopfer et al. (1954) noted that *FM* "indicates impulses for immediate need gratification" and is "closely associated with the handling of 'stress tolerance'" (p. 578). Klopfer et al. further suggested that "the unfolding of emotional integration is dependent upon the development of stress tolerance because only in the extent to which immediate need gratification can be postponed are opportunities provided for the facilitation of this process" (p. 578). Therefore, *FM* is said to reflect an individual's management of drive impulses as well as the level of comfort felt with those impulses.

This finding may suggest that patients in this sample demonstrated an increase in capacity for stress tolerance, as measured by the *FM* score. Because this factor was also found to significantly predict fewer neurotic symptoms at 15 months, *FM* may provide important information, not revealed with the Total Prognostic score alone, about the way patients change during treatment. It is not difficult to imagine that an increase in stress tolerance could be a key factor in the reduction of neurotic symptoms in this population. This would certainly be a very important component in the context of therapy given that one goal of psychodynamic psychotherapy is often to improve a patient's ability to organize conflicting thoughts and feelings better by integrating them into a more manageable, ego-syntonic whole.

For example, the increase in *FM* occurred at the same time these patients were experiencing an increase in primary process material, as reflected in lower Form Level scores for the entire sample. Thus, these two factors, in conjunction, may explain why patients in the current sample demonstrated lower scores on Form Level while simultaneously demonstrating fewer overt psychotic and neurotic symptoms. In combination, these findings may indicate that patients were becoming better able to tolerate the emergence of loose thinking via improved stress tolerance, possibly resulting in improved capacity for exploration of unconscious drives and wishes. Furthermore, because patients demonstrated a reduction in symptoms from admission to 15 months, they may have achieved some success in producing this material in the testing session, but managed it better when on the ward.

In addition, the RPRS was able to detect differences among patients with introjective and anaclitic pathology in this sample. Anaclitic patients demonstrated main effect differences when compared to patients with introjective pathology on *C* subscale scores from Time 1 to Time 2, with introjective patients demonstrating significantly higher scores on *C* than the anaclitic patients. A main effect for group type was also found on ratings of *m*, again with introjectives scoring significantly higher than anaclitics. Because introjective psychopathology is conceptualized as a tendency to exhibit excessive concern regarding issues of self-control and containment of affect, it is not surprising to find that introjective types scored significantly higher on both *m* and C than did anaclitics. This finding supports the conceptualization of these two groups as differing psychologically and reflects the ability of the RPRS to detect such differences between them.

Child Clinical Samples

In an investigation of the ability of the RPRS to predict improvement in play therapy, Johnson (1953) examined Rorschach protocols of a sample of 21 mentally retarded children (ages 9–16) receiving therapy at a residential school that offered milieu therapy and "reeducation." Children chosen for the study were referred to more intensive clinical treatment due to significant problems with behavior, learning, or "undue tension" (Johnson, p. 321). Johnson divided the participants into groups described as "improved" and "unimproved," and RPRS scores at the beginning of treatment and at the time of therapy termination were examined. Improvement was determined by therapist ratings of clinical progress and teacher ratings of social behaviors. Changes in RPRS scores from beginning of treatment to termination were in the expected direction, with those in the improved group demonstrating a mean change of +0.9 and those in the unimproved group averaging a change of –0.5 ($p < .01$).

Novick (1962) examined the ability of the RPRS to predict positive change in behavior of 44 "mildly disturbed" children (age range 8 to 10 years old) participating in brief psychotherapy. Significant improvement was correlated with RPRS scores after 20 sessions.

Nonclinical Samples

Although much of the previous research investigated the use of the RPRS with clinical populations, a few studies have examined the ability of the RPRS to assess ego strength of those not involved in psychotherapy. Greenberg's (1969) interesting study examined ego strength in children who had been separated from their natural mothers. Participants were 60 male adolescents divided into three groups of 20, based on age at the time of separation from their mothers. The subjects in the first group were placed in foster care between the ages of 8 months and 3 years; the second group of children were separated from their mothers between the ages of 4 and 9 years. A third group were raised by their natural mothers. The results indicated that the RPRS scores were significantly higher for the natural-mother group than for the two groups of foster-home children (p = .01 for both comparisons), as was predicted. No significant difference was found between the two foster-home groups.

Brawer and Cohen (1966) investigated the ability of the RPRS to predict vocational adjustment among a sample of 20 beginning teachers. The correlation between pretraining RPRS scores and supervisors' ratings of performance after 1 year of teaching was $r = .39$ ($p < .10$). In a somewhat similar study, Mindess (1957) investigated a sample of 68 young women in the process of training in nursing at a Canadian hospital. The RPRS and the Wechsler-Bellevue examined the ability of these instruments to predict success during training as measured by academic performance and supervisor ratings. The RPRS was significantly correlated with academic grades ($r = .28, p < .05$) and with Total Nurse Grade ($r = .41, p < .01$). Multiple correlation using both scores predicted the Total Nursing Grade at the .01 level of significance ($r = .59$). This is especially interesting given that IQ scores were very weakly correlated with RPRS scores, suggesting that each was tapping distinct aspects of functioning, and that together, these scores were quite effective in predicting overall success in training. Mindess concluded that the RPRS could be quite useful if applied more generally to other areas of vocational assessment in the selection and evaluation of future employees.

Meta-Analysis

Meyer and Handler's (1997) exhaustive search of the literature uncovered 22 studies, containing 24 independent samples in which the RPRS was used as a predictive instrument. Four of the 22 studies were excluded from the analysis because the authors used only part of the RPRS, or because they did not report statistics necessary for the RPRS meta-analysis. This left 18 studies with 20 independent samples obtained from a total of 752 participants.

In meta-analysis it is important to identify and correct statistical artifacts (Hunter & Schmidt, 1990) in the data. Correction decisions were made in a conservative manner, so they would result in an underestimate rather than an overestimate of the effect size. Following accepted psychometric tradition (Huffcutt & Arthur, 1995; Hunter & Schmidt) four outliers were removed from the analysis. After correction the effect size was found to be .560, a rather robust finding (Meyer & Handler, 1997, 2000). Removal of the outliers had a trivial effect on the effect size. The chance that this effect size is due to chance is one in a billion!

The presence of substantial moderating variables was investigated. There was no difference in the results when the raters were or were not blind to the Rorschach findings. No differences were found when the analysis was limited to just the studies from patients who received psychotherapy. Using an effect size of .56, 78% of the patients with high scores on the RPRS would be predicted to have a successful therapeutic experience, whereas only 22% of the patients with low RPRS scores would be rated as successful. Meyer and Handler (1997) concluded that the obtained data indicate that:

> [The] RPRS is equally effective when used with children or adults, with schizophrenics or healthier outpatients, with those who are court referred or those who elect treatment on their own, with those who are followed for 6 months or 36 months, and when the outcome is determined by therapists or by researchers. The RPRS also seems to be an effective predictor of outcome regardless of whether outcome is measured as change over the course of treatment or functional capacity at the end of treatment. (p. 25)

It is difficult indeed to find another measure that predicts so well in all these diverse situations.

To put the effect size of .56 in perspective, Meyer and Handler (1997) compared this statistic to other meta-analytic statistics for physical, academic, medical, and psychological tests. The RPRS effect size exceeds all but three of the 28 listed comparisons. It greatly exceeds the ability of the Barron Ego Strength scale (Es) of the MMPI to predict subsequent treatment outcome (effect size = .02), several medical relationships involving trusted medical tests, the ability of the SAT and the GRE verbal scores to predict grade point averages (.27 and .28, respectively), and even some physical variables, such as gender and concurrent weight (.47) and concurrent arm strength (.52). In addition, the relationship between the RPRS scores and subsequent outcome is slightly larger than the association between intelligence and school grades (r = .47). The RPRS predicts psychotherapy outcome better than many medical tests and procedures. This led the authors to state, "In fact, we are aware of no other personality scale that demonstrates such consistently strong prognostic abilities" (Meyer & Handler, 1997, p. 28).

Generally, the body of research reviewed herein suggests that Klopfer, et al. (1951) designed a scoring system that detects a number of subtle ego variables related to therapy prognosis and integrates them to reflect an individual's likelihood for improvement as a result of psychotherapy. The RPRS Total Prognostic Score is consistently significantly correlated with improvement in therapy, with only a few exceptions in which the correlation is positive but not significant (Filmer-Bennett, 1955; Luborsky et al., 1979; Schulman, 1963) and only one in which the correlation was negative and nonsignificant (Fiske et al., 1964). Furthermore, the RPRS demonstrated an ability to assess ego strength not only among individuals seeking psychotherapy, but also in those pursuing occupational training. In fact, the RPRS predicts success in vocational adjustment as well as it predicts improvement in psychotherapy. Evidently, the RPRS is an instrument that may not be limited to the evaluation of psychotherapy potential alone, but may also be an effective tool for measuring ego strength as it pertains to a variety of areas of functioning in which the level of ego strength can contribute to success or failure. An impressive example of this is the ability of the RPRS to detect differences in foster-home children when compared to children raised by their natural mothers. These findings are promising and indicate that the RPRS may be used to detect ego strength in a number of important contexts.

Subscale Scores

Several authors have sought to find subscale scores for the RPRS that would more accurately and more efficiently predict prognosis. The results have been mixed and have rarely resulted in consistencies across patient groups. For example, Cartwright (1958) attempted to create a "strength score" using those RPRS variables that contributed most significantly to the prediction of success in therapy in her sample of outpatients at a university counseling center. She identified *M*, *C*, and Form Level as the variables that correlated most highly with success, and calculated a simple scoring method (adding the two highest of the three subscale scores) to determine the strength score. The correlation was quite high (tau = .73; p = .003) between the strength score and rated success. This finding is questionable, however, given the ad hoc nature of the analyses and the application of the new variable to the same dataset from which it was derived. To further examine the possible use of this strength score, Cartwright (1959) reanalyzed the data presented by Kirkner et al. (1953) in a second article, in which she applied to their sample her formula for computing the strength score. She found the strength score to be correlated with improvement in therapy at $r = .85$. Although this correlation is quite high, it is slightly smaller than the RPRS total score for this sample when examined in regard to improvement. The strength score was slightly less effective than the total RPRS score, but still demonstrated a very high correlation. In examining the results from the Kirkner et al. study, it is clear, however, that the weighted subscale scores of *m*, Shading, and *M* are good stand-alone predictors of improvement in this sample ($p = .01$, .01, and .02, respectively), whereas *C* and Form Level failed to reach statistical significance individually. This suggests that in the Kirkner et al. study, the best individual predictors of progress are different from those defined by Cartwright's (1958) strength score.

Schulman (1963) later attempted to replicate the Cartwright (1958, 1959) studies using a similar sample. In his investigation, the correlation between the strength score and movement was "essentially zero." Given the absence of consistent replication for the strength score, this configuration of scoring appears to lack the level of validity required for confident use in predicting psychotherapy outcome.

Whiteley and Blaine (1967) applied only the movement and shading scores (omitting Form Level and Color) in the calculation of the RPRS, following the Kirkner et al. (1953) study. Using this configuration, they found no significant differences among improvers and nonimprovers in psychotherapy. Only one variable, Shading, was found to differentiate significantly the long- and short-term therapy groups ($p < .05$).

Indeed, additional studies of subscale scores as predictors of progress have demonstrated further discrepancies. In a study of stutterers in outpatient treatment, Sheehan et al. (1954) found that *M*, *m*, and *FM* tended to exhibit the strongest relationship with improvement, with significance levels equivalent to that of the RPRS score ($p = .02$ for all). Sheehan and Tanaka (1983) again examined the prognostic validity of RPRS subscale scores in a replication study of 50 stutterers, using logistic regression analysis, and found that *M*, *FM*, and Shading significantly predicted improvement ($p < .05$ for all).

Of the individual determinants included in the RPRS, results from the Mindess (1953) study indicated that Form Level demonstrated the highest correlation with improvement, followed by *M* in a mixed sample of inpatients, outpatients, court-referred, and non-court-referred individuals. In a large sample of schizophrenic inpatients (Seidel, 1960), Form Level predicted improvement better than the RPRS score ($r = .44$ and $r = .36$, respectively), and in a sample of military personnel and their dependents seeking outpatient treatment (Endicott & Endicott, 1964), RPRS variables (raw scores) found to be most highly correlated with improvement were Shading, C, and Number of Responses.

Further discrepancies were reported in a sample of outpatients participating in behavior modification therapy (Newmark et al., 1973). Individual RPRS variables were examined, and none was found to significantly predict improvement alone. A combination of *M* and *C* was significantly correlated with outcome (point-biserial $r = .37$, $t = 2.08$, $p < .05$). Again, it appears that the individual variables cannot do what the complete RPRS Total Prognostic Scale score achieves.

From this body of research, it seems that in the prediction of progress, variables contribute to different degrees to the Total Prognostic Score, depending on the sample being investigated. Furthermore, among many of the studies cited here, methodological concerns limit the interpretation of results due to the application of ad hoc analyses. At this time, the research community has yet to discover a condensed set of variables to predict progress as accurately as does the RPRS Total Prognostic Score.

CONVERGENT VALIDITY STUDIES

Few studies have investigated the relationship between the RPRS and other scales purported to measure ego strength. Of this limited number of studies, most have investigated the relation between the RPRS and Barron's Ego Strength (Es) Scale (Barron, 1953) from the MMPI. The Es scale was initially created to predict neurotic patients' responses to psychotherapy (Barron), and thus, may be a reasonable measure for investigating the convergent validity of the RPRS.

Endicott and Endicott (1964) were the first to investigate the relationship between scores on the RPRS and scores on the Es scale among samples of treated and untreated outpatients. Surprisingly, only small nonsignificant correlations were found between the rating scales, resulting in a correlation of $r = .12$ for the untreated waitlist group and $r = .22$ for the group receiving weekly outpatient treatment.

Adams and Cooper (1962) obtained similar results among a group of 36 VA hospital patients. In their study, the Es scale was positively but nonsignificantly correlated with the RPRS, at $r = .13$. Given this finding, the authors concluded that the two scales may not be measuring the same personality construct. However, using the same dataset under investigation in the Adams and Cooper study, Adams, Cooper, and Carrera (1963) conducted further analyses examining the relationship among the RPRS subscale scores and all of the remaining MMPI scale scores. Numerous correlational analyses among these scales were conducted, and Adams et al. obtained correlations all in the expected direction. Of those, 23 were significant at $p < .10$ or better; "the number of statistically significant correlations was about twice chance expectancy" (p. 33). Significant relationships among scale scores were discussed, and Adams et al. concluded that additional ego strength indicators on the MMPI (beside the Es scale) reflect the concurrent validity of the RPRS.

Adding to the small body of studies investigating the relationship between the Es scale and the RPRS, Newmark et al. (1974) examined the two scales as applied to groups of outpatients receiving two different types of psychotherapy. Comparisons of the RPRS with the Es scale resulted in nonsignificant correlations of .06 for patients receiving behavior modification therapy and .23 for patients receiving rational emotive therapy. Taken together, these findings suggest that the RPRS scale and the Es scale may be measuring primarily distinct constructs.

Another scale used to study the convergent validity of the RPRS was Phillips' Case History Prognostic Rating Scale (Phillips, 1953). The Phillips scale was designed to predict the outcome of shock treatment therapy with schizophrenic patients. Using this scale, Seidel (1960) administered the Rorschach to 100 adult Caucasian male inpatients diagnosed with schizophrenia within 4 months of hospitalization. Patients' premorbid social and sexual adjustment, as measured by section I of the Phillips scale, were compared to ratings of patients' ego strength as measured by the RPRS. Ratings on the RPRS Total Prognostic Score correlated with ratings on the Phillips scale at $r = .24$ ($p < .05$), suggesting that higher premorbid level of adjustment was related to higher RPRS scores. Thus, in this study, the RPRS's measurement of adjustment potential is partially validated by Phillips' scores of patients' premorbid adjustment, providing the most solid data yet for the convergent validity of the RPRS.

Convergent validity studies have also included examinations of observer ratings of adjustment in relation to RPRS scores in a variety of samples. Williams et al. (1967) investigated psychiatrist and social worker ratings of prognosis for 42 children referred to a juvenile court clinic. Social worker ratings of prognosis for therapy were based on interviews with parents, and psychiatrist ratings were based on interviews with both parents and the child. These ratings were compared to RPRS protocols for this sample. Results were small and nonsignificant for correlations between the RPRS and social worker ratings of prognosis ($r = .10$ with Psychologist I; $r = .09$ with Psychologist II), but were higher for psychiatrist ratings of prognosis ($r = .29$ with Psychologist I; $r = .32$, $p < .05$ with Psychologist II).

Edinger and Bogan (1976) compared ratings of adjustment in several settings with RPRS scores in a sample of 25 male incarcerated offenders participating in a therapeutic drug abuse program. Group therapy ratings by staff counselors correlated with the RPRS at $r = .31$. Work progress ratings correlated with the RPRS at $r = .37$. None of the correlations reached significance. Edinger and Bogan noted that care should be taken in interpreting the results, given that 11 of the 25 Rorschach protocols would be considered "underproductive" with 15 or fewer responses.

RPRS AND IQ

The relationship between RPRS scores and intelligence have been somewhat discrepant, with correlations of $r = .10$ (Mindess, 1957), $r = .51$ (Rockberger, 1953), $r = .66$ (Hathaway, 1982), and $r = .72$ (Edinger & Weiss, 1974) in previous studies. In the Williams et al. study (1967), the relationship between IQ and RPRS scores was "essentially zero" for the entire sample. However, when subgroups were examined by race, IQ scores were significantly correlated with RPRS scores for Caucasians ($r = -.40$, $p < .05$ for Psychologist I; $r = -.43$, $p < .05$ for Psychologist II), but not for African Americans in the sample.

Incremental Validity

In an investigation of the ability of the RPRS to predict outcome after accounting for scores on the MMPI Es scale (Meyer, 2000), the RPRS demonstrated clear incremental validity over scores on this scale. The RPRS predicted outcome at $r = .40$, compared to the MMPI Es scale at $r = .02$. When the incremental validity of the RPRS with measures of IQ was examined, the RPRS demonstrated clear incremental validity over IQ scores, with an average weighted incremental effect size of .36. Therefore, despite the discrepant findings regarding the correlational relationships between IQ and the RPRS in previous studies, it is clear from the Meyer study that the RPRS offers distinct and useful information regarding potential response to treatment.

A review of the reliability and validity studies of the RPRS shows that the empirical validity of the RPRS scale is robust. As recommended by Meyer and Handler (1997), the next step in doing research with the RPRS would be to explore the relationship of this scale to more contemporary prognostic indicators from the Rorschach (p. 33), as well as to continue to investigate the ability of the RPRS concerning various aspects of psychotherapy process and outcome. Studies are needed to account for base-rate predictions in the study of outcome. In addition, it is important to translate the subtle scoring variables of the Klopfer system into the Exner system, so that the scale might be used more often in research. One such manual was recently created by Garlan, MacAllister, and Hibbard (2004).

The importance of these subtle variables in the ability of the RPRS to predict psychotherapy outcome also needs to be examined. If an effective translation is not possible, learning to score the scale reliably is not as difficult as it seems at first. We were able to train first- and second-year students to score reliably with three or four training sessions of several hours' duration. Because there are no standardization data available, it is not possible to determine what constitute good and poor scores. Nevertheless, the RPRS, a scale from the distant past, yields significant and impressive reliability and validity data. It has the potential to become an important scale in the future to predict success in psychotherapy and in various areas of training.

REFERENCES

Adams, H. B., & Cooper, G. D. (1962). Three measures of ego strength and prognosis for psychotherapy. *Journal of Clinical Psychology, 18,* 490–494.

Adams, H. B., Cooper, G. D., & Carrera R. N. (1963). The Rorschach and the MMPI: A concurrent validity study. *Journal of Projective Techniques, 27,* 23–34.

Barron, F. (1953). An ego-strength scale which predicts response to psychotherapy. *Journal of Consulting Psychology, 17,* 327–333.

Bergin, A., & Garfield, S. (1994). *Handbook of psychotherapy and behavior change* (4th ed.). Oxford, England: Wiley.

Blatt, S. J., & Ford, R. Q. (1994). *Therapeutic change: An object relations perspective.* New York: Plenum Press.

Blatt, S. J., & Shichman, S. (1983). Two primary configurations of psychopathology. *Psychoanalysis and Contemporary Thought, 6,*187–254.

Bloom, B. L. (1956). Prognostic significance of the underproductive Rorschach. *Journal of Projective Techniques, 20,* 366–371.

Brawer, F. B., & Cohen, A. M. (1966). Global and sign approaches to Rorschach assessment of beginning teachers. *Journal of Projective Techniques and Personality Assessment, 30,* 536–542.

Cartwright, R. D. (1958). Predicting response to client-centered therapy with the Rorschach Prognostic Rating Scale. *Journal of Counseling Psychology, 5,* 11–17.

Cartwright, R. D. (1959). A note on the Rorschach Prognostic Rating Scale. *Journal of Counseling Psychology, 6,* 160–162.

Clemence, A. J. (2003). *Use of Rorschach variables in the assessment of psychotherapy progress.* (PhD dissertation, University of Tennessee, Knoxville).

Clemence, A. J., Handler, L., Blatt, S. J., Ford, R. Q., Martin, B., Campbell, A., et al. (2003). *Rorschach Prognostic Rating Scale as a measure of progress in long-term inpatient psychotherapy.* Manuscript submitted for publication.

Edinger, J. D., & Bogan, J. B. (1976). The validity of the Rorschach Prognostic Rating Scale with incarcerated offenders. *Journal of Clinical Psychology, 32,* 877–880.

Edinger, J. D., & Weiss, W. U. (1974). The relation between the altitude quotient and adjustment potential. *Journal of Clinical Psychology, 30,* 510–513.

Endicott, N. A., & Endicott, J. (1964). Prediction of improvement in treated and untreated patients using the Rorschach Prognostic Rating Scale. *Journal of Consulting Psychology, 26,* 342–348.

Filmer-Bennett, G. (1955). The Rorschach as a means of predicting treatment outcome. *Journal of Consulting and Clinical Psychology, 19,* 331–334.

Fiske, D. W., Cartwright, D. S., & Kirtner, W. L. (1964). Are psychotherapeutic changes predictable? *Journal of Abnormal and Social Psychology, 69,* 418–426.

Fleiss, J. (1981). *Statistical methods for rates and proportions* (2nd ed.). New York: Wiley.

Garlan, R., MacAllister, W., & Hibbard, S. (2004, March). *Reviving Klopfer's RPRS for Comprehensive System users: Manual Creation, rater training and reliability.* Paper presented at the Annual Meeting of the Society for Personality Assessment, Miami, FL.

Greenberg, N. (1969).The use of the Rorschach Prognostic Rating Scale with foster-home children. *Journal of Projective Techniques and Personality Assessment, 33,* 451–453.

Harris, R., & Christiansen, C. (1946). Prediction of response to brief psychotherapy. *Journal of Psychology, 21,* 269–284.

Hathaway, A. P. (1982). Intelligence and non-intelligence factors contributing to scores on the Rorschach Prognostic Rating Scale. *Journal of Personality Assessment, 46,* 8–11.

Hunt, J. M., & Kogan, L. S. (1950). *Assessing the results of social case work: A manual on judging movement.* New York: Family Services Association of America.

Hunter, J. E., & Schmidt, F. L. (1990). *Methods of meta-analysis: Correcting error and bias in research findings.* Newbury Park, CA: Sage.

Huffcutt, A., & Arthur, W. (1995). Development of a new outlier statistic for meta-analytic data. *Journal of Applied Psychology, 80,* 327–333.

Johnson, E. (1953). Klopfer's Prognostic Rating Scale used with Raven's Progressive Matrices in play therapy prognosis. *Journal of Projective Techniques, 17,* 465–470.

Kirkner, F. J., Wisham, W. W., & Giedt, F. H. (1953). A report on the validity of the Rorschach Prognostic Rating Scale. *Journal of Projective Techniques, 17,* 465–470.

Klopfer, B., Ainsworth, M., Klopfer, W., & Holt, R. (1954). *Development in the Rorschach technique* (Vol. 1). New York: World Book.

Klopfer, B., Kirkner, F. J., Wisham, W., & Baker, G. (1951). Rorschach Prognostic Rating Scale. *Journal of Projective Techniques, 15,* 425–428.

Kotkov, B., & Meadow, A. (1953). Rorschach criteria for predicting continuation in individual psychotherapy. *Journal of Consulting Psychology, 17,* 16–20.

Lipton, M., Tamarin, S., & Lotesta, P. (1951). Test evidence of personality change and prognosis by means of the Rorschach and Wechsler-Bellevue tests on 17 insulin-treated paranoid schizophrenics. *Psychiatric Quarterly, 25,* 434–444.

Luborsky, L., Mintz, J., & Christoph, P. (1979). Are psychotherapeutic changes predictable? Comparison of a Chicago counseling center project with a Penn psychotherapy project. *Journal of Consulting and Clinical Psychology, 47,* 469–473.

Lundin, W. H., & Schpoont, S. (1953). The application of the Rorschach Prognostic Rating Scale to one intensively followed case. *Journal of Projective Techniques, 17,* 295–299.

Meyer, G. J. (2000). Incremental validity of the Rorschach Prognostic Rating Scale over the MMPI Ego Strength Scale and IQ. *Journal of Personality Assessment, 74,* 356–370.

Meyer, G. J., & Handler, L. (1997). The ability of the Rorschach to predict subsequent outcome: A meta-analysis of the Rorschach Prognostic Rating Scale. *Journal of Personality Assessment, 69,* 1–38.

Meyer, G., & Handler, L. (2000). The ability of the Rorschach to predict subsequent outcome: A meta-analysis of the Rorschach Prognostic Rating Scale: Correction. *Journal of Personality Assessment, 74,* 504–506.
Miles, H. H. W., Barrabee, E., & Finesinger, J. E. (1951). Evaluation of psychotherapy. *Psychosomatic Medicine, 13,* 82–105.
Mindess, H. (1953). Predicting patient's response to psychotherapy: A preliminary study designed to investigate the validity of the Rorschach Prognostic Rating Scale. *Journal of Projective Techniques, 17,* 327–334.
Mindess, H. (1957). Psychological indices in the selection of student nurses. *Journal of Projective Techniques, 21,* 37–39.
Newmark, C. S., Finkelstein, M., & Frerking, R. A. (1974). Comparison of the predictive validity of two measures of psychotherapy prognosis. *Journal of Personality Assessment, 38,* 144–148.
Newmark, C. S., Hetzel, W., Walker, L., Holstein, S., & Finklestein, M. (1973). Predictive validity of the Rorschach Prognostic Rating Scale with behavior modification techniques. *Journal of Clinical Psychology, 29,* 246–248.
Newmark, C. S., Konanc, J. T., Simpson, M., Boren, R. B., & Prillaman, K. (1979). Predictive validity of the Rorschach Prognostic Rating Scale with schizophrenic patients. *Journal of Nervous and Mental Disease, 167,* 135–143.
Novick, J. I. (1962). Effectiveness of the Rorschach Prognostic Rating Scale for predicting behavioral change in children following brief psychotherapy. *American Psychologist, 17,* 359–360.
Owen, P., & Kohutek, K. C. (1981). The rural mental health dropout. *Journal of Rural Psychology, 2,* 38–41.
Phillips, L. (1953). Case history date and prognosis in schizophrenia. *Journal of Nervous and Mental Disorders, 117,* 515–525.
Piotrowski, Z. (1941). The Rorschach method as a projective aid in the insulin shock treatment of schizophrenics. *Psychiatric Quarterly, 15,* 807–822.
Piotrowski, Z., & Lewis, N. (1952). An experimental criterion for the prognostication of the status of schizophrenia after a three year interval based on Rorschach data. In P. Hoch & J. Zubin (Eds.), *Relation of psychological tests to psychiatry* (pp. 51–72), Oxford, England: Grune & Stratton.
Pollins, B. (1951). The relationship between psychological data and prognosis in psychotherapy [Abstract]. *University Microfilm Abstracts, 11,* 750–752, Abstract No. 2511.
Rockberger, H. (1953). The effectiveness of a Rorschach Prognostic Scale for predicting results in psychotherapy: A study of the relationship between a Rorschach Prognostic Rating scale and the improvement status of psychoneurotic and ambulatory schizophrenic veterans undergoing individual psychotherapy. *Dissertation Abstract, 1954,* 14: 399–400.
Rogers, L., Knauss, J., & Hammond, K. (1951). Predicting continuation in psychotherapy by means of the Rorschach test. *Journal of Consulting Psychology, 15,* 368–371.
Schulman, R. E. (1963). Use of the Rorschach Prognostic Rating Scale in predicting movement in counseling. *Journal of Counseling Psychology, 10,* 198–199.
Seidel, C. (1960). The relationship between Klopfer's Prognostic Rating Scale and Phillips' Case History Prognostic Rating Scale. *Journal of Consulting Psychology, 24,* 46–49.
Sheehan, J. G., Frederick, C. J., Rosevear, W. H., & Spiegelman, M. (1954). A validity study of Rorschach Prognostic Rating Scale. *Journal of Projective Techniques, 18,* 233–239.

Sheehan, J. G., & Tanaka, J. S. (1983). Prognostic validity of the Rorschach. *Journal of Personality Assessment, 47*, 462–465.
Strauss, J. S., & Harder, D. W. (1981). The Case Record Rating scale: A method for rating symptom and social function data from case records. *Psychiatry Research, 4*, 333–345.
Whiteley, J. M., & Blaine, G. B. (1967). Rorschach in relation to outcome in psychotherapy with college students. *Journal of Consulting Psychology, 31*, 595–599.
Williams, G. J., Monder, R., & Rychlak, J. F. (1967). A one-year concurrent validity study of the Rorschach Prognostic Rating Scale. *Journal of Projective Techniques and Personality Assessment, 31*, 30–33.

Appendix
Rorschach Prognostic Rating Scale (RPRS)

A. Human Movement Responses

Each *M* response is rated according to the three criteria that follow; then the average of these three ratings is assigned to that response.

Criteria **Rating**

1. Amount of movement in space, described or implied
   a. Increasing living space (dancing, running, talking together, pointing). 1
   b. Decreasing living space (bowing, kneeling, crying, crouching, and all Hd responses). . ½
   c. Merely alive (sleeping, lying down, sitting, balancing) 0
2. Freedom in seeing movement
   a. Spontaneously sees action. 1
   b. Uses intermediary means of representing movement . . . . ½
   c. Reluctantly given in Inquiry or follows only from the logic of the situation. 0
3. Cultural distance
   a. Real people of immediate cultural milieu 1
   b. Culturally distant real people, culturally popular fantasy figures, and figures whose clothing or equipment practically conceals their human form (Ubangis, Mickey Mouse, Superman, diver in diving suit). . . . ½
   c. Unusual fantasy figures, or culturally or historically extremely distant figures (Neanderthal men) 0

The average ratings of all the M responses are added algebraically, counting each *M*– response as –1. The resulting raw score is converted into a weighted score as follows:

M Raw Score	Weighted Score
5 to 10.9	3
3 to 4.9 or 11 to 15.9	2
1 to 2.9 or 16 to 20.0	1
Less than 1 or more than 20.0	0
Less than 0 (any minus score)	–1

B. Animal Movement Responses

Each *FM* response is rated according to the three criteria that follow and then the average of these three ratings is assigned to that response.

Criteria	Rating
1. Amount of movement in space	
a. Increasing living space (running, jumping, growling at each other)	1
b. Decreasing living space (crouching, stooping, bending over)	½
c. Merely alive (sleeping, lying down, sitting, standing)	0
2. Freedom in seeing movement	
a. Spontaneously sees action	1
b. Uses intermediary means of representing movement (picture of an animal flying or climbing, totem animal)	½
c. Reluctantly given in inquiry or follows only from the logic of the situation	0
3. Cultural distance	
a. Existing animals common to the culture (dog, bear, crab, elephant, lion, spider, cat, monkey)	1
b. Existing rare animals, common extinct animals, or culturally popular fantasy animals (octopus, dinosaur, Mickey Mouse)	½
c. Unusual fantasy or culturally extremely distant animals (Pegasus, push-me-pull-me, Cerberus, amoeba)	0

The average ratings of all the FM responses are added algebraically, counting each *FM*– response as –1. The resulting score is converted into a weighted score as follows:

FM Raw Score	Weighted Score
2 or more, except in cases where the rule applies, which immediately follows	1
1 to 1.9; or if raw score *FM* is twice raw score *M* or more	0

0 to 0.9 . . . . –1
Less than 0 (any minus score) . . . . –2

C. Inanimate Movement Responses

Each *m* response is rated according to one of the following criteria.

Criteria	**Rating**
1. Natural and mechanical forces	
a. Counter-gravity (explosion, rocket, mechanical motion, geyser, volcano)	1
b. Due to gravity (falling, rock poised precariously)	½
2. Abstract forces	
a. Expressions projected onto inanimate objects (pumpkin with devilish expression)	1
b. Repulsion or attraction (keeps two people apart or brings them together; is the center from which all power emanates)	½
c. Dissipation (Card VIII, lower D, melting ice cream; Card IX, deteriorating mess)	0

The ratings of all the m responses are added algebraically, counting each *Fm–* as –1. The *m* raw score is then converted into a weighted score as follows:

Raw Score	**Weighted Score**
3 to 5.9	2
1 to 2.9 or 6 to 10.0	1
0 to 0.9 or more than 10.0	0
Less than 0 (any minus score)	–1

D. Shading Responses

Each shading item is rated according to the weightings that follow. The individual ratings are added algebraically. The total thus obtained is multiplied by 3 and divided by the total number of shading entries. This is done regardless of whether these entries are ratings for single responses or for characteristics of the total record. This figure is then used as the total weighted score for shading responses.

Responses	**Rating**
Fc (warm, soft, or transparent)	1
FK	1
Fc denial	½

Fc (cold or hard). . . . . ½
K, KF. 0
Fc (shading used as color). . . . . –½
Fk, kF, k. . . . . –½
cF. . . . . –½
Fc- . . . . –1
FK-. . . . . –1
Fc (diseased organ). . . . . –1
c . . . . –1
Characteristics of total record:
Shading evasion . . . . –½
Shading insensitivity . . . . –1

E. Color Responses

Each color item is rated according to the weightings that follow. The individual ratings are added algebraically. The total thus obtained is multiplied by 3 and divided by the total number of color ratings. This figure is then used as the total weighted score for color responses.

Responses **Rating**

FC (color is important, essential,
and meaningful part of the concept) 1
CF (explosive or passive) . . . . ½
C_{des} . . . . ½
Color denial . . . . ½
C_{sym} (euphoric) . . . . ½
Unscorable color remarks expressing discomfort . . . . ½
(Card II: "that red doesn't mean anything")
F ↔ C (forced, overeasy bland). 0
F/C, C/F 0
C_{sym} (dysphoric). . . . . –½
Color in diseased organ. . . . . –½
CF (explosive but given without any sign of affect). . . . . –½
FC– . . . . –1
CF– . . . . –1
C, C_n. . . . . –1
Color contamination. . . . . –1

F. Form Level

Each response is rated for Form Level in the usual manner. Then the average Form Level rating is used as a weighted score except for the following modifications:

1. The occurrence of any "weakening" specifications anywhere in the record (specifications where 0.5 is subtracted from the Form Level rating of any response) reduces the weighted Form Level rating for the entire record by 0.5.

2. The existence of discrepancies between the lowest Form Level rating for any response in a record, provided it is a minus score, and the highest Form Level rating for any response in the same record of at least 3.0, reduces the weighted Form Level rating for the same record by 1.0.

3. These two may be cumulative in the same record. That is, where both occur in a record, 1.5 is subtracted from the average Form Level rating.

G. Final (Total) Prognostic Score

The final (Total) Prognostic Score is the sum of the six separate weighted scores described previously. Tentatively, the following meanings have been assigned to different ranges of prognostic score:

Range	Group	Meaning
17 to 13	I	The person is almost able to help himself. A very promising case that just needs a little help.
12 to 7	II	Not quite so capable as the previous case to work out his problems himself but with some help is likely to do pretty well.
6 to 2	III	Better than 50-50 chance; any treatment will be of some help.
1 to –2	IV	50-50 chance.
–3 to –6	V	A difficult case that may be helped somewhat but is generally a poor treatment prospect.
–7 to –12	VI	A hopeless case.

By examining the positive and negative weights Klopfer et al. (1954) assigned to each variable, it is easy to see which variables they theorized to be most associated with good actual or potential ego strength, and which they believed were associated with poor ego strength.

3

The Use of the Rorschach Technique for Assessing Formal Thought Disorder

Philip S. Holzman
Deborah L. Levy
Harvard University

Mary Hollis Johnston
University of Chicago

In this chapter, we present a method we developed to quantify and characterize the amount and types of thought pathology in responses to the Rorschach inkblots. This work is part of our laboratory's broader investigation of schizophrenia, which employs psychophysiological, neurocognitive, and genetic probes.

Even a naive observer who, for the first time, encounters a patient suffering from a schizophrenic psychosis, will be impressed by at least some of the following: a jarring disconnection between words spoken and their consensual meaning, sudden, unexpected changes in the topic under discussion, a rhythmic repetition of phrases, obscure references to tangential topics, and even neologisms, or newly coined words. In one of his most influential articles, Paul Meehl (1962) asked what kind of behavioral fact about a patient leads us to the diagnosis of schizophrenia. After considering a range of symptoms that include intense ambivalence, social withdrawal, inappropriate affect, and idiosyncratic belief systems, Meehl held that formal thought disorder wins the race. If the patient says, "Naturally, I am growing my father's hair," one has, in Meehl's words, the diagnostic "bell ringer."

Since the middle of the nineteenth century, when psychiatrists began to examine systematically patients who later would be viewed as suffering from schizophrenia, the strangeness in the language of these patients has been a central topic of study. Kraepelin (1919), who first brought together, under a single diagnostic rubric called *dementia praecox,* the several psychotic conditions of *demence précoce* (of Morel), *hebephrenia* (of Hecker), and *katatonia* (of Kahlbaum), called attention to these "derailments" in speech and thought. He cited them as evidence for the dementia he assumed to be characteristic of these conditions. Influenced by the British associationist school of psychology, Bleuler (1911/1950) attributed these disorders of thinking to a disorder of association. He wrote that when associative links and relationships between ideas and thoughts are lost, confusion and illogic result, and thinking becomes bizarre (p. 9).

Other theorists followed Kraepelin's (1919) and Bleuler's (1911/1950) interest in the thought slippage in these psychotic conditions, and most of them offered their own explanations of the cognitive aberrations. Storch (1924) and Werner (1940) emphasized links between the thinking of schizophrenic patients and that of children and "primitives." Goldstein (1944) was impressed by the replacement of abstract thinking with concreteness, and von Domarus (1944) focused on the syllogistic errors in the thinking of schizophrenic patients. Writers from a psychoanalytic perspective considered that the peculiarities in language and thought were examples of "primary process," and concluded that schizophrenia must represent a regressive return to earlier developmental stages of mental life (Fenichel, 1945).

The several theories of formal thought disorder in psychosis approach the phenomenon from different vantage points. Their variety makes it clear that we cannot adequately describe, let alone explain, the phenomenon in terms of a single dichotomy, whether it is loosened association, primary versus secondary process, abstract versus concrete thinking, and so forth. We recognize now that there is a continuum between the extremes of each of these qualities of thought; they are dimensions rather than categories. Thought disorder also is not a uniform condition. All or any of these qualities, and others as well, may characterize the thinking process of any particular psychotic patient. Some of these dimensions characterize some of the patients some of the time; not all schizophrenic patients manifest the same type of thought disorder; nor are all kinds of thought disorders present in any particular patient. The classical theorists of thought disorder obtained their data from clinical observation, principally from talking with schizophrenic patients, and they did not attempt to reconcile their formulations with those of other theorists. Consequently, there was no agreement about which aspects of schizophrenic thinking are of primary and which are of secondary importance. We began our work in the confines of what amounted to an analog of the Tower of Babel; the notable theorists, located in different psychiatric centers as occupants of this tower, spoke different national languages as well as different psychiatric languages that were not mutually understandable.

EFFORTS TO MEASURE FORMAL THOUGHT DISORDER

A survey of those aspects of thought that have been singled out as constituting an underlying, fundamental deficit turns up several candidates. Chapman and Chapman (1973) reviewed several that had been investigated empirically. The deficits can be ordered into five areas of thinking: concept formation, cognitive focusing, reasoning, modulation of affect, and reality testing. Because of the multiple aspects and multidimensionality of thought disorder, some investigators constructed scales for rating all aspects of thought disorder as they occurred in interviews or structured tests. These include rating scales by Cancro (1968), Harrow, Harkavy, Bromet, and Tucker (1973), Harrow, Tucker, Himmelhoch, and Putnam (1972), and Harrow and Quinlan (1977); methods developed by Perry, Geyer, and Braff (1999) and Docherty, Gordinier, Hall, and Cutting (1999); as well as the widely used "Thought, Language, and Communication" (TLC) Scale developed by Andreasen and colleagues (Andreasen, 1979a, 1979b; Andreasen & Grove, 1986). All of these authors endorsed the idea of a continuum of thought disorder from mild slippage to bizarre disorganization. Thus individuals can be placed appropriately on a continuum and compared with respect to severity of thought disorder as well as with themselves over time. The consensus position is that thought disorder is not unitary and that there are many different ways and degrees to which thinking can become disordered.

The rating scale or other instrument used by investigators determines the range and kind of thought disorder they can identify. For example, if the investigator relies solely on an object-sorting test, the dimension of abstractness-concreteness will assume primacy; if reliance is on a word-association test, looseness of associations will move to the forefront. The effort to characterize pathological thinking advanced significantly with the study of diagnostic psychological testing by Rapaport, Gill, and Schafer (1968). Their study employed a battery of projective (including the Rorschach and Thematic Apperception Test [TAT]) and nonprojective instruments (including the Wechsler Adult Intelligence Scale [WAIS] and an object-sorting task) to identify differences in responses among classes of psychiatric patients. In addition to a careful discussion of the rationales of the determinants, form level, location, and content of Rorschach responses, Rapaport et al. introduced a "fifth scoring category" that focused on patients' verbalizations and their interrelations with the perceptual process that gave rise to the response. They wrote that peculiarities in verbalization reflect a disturbance in the person's reality attunement. Indeed, they defined deviant thinking as thinking that does not adhere to the consenually agreed-on constraints implicit in the test situation, as defined by "attitudes, responses, and verbalizations of the general normal population" (Rapaport et al., p. 427).

Rapaport et al. (1968) did not develop a quantitative scheme to rate the various types of deviant verbalizations that make up this "fifth scoring category" of Rorschach responses. They did, however, identify several classes of deviant verbalizations, such as peculiar, queer, absurd, and neologisms. They also identified clangs, fluidity, autistic logic, and contaminations as additional manifestations of thought disorder. Watkins and Stauffacher (1952) quantified the Rapaport et al. categories of thought disturbance to derive a "Delta Index," the term *Delta* denoting deviation. They assigned weights on a 4-point scale to instances of formal thought disorder. Minor deviations, such as the peculiar use of a word, received the lowest weight (0.25), and major instances of thought disturbance, such as a neologism or an absurd response, received the highest weight (1.0). The Delta Index was computed as the sum of the instances of thought disorder multiplied by their assigned weights, divided by the number of Rorschach responses. They reported interscorer reliabilities of 0.78 for psychotic patients, and 0.04 for normal controls. The poor reliability in scoring the records of normal controls reflected the relative infrequency of scorable instances of pathological verbalizations and the constricted range of variability. They found that all normal controls had a Delta Index of 5 or below.

FORMAL THOUGHT DISORDER IN NON-PSYCHOTIC INDIVIDUALS

Most clinicians are aware that some of the biological relatives of schizophrenic patients manifest some peculiarities in thinking, although they may show no other indications of psychiatric illness. It is also noteworthy that many persons who later developed a schizophrenic illness showed these same peculiarities of thought even before the appearance of their manifest illness. Bleuler identified some individuals as having a "latent schizophrenia" (Bleuler, 1911/1950). These were people who shared some personality features with their schizophrenic relatives, yet never went on to experience a psychotic episode and even seemed to live rather stable lives. This observation gave rise to the concept of the "schizophrenia spectrum" (Kety, Rosenthal, & Wender, 1978). It implies that, although schizophrenia runs in families, there is good evidence that a genetic component plays a significant role in its transmission. Indeed, most observers accept the position that it is not the schizophrenic psychosis by itself that is inherited, but some disposition that is yet to be identified.

We propose that thought disorder is part of that disposition and have developed a technique to measure the presence and degree of thought disorder in its several guises. It is applicable to the various types of thought disorder and permits an evaluation of their relative significance and importance in a particular record. Watkins and Stauffacher's (1952) simple method of quantifying the Rapaport et al. (1968) Rorschach response categories provided the template on which we constructed our scale to measure the types and extent of formal thought disorder in several psychiatric conditions. We named the metric the Thought Disorder Index (Johnston & Holzman, 1979), or TDI. Although the TDI can, in principle, be used to score the presence of thought disorder in any extended verbal sample, such as the written record of a psychological test or psychiatric interview, the use of the relatively standardized verbal sample of the protocol of an individual's Rorschach test offers many advantages over such opportunistic situations. Tests like a sorting test or the WAIS rely on overlearned responses, which can result in stereotypical answers to standardized questions and thus limit the possibility to produce instances of thought disorder. Similarly, the psychiatric interview frequently taps into conventional and overpracticed responses. We settled on the use of the Rorschach test because it provides a relative balance between an unstructured and unfamiliar situation that minimizes overlearned and overpracticed responses, and because, to the examiner, it is quite familiar because of experience with many protocols. The frame of reference and social expectations of the Rorschach are less obvious to the person taking the test than those of the WAIS or of a psychiatric interview, and therefore can more easily elicit the person's own organizing efforts, efforts that are more likely to be impaired by psychopathology.

THE THOUGHT DISORDER INDEX

The TDI classifies and weights responses to the Rorschach blots according to their pathological significance. The 23 categories of thought disorder and responses can be given weights according to their severity on a 4-point scale (0.25, 0.50, 0.75, and 1.0). Johnston and Holzman (1979) presented a detailed description of the TDI, which has been subsequently modified in minor ways (see, e.g., Solovay et al., 1986). The rationale for the presumed sensitivity to thought disorder of the TDI assumes that patients responding to the Rorschach plates first have an associative apprehension of the amorphous stimuli. This associative process is followed by an effort to organize and elaborate the initial impression. Finally, patients attempt to verbalize the confluence of the perceptual and associative impressions in their responses (Rapaport et al., 1968, p. 276). Interference by psychopathology with the process of organizing a response at any of these stages will result in thought slippage, such as inappropriate reasoning and disruptions in attending, or peculiarities in concept formation, perceptual organization, and verbalization.

In our laboratory, we administer the Rorschach according to the Rapaport et al. (1968) instructions. Inquiry into the responses should be brief and unintrusive, but sufficiently focused so that it yields enough information to score a response for location, determinants, form level, and content. When there is any suspicion of thought slippage, as in deviant verbalization, elliptical responses, and responses with very poor form level, it is important to inquire into the thought process that went into the response. Leading questions are to be avoided; instead, questions such as, "What did you mean by ... ?" or "When you said such and such a word, what did you have in mind?" are preferable. The inquiry is conducted as soon as the patient is finished responding to a card (not, as in some systems, after all ten cards are responded to), and the examiner should be aware that deviant verbalizations might occur during the response period, during the inquiry or during the location period.

It is our practice, especially in a research context, to tape record the protocol, which is then transcribed verbatim and checked for accuracy against the notes taken by the examiner during testing. Tape recording the test is important because we have found that at times it is not possible for the examiner to accurately record the content of deviant responses and other verbalizations without slowing the discourse, for example, when testing manic patients who often speak very rapidly. If, as in many clinical situations, tape recording is not practicable, it is critical that the examiner obtain a near-verbatim record and not edit deviant responses so that they make better sense.

With experience, examiners are able to use the TDI more effectively. To improve the sensitivity of examiners to the nuances of deviant verbalizations and poor perceptual responses, we have found it advisable to score protocols in a group of two or three examiners that includes at least one person who has broad experience with this metric. It should be clear from these cautions that the TDI is neither a self-scoring instrument, nor is it quickly learned. To become proficient requires training and experience. As with most clinical methods that require subjective judgment, such as reading electrocardiograms or recognizing the presence of a neoplastic lesion in an x-ray, there is no substitute for exposure to many protocols, so that the examiner becomes sensitive not only to what the patient says, but also to how the patient says it. Instances of pathological verbalization are exemplars of natural categories (Rosch, 1973) and learning to distinguish one natural category from another is like learning to distinguish oak leaves and maple leaves, Chevrolets and Dodges, the music of Mozart and that of Haydn, or a Bordeaux wine and a Burgundy. The differences the examiner must become attuned to are subtle; varieties of thought disorder are not members of proper sets, as are geometric shapes. To accurately identify members of a natural category such as leaves, one must be trained, for instance, to distinguish the many varieties of oak leaves, some of which are quite similar to the leaves of other species. One must learn to recognize both the prototype and its alternative presentations. In contrast, in the case of proper sets, one can learn to distinguish any square from any triangle after only one exposure.

THOUGHT, LANGUAGE, OR SPEECH DISORDER

We consider that deviant verbalizations of patients reflect disorders of thought, rather than disorders of language or of speech, a choice that is tinged with controversy (Brown, 1973; Chaika, 1974; Chaika & Lambe, 1985; Fromkin, 1975). We adopt the position that language is a medium through which thought is communicated. This view is influenced by Heider's (1959) analysis of the perception of things and the media through which they are conveyed. Sizes, shapes, textures, constancies, contrasts, and colors are examples of media through which we perceive things. When we look at a chair, we do not "see" the chair's retinal size, or its changes in shape as we approach it, or how its color changes as fluorescent light rather than sunlight bathes it. The chair retains its "object constancy." We either see the chair we are expecting to see at the breakfast table or perhaps another, one we put there for a guest. The perception of that specific chair is mediated by its properties of size, shape, slant, texture, and color. At any time, of course, we can voluntarily direct our attention to the retinal image size of the chair or to any of its attributes or mediators, and by changing our intention, we transform them into things or objects of perception.

The process is the same with language. From the earliest moments of life, we are trained to look through language at the thoughts it conveys. In use, language is transparent, although it can be made an object of examination, as when a linguist examines language usage, grammar, and syntax. As with the perception of concrete objects, when we listen to a person speaking, we grasp the thoughts the person is trying to transmit. We attend primarily to the thoughts and only secondarily, if at all, to the language in which they are couched. Therapists gifted in treating psychotic patients are able to perform these dual acts of understanding better than most of us.

Psychotic patients do not speak a shared language or even a shared dialect. There is no such thing as a schizophrenic language or a manic patois. There is no culture of schizophrenia. Indeed, schizophrenic patients have as much difficulty as nonschizophrenic individuals in understanding the elliptical speech of another schizophrenic person (see, e.g., Hunt & Walker, 1966) or even their own.

The observation that disorders of language and disorders of thought are not only conceptually but empirically separable provides yet another argument for our position. Thought disorders exist independently of language disorders, and language disorders can exist without thought disorders. Cases of pure paranoia are instances of disturbed thinking without a trace of language disorder. The delusions voiced by such patients generally are couched in language that is syntactically and grammatically correct. With increasing degrees of psychological disorganization, people suffering from psychosis tend to manifest disturbance of language along with thought disorder. Then one can see thought disorder in a setting of deviant language. Of course, one can see evidence of serious thought disorder when little or no language is involved, as in instances of bizarre and disorganized behaviors and in the responses of psychotic patients to nonverbal tests such as the Ravens Matrices, sorting tests, or the performance subtests of the WAIS (e.g., digit symbol, block design, and picture arrangement).

There are, to be sure, conditions of serious language disturbance without any thought disorders, as in the case of the congenitally deaf. These people are generally able to read at no better than a fifth-grade level, and their spoken speech tends to be laden with grammatical and syntactic errors. Yet, when communicating in sign language, their thinking is as well organized as that of a person with no hearing impairment.

Our late colleague, Roger W. Brown, expanded on the separability and overlap of language and thought (Brown, 1973). Brown called attention to linguistic factors that are independent of thought; these factors include phonotactics, morphology, and syntactics. *Phonotactics* refers to phonemes that are more or less acceptable within a particular language, such as the gutteral "ch" sound in Hebrew or the similar one in German, called by linguists a velar fricative, the "ϕ" sound in Norwegian, the throaty "r" sound in French, and the click sound in some African languages. In English, there are many tolerable combinations of consonantal sounds, such as *pr* (as in "prawn"), *dr* (as in "drawer"), and *tr* (as in "trill"). But *sr* is not such a tolerable combination in English, although it is in Serbian. It is remarkable that schizophrenic patients, even when they invent words (neologisms), do not violate these phonotactic strictures. Rather, they stay within the forms that are permissible in their spoken language.

Morphology refers to the rules for language inflection, such as "go, going, gone," "build, building, built," "toy, toys," and "man, men." Psychotic patients tend to adhere to the rules for regular and irregular inflections as most people do. Similarly, *syntactics*, which refers to the rules for meaningful word order in a language, remain within the permissible confines of the language, and no study has shown either morphologic or syntactic structures in schizophrenics that deviate from those of people who are not schizophrenic.

One may apply the same analysis to the issue of whether there is an essential speech disorder in schizophrenia. There are central nervous system disorders that produce speech disorders, such as Broca's aphasia. The several types of aphasia can be divided into receptive and expressive aphasias, both of which produce disturbances that differ from those shown by patients with schizophrenia or other psychotic disorders.

For all of these reasons, and in the absence of convincing demonstration that psychotic conditions can produce a purely linguistic or speech disorder, we believe it is more heuristic and more conducive to deepening our understanding of the nature of psychotic disorganization to regard the odd verbal productions of psychotic persons as the outcome of disordered thinking. The strangeness of their speech involves the semantics of communication.

THE TDI SCORING CATEGORIES

Earlier in this chapter, we proposed that no single measure would suffice to reflect the complexity and heterogeneity of thought disturbances in psychotic disorders. The TDI, however, which taps a wide variety and range of manifestations of thought disorder, permits us to distinguish among types of thought pathology and degrees of severity within types. Like Rapaport et al. (1968), we distinguish two major classes of deviance. The first class is based on the degree of perceptual support the blot supplies for the response. The second class is based on the verbalizations with which those responses are expressed to the examiner.

An example of a response from the first category is "A beetle's eye" to Card I in a location that provides no perceptual justification for the response. Experience in reading many Rorschach protocols also shows that no other person has responded in that way to that area of the blot. One therefore may infer that it resulted from severe slippage in thinking. The TDI scoring scheme would place such a response in the category of absurd responses.

Thought disorder may also be inferred when two responses, each justified by reasonable formal resemblance to an area of the blot, are combined in a capricious manner, and it is the combination rather than either percept that violates reality constraints. An example is the response to Card VIII, "two bears" (an appropriate response) and a "ball-point pen" (a small area in the center of the card); "The bears are dancing on the point of the pen." Here the respondent takes too literally the spatial arrangement of the blot and produces a response that stretches reality constraints. One might object that the judgment made here is too subjective to permit a reliable consensus about the deviance of such a response. Like Rapaport et al. (1968), we argue that, although scoring is unavoidably subjective, normal subjects understand implicitly that they are to give responses for which "sufficient justification may be found in the perceptual qualities of the inkblot ... [and] that their responses must be completely acceptable to everyday conventional logic ... [or to] critical control, and thus [not be] absurdly combined or absurdly integrated" (Rapaport et al., p. 429).

The second major class of deviance reflects the way in which the response is verbalized, and thus represents the outcome of the deviant thought process. These verbalizations are denoted in the TDI as peculiar, queer, neologism, and absurd. Many deviant verbalizations are easily overlooked during the course of ordinary conversation or even during the course of psychiatric interviews. In nonpathological instances these peculiarities of speech are generally mild and are usually spontaneously corrected, much like a slip of the tongue. It is the accumulation of these mild peculiarities or even the appearance of a single queer response or neologism that alerts the listener to something more than the presence of a benign slip of the tongue.

We list in Table 3.1 the scoring categories of the TDI, after which we elaborate on some of them. A fuller description of most of the categories can be found in Johnston and Holzman (1979). Since the publication of that book, the TDI has been modified to include some new categories because of experiences testing patients with bipolar disorder, particularly, manic psychosis (Solovay, Shenton, & Holzman, 1987), schizoaffective disorder (Shenton, Solovay, & Holzman, 1987), and right hemisphere cortical lesions (Kestnbaum Daniels et al., 1988). A few categories were removed because they were difficult to score reliably or occurred too rarely to justify their continued use (Solovay et al., 1986).

The metric for the TDI as a percentage is computed as the sum of the instances of thought disorder that occur at each of the four severity levels, multiplied by the weights of those levels, divided by the number of Rorschach responses. This measure is summarized in the following formula:

$$\frac{\textbf{Total TDI} = \Sigma\,[0.25(A) + 0.50(B) + 0.75(C) + 1.0(D)]}{\textbf{Total } R} \times 100$$

Where A = number of thought disordered responses at the 0.25 level
B = number of thought disordered responses at the 0.50 level
C = number of thought disordered responses at the 0.75 level
D = number of thought disordered responses at the 1.0 level
R = total number of Rorschach responses

Dividing by the total number of Rorschach responses provides a control over verbosity, a control that is needed because psychopathology

TABLE 3.1
Scoring Categories of the TDI

Severity Level	*Examples*
0.25	Inappropriate distance (loss or increase of distance, tendency to looseness, concreteness, overspecificity) Flippancy Vagueness Peculiar verbalizations and responses (stilted, inappropriate, or peculiar expressions, idiosyncratic word usage, peculiar verbalizations) Word-finding difficulty Clangs Perseveration Incongruous combinations (composite response, arbitrary form-color response, inappropriate activity response, external-internal response) Relationship verbalization Idiosyncratic symbolism
0.50	Queer responses Confusion Looseness Fabulized combinations, impossible or bizarre Playful confabulations Fragmentation
0.75	Fluidity Absurd responses Confabulations (extreme elaboration without objective support from the blot, details in one area generalized to a larger area without support) Autistic logic
1.0	Contaminations Incoherence Neologisms

affects verbal productivity. People with depressive disorders, for example, tend to give far fewer responses than normals, and those suffering from manic symptoms tend to give many more. Similarly, some patients with schizophrenia display a disabling constriction, whereas others show a disinhibited posture while responding to the Rorschach test. We have found that dividing by the number of responses corrects for verbal productivity to about the same extent as correcting for the total number of words spoken in the course of the testing, and, of course, is much more efficient than counting words.

ELABORATIVE REMARKS ON THE TDI CATEGORIES

The book that introduced the TDI (Johnston & Holzman, 1979) is out of print and not easily available. We therefore repeat here some of the explanatory comments that appeared in that book. Some of the examples that follow appeared in that publication, but others are new.

The 0.25 level of severity represents minor breaks in ordinary conversation that generally attract only passing notice. The listener may experience a lack of clarity about what the speaker intends, but may be able to overlook the aberrant word or phrase and infer the intention. However, an accumulation of mildly idiosyncratic uses of words and phrases, especially if they cloud the message or lead to a loss of focus, may alert the listener to recognize that a disorder of thinking is present. Following are some examples:

1. *Inappropriate distance*. We have grouped four kinds of inappropriate distance under this category. Rapaport et al. (1968) distinguished an increase of distance from a loss of distance. In *increase of distance*, the subject fails to recognize that the inkblot is merely a stimulus for a response, and is unable to adopt the set of "it looks like" and instead tries to think of what "it is." In *loss of distance*, the subject becomes personally involved with the inkblot, and comments, for instance, that the blot is too disturbing or horrible ("I can't stand looking at it"). *Concreteness* is scored when the subject loses perspective, and awards undeserved reality to incidental aspects of the blot. Examples are: "A large size moth. It's large, because it's approximately seven inches by five inches" and "An enormous bee, because it was so big and the bears were so small." *Overspecificity* is scored when a response involves an effort at excessive and unwarranted precision, perhaps implying the misfiring of an obsessional disposition, for example, "This is a dog's tibia."

2. *Flippancy*. Here the respondent departs from the usual social restraints of a testing situation, one that implicitly calls for a professional relationship with the examiner and a task-oriented set. Flippant remarks, gratuitous joke telling, or wise cracks step beyond the informal limits, for example, "Is this helping you? Good, 'cause I wouldn't do it if it wasn't helping you. Being my generous personality."

3. *Vagueness*. A vague response may mask an attempt to avoid offering an inappropriate response or perhaps an unwillingness to engage in the task. The vague response contains too little information to score as a Rorschach response. A vague response may be a short, cryptic phrase or a long, meandering, circumstantial paragraph. It may result from the inability to organize and communicate informa-

tion. Examples are: "Two figures" (What made them look like that?) "I don't know. I don't know what they are. Two smears," and "Picture of like depth, and stuff, like distance."

4. *Peculiar verbalizations and responses*. This category is intended for odd words or phrases that may have a recognizable meaning but do not fit the context in which they are used. Sloppiness in speech, characteristic of people with a hysterical character disposition, or the carelessness and cavalier use of language by sociopathic persons, can result in peculiar verbalizations. People with psychotic disorders, and many unaffected relatives of patients with schizophrenia, often produce stilted, unusual, strained, and unconventional expressions that belong in this category. Examples are: "half heads," "beak-like obstructions," "potential ears," "cranial skull," "contemporary view of a person," "There's a segregation between mouth and nose," and "They are in descending motion [sitting down]."

5. *Word-finding difficulty*. We distinguish blocking—the subject knows the word, but cannot recall it—from a simple absence of knowledge about what word to use. "It's a ... what is it, it's a ... not a beetle, but oh, it's a sca ... it's in the desert. I can't think of it."

6. *Clang*. Clangs are scored when the subject uses rhyming or alliterative phrases, and in that manner plays with words: "... and that's what the nature of his loins is ... he's organizing in his organs," "Really busy. Busy Lizzie."

7. *Perseveration*. Perseveration is scored if a response that has very poor form is repeated at least three times, for example, "an airplane" to Cards I, II, and IV.

8. *Incongruous Combinations*. Single details of a blot that are contiguous with each other are merged into a single response. Here, as Weiner (1966) noted, the respondent imparts too much reality to the images. We follow Weiner's suggestions in distinguishing four subcategories: composite, arbitrary form-color, inappropriate activity, and external-internal. "Some type of phallic figure with wings" and "a lizard with cat's legs" are examples of the first category. In the arbitrary form-color response (scored by Rapaport et al. (1966) as FC_{arb}), the subject must be unaware of the inappropriateness of the combination of form and color, for example, "An orange pelvic bone. Or a small guy with two orange arms." Inappropriate activity denotes an image that is impossible or distorts reality, for example, "a beetle crying." The external-internal response denotes the simultaneous depiction of external and internal parts of an object. For example, "internal organs of the body" would be scored if the subject saw a person or animal and was looking through the skin to see the internal organs such as the heart or kidney.

9. *Relationship verbalization*. The subject links the current response to a prior one on a previous card and relates the two separate percepts, for example, "the previous bat [i.e., the bat seen on a previous card], in flight."

10. *Idiosyncratic symbolism*. An example is: "Red is trouble, and Africa being red symbolizes that maybe the origin of man was in Africa and that's why it looks red."

In contrast to the 0.25 level of severity, which indicates a somewhat shaky but by no means broken hold on reality, responses at the 0.50 severity level convey a loss of stable mooring in reality, as shown in the following:

1. *Queer verbalizations or responses*. These responses are on a continuum with peculiar responses, but they represent a clear increase in severity and strangeness. (Further worsening in severity are the categories of absurd at the 0.75 severity level, and neologism at the 1.0 level.) With respect to queer responses, the examiner is generally uncertain about what is meant by the word or phrase used by the respondent. Examples are: "a foxed comic dog," "both sides, left and right, seemed to be totally equal in shape and culture," "the echo of a picture," "the outside lookers, the onlookers of the outside," "these are the posterior pronunciations," "the adhesive adjunctive extensions," and "a tree head kind of a person."

2. *Confusion*. Subjects lose the train of thought and are not sure what they are seeing or saying, indicating some disorientation, for example, "like a backbone, when you listen to an x-ray, part of one."

3. *Looseness*. This category is scored when the respondent loses the focus of the communication, and takes off into an unrelated, tangentially related, or arbitrarily related area. It is often possible, however, to identify the original starting point of this tangential chain of ideas. Examples are: "Because it's black, dark, darkness, lovemaking," "A little bit of the phallus ... symbol. That's very prominent today, for some reason. If you may have read in the paper the other night, remember when you used to go to the movies, the saltiest thing in the movies was the popcorn," and "A flower. Reminded me of when I gave a flower to someone before. Plus, I like roses... Didn't never really get to ... express myself the way I wanted to."

4. *Fabulized combinations, impossible or bizarre*. This category represents part of a continuum of combinatory thinking that inappropriately infers relations between unrelated things. Here percept and ideas are condensed into conclusions that violate reality considerations about relationships between images, blot qualities, and ob-

jects. At the mildest end of the combinatory spectrum (0.25 level) are incongruous combinations. Fabulized combinations are scored at the 0.50 level, confabulations at the 0.75 level, and contaminations at the 1.0 level. Many respondents produce fabulized combinations that do not distort reality, and represent creative organization of the percepts, for example, "two women bending over to pick up baskets" (Card III). Such responses are not scored, because they result from the combination of two accurately perceived images that are realistically possible. Fabulized combinations are scored when the respondent forces two contiguous, more or less separate, percepts into unrealistic relationships. The form quality of the separate percepts may be good, but the spatial relationship between them is taken as real, and the final combined image is realistically impossible. Examples are: "Two crows with Afros and they're pushing two hearts together," "the doctor holding his bag in front of a red butterfly, fixing the embryo," and "two fetal bears on a coral reef."

5. *Playful confabulations*. Playful confabulations are fabulized combinations that are fancifully overelaborated. They typically involve humorous and playful images. They are less extreme than a confabulation. Examples are: "A fat insect in a tuxedo. Got a nice red bow tie. His stomach was hangin' over. Like one of those guys who watches football Sunday afternoon ....," "a butterfly on steroids," and "dancing bears who've just stepped on broken glass, perhaps at a Jewish wedding. They've been toasting each other, talking animatedly."

6. *Fragmentation*. In scoring fragmentation, one should notice a clear inability on the part of the respondent to integrate separate elements into a whole percept. We were first struck by this inability when testing patients with right hemisphere cortical damage (Kestnbaum Daniels et al., 1988). An example is: "A masquerade party costume ... cha-cha ... clap hands ... let's dance." The patient was able to integrate these fragments into one response only after the examiner asked whether she was seeing a couple dancing. Fragmentation is also scored when the focus is on a small detail of a typically larger percept, which Rorschach (1922/1942) labeled the "Do" response.

At the 0.75 level, we score obvious thought disturbances that clinicians identify with psychotic thinking, including unstable percepts, absurd responses, personalized logic, and undisciplined and arbitrary combinations.

1. *Fluidity*. Whereas looseness means that the respondent seems unable to focus on a single topic, wanders discursively from one idea

to another, and is only tenuously tied to any of the previous ideas, fluidity means that something seen as one thing at one instant will be seen as a different object at the next instant. Fluidity indicates that object constancy is weakened. In order to be scored as fluidity, the subject must state that the percept appears to be changing into another, rather than one response merely following quickly on the next, for example, "Two poodles. Two ladies. They are the same place and I couldn't tell if they were poodles or ladies." "When I first looked at it, it looked like a bat flying away, then I looked at it again, it looked like a bat flying toward me."

2. *Absurd responses*. Responses scored as absurd are almost totally arbitrary, and bear little if any resemblance to objective reality. The examiner or scorer is unable to form an idea about the source of the response, which reflects more about the ideation of the responder than the reality of the blot. Examples are: "Altogether we can fly and understand God. Altogether we are the butterfly," "I think wolves are usually synonymous with bears," "the eye of a spider," and "a nonverbal misrepresentation leading to an unformulated thought."

3. *Confabulations*. The TDI recognizes two classes of confabulation. In extreme elaboration, the respondent carries to an extreme an elaborative ideational tendency that extends the percept beyond the bounds of reality constraints. Examples are: "Two people looking at each other and feeling something heart-to-heart," "Looks like a beetle that's been injured. It looks frightened, angry, aggressive. And uh ... very intent on ... attacking in ... retaliation for something that's bothering it," and "Two women sitting at a café and they're eating something that looks like hearts. Sort of half-women, half-birds ... maybe they're having babies because this looks like it could be a baby or they're pregnant and talking and thinking about babies. See how their thoughts are shaped like a fetus." The category of details in one area generalized to a larger area is the same as that scored by Rorschach as a DW response, which denotes that a single, small detail is clearly perceived, but is then used to interpret the entire inkblot in a way that violates the shape of the larger area (Rorschach, 1922/1942, pp. 37–38). An example is: " A basketball player" (What makes it look like a basketball player?) "Here's the ball, then it's not clear where the basketball player is, but I can see the ball, it must be somewhere in there."

4. *Autistic Logic*. The respondent justifies a response by rationalizing it with a "because" statement that is illogical or based on private, autistic reasoning processes rather than on conventional, logical reasoning. To score autistic logic requires that the response be based explicitly on faulty logic. Examples are: "Two pant legs" (What made it

look like that?) "Well ... because it wasn't the skull, it's gotta be pant legs." (Could you explain that a little more?) Well, skulls deteriorate and ... pant legs don't" and ("Japanese silk screen") "Well, Japanese like the color red so I picked the red color because their flag has the rising sun on it which is red."

At the 1.0 level, which represents the most disordered thinking in the TDI, reality constraints appear to have collapsed and bizarre ideation occurs.

1. *Contamination.* In this response, two separate and unrelated percepts are merged into one. This category represents the extreme of the continuum of combinatory responses. In contrast to fabulized combinations, incongruous combinations, confabulations, and playful confabulations, in which individual percepts retain their original identity, in a contaminated response the original identity of each percept is merged into a composite. The two discrete images are usually seen in the same area of the inkblot, but are fused into a single percept. Examples are: "Looks like two rats. Or demons again. Two rat demons" and "a butterfly. Or blood. A bloody butterfly."

2. *Incoherence.* The response is unrelated to the task and it is not possible for the examiner or scorer to understand it in any context. Examples are: "Tears go up in the air. Blood, and break their neck, you know, reject" and "All centered around a compass or a gyroscope or a bottle. Inside the bottle comes all, inside the bottle comes all. (Can you explain?) It looks like inside the bottle it all came out of."

3. *Neologisms.* These are new word coinages that could be actual words, except that they are not. Because they do not violate English morphology or phonotactics, they remain within the English language (if English is the language being spoken). They are, nevertheless, invented words, perhaps as a result of condensations, or of a private language. The Joycean epic *Finnegans Wake* (1939) contains many neologistic word formations; but these are the product of effortful composing, ingenious punning, and portmanteau words, such as "When I was jung and unafreud" and "Three quarks for Muster Mark." At the time *Finnegans Wake* was published, *quark* was not a real English word. It entered our vocabulary through Murray Gell-Mann's (1964) work on the basic building blocks of matter, one of which he dubbed the *quark*. Gell-Mann pointedly took the word from *Finnegans Wake*. These deliberate wordplays display a quality of originality and ingenious inventiveness, as does a clever puzzle or a well-crafted poem. In the neologisms of psychotic patients, on the other hand, this deliberate playfulness is absent, and the product re-

sembles a verbal contamination in which two words are combined into a third, but the meaning may be only vaguely glimpsed, if at all. In contrast to the Joycean constructions, subjects seem unaware that the word uttered is unusual and that it has meaning only to them. Examples are: "Two people juggling. People tobbling like on TV," "The property is more closely centulated to the trailroads," "skullogy," and "levatory steps ..." [*levatory* means "sort of coming in at a different angle"].

As we emphasized earlier, ability to use the TDI increases with experience. Scoring, which requires about 20 minutes, is best learned in groups of at least two people, one of whom is an experienced scorer. Training and practice sensitize people to the formal characteristics of verbalizations, that is, to the way people express themselves.

THE RELIABILITY OF THE TDI

Studies of cognitive and physiological performance of schizophrenic patients almost universally report that the patients' performance is highly variable. This variability does not result from changes in clinical state, which can positively or negatively affect almost any behavior. The variability in question occurs independently of clinical state, not only within the group of psychotic patients being tested, but also within individual patients. A patient's performance will vary from moment to moment whether one is testing reaction-time latencies (some normal latencies occur in the setting of generally raised latencies), eye-tracking dysfunction (epochs of normal pursuit tracking are interspersed among abnormalities in tracking), or thought disorder. Disruptions in thinking occur intermittently, not regularly and not continuously. Both their severity and their prevalence fluctuate. They may also vary in their form from moment to moment. We believe that this aspect of schizophrenic response—it appears to occur in schizophrenia more than in other psychoses—deserves special study because it sets schizophrenia apart from other diseases in which intermittency is not the rule. A lesion in Broca's area of the brain, for example, shows no intermittency in the aphasic disorder it causes. We have referred to this intermittent degradation in performance as *dialipsis*, our own intentional neologism, derived from the Greek to denote a deviation from that which is regularly expected. It is important to be able to measure this intermittent variability in order to appreciate many aspects of schizophrenic behavior, including thought disorder. Elsewhere instructions were provided for its statistical measurement (Matthysse, Levy, Wu, Rubin, & Holzman, 1999). The importance of the phenomenon of dialipsis in assessing the internal consistency of the TDI is that we do not expect that thought disruptions will necessarily occur on every Rorschach card, or with the same type of thought disorder, or with the same severity. This phenomenon makes interpreting split-half reliabilities of internal consistency of the TDI difficult. It can happen, for example, that a schizophrenic patient will produce no scorable instances of thought disorder on the first nine cards, and on the tenth card may produce a single contamination. Nevertheless, the split-half correlation within a group of 49 schizophrenic patients was 0.78 and statistically significant (Johnston & Holzman, 1979, pp. 132–133).

Another characteristic of the TDI scores that affects estimates of reliability is that the scores do not form a normal distribution. Most normal controls have no thought disorder, and psychiatric patients with nonpsychotic disorders tend to have scores that cluster at the lower end of the TDI continuum. For this reason statistical analyses must be undertaken with transformed scores. With adequately large samples, a log transformation yields an acceptable approximation to a normal distribution that permits parametric treatment of the data.

The study from which the TDI emerged (Johnston & Holzman, 1979) included 237 subjects, made up of 20 chronically hospitalized schizophrenics, 80 recently hospitalized schizophrenics, 10 patients with bipolar disorder, 21 patients with nonpsychotic disorders, 110 relatives of the hospitalized patients, and 27 nonpatient controls. No significant relationship was found between the TDI and IQ, sex, ethnicity, age, and socioeconomic class. Inasmuch as the TDI evaluates a number of deviant language patterns, and considering that ethnic speech patterns and dialects might be erroneously scored as pathological, we were particularly interested in whether the TDI could distinguish racial and ethnic dialects from thought disorder. We found that normal language patterns from other ethnic and racial groups are clearly distinguishable from patterns that we would score for thought disruption. Thus, subcultural language style does not interfere with accurate detection of thought disorder, and cultural dialect is not mistaken for thought disorder (Haimo & Holzman, 1979).

In Johnston and Holzman's (1979) study, two raters independently scored the Rorschach protocols in accordance with the TDI categories. The Pearson product-moment correlations were all highly significant and ranged from 0.93 for nonpsychotic patients and 0.90 for schizophrenic patients to 0.82 for nonpsychiatric controls. A later study of reliability employed a different method of assessing reliability (Coleman et al., 1993). Twenty Rorschach records were randomly selected from a large pool of protocols obtained from records of subjects who had participated in a research project on the major psychoses. Four teams of raters at three different institutions scored the protocols independently of each other. The intraclass correlation among the four teams was 0.74, and Spearman rank order correlations among the teams ranged from 0.81 to 0.90. The ratings of absolute amounts of thought disorder varied among the teams, a factor that reflects the differing thresholds held by the teams for detecting thought disorder. Nevertheless, all teams showed high agreement about which protocols displayed thought disorder and about ranking the records with respect to the amount of thought disorder.

Another study compared four-card sets of the Rorschach cards with each other and with the standard ten-card set (Carpenter et al., 1993). Correlations among sets and with the complete ten-card set ranged from 0.79 to 0.97. However, the correlations among sets with respect to individual categories of the TDI ranged widely, a finding that reflects the presence of dialipsis. We conclude that if one were seeking time-efficient serial testing, the four-card combinations described by Carpenter et al. could provide useful estimates of the total amount of thought disorder. For in-depth examinations of quality and amount of thought disorder, we prefer the ten-card test.

CLINICAL VALIDITY STUDIES OF THE TDI

Prior to the advent of specific psychopharmacologic agents for psychiatric conditions in the 1950s, it mattered very little what diagnosis was given to a patient's condition. This state of affairs was particularly true for the several psychotic conditions—schizophrenia, mania, and psychotic depression—that were once referred to as the "functional psychoses" to distinguish them from psychoses that were symptoms of diagnosable organic brain conditions. In contemporary clinical practice, however, accurate diagnosis makes a substantial difference because of the pharmacological choices that are now available to aid in the treatment of a specific disorder. In its clinical application within psychiatric settings, the TDI can distinguish between bipolar disorders (e.g., manic psychosis) and schizophrenia in both adolescent and adult patients (Makowski et al., 1997; Solovay et al., 1987), and has become an important tool in making treatment decisions (Kleiger, 1999). The instrument has also been used to identify psychotic conditions that are otherwise difficult to classify, such as schizoaffective disorder, as well as nonpsychotic conditions that are related to schizophrenia, such as psychometrically defined schizotypy (Coleman, Levy, Lenzenweger, & Holzman, 1996; Holzman et al., 1995). It is sensitive enough to detect clinical changes prior to their detection by clinicians (Hurt, Holzman, & Davis, 1983). Each of these findings is now examined.

In their initial study, Johnston and Holzman (1979) compared the diagnosis assigned by the clinician in charge of the patient with the diagnosis assigned by an experienced clinician on the basis of inspecting the TDI, without ever having seen the patient or having reviewed the patient's chart (a "blind diagnosis"). An analysis of variance indicated that similar overall classifications obtained whether one used the clinician's diagnosis or the TDI-based diagnosis. Both methods distinguished the schizophrenic patients from the nonpsychotic patients and from controls at high levels of statistical significance. The psychotic patients as a group had significantly higher total TDI scores than did the nonpsychotic patients. The TDI-based diagnoses, however, which are attuned to subtle nuances in thought disruption and not to clinical symptoms, classified some patients differently from the clinical assessment. Clinicians often failed to identify patients with significant amounts of thought disorder as schizophrenic; because these patients did not report delusions, hallucinations, or other gross psychotic symptoms, the clinicians tended to classify them as nonpsychotic. The ability of the TDI to identify the quality of thought disorder complements the clinical diagnostic process. Increasingly, clinicians rely on consultation from a tester who is experienced with the TDI. Because the TDI requires verbatim protocols, whether tape recorded or hand written, and can be reviewed for all instances of thought slippage, it is able to document subtle instances of thought disorder that may have eluded detection even by experienced clinicians.

Effects of Treatment

Hurt et al. (1983) examined the capacity of the TDI to track changes in the quantity of thought disorder as a function of pharmacological treatment. The study was undertaken at a time when hospital stays were much longer than they are now. Twenty-four patients who met criteria for a Diagnostic and Statistical Manual of Mental Disorders (American Psychiatric Association, 1980) diagnosis of schizophrenia were enrolled in the study. They were withdrawn from all antipsychotic drugs for 3 weeks and then were randomly assigned to a high or low dose of haloperidol. One control group of 8 patients was drawn from the same patient population from which the experimental group was drawn. They, too, were consecutively admitted patients who met *DSM-III* criteria for schizophrenia, and they were also withdrawn from antipsychotic drugs for 3 weeks; then half of this group was placed on placebo and half in a no treatment condition, with a crossover after 1 week. These conditions were designed to estimate the effect of a placebo condition on the TDI as well as to provide an estimate of the test-retest effects that are independent of active medication. A second control group consisted of unmedicated volunteers who were psychiatrically asymptomatic;

they were recruited to provide an estimate of test-retest effects in a nonpsychiatric population and to provide a baseline from which to observe deviations from normal levels on the TDI. Testing was conducted at the end of the washout period, at 3, 5, 12, and 19 days after initiation of drug treatment, and at discharge from the hospital. Independent ratings of clinical condition were assessed using the Brief Psychiatric Rating Scale (BPRS, Overall & Gorham, 1962) at the same intervals at which the TDI was administered.

Following the drug washout period, all patients showed high levels of thought disorder, averaging almost seven times as much as the normal control group did at baseline. Statistically significant reductions in total amount of thought disorder were apparent by the third day of treatment, with a sharp drop on the fifth day. A similar drop in symptom severity was measured by the BPRS, but the TDI changes tended to precede those detected by the BPRS. In contrast, the no-treatment and placebo conditions showed no significant changes on either the TDI or BPRS. The normal controls showed no significant changes in total TDI scores on repeated testing. At both the end of the study and at discharge, the total TDI scores of the treated patients remained significantly above those of the normal controls, although they were clearly below their initial levels. The TDI was an effective monitor of change in thought disorder brought about by pharmacological treatment.

Spohn et al. (1986) examined the effects of withdrawing antipsychotic drugs on thought disorder. Two groups of chronic schizophrenia patients (which included schizoaffective patients) were compared; one group was withdrawn from antipsychotic medication and the other continued on the prescribed drug regimen. These patients were also compared with medicated bipolar patients and with nonpsychiatric controls. All psychotic patients had significantly higher total TDI scores than controls, and schizophrenia and schizoaffective patients had a significantly higher amount of thought disorder than bipolar patients. The thought disorder of the schizoaffective patients resembled that of the schizophrenia patients rather than that of the patients with affective disorders, a finding that is similar to that of Shenton et al. (1987). Neuroleptic discontinuation produced a significant increase in total amount of thought disorder, whereas continuously medicated schizophrenia patients and bipolar patients showed no change in total TDI scores. Antipsychotic medication reduced the manifestations of the more severe kinds of thought disturbance (i.e., at the 0.50, 0.75, and 1.0 levels) but had little effect on the milder thought disorders scored at the 0.25 level. Spohn et al. concluded that the more severe kinds of thought disorder are state related, whereas the milder instances of thought slippage are present in all clinical states, including remission, and appear to be a trait-related feature of the illness.

Distinguishing Mania From Schizophrenia

The Johnston and Holzman (1979) study found that total TDI scores were significantly elevated in all groups of psychotic patients, including both chronically hospitalized and recently hospitalized schizophrenic patients, as well as patients with bipolar and other psychotic disorders. Nonpsychotic hospitalized patients showed less total thought disorder than the psychotic patients, and the normal controls had the lowest total TDI scores. Sex differences, ethnicity (Haimo & Holzman, 1979), social class, and intellectual level did not account for these differences, nor did verbal productivity.

The next step in clinical validation of the TDI was to study its effectiveness in discriminating between schizophrenia and manic psychosis. In this effort, Solovay et al. (1987) included only patients who met diagnostic criteria for three classification systems that were in use at the time of the study: *DSM-III*, the Research Diagnostic Criteria (Spitzer, Endicott, & Robins, 1978), and the Washington University criteria (Feighner, Robins, & Guze, 1972). Twenty manic and 43 schizophrenic patients were thus selected, and compared with 22 normal controls.

The scores for the individual TDI categories were subjected to a principal components factor analysis with a variance maximization rotation using 97 patients, a group that included the 63 psychotic patients selected by the three diagnostic criteria and an additional 34 psychotic patients who did not meet criteria for either schizophrenia or mania on all three diagnostic schemes, but all of whom were psychotic. Six factors that made conceptual sense and that had Eigen values above 1.0 emerged from this analysis. We named them Combinatory Thinking, Idiosyncratic Verbalizations, Autistic Thinking, Fluid Thinking, Absurdity, and Confusion. It was striking that this empirically derived factor analysis was very similar to Johnston and Holzman's (1979) arrangement of the TDI categories on the basis of an a priori grouping of the categories as conceptually related. That grouping included four categories: Associative Looseness, Combinatory Thinking, Disorganized Responses, and Unconventional Verbalizations. The scorers in the Solovay et al. (1987) study had an interrater reliability of 0.89, similar to that of Johnston and Holzman; reliabilities with the Spearman-Brown correction were 0.84 for the a priori grouping and 0.89 for the empirically derived factors.

The results showed that the total TDI scores did not differ between the two groups of psychotic patients, and both were significantly higher than the normal group. The data were analyzed in several ways, resulting in similar conclusions, regardless of which factor structure was used: Both groups gave similar amounts of vague, perseverative, and inappropriate distance responses. It was characteristic of the manic group, however, to give extravagantly combinatory responses, usually with humor, flippancy, and playfulness. The thought disorder of schizophrenic patients appeared disorganized, confused, and ideationally fluid, with many peculiar or queer words and phrases. A discriminant function analysis correctly classified 76.5% of the patients, a level of accuracy that is significantly above chance.

Studies of Schizoaffective Disorder

In the study by Solovay et al. (1987), 34 patients did not meet criteria for schizophrenia or manic psychosis on all three diagnostic schemes. Of these 34, 22 met criteria for schizoaffective disorder, using the Research Diagnostic Criteria of Spitzer et al. (1978), which was the only diagnostic scheme at that time to include the category of schizoaffective disorder. Of these 22 patients, 10 met criteria for schizoaffective depressed and 12 for schizoaffective manic.

The schizoaffective patients had significantly higher total TDI scores than the normal controls, and they did not differ from the other psychotic groups. Factor analytic and discriminant function techniques discovered that only 14% of the schizophrenics were misclassified as manic, and only 5% of the manics were misclassified as schizophrenic. When misclassified, a manic or a schizophrenic patient tended to be categorized as schizoaffective on the basis of the TDI profile. Overall, the schizoaffective patients tended to resemble both the schizophrenic and the manic patients in some respects. Schizoaffective depressed patients appeared to be distinctly different from schizoaffective manic patients in that a few flagrant bursts of major thought disorder (e.g., absurd, confusion, queer, contamination) occurred in a setting of relative constriction. Schizoaffective manic patients, on the other hand, were much more verbally productive, but their thought disorder patterns strongly resembled those of the schizophrenic patients and their resemblance to the thought disorder of the manics was qualitatively superficial. That is, although schizoaffective manic patients resembled manic patients in producing a noteworthy amount of combinatory thinking and looseness, they failed to show the flippancy and playfulness of manic patients. Bleuler (1916/1924) noted this quality about some schizophrenic patients. He wrote that, although "manic affects" do occur in schizophrenic patients, "the fresh joyousness of the manic is lacking" (p. 410). The schizoaffective manic patients, moreover, resembled schizophrenic patients in their autistic logic and idiosyncratic thinking and in their propensity for confusion, qualities that are conspicuously absent in manics. Shenton et al. (1987) concluded that, although schizoaffective patients resemble patients with affective disorders, the resemblances are principally in overt symptoms. The principal qualities of their thought disorder, however, suggested a close relationship to schizophrenia.

These validation studies raise a question about the data on which we make diagnoses of mental disorders. Neither we nor the authors of the various studies cited here propose that thought disorder should be the sole basis for the diagnosis of one or another psychotic condition. Rather, the issues raised by the studies of thought disorder strongly indicate that a productive science of psychopathology should rely less heavily on essentially descriptive phenomenological data, which diagnostic manuals such as the *DSM* base themselves (American Psychiatric Association, 1968, 1980, 1987). Many symptom patterns are nonspecific. Delusions, for example, can occur in many different psychotic conditions, and are pathognomonic for none. A comprehensive approach to diagnosis would include phenomena from physiology, psychology, genetics, and other sciences that address simpler and more fundamental processes.

Thought Disorder in Biological Relatives

Johnston and Holzman (1979) reported that parents of schizophrenic patients showed more thought disorder than did parents of nonpsychotic patients or parents of normal controls. The sibling groups in that study did not differ significantly from each other, most likely because of large standard deviations within the groups. The authors also noted a modest but significant tendency for parents with high total TDI scores to have adult offspring with high TDI scores. Similar trends were reported by Singer and Wynne (1966) and by Hirsch and Leff (1975) for communication deviance, a measure of interpersonal communication that overlaps to some extent with the low end of the severity spectrum of the TDI. Shenton, Holzman, and Solovay (1989) undertook to examine the thought disorder of first-degree relatives of patients with schizophrenia, mania, and schizoaffective disorder. They sought to determine whether thought disorder runs in families and also whether the specific qualities of thought disorder that characterized each patient group were found in their corresponding relatives. The subjects included 107 individuals from 84 separate families. They included approximately equal numbers of parents and siblings. None of these family members had been hospitalized for a psychiatric problem or was being treated for a psychiatric condition.

The results showed that the relatives of the psychotic patients, whether considered individually or as a family group, showed significantly higher total TDI scores than did the controls. Relatives rarely gave a response that was scored above the 0.25 severity level. Probands with high total TDI scores showed a tendency to have family members with high TDI scores. With respect to the qualitative scores, only the Idiosyncratic Verbalizations factor differed among the groups of relatives. The relatives of the chronic schizophrenic patients and of schizoaffective manic patients gave significantly more of these responses than did the other relative groups. Relatives of the schizoaffective depressed patients produced the fewest deviant verbalizations, although the number of such responses was higher than that of the normal group. Moreover, relatives of the manic patients, like the manic probands, gave significantly more combinatory responses than did the relatives of the other patients. It was striking that the same qualitative features of thought disorder that characterized the probands were found in an attenuated degree in their first-degree biological relatives.

The TDI and Children at Risk for Psychosis

The finding that the TDI detected similar but milder instances of thought disorder in nonpsychotic adult relatives of schizophrenic and manic patients raises the question of whether particular kinds of thought disorder might serve as a marker of vulnerability for psychotic disorder. If so, we would expect to find significant amounts of thought disorder in children at risk for major psychotic conditions. Arboleda and Holzman (1985) used the TDI in a cross-sectional study of thought disorder in children born to schizophrenic and manic depressive parents. They compared the total TDI scores of children who were presumed to be at risk by virtue of having a biological parent with a psychotic condition with the TDI scores of currently psychotic children and with those of normal children. The group of normal children served to control for the possibility that loose, fabulized, tangential, or syncretic thinking might be found in young children and yet have no pathological significance. Instances of developmentally immature thinking may easily be confused with instances of disordered thinking in children and in adults. For example, instances of incongruous combinations and perservations in Rorschach protocols have been reported in nonpatient adolescents and labeled as "disordered thinking." (Weiner & Exner, 1978).

The normal group in the Arboleda and Holzman (1985) study included 79 children from four age groups: 5 to 7, 8 to 10, 11 to 13, and 14 to 16. A second group of 18 children, ages 6 to 16, were patients on an inpatient unit of a private psychiatric hospital. A third group of 12 children, ages 13.5 to 15, hospitalized for nonpsychotic behavioral problems, were recruited from the same hospital. A fourth group, containing 20 children between the ages of 5 and 16, were children of psychotic mothers. The diagnostic classifications of the mothers were equally divided between schizophrenic and bipolar manic (one mother, however, was given the diagnosis of unipolar affective disorder).

The results showed that the normal children could be easily distinguished from the at-risk and psychotic children. The normal children had TDI scores that ranged from an average of 9.30 (at the youngest age) to 5.34 at age 14 to 16, whereas the psychotic children and the high-risk children had TDI scores that averaged above 16, statistically significantly higher than all of the other groups. The children with nonpsychotic conditions had a mean TDI score of 8.82. A large number of the children in the high-risk and psychotic groups gave more than one response that was scored as autistic logic, confabulation, fluidity, incoherence, absurd, or neologism. None of the normal children or the nonpsychotic hospitalized children gave responses in those categories. The study concluded that the TDI is a useful adjunct in diagnostic studies of children.

The TDI and Adolescent Onset Psychosis

Makowski et al. (1997) used the TDI to characterize the nature of the thought disorder found in adolescent-onset psychiatric conditions. They addressed whether schizophrenics with an unusually early age of onset show the same characteristic features of thought disorder as adult-onset schizophrenics.

Adolescent-onset psychiatric inpatients with *DSM-III-R* (1987) diagnoses of schizophrenia, major depression with psychotic features, and nonpsychotic conditions (e.g., major depression without psychotic features, or adjustment reaction) were compared with nonpsychiatric adolescents (as controls) who were hospitalized for non-life-threatening medical conditions. The average age of the subjects was 15. The results showed that all of the adolescents who had been hospitalized for psychiatric disorders had significantly higher total TDI scores than the controls, although the greatest increase occurred in the schizophrenic and psychotic depressed groups. Control adolescents showed very low levels of thought disorder. The thought disorder of the adolescent-onset schizophrenics was qualitatively different from the thought disorder of the adolescent-onset affective disorders, but very similar to that of adult-onset schizophrenics, with significant amounts of idiosyncratic word usage, illogical reasoning, perceptual confusion, loss of realistic attunement to the task, and loosely related ideas. Combinatory thinking was also a prominent feature of the schizophrenic and psychotically depressed adolescents, as it is in patients with adult-onset psychotic disorders. Neither group showed the playfulness and extravagance seen in manic conditions. The results were similar to those described by Arboleda and Holzman (1985), whose sample of psychotic children and adolescents was diagnostically more heterogeneous.

These results strongly support the interpretation that, from the vantage point of thought disorder, adolescent-onset and adult-onset schizophrenia seem to be the same disorder. The distinctive features of schizophrenic thought disorder can be identified in early-onset cases and distinguished from the thought disorder of affective psychosis as well as from indications of developmental immaturity.

The TDI and Schizophrenia Spectrum Disorders

The awareness that schizophrenia runs in families prompted many investigators to examine the nature of the family connection. One set of studies scrutinized conditions that resemble schizophrenia, but do not meet the criteria for a diagnosis of schizophrenia. Bleuler (1911/1950) called some of these people "latent schizophrenics" and noted that they tended to be in the families of schizophrenic patients. This observation spawned such terms as *schizophrenic character, schizotypal personality,* and *schizoid personality,* among others. The presumption was that people with some of the personal qualities of otherwise schizophrenic patients were part of the broader syndrome of schizophrenia. The relationship of schizotypic psychopathology and schizophrenia, however, remains unclear. It appears to many observers that schizotypy is a less malignant, and probably more prevalent, form of schizophrenia.

One strategy for looking for links between these less malignant conditions and schizophrenia is to compare the quality of thought disorder of schizotypic individuals with that occurring in schizophrenic patients. Coleman et al. (1996) and Holzman et al. (1995) tested a randomly selected sample of first-year college students who had taken a 250-item inventory, including a 35-item subset that tapped perceptual aberrations and distortions that had been associated with schizotypy by both Rado, Buchenholz, Dunton, Karlen, and Senescu (1956) and Meehl (1990). The groups were chosen according to the procedures outlined by Chapman, Chapman, and Raulin (1976) and Chapman, Chapman, and Raulin (1978). The TDI scores of students whose PerAb (perceptual aberrations) scores were more than two standard deviations above the mean ($n = 30$) were compared with students who had PerAb scores in the average range ($n = 26$).

The students were screened for psychosis at the time of testing, and none of them was psychotic. All the students were in good academic standing. The students in the high-PerAb group had significantly elevated total TDI scores. Furthermore, they had an increased number of idiosyncratic verbalizations scored as peculiar or queer as well as autistic logic. It thus appeared that psychometrically identified schizotypal individuals selected by the Chapman and Chapman scales (e.g., Chapman, Chapman, & Raulin, 1976) can serve as tools for exploring schizophrenia-related behavior. Furthermore, the study presents additional evidence that the TDI is sensitive to thought slippage in asymptomatic persons and in this way can help identify people with a schizophrenic disposition who might escape detection because they do not have the glaring symptoms of a psychotic condition.

Another strategy for ascertaining individuals with schizotypal personality disorder (SPD) recruits community members who endorse certain symptoms associated with SPD and then screens them for meeting specific diagnostic criteria. In a follow-up study of the association between elevated amounts of thought disorder and left superior temporal gyrus (STG) volume reduction in schizophrenia patients (see later discussion), Dickey et al. (1999) studied individuals who met criteria for SPD. They found that left-STG gray matter volume was reduced and that TDI scores were increased in these SPD subjects, a finding similar to reports on schizophrenic patients. These findings are consistent with the interpretation that SPD is on a continuum with schizophrenia, but represents a milder form of the disorder. Unlike schizophrenics, however, left-STG volume was not significantly correlated with amount of thought disorder in SPD. In a second follow-up study, Dickey et al. (2002) separately measured the volume of different parts of the STG, specifically, Heschl's gyrus and the planum temporale. Only the left Heschl's gyrus showed a volume reduction (21%) in SPD subjects, but the volume of neither region was significantly associated with amount of thought disorder. Thus, although there are some similarities between schizophrenic patients and individuals with SPD, the overlap is only partial.

Thought Disorder Associated With Right Hemisphere Cortical Damage

Kestnbaum Daniels et al. (1988) administered a subset of Rorschach cards to 23 patients with right hemisphere lesions. They compared the TDI scores and categories obtained from these patients with those from a sample of 25 schizophrenia and 20 bipolar manic patients. Total TDI scores did not differ among the groups, but the categories of thought disorder distinguished the groups. The schizophrenia and bipolar patients showed thought disorder that was consistent with that reported by Solovay et al. (1987) and Shenton et al. (1987). The patients with the right hemisphere cortical lesions, however, were distinguished from the other patients by fragmented thinking, a clear inability to integrate disparate elements into a coherent whole. This fragmentation was manifested in a tendency to focus on one small part of the inkblot, while ignoring the remainder. One of the commonly recognized effects of right hemisphere cortical damage is constructional apraxia, which, in the visuospatial domain, is like that seen in fragmentation responses, and reflects an inability to appraise relationships among elements in a pattern.

In summary, the several studies reported here indicate that the total TDI level is elevated almost to the same degree in people with schizophrenia, schizoaffective disorder, bipolar (manic) disorder, and right hemisphere lesions. This equivalency illustrates that a variety of pathological conditions are accompanied by increases in the amount of thought disorder. Although the sheer quantity of thought disorder marks the presence of psychopathology, it does not indicate the nature of the pathological condition. The specific TDI categories associated with the increased thought disorder serve as effective diagnostic indicators of the specific pathological condition. In the case of schizophrenia, it is idiosyncratic verbalizations; in the case of bipolar affective disorder, it is combinatory thinking; in the case of right hemisphere lesions, it is fragmentation. Both the magnitude of the total TDI score and the qualitative features of the index should be considered when using the TDI for diagnostic purposes.

THE TDI AS A RESEARCH TOOL

Thus far, we have described research about the TDI itself, particularly its reliability and its validity in helping to distinguish one psychotic disorder from another. The true measure of a tool's worth is its capacity to advance new research. The TDI has, indeed, launched new research probes in several different directions and areas, in the United States and in many other countries, including, Denmark, Finland, Italy, Germany, France, Holland, and Japan.

The TDI and Brain Morphology

Using structural magnetic resonance imaging scans, Shenton et al. (1992) found that three regions in the temporal lobes of chronically ill schizophrenic patients showed significantly reduced tissue, although there were no differences in absolute brain volume. The tissue reduction was particularly striking in the left superior temporal area, in the STG, located in the auditory association cortex. The greater the amount of thought disorder, as measured by the TDI, the smaller the STG volume. In a follow-up study, Nestor et al. (1998) showed that TDI scores of these same schizophrenics were not correlated with relative gray matter volume in basal ganglia or prefrontal regions, suggesting that the association between increased thought disorder and gray matter volume reduction is selective for regions within the temporal lobe. An earlier, independent study showed that the severity of auditory hallucinations was related to tissue reduction in that same area (Barta, Pearlson, Powers, Richards, & Tune, 1990). These studies suggest that the STG is implicated in disturbances of effective thinking in schizophrenic patients.

Now that functional magnetic resonance scanning and magnetoencephalography are available to observe brain activation while the mental processes under study are actually occurring, we can look forward to studies of the functional network of brain areas involved when thinking is normal and when it is disturbed.

Kircher et al. (2001) performed an investigation very similar to that of Shenton et al. (1992). Using functional MRI, they compared brain areas in schizophrenia patients and controls using a scale similar to the TDI to quantify thought disorder. They reported that severity of thought disorder in schizophrenic patients was negatively correlated with activation in the left superior and middle temporal gyri, a result congruent with the structural findings of Shenton et al. (1992). Total TDI scores have been reported to be significantly associated with auditory P300 abnormalities in some studies (McCarley et al., 1993; Shenton, Faux et al., 1989), but not others (Bruder et al., 2001).

The TDI and The Dopamine Hypothesis

Soon after the introduction of the phenothiazines in the 1950s for the treatment of schizophrenia (see Davis, 1976, for a review), the mechanism of their action was attributed to their effect on the dynamics of the neurotransmitter dopamine. Carlsson (1988) was the first to note that these therapeutic compounds appeared to block postsynaptic dopamine receptors. The dopamine hypothesis remains heuristically viable, although it is not a complete explanation for the emergence of psychotic symptoms or their alleviation with psychoactive medications. According to the dopamine hypothesis, this neurotransmitter plays a role in the emergence of psychotic symptoms and in their effective treatment. Psychostimulant drugs such as methylphenidate increase the transmission of dopamine and other catecholamines and, because they seem to produce psychotic symptoms in some people, have been called "psychotomimetic." Antipsychotic drugs like the phenothiazines, on the other hand, antagonize the effects of psychostimulants and ameliorate psychotic symptoms.

Hurt et al. (1983) showed that thought disorder abates during neuroleptic drug treatment, and Spohn et al. (1986) showed that thought disorder worsens during an acute exacerbation of psychotic symptoms. Levy et al. (1993) compared the effects of the dopamine agonist, methylphenidate, on thought disorder in unmedicated first-episode schizophrenia patients and in nonpsychiatric controls. If administration of methylphenidate produced increased amounts of thought disorder and of other psychotic symptoms, these increases could be attributed to changes in aminergic tone in the central nervous system. Levy et al. administered the TDI prior to drug administration and 45 minutes after administration of methylphenidate. They also assessed thought disorder from another instrument using items from the Schedule for Affective Disorders and Schizophrenia (Endicott & Spitzer, 1978), including illogical thinking, poverty of content, neologisms, impaired understandability, and loosening of associations. They found that administration of methylphenidate was followed by worsened thought disorder in the schizophrenia patients but not in controls, whether measured by the TDI or clinical ratings. The methylphenidate-induced increase in TDI scores in the schizophrenia patients parallels the TDI changes associated with discontinuation of antipsychotic treatment described by Spohn et al. and initiation of antipsychotic drug treatment by Hurt et al. That is, TDI scores increase significantly following both drug discontinuation and administration of methylphenidate.

Psycholinguistic Approaches to Thought Disorder

Although earlier we argued that formal thought disorder should be regarded as disorder of thinking and not of language, for the most part, we detect thought disorder through language. And language itself can be distorted by disorders in thinking. For example, when a phrase strikes the listener as odd or peculiar, there is a clash between the word and the meaning that is implied in the usage. When a patient remarks that an area of a Rorschach card looks like "potential ears" or "two pointed obtrusions," the listener is puzzled by the ambiguity. The patient has used recognizable English words, but in a way that is sufficiently off the mark so that one is not quite sure what the speaker intends. In social listening, one does, of course, try to understand the speaker's intention by imputing a presumed meaning while ignoring the peculiarities.

Many aspects of language convey ambiguity and uncertainty about meaning. In English, for example, the words *him* and *hymn* are homonyms, and only when they are used in a sentence is one able to decide whether the speaker is referring to a male friend or to a song of praise. There are many examples of such ambiguities in English, and Chapman, Chapman, and Daut (1976) reported that schizophrenic patients showed a significant tendency to impute the more frequent or the more usual meaning of a word than did normal subjects. Titone, Levy, and Holzman (2000) used a semantic priming task that allowed them to assess how schizophrenic patients process the relevant and irrelevant meanings of words. Schizophrenic patients and controls listened to 64 noun-noun homonyms, placed within phrase contexts that were either moderately biased or strongly biased toward the subordinate meaning of the words. Immediately after the presentation of the spoken prime, the subjects viewed targets that were related to either the dominant or the subordinate meaning of the word. The task was to decide whether the targets were words or nonwords, and to press a button upon making a decision.

The biasing was done to make the subordinate meaning always contextually relevant and the dominant meaning always contextually irrelevant. Thus, subjects had to respond to the subordinate meanings of targets in order to detect the relevant information in the sentence. The results showed that, when the context was strongly biased toward the subordinate meaning of the homonym, both schizophrenic patients and controls showed priming of the subordinate meaning. When, however, the context was only moderately biased toward the subordinate meaning, the schizophrenic patients showed priming of the dominant target; they failed to inhibit the inappropriate meaning. Here, then, is evidence that although schizophrenic patients are able to use context for regulating behavior, the clues to context must be stronger for them to inhibit inappropriate responses.

Use of the TDI in Linkage Studies

Both the excess of thought disorders in the relatives of schizophrenia patients and the similarity of types of thought disorder in the probands and relatives suggest that the presence of formal thought disorder can potentially identify gene carriers to help in linkage studies. Vuchetich et al. (2004) conducted a segregation analysis of the inheritance of thought disorder in five large Danish families selected for multiple cases of schizophrenia. They found strong evidence of a major gene effect on the expression of thought disorder (as measured by the TDI), particularly deviant verbalizations. The presence of formal thought disorder can now be useful as an endophenotypic indicator (Gottesman & Shields, 1972) that can increase the power of linkage studies in a search for genes involved in the transmission of schizophrenia.

Many studies have shown that the likelihood of finding other sufferers from schizophrenia in the family of a proband—called the "recurrence risk rate"—is rather low, probably not more than about 6% (Kendler et al., 1993; Tsuang, Winokur, & Crowe, 1980). This rate is far too low to afford the power needed to conduct successful linkage studies. In contrast, in families with one member having a disease such as Huntington's or cystic fibrosis, we are likely to find a larger number of afflicted relatives. These diseases have a dominant or recessive pattern of transmission and linkage strategies have been spectacularly successful in identifying susceptibility loci. A better strategy for diseases such as schizophrenia, with a low recurrence risk rate and that are likely caused by several genes, is to broaden the phenotype by including traits that have a higher recurrence risk rate than does clinical schizophrenia in the families of a schizophrenic proband. Defective eye tracking is such a trait that we are using to improve the sensitivity of linkage studies of schizophrenia (Matthysse, Holzman, & Lange, 1986; Matthysse & Parnas, 1992; Matthysse et al., 2004). The TDI is also serving in ongoing research as another such endophenotypic marker.

The TDI and Adoption Studies

We have presented evidence that deviant TDI scores can identify not only persons with clinical schizophrenia, but also persons without clinical schizophrenia who carry genes for the disease. It is important to address the possibility that thought disorder appearing in the relatives of schizophrenic patients might reflect environmental factors in the rearing families. For example, deviant communication patterns within families also may contribute to the development of schizophrenic pathology, as suggested, for example, by the work of Singer and Wynne (1966), Hirsch and Leff (1975), and Tienari and colleagues (Tienari, Sorri, Lahti, Naarala, Wahlberg, Pohjola et al., 1985; Tienari, Sorri, Lahti, Naarala, Wahlberg, Ronkko, et al., 1985).

To reduce the likelihood that environmental factors are responsible for the higher TDI scores in the relatives of schizophrenic patients, one would need to use a strategy that separates the effects of biological or genetic risk from the effects of environment. Comparing the TDI scores of biological relatives of the schizophrenic adoptees (who share genes but not environment with the patient) with those of the adoptive relatives of schizophrenics (who do not share the genes with the schizophrenic adoptee) can help to unravel this knotty issue. Kinney et al. (1997) employed this adoption strategy to tease apart genetic and environmental factors using the TDI as the principal dependent variable. If the TDI scores proved to be higher in the biological relatives of persons with schizophrenia than in the biological relatives of adopted children raised in the same family with the schizophrenic patient, that finding would support a genetic hypothesis.

The subjects were drawn from the population of a large adoption study in Denmark. The adoptees were separated at birth from their biological mothers, and had little or no contact with them. The Rorschach test was administered in Danish, and the scoring team was trained in the use of the TDI, with frequent calibration sessions, using translated protocols, which were scored blind to group membership. In a subset of 30 protocols, interrater reliability was 0.90. The results showed: (a) The average total TDI score of adoptees with schizophrenia (probands) was significantly higher than that of adoptees without schizophrenia, (b) the mean TDI scores for the biological relatives (including parents, sibs, and half-sibs) of the schizophrenic adoptees were significantly higher than the scores of the adoptive family and their relatives, and (c) the biological sibs and half-sibs of the schizophrenic adoptees, who did not share the same rearing environment with the schizophrenic adoptees, had significantly higher total TDI scores than the biological sibs and half-sibs of nonschizophrenic adoptees who were raised elsewhere. In contrast, the scores of the adoptive parents of the noncontrol probands and schizophrenic probands did not differ from each other.

The significantly elevated TDI scores of biological sibs and half-sibs of schizophrenic probands who did not share the same rearing environment with the schizophrenic adoptees support the likelihood of genetic factors in the transmission of thought disorder. It was noteworthy, moreover, that the TDI scores were elevated not only in the relatives with schizophrenia spectrum disorders, but also among the biological sibs and half-sibs with no spectrum disorder. This finding supports the possibility that mild or subtle forms of thought disorder may represent a subclinical indicator of increased liability to schizophrenia, as argued by Bleuler (1916/1924) and Meehl (1962).

Using an adoption strategy similar to that of Kinney et al. (1997), Wahlberg et al. (2000) compared adult offspring in a Finnish sample of schizophrenic mothers and control mothers. The offspring had been adopted on average within 15 months after birth. None of these adoptees had schizophrenia or a schizophrenia spectrum disorder. Although total TDI scores did not differ in the two groups of adoptees, a significantly larger proportion of adopted offspring of schizophrenic mothers showed idiosyncratic verbalizations than did adopted offspring of control mothers. Both the Kinney et al. and Wahlberg et al. studies show that the TDI can distinguish individuals who are and who are not at genetic risk for schizophrenia.

Hermann Rorschach (1922/1942) introduced his method as a "psychological experiment" that is of value in research and in clinical testing. He recognized that the yield from his method was entirely empirical, and therefore provisional. His focus was primarily on diagnosis of psychiatric disorders, and to that end he searched for regularities in responses of patients that could aid in diagnosis. He began his experiments in 1911 and when he died prematurely in 1922, he was still studying the yield of his method. Almost 100 years have elapsed since the time he began his first studies, and it is to be expected that, as with any method that has a time-tested usefulness, it will evolve as our needs for its use will surely evolve.

The kind of fine-grained personality description that can be drawn from responses to Rorschach's plates seems to be less favored in the contemporary era of neuroscience. Neuroimaging and neurogenetics—unencumbered by Cartesian dualism—may provide a more direct route to what is going on in a patient's head. Still, there is much that Rorschach's simple yet astoundingly original technique can contribute to contemporary experimental psychopathology. The TDI provides a metric for the quantity and quality of disturbance of thinking based on responses to Rorschach's plates. It is sensitive to the various forms of thought disorder found in putatively different conditions, such as schizophrenia and mania. That achievement, too, is a beginning. The categories in which we now classify thought disorder are gross and must be parsed into simpler components to advance our ability to penetrate the mystery of how mental disorders affect cognitive and emotional functioning. We must study further the phenomena of peculiar words and phrases, looseness of ideation, and fluid percepts to discover their roots in mental life and in brain functioning. The search might lead to the discovery of errors in neuronal firing or neurotransmission gone awry, events that are both more complex and yet simpler than the thoughts that they underlie. The almost 100-year-old technique of Hermann Rorschach may be finding a new place alongside the technical marvels of contemporary cognitive neuroscience, where they may complement each other. As Einstein is reputed to have said, "Everything should be made as simple as possible, but not simpler."

ACKNOWLEDGMENTS

Preparation of this chapter was supported by funds from USPHS Grants MH 31340, 49487, 31154, and 01020, and by grants from the Roy A. Hunt Foundation and the Essel Foundation. We are grateful to our colleague Herbert J. Schlesinger, who made valuable comments on a previous version of this chapter.

REFERENCES

American Psychiatric Association. (1968). *Diagnostic and statistical manual of mental disorders* (2nd ed). Washington, DC.

American Psychiatric Association. (1980). *Diagnostic and statistical manual of mental disorders* (3rd ed.). Washington, DC.

American Psychiatric Association. (1987). *Diagnostic and statistical manual of mental disorders* (3rd ed., rev.). Washington, DC.

Andreasen, N. C. (1979a). Thought, language, and communication disorders I. Clinical assessment, definition of terms, and evaluation of their reliability. *Archives of General Psychiatry, 36,* 1315–1321.

Andreasen, N. C. (1979b). Thought, language, and communication disorders II. Diagnostic significance. *Archives of General Psychiatry, 36,* 1325–1330.

Andreasen, N. C., & Grove, W. (1986). Thought, language and communication in schizophrenia diagnosis and prognosis. *Schizophrenia Bulletin, 12,* 348–359.

Arboleda, C., & Holzman, P. S. (1985). Thought disorder in children at risk for psychosis. *Archives of General Psychiatry, 42,* 1004–1013.
Barta, P. E., Pearlson, G. D., Powers, R. E., Richards, S. S., & Tune, L. E. (1990). Auditory hallucinations and smaller superior temporal gyral volume in schizophrenia. *American Journal of Psychiatry, 147,* 1457–1462.
Bleuler, E. (1916/1924). *Textbook of psychiatry* (A. A. Brill, Trans.). New York: MacMillan. (Original work published 1924)
Bleuler, E. (1950). *Dementia praecox or the group of schizophrenias* (H. Zinkin, Trans.). New York: International Universities Press. (Original work published 1911)
Brown, R. W. (1973). Schizophrenia, language, and reality. *American Psychologist, 28,* 395–403.
Bruder, G. E., Kayser, J., Tenke, C. E., Friedman, M., Malespina, D., & Gorman, J. M. (2001). Event-related potentials in schizophrenia during total and phonetic oddball tasks: Relations to diagnostic subtype, symptom features and verbal memory. *Biological Psychiatry, 50,* 447–452.
Cancro, R. (1968). Thought disorder and schizophrenia. *Diseases of the Nervous System, 28,* 846–848.
Carlsson, A. (1988). The current status of the dopamine hypothesis of schizophrenia. *Neuropsychopharmacology, 1,* 179–188.
Carpenter, J. T., Coleman, M. J., Waternaux, C. M., Perry, J., Wong, H., O'Brian, C., et al. (1993). The Thought Disorder Index: Short-form assessments. *Psychological Assessment, 5,* 75–80.
Chaika, E. (1974). A linguist looks at "schizophrenic" language. *Brain and Language, 1,* 257–276.
Chaika, E., & Lambe, R. (1985). The locus of dysfunction in schizophrenic speech. *Schizophrenia Bulletin, 11,* 8–15.
Chapman, L., & Chapman, J. (1973). *Disordered thought in schizophrenia.* New York: Appleton-Century-Crofts.
Chapman, L., Chapman, J., & Raulin, M. L. (1976). Scales for physical and social anhedonia. *Journal of Abnormal Psychology, 85,* 374–382.
Chapman, L. J., Chapman, J. P., & Daut, R. L. (1976). Schizophrenic inability to disattend from strong aspects of meaning. *Journal of Abnormal Psychology, 85,* 35–40.
Chapman, L. J., Chapman, J. P., & Raulin, M. L. (1978). Body-image aberrations in schizophrenia. *Journal of Abnormal Psychology, 87,* 399–407.
Coleman, M. J., Carpenter, J. T., Waternaux, C., Levy, D. L., Shenton, M. E., Perry, J., et al. (1993). The Thought Disorder Index: A reliability study. *Psychological Assessment, 3,* 336–342.
Coleman, M. J., Levy, D. L., Lenzenweger, M. F., & Holzman, P. S. (1996). Thought disorder, perceptual aberrations, and schizotypy. *Journal of Abnormal Psychology, 105,* 469–473.
Davis, J. M. (1976). Recent developments in the treatment of schizophrenia. *Psychiatric Annals, 6,* 33–50.
Dickey, C. C., McCarley, R. W., Voglmaier, M. M., Frumin, M., Niznikiewicz, M. A., Hirayasu, Y., Fraone, S., Seidman, L. J., & Shenton, M. E. (2002). Smaller left Heschl's gyrus volume in patients with schizotypal personality disorder. *American Journal of Psychiatry, 159,* 1521–1527.
Dickey, C. C., McCarley, R. W., Voglmaier, M. M., Niznikiewicz, M. A., Seidman, L. J., Hirayasu, Y., Fischer, I., The, E. K., Rhoads, R. V., Jakab, M., Kikinis, R., Jolescz, F. A., & Shenton, M. E. (1999). Schizotypal personality disorder and

MRI abnormalities of temporal lobe gray matter. *Biological Psychiatry, 45,* 1393–1402.

Docherty, N. M., Gordinier, S. W., Hall, M. J., & Cutting, L. P. (1999). Communication disturbances in relatives beyond the age of risk for schizophrenia and their associations with symptoms in patients. *Schizophrenia Bulletin, 25,* 851–862.

Endicott, J., & Spitzer, R. L. (1978). *Schedule for affective disorders and schizophrenia-lifetime version.* New York: New York State Department of Mental Hygiene.

Feighner, F. P., Robins, E., & Guze, S. B. (1972). Diagnostic criteria for use in psychiatric research. *Archives of General Psychiatry, 86,* 57–63.

Fenichel, O. (1945). *The psychoanalytic theory of neurosis.* New York: Norton.

Fromkin, V. A. (1975). A linguist looks at "A linguist looks at 'schizophrenic' language." *Brain and Language, 2,* 498–503.

Gell-Mann, M. (1964). Nonleptonic weak decays and the eightfold way. *Physical Review Letters, 12,* 155–156.

Goldstein, K. (1944). Methodological approach to the study of schizophrenic thought disorder. In J. S. Kasanin (Ed.), *Language and thought in schizophrenia* (pp. 17–40). New York: Norton.

Gottesman, I. I., & Shields, J. (1972). *Schizophrenia and genetics: A twin study vantage point.* New York: Academic Press.

Haimo, S., & Holzman, P. S. (1979). Thought disorder in schizophrenics and normal controls: Social class and race differences. *Journal of Consulting Clinical Psychology, 47,* 963–967.

Harrow, M., Harkavy, K., Bromet, E., & Tucker, G. J. (1973). A longitudinal study of schizophrenic thinking. *Archives of General Psychiatry, 28,* 179–182.

Harrow, M., & Quinlan, D. (1977). Is disordered thinking unique to schizophrenia? *Archives of General Psychiatry, 34,* 15–21.

Harrow, M., Tucker, G., Himmelhoch, J., & Putnam, N., Jr. (1972). Schizophrenic "thought disorders" after the acute phase. *American Journal of Psychiatry, 128,* 824–829.

Hecker, E. (1871). Die hebephrenie. *Archiv für pathologische anatomie und physiologie und für klinische medizin, 52,* 394–429.

Heider, F. (1959). On perception, event structure, and the psychological environment. *Psychological Issues, 1,* 1–35.

Hirsch, S. R., & Leff, J. P. (1975). *Abnormalities in parents of schizophrenics.* London: Oxford University Press.

Holzman, P. S., Coleman, M., Lenzenweger, M. F., Levy, D. L., Matthysse, S., O'Driscoll, G., et al. (1995). Working memory deficits, antisaccades, and thought disorder in relation to perceptual aberration. In A. Raine, T. Lencz, & S. Mednick (Eds.), *Schizotypal personality* (pp. 353–381). Cambridge, England: Cambridge University Press.

Hunt, W. A., & Walker, R. E. (1966). Schizophrenics' judgements of schizophrenic test responses. *Journal of Clinical Psychology, 22,* 118–120.

Hurt, S. S., Holzman, P. S., & Davis, J. M. (1983). Thought disorder: The measurement of its changes. *Archives of General Psychiatry, 40,* 1281–1285.

Johnston, M. H., & Holzman, P. S. (1979). *Assessing schizophrenic thinking* (Vol. 310). San Francisco: Jossey-Bass.

Joyce, J. (1939). *Finnegans wake.* London: Faber and Faber.

Kahlbaum, K. (1874). *Die Katatonie oder das Spannungsirresein.* Berlin: Hirschwald.

Kendler, K. S., McGuire, M., Gruenberg, A. M., Spellman, M., O'Hare, A., & Walsh, D. (1993). The Roscommon family study I. Methods, diagnosis of probands, and risk of schizophrenia in relatives. *Archives of General Psychiatry, 50,* 527–540.

Kestnbaum Daniels, E., Shenton, M. E., Holzman, P. S., Benowitz, L. I., Coleman, M. J., Levin, S., et al. (1988). Patterns of thought disorder associated with right cortical damage, schizophrenia, and mania. *American Journal of Psychiatry, 145,* 944–949.

Kety, S. S., Rosenthal, D., & Wender, P. H. (1978). Genetic relationships within the schizophrenia spectrum: Evidence from adoption studies. In R. L. Spitzer & D. F. Klein (Eds.), *Critical issues in psychiatric diagnosis* (pp. 213–223). New York: Raven Press.

Kinney, D. K., Holzman, P. S., Jacobsen, B., Jansson, L., Faber, B., Hildebrand, W., et al. (1997). Thought disorder in schizophrenic and control adoptees and their relatives. *Archives of General Psychiatry, 54,* 475–479.

Kircher, T. T. J., Liddle, P. F., Brammer, M. J., Williams, S. C. R., Murray, R. M., & McGuire, P. K. (2001). Neural correlates of formal thought disorder. *Archives of General Psychiatry, 58,* 769–774.

Kleiger, J. H. (1999). *Disordered thinking and the Rorschach: Theory, research, and differential diagnosis.* Hillsdale, NJ: Analytic Press.

Kraepelin, E. (1919). *Dementia praecox and paraphrenia* (M. Barclay, Trans). Edinburgh: E. & S. Livingstone.

Levy, D., Smith, M., Robinson, D., Jody, D., Lerner, G., Alvir, J., et al. (1993). Methylphenidate increases thought disorder in recent onset schizophrenics, but not in normal controls. *Biological Psychiatry, 34,* 507–514.

Makowski, D. G., Waternaux, C., Lajonchere, C. M., Dicker, R., Smoke, N., Koplewicz, H., Min, D., Mendell, N. R., & Levy, D. L. (1997). Thought disorder in early-adolescent onset schizophrenia. *Schizophrenia Research, 23,* 147–165.

Matthysse, S., Holzman, P. S., Gusella, J., Levy, D. L., Harte, C., Jørgensen, A., Møller, L., & Parnas, J. (2004). Linkage of eye movement dysfunction to chromosome 6p in schizophrenia: A confirmation. *American Journal of Medical Genetics, 128B,* 30–36.

Matthysse, S., Holzman, P. S., & Lange, K. (1986). The genetic transmission of schizophrenia: Application of Mendelian latent structure analysis to eye tracking dysfunctions in schizophrenia and affective disorder. *Journal of Psychiatric Research, 20,* 57–65.

Matthysse, S., Levy, D. L., Wu, Y., Rubin, D. B., & Holzman, P. S. (1999). Modeling intermittent degradation in schizophrenic performance. *Schizophrenia Research, 40,* 131–146.

Matthysse, S., & Parnas, J. (1992). Extending the phenotype of schizophrenia: Implications for linkage analysis. *Journal of Psychiatric Research, 26,* 329–344.

McCarley, R. W., Shenton, M. E., O'Donnell, B. F., Faux, S. F., Kikinis, R., Nestor, P. G., et al. (1993). Auditory P300 abnormalities and left posterior superior temporal gyrus volume reduction in schizophrenia. *Archives of General Psychiatry, 50,* 190–198.

Meehl, P. E. (1962). Schizotaxia, schizotypy, schizophrenia. *American Psychologist, 17,* 827–838.

Meehl, P. E. (1990). Toward an integrated theory of schizotaxia, schizotypy, and schizophrenia. *Journal of Personality Disorders, 4,* 1–99.

Morel, B. A. (1860). *Traite de maladies mentales.* Paris: V. Masson.

Nestor, P. G., Shenton, M. E., Wible, C., Hokama, H., O'Donnell, B. F., Law, S., & McCarley, R. W. (1998). A neuropsychological analysis of schizophrenic thought disorder. *Schizophrenia Research, 29,* 217–225.

Overall, J. E., & Gorham, D. R. (1962). Brief Psychiatric Rating scale. *Psychological Reports, 10,* 799–812.

Perry, W., Geyer, M. A., & Braff, D. L. (1999). Sensorimotor gating and thought disturbance measured in close temporal proximity in schizophrenic patients. *Archives of General Psychiatry, 56,* 277–281.

Rado, S., Buchenholz, B., Dunton, H., Karlen, S., & Senescu, R. (1956). Schizotypal organization: Preliminary report on a clinical study of schizophrenia. In S. Rado & G. Daniels (Eds.), *Changing concepts of pychoanalytic medicine* (pp. 225–235). New York: Grune & Stratton.

Rapaport, D., Gill, M. M., & Schafer, R. (1968). *Diagnostic psychological testing* (rev. ed.). New York: International Universities Press.

Rorschach, H. (1942). *Psychodiagnostics* (P. Lemkau & B. Kronenberg, Trans.). Bern, Switzerland: Huber. (Original work published 1922)

Rosch, E. (1973). On the internal structure of perceptual and semantic categories. In T. E. Moore (Ed.), *Cognitive development and the acquisition of language* (pp. 111–144). New York: Academic Press.

Shenton, M. E., Faux, S. F., McCarley, R. W., Ballinger, R., Coleman, M., Torello, M., et al. (1989). Correlations between abnormal auditory P300 topography and positive symptoms in schizophrenia: A preliminary report. *Biological Psychiatry, 29,* 710–716.

Shenton, M. E., Holzman, P. S., & Solovay, M. (1989). Thought disorder in the relatives of psychotic patients. *Archives of General Psychiatry, 46,* 897–901.

Shenton, M. E., Kikinis, R., Jolescz, F. A., Pollak, S., LeMay, M., Wible, C. G., et al. (1992). Abnormalities of the left temporal lobe and thought disorder in schizophrenia. *New England Journal of Medicine, 327,* 604–612.

Shenton, M. E., Solovay, M. R., & Holzman, P. S. (1987). Comparative studies of thought disorder: II. Schizoaffective disorder. *Archives of General Psychiatry, 44,* 21–30.

Singer, M. T., & Wynne, L. C. (1966). Communication styles in parents of normals, neurotics, and schizophrenics. *Psychiatric Research Reports, 20,* 25–38.

Solovay, M. R., Shenton, M. E., Gasperetti, C., Coleman, M., Kestnbaum, E., Carpenter, J. T., et al. (1986). Scoring manual for the Thought Disorder Index (Revised Version). *Schizophrenia Bulletin, 12,* 483–496.

Solovay, M. R., Shenton, M. E., & Holzman, P. S. (1987). Comparative studies of thought disorder: I. Mania and schizophrenia. *Archives of General Psychiatry, 44,* 13–20.

Spitzer, R. L., Endicott, J., & Robins, E. (1978). *Research diagnostic criteria (RDC) for a selected group of functional disorders.* New York: Biometric Research.

Spohn, H. E., Coyne, L., Larson, J., Mittleman, F., Spray, J., & Hayes, K. (1986). Episodic and residual thought pathology in chronic schizophrenics: effects of neuroleptics. *Schiz ophrenia Bulletin, 12,* 394–407.

Storch, A. (1924). *The primitive archaic forms of inner experiences and thought in schizophrenia.* New York: Nervous and Mental Disease Monographs.

Tienari, P., Sorri, A., Lahti, I., Naarala, M., Wahlberg, K. E., Pohjola, J., et al. (1985). Interaction of genetic and psychosocial factors in schizophrenia. *Acta Psychiatrica Scandinavica, 71,* 19–30.

Tienari, P., Sorri, A., Lahti, I., Naarala, M., Wahlberg, K. E., Ronkko, T., et al. (1985). The Finnish adoptive family study of schizophrenia. *Yale Journal of Biology and Medicine, 58,* 227–237.

Titone, D., Levy, D. L., & Holzman, P. S. (2000). Contextual insensitivity in schizophrenic language processing: Evidence from lexical ambiguity. *Journal of Abnormal Psychology, 109,* 761–767.

Tsuang, M. T., Winokur, G., & Crowe, R. R. (1980). Morbidity risks of schizophrenia and affective disorders among first degree relatives of patients with schizophrenia, mania, depression and surgical conditions. *British Journal of Psychiatry, 137,* 497–504.

von Domarus, E. (1944). The specific laws of logic in schizophrenia. In J. S. Kasanin (Ed.), *Language and thought in schizophrenia* (pp. 104–114). New York: Norton.

Vuchetich, J. P., Levy, D. L., Holzman, P. S., Perlt, D., Parnas, J., & Matthysse, S. (2004). *Evidence for a major gene effect on thought disorder in schizophrenia pedigrees.* Manuscript submitted for publication.

Wahlberg, K. E., Mynne, L. C., Oja, H., Keskitalo, P., Anais-Tanner, H., Koistinen, P., et al. (2000). Thought disorder index of Finnish adoptees and communication deviance of their adoptive parents. *Psychological Medicine, 30,* 127–136.

Watkins, J. G., & Stauffacher, J. C. (1952). An index of pathological thinking in the Rorschach. *Journal of Projective Techniques, 16,* 276–286.

Weiner, I. B. (1966). *Psychodiagnosis in cchizophrenia.* New York: Wiley.

Weiner, I. B., & Exner, J. (1978). Rorschach indices of disordered thinking in patient and nonpatient adolescents and adults. *Journal of Personality Assessment, 42,* 339–343.

Werner, H. (1940). *Comparative psychology of mental development.* New York: Harper.

4

Concept of the Object on the Rorschach Scale

Kenneth N. Levy
Pennsylvania State University

Kevin B. Meehan
City University of New York

John S. Auerbach
Mountain Home VA Medical Center

Sidney J. Blatt
Yale University

Relational models of personality development and psychotherapy—that is, theories emphasizing the centrality of relationships, both fantasied and real, with other human beings—are now commonplace in psychoanalysis (e.g., Aron, 1996; Atwood & Stolorow, 1984; Benjamin, 1995; Bromberg, 1998; Mitchell, 1988; Mitchell & Aron, 1999; Ogden, 1997; Orange, Atwood, & Stolorow, 1999; Skolnick & Warshaw, 1992). Such models are widely seen as deriving from a complex mix of British object relations theory, American interpersonal theory, and Kohutian self psychology (see Greenberg & Mitchell, 1983). Indeed, a chief argument of Greenberg and Mitchell's now-classic summary of object relations theories in psychoanalysis is precisely that there is a bifurcation between the drive model posited by classical psychoanalysis and ego psychology on the one hand and the relational models variously proposed by the British theorists, the interpersonal school, and the Kohutians on the other.[1]

[1] A parallel evolution has taken place outside psychoanalysis as well. For example, various cognitive- and schema-based models of personality have begun to integrate more explicitly an interpersonal component (Safran & Segal, 1990).

Unfortunately, this version of psychoanalytic history omits the contributions of psychoanalytic scholars who were influenced by the work of David Rapaport and his colleagues (Rapaport, 1951, 1967; Rapaport, Gill, & Schafer, 1945–1946), and yet these theorists (e.g., Gill & Holzman, 1976; Holt, 1989; Klein, 1976; Schafer, 1976), by rigorously challenging the Freudian metapsychology they learned from Rapaport, were just as essential as were figures like Fairbairn (1952), Sullivan (1953), Winnicott (1958, 1965), and Kohut (1971, 1977, 1984) to the transformation of psychoanalysis from a one-person psychology focused on drive, energy, and structure to a two-person psychology in which the vicissitudes of human relationships are primary. Furthermore, another crucial aspect of the work of many of these post-Rapaportian theorists was their reliance on empirical research as an impetus to their theoretical revisions. Thus, Greenberg and Mitchell's (1983) account of post-Freudian developments in drive and energy theory contains chapter-length discussions of the work of Heinz Hartmann, Edith Jacobson, Otto Kernberg, and Margaret Mahler, all theorists whose ideas in some significant way descend from classic psychoanalytic drive theory, but has scarcely a word about either Rapaport's attempt to systematize the Freudian metapsychology—to wed drive theory and cognitive psychology, motives and thought—or his students' eventual rejection of this effort in favor of what Gill (1983) termed the *person point of view* in psychoanalysis. In their discussion, which Greenberg and Mitchell regarded as a dichotomy between drive/structure and relational/structure theories, they also are explicitly silent on the role of empirical research in sorting out the differences between drive and relationship views and potentially integrating them. Meanwhile, traditional psychoanalytic theorists (e.g., Arlow & Brenner, 1964), in their classic attempt at systematizing Freud's structural and drive theories, did not mention at all Rapaport's efforts at constructing a more rigorous account of the metapsychology.

The purpose of this chapter is to describe the concept of the object on the Rorschach (COR) scale developed by Blatt, Brenneis, Schimek, and Glick (1976) to assess human representation on the Rorschach. Blatt et al.'s development of this scale, like the contributions of other Rapaport-influenced theorists of the time (e.g., Gill & Holzman, 1976; Klein, 1976; Schafer, 1976), is best understood as part of the general shift in psychoanalysis of the 1970s from a psychology dominated by metapschological abstractions to one that focused on the lived experience, once again both real and fantasied, of human relationships or, to use the psychoanalytic term, *object relations*. Readers of this chapter will therefore have a much better grasp of the COR scale if they understand its Rapaportian lineage. Specifically, insofar as it focuses on the developmental construction of Rorschach percepts of human figures instead of on classical metapsychological concepts like drive-defense expression, the COR scale reflects, as did the work of figures like Gill, Klein, Holt, and Schafer, a break with the Rapaportian past from which it descends. Yet at the same time, it continues this heritage in at least four ways.

First, the COR scale developed out of the Rapaport approach (e.g., Allison, Blatt, & Zimet, 1968; Rapaport et al., 1945–1946; Rapaport, Gill, & Schafer, 1968) to the Rorschach and to psychological testing more generally. Rapaport used psychoanalytic theory to understand not only the ego functions and cognitive capacities but also the experiential world of the testing subject. To understand the testing subject, Rapaport moved from analysis of ordinary verbalizations uttered in the testing context to a hierarchical integration based on a highly sophisticated understanding of the cognitive operations underlying the subject's test responses. Because Rapaport articulated his approach to testing well before the emergence of post-Freudian object relations theories, the COR scale may be seen as an expansion of his approach to consider more recent theoretical contributions not available in the early 1940s. Second, contrary to Greenberg and Mitchell's (1983) argument that drive-based developmental psychologies (e.g., those of Freud,1965; Jacobson, 1964; Mahler, 1968; and Mahler, Pine, & Bergman, 1975) cannot be combined with developmental psychologies derived from object relations theories, Blatt et al. (1976) integrated ego-psychological and object relations concepts in constructing their scale. The development of this scale, as well as the theoretical work by Blatt and colleagues from the 1970s and 1980s (e.g., Behrends & Blatt, 1985; Blatt, 1974; Blatt & Behrends, 1987; Blatt & Shichman, 1983), was quite clearly a part of the growing movement at that time toward a more experiential and relational psychoanalysis. Third, the COR scale relies equally heavily on the cognitive developmental theories of Piaget (1937/1954) and Werner (1957; Werner & Kaplan, 1963) and psychoanalytic object relations theories for its conceptual underpinnings. That is, this measure sees object representation as growing and changing in accordance with the trajectory of cognitive development. Werner's concepts of differentiation, articulation, and integration are central to its logic. Fourth, therefore, like many theorists whose views descended from the work of Rapaport, Blatt et al. were concerned with developing a measure that was not only theoretically and clinically sophisticated but also empirically sound. Thus, in constructing the COR scale, Blatt et al. were entirely consistent with Rapaport's project of integrating psychoanalytic and cognitive theory. In essence, the COR Scale, unlike Exner's (2002) Comprehensive System, derives from a sophisticated theoretical understanding of the link between human relationships and the representation of those relationships on the Rorschach (see Auerbach, 1999). Indeed, this measure prefigures the movement among post-Rapaportian Rorschach theorists (e.g., Blatt, 1990, 1999a, 1999b; Leichtman, 1996; Lerner, 1998) toward understanding the Rorschach as a representational, rather than perceptual, test.

In this chapter, therefore, we present the COR scale as reflecting a post-Rapaportian theoretical approach to the Rorschach and, more generally, an approach to object relations. First, we discuss the development of the scale. Second, we describe the scoring and interpretation of this measure. Third, we review empirical data pertaining to the scale's validity. Fourth, we evaluate the strengths, weaknesses, and limitations of the COR scale. Finally, we consider directions for further research using this measure.

DEVELOPMENT OF THE COR SCALE

Using a theoretical conceptualization derived from developmental psychology (Werner, 1957; Werner & Kaplan, 1963), Blatt et al. (1976) developed an extensive procedure for evaluating properties of human responses on the Rorschach. They identified three developmentally derived, primary dimensions of responses: differentiation, articulation, and integration. *Differentiation* was defined as the nature of the response with human content, from unrealistic human details through realistic whole humans; *articulation* was the degree to which perceptual and functional characteristics of the response were elaborated; and *integration* was the ways in which the concept of the human object was integrated into a context of action and interaction with other objects.

Specifically, the system calls for scoring human or humanoid responses according to developmental principles of differentiation (i.e., types of human figures perceived: quasi-human part properties, human part properties, quasi-human full figures, and full human figures), articulation (i.e., number and type of perceptual and functional features attributed to figures), degree of internality in the motivation of action attributed to the figures (i.e., unmotivated, reactive, and intentional action), degree of integration of the object and its action (i.e., fused, incongruent, nonspecific, and congruent action), content of the action (malevolent, benevolent), and the nature of any interaction (i.e., active-passive, active-reactive, active-active interactions) between human or humanoid figures. In each of these six categories, responses are scored along a developmental continuum. This developmental analysis is made separately for those human or humanoid responses that are accurately perceived ($F+$) and for those that are inaccurately perceived ($F-$).

Differential weighting for scores within each of the six categories assessing the concept of the object reflects a developmental progression, with higher scores indicating higher developmental levels. Score values are as follows. For differentiation: For a quasi-human detail, $Hd = 1$;

for a human detail, *Hd* = 2; for a full quasi-human figure, *H* = 3; and for a full human figure, *H* = 4. For articulation, perceptual attributes = 1, and functional attributes = 2. For motivation, unmotivated = 1, reactive = 2, and intentional = 3. For integration of object and action, fused = 1, incongruent = 2, nonspecific = 3, and congruent = 4. For content of action, malevolent = 1, and benevolent = 2. For nature of interaction, active-passive = 1, active-reactive = 2, and active-active = 3. A detailed presentation of this scoring system is provided in the next section. Table 4.1 summarizes the COR scale.

This developmental analysis is made for those responses with any human features that are accurately perceived (*F*+) or inaccurately perceived (*F*–). Scores in the six categories are converted to standard scores,[2] and a residualized weighted sum and an average developmental score (mean) for each of the six categories is obtained for *F*+ and *F*– responses separately. The composite weighted sum (developmental index) and the developmental average (mean) of the differentiation, articulation, and integration of accurately perceived human forms (*OR*+) assess the capacity for investing in appropriate interpersonal relationships; the composite weighted sum (developmental index) and the developmental average (mean) of differentiated, articulated, and integrated inaccurately perceived human forms (*OR*–) assess the degree of investment in inappropriate, unrealistic, possibly autistic fantasies, rather than realistic relationships.

CURRENT CONTROVERSY REGARDING THE RORSCHACH

Much of the current criticism of the Rorschach focuses on the validity of Exner's Comprehensive System and the use of the Rorschach for making clinical diagnostic distinctions (Dawes, 1994; Garb, 1998; Garb, Wood, Lilienfeld, & Nezworski, 2002; Grove & Barden, 1999; Hunsley & Bailey, 1999; Wood & Lilienfeld, 1999). In addition to concerns about reliability, Wood, Lilienfeld, Garb, and Nezworski (2000) suggested that six methodological issues may be especially widespread and problematic for Rorschach researchers: (a) comparing diagnostic groups to normative data (rather than a comparison group), (b) basing criterion diagnoses on procedures other than clinical or structured interviews, (c) failing to blind diagnosticians thoroughly to both direct and indirect influence of Rorschach scores, (d) failing to blind Rorschach administrators and scorers to study hypotheses, (e) performing large numbers of statistical tests without adequate adjustment of alpha, and (f) using parametric rather than nonparametric tests for skewed data and small

[2]Standard scores are a way of placing a series of raw scores into a common context by converting them to *z* scores with a mean of 0 and a standard deviation of 1.

TABLE 4.1
Summary of the Concept of the Object Scale

Categories of Analysis	*Subcategory I*	*Subcategory II*
Accuracy of response	*F+ or F–*	
Differentiation	Types of figures perceived	Quasi-human detail Human detail Quasi-human Human
Articulation	Perceptual attributes	Size or physical structure Clothing or hairstyle Posture
	Functional attributes	Sex Age Role Specific identity
	Degree of articulation	Number of features articulated Number of responses
Integration	Motivation of action	Unmotivated Reactive Intentional
	Integration of object and action	Fusion of object and action Incongruent action Nonspecific action Congruent action
	Content of action	Malevolent Benevolent
	Nature of interaction with another object	Active-passive Active-reactive Active-active

samples. We address each of these issues in evaluating the validity of the COR scale.

VALIDITY OF THE COR SCALE

Reliability

In Blatt et al.'s (1976) initial study, reliability was assessed with percentage of agreement, with a minimum of 90% agreement found between two raters in all but two categories. For those two categories, the agreement figures were 84% and 82%. Ritzler, Zambianco, Harder, and Kaskey

(1980) also used agreement percentages to assess reliability and found values between 75% and 91%. Lerner and St. Peter (1984) reported similar reliabilities on a subset of twenty protocols. Thus, the early studies of the COR scale reported agreement percentages as the reliability metric. Although at the time of the Blatt et al. and Ritzler et al. studies, agreement percentages was an acceptable metric of reliability, it is now considered a problematic statistic because it ignores chance agreements and does not allow for testing statistical significance. Three studies have used the kappa (*K*) or the Pearson *r* in addition to agreement percentage to calculate reliability (Greco & Cornell, 1992; Hibbard, Hilsenroth, Hibbard, & Nash, 1995; Stuart et al., 1990). Greco and Cornell found 98.5 % agreement between two raters and a *K* of = .97, and Stuart et al. found *K*s ranging from .62 to .96, with an average *K* of .80. These levels of reliability are in the good to excellent range (Fleiss, 1981). Hibbard et al. found 84% agreement and Pearson correlations ranging from .89 to .95. Thus, prior research indicates that these COR variables can be scored reliably and that the reliability of the subscales has been consistently replicated.

Blatt, Ford, Berman, Cook, and Meyer (1988; cf. also Blatt & Ford, 1994) trained a senior undergraduate, untrained with and uninformed about the Rorschach, to score the COR scale on data collected at the Austen Riggs Center. This student achieved an item alpha intraclass correlation coefficient (ICC) of .70 or greater in scoring all six categories of the COR scale when her ratings were compared with those of an expert scorer. This same student also scored the COR scale on Rorschach data collected as part of the Menninger Psychotherapy Research Project (MPRP; Blatt, 1992; Wallerstein, 1986), and in both of these investigations, this rater scored only the COR scale. The evaluations of the other Rorschach dimensions (e.g., thought disorder, accuracy of the responses) were scored by separate raters.

Construct Validity

Developmental Changes. The COR scale was first used to study the development of human responses on the Rorschach in a longitudinal study of normal subjects over a 20-year period from early adolescence to young adulthood (Blatt et al., 1976). Thirty-seven normal subjects had been given the Rorschach at ages 11–12, 13–14, 17–18, and 30; these protocols were analyzed in a repeated measures design. The results indicated that formal properties of the human responses show consistent changes with development. The number of well-differentiated, highly articulated, and integrated human figures increased significantly with normal development, from preadolescence (age 11–12) to adulthood (age 30). The attribution of activity congruent with important characteristics of the figures and the degree to which the object was seen as involved in constructive and positive interactions also increased significantly with age. Developmentally, differentiation of the object, fuller articulation of attributes, integration of action, and interactions that were reflective, motivated, purposive, and benevolent significantly increased with age. The number of inactive human figures decreased significantly over time, with a trend toward less distorted or partial human figures. This developmental progression in the quality of human responses with age is consistent with the developmental model upon which the COR scale is based, and it demonstrates the construct validity of this scoring system for the Rorschach as an assessment of psychological development.

Comparisons Across Diagnostic Groups. The COR scale was also used to study the human response in the Rorschach protocols of a sample ($N = 48$) of seriously disturbed adolescents and young adults hospitalized in a long-term, intensive treatment facility (Blatt et al., 1976). Although no significant relationships were found between the degree of thought disorder on the Rorschach and any aspects of accurately perceived human responses, more seriously disturbed patients, as compared with both less seriously disturbed patients and normal participants, gave significantly more inaccurately perceived human responses that were more fully articulated, had more unmotivated and nonspecific action, depicted interactions that were primarily active-passive and active-reactive, and contained both benevolent and malevolent content. Thus, significant relationships were found in seriously disturbed patients between severity of psychopathology and aspects of inaccurately perceived human figures (Blatt et al.). Unexpectedly, the patient group provided developmentally lower level responses when they gave accurately perceived human responses and developmentally higher level responses to more inaccurately perceived human responses. These unexpected findings led Blatt et al. to hypothesize two independent dimensions in the psychotic experience. First, psychotic individuals trying to grapple with consensual reality maintain interpersonal contact function at a developmentally lower level, in which reality is experienced as distorted, malevolent, and destructive. Second, when such persons are absorbed in unrealistic fantasies, they are able to function at a developmentally higher level, in which the world is experienced as benevolent. For only the most seriously disturbed patients, as defined by severity of thought disorder, were both inaccurately and accurately perceived humans experienced as distorted and malevolent. These findings were replicated by Ritzler et al. (1980).

The COR scale has been used in several studies of clinical samples. Blatt, Berman, et al. (1984) and Blatt and Berman (1990) applied the measure to a sample of 53 patients with opiate dependence in an attempt to differentiate subgroups in this population, rather than regarding the population of opiate-dependent patients as homogeneous. Cluster analysis identified three subgroups that could be distinguished along dimensions derived from the COR scale: a first group characterized primarily by disturbances in interpersonal relatedness, a second group characterized primarily by affective lability, and a third group characterized by an orientation toward fantasy-generated perceptions. Blatt et al. (1988) and Blatt and Ford (1994) applied the COR scale to identify changes in 90 seriously disturbed, treatment-resistant patients in long-term inpatient treatment. They distinguished between two clinical groups, anaclitic patients preoccupied with issues of interpersonal relatedness and introjective patients preoccupied with issues of self-definition and self-worth (e.g., Blatt, 1974, 1990, 1995b; Blatt & Shichman, 1983). Blatt et al. (1988) found that clinical change in introjective patients was associated with improved cognitive functioning, whereas clinical improvement in anaclitic patients was associated with improved interpersonal relationships, as indicated by a reduction in both the developmental mean and the developmental index for *OR*– responses on the COR scale. Greco and Cornell (1992) compared the Rorschach protocols of 55 adolescents who committed either homicide or nonviolent offenses. Although the adolescents who committed homicide did not differ from nonviolent delinquents in the quality of their object differentiation, adolescents who committed a homicide during another crime (such as robbery) had worse object differentiation than adolescents who committed a homicide in the context of an interpersonal dispute. Piran (1988) applied the COR scale to differentiate between 65 restricting and bulimic anorexics. Although the two groups did not differ in terms of differentiation, the bulimic group produced significantly more malevolent responses.

Research on the COR scale has contributed to the construction of a developmental model of representation (e.g., Blatt, 1991, 1995b; Blatt & Shichman, 1983) that posits a continuum of psychopathology from neurotic to borderline to psychotic. Spear and Lapidus (1981) studied 55 inpatients that they classified into three groups: obsessive-paranoid borderline personality, hysterical-impulsive borderline personality, and nonparanoid, undifferentiated schizophrenia. The obsessive-paranoid borderline group had developmentally higher levels of object representation. Farris (1988) applied the COR scale to differentiate between 18 narcissistic and 18 borderline patients. He found that narcissistic participants produced significantly more differentiated, articulated, and integrated responses than did borderline participants. Hymowitz, Hunt, Carr, Hurt, and Spear (1983) found that borderline patients diagnosed by the Diagnostic Interview for Borderlines (Gunderson, Kolb, & Austin, 1981) evidenced higher total developmental scores on the COR scale, as compared to schizophrenic patients. Johnson and Quinlan (1993) compared 31 normal subjects with 42 schizophrenic patients on a role-playing task scored with the COR scale (16 paranoid, 11 intermediate, and 15 nonparanoid). They reported that, although the normal group's representations were the most differentiated, integrated, and complex, no differences were found between normal and paranoid schizophrenic patients on the developmental level of representation. The paranoid schizophrenic patients, however, were found to be at a higher developmental level on the COR scale than were the nonparanoid schizophrenic individuals. This finding is consistent with research indicating that a paranoid orientation can be organizing, as compared with the more diffuse orientation of nonparanoid schizophrenic patients (Blatt & Wild, 1976; Blatt, Wild, & Ritzler, 1975).

Lerner and St. Peter (1984) studied the Rorschach protocols of 70 patients classified into four groups: outpatient neurosis, outpatient borderline personality, inpatient borderline personality, and inpatient schizophrenia. They found that, as predicted, less severe psychopathology was correlated with developmentally higher level responses on responses with good form level accuracy. The inpatient borderline group, however, had greater investment in responses with poor form level. They had high levels of differentiation on inaccurately perceived human responses. The inpatient borderline group also had the most malevolent content and was the only group to produce inaccurate malevolent responses. In contrast, the outpatient borderline group's responses were more accurate but were primarily quasi-human figures, rather than whole humans. Lerner and St. Peter noted that the outpatient borderline group may defensively maintain distance from people to avoid painful interactions that might threaten their connection to reality. In contrast, because the inpatient borderline group seems unable to mobilize defenses that would allow them to establish this distance, their contact with reality suffers.

In comparing the two inpatient groups, Lerner and St. Peter (1984) found that the inpatient borderline groups produced significantly more (accurate and inaccurate) human responses and significantly more malevolent responses than did the inpatient schizophrenic group. Citing Blatt et al. (1976) and Ritzler et al. (1980), they noted that, unlike schizophrenic patients, who could withdraw from a painful reality filled with malevolent objects into an idiosyncratic but benevolent internal reality, inpatient borderline patients seemed unable to mobilize defenses that would protect them from a malevolent world.

Psychotherapy Effects. Blatt and his colleagues also used the COR scale as an outcome measure of change in psychotherapy research. In a reanalysis of the data from the MPRP, Blatt (1992) evaluated 33 Rorschach protocols obtained before the beginning and at the end of either a supportive-expressive psychotherapy (SEP) or psychoanalysis. Statistically significant differences were found between anaclitic and introjective patients at the beginning of treatment, with introjective patients showing a greater investment in inappropriate, unrealistically perceived human forms than did anaclitic patients. Furthermore, a significant treatment main effect was found for the developmental level of accurately perceived figures, with greater improvement for introjective patients in psychoanalysis, rather than in psychotherapy. A similar nonsignificant trend was noted for anaclitic patients, with greater change also in psychoanalysis, as opposed to psychotherapy.

Further analyses of the data from the MPRP by Blatt and Shahar (2004) indicated a significant treatment effect, as evidenced by a significant increase in adaptive representations, measured by the developmental index of *OR+* responses for both anaclitic and introjective patients in psychoanalysis, rather than in SEP. Whereas these two treatments had different effects on changes in the two groups' adaptive interpersonal schemas, as measured by the developmental mean of *OR+*, no significant changes were noted for *OR–* in either anaclitic or introjective patients in psychoanalysis and SEP. It is important to note that the developmental level of accurately perceived human responses (*OR+*) was more relevant in the study of the therapeutic response of outpatients, the groups studied in the MPRP, whereas the developmental level of inaccurately perceive human responses (*OR–*) was more relevant in the study of the therapeutic response of the more seriously disturbed inpatients in the Riggs-Yale project (Blatt & Ford, 1994).

Critique and Future Directions

Several studies have examined the relationship between the quality of human object representation, as measured by the COR scale, and psychopathology. Hibbard et al. (1995) evaluated Rorschach protocols, using the COR scale, and Thematic Apperception Test (TAT; Morgan & Murray, 1935) protocols, using the Social Cognition and Object Relations scales (SCORS; Westen, 1989), of 94 patients from the University of Tennessee clinic files and 15 participants from a previous study of children of alcoholics. The structural scales of the COR significantly correlated with the structural scales of the SCORS, independent of IQ. Although the COR scale as a measure of object representations was validated, little support was found for a relationship between developmentally low-level responses as indicated by the COR scale and pathology as indicated by the Minnesota Multiphasic Personality Inventory (MMPI; Hathaway & McKinley, 1983). No significant correlation was found between the structural scales of the COR and the individual scales of the MMPI. In addition, no correlation was found between the COR Scale and the Psychotic Triad, which aggregates the MMPI Paranoia, Schizophrenia, and Hypomania scales as an index of more severe psychopathology.

When Hibbard et al. (1995) related the COR scale to the Millon Clinical Multiaxial Inventory (MCMI; Millon, 1983), they found a significant correlation between the Motivation and Content of Interaction scales of the COR and a participant's highest score on the MCMI's three severe personality disorder scales (Schizotypal, Borderline, and Paranoid).[3] Stuart et al. (1990) compared the Rorschach protocols of 9 borderline patients, 13 depressed patients, 12 depressed borderline patients, and 26 normal participants. Like Lerner and St. Peter (1984), Stuart et al. found that borderline participants provide cognitively sophisticated but distorted and malevolent representations of human objects.

Westen (1990) cited evidence that borderline patients construct more malevolent representations than even do schizophrenic individuals but also exhibit cognitive sophistication that exceeds that produced by healthier participants. Westen noted that such findings contradict traditional notions of pathology as falling along a single developmental continuum from neurotic to psychotic. He contended that different pathologies are best understood as each having progressed differently along multiple developmental lines. With regard to the development of object relations, Westen noted the need for a distinction between cognitive and affective development. However, his own research (Stuart et al., 1990) raises the question of the degree to which borderline patients evidence actual cognitive sophistication. Westen himself noted that borderline patients often evidence a hypercomplexity or pseudocomplexity, but the program of empirical research on projective measures that Westen described does not seem to include any correction for this.

---

[3]These modest relationships between projective scores and self-report test scores could be interpreted as representing evidence for the discriminant validity of the measure (Bornstein, 1999; McClelland, Koestner, & Weinberger, 1989). This interpretation is consistent with findings across a number of subfields of psychology (e.g., studies of memory, personality, attachment, emotion, motivation, psychopathology, and attitudes) that have found a distinction between measurement of explicit and implicit processes. For example, research on self-esteem finds that self-report measures and priming procedures tend to correlate minimally with one another but that both predict relevant criterion variables (Bosson, Swann, & Pennebaker, 2000). Similarly, research on adult attachment finds that self-report measures and interview measures scored primarily by noting awkward pauses, gaps in memory, incoherent discourse, and other signs of defensiveness are only moderately correlated (Shaver, Belsky, & Brennan, 2000) but that both also predict relevant criterion variables (Bartholomew & Shaver, 1998; Crowell, Fraley, & Shaver, 1999). Thus, projective test scores should correlate modestly with self-reports; strong correlations would be conceptually problematic in most instances (Bornstein, 2001; McClelland et al., 1989).

Fonagy, Gergely, Jurist, and Target (2002) noted the hypercomplexity of some patient groups and the impact this style has on an individual's ability to reflect on the mental state of another person (see also Louis Sass, 1992, in this regard). For example, in the scoring of Reflective Function (Fonagy, Target, Steele, & Steele, 1998)—that is, the ability to reflect on one's own mental states and those of others—on the Adult Attachment Interview (George, Kaplan, & Main, 1985), the rater is instructed to consider factors like a hyperanalytic quality and a sureness of the other's mental state as signs that genuine mentalization (i.e., genuine understanding of mental states) might not be present.

Fritsch and Holmstrom (1990) applied a modification of the COR scale scoring that corrects for this very issue. In a sample of 84 adolescent inpatients, they found that, although good form accuracy correlated with adjustment potential, poor form accuracy did not have such a linear relationship. As Blatt et al. (1976), Ritzler et al. (1980), and Lerner and St. Peter (1984) noted, individuals with severe psychopathology may be able to display good differentiation, but only in the context of inaccurate responses. Fritsch and Holmstrom modified the COR scale to weight form level to correct for decreased maturity of inaccurate responses, whether differentiated or not, because such responses do not conform to consensual reality. In other words, a highly differentiated, integrated, and articulated response with poor form would receive a low weighted value, despite its high absolute value on the structural scale. With this modification, they found that developmentally advanced levels of human responses differentiated nonpsychotic from psychotic patients and correlated significantly with independent ratings of high interpersonal relatedness and less severe psychopathology.

We have contended in this chapter that, in contrast to the approach embodied in the Comprehensive System, the Rorschach is best viewed as a theory-driven evaluation of the content and structural organization of an individual's representational capacities, rather than an atheoretical, empirically based test. Although it is of course also our belief, as this chapter demonstrates, that empirical validation is still necessary for clinical propositions derived from the Rorschach, we nevertheless argue that the clinical information obtained through the Rorschach is meaningful only to the extent that one has a theoretical understanding of the psychological operations involved in constructing responses to the test. Alternatively, the Rorschach is best regarded as a representational assessment (Blatt, 1990, 1999b; Leichtman, 1996), a task through which the testing participants construct or reveal their representational, relational, and experiential worlds (see Lerner, 1998). On this perspective, the many scores and ratios that constitute the Comprehensive System would have greater meaning if they had some underlying theoretical perspective. And it is precisely a theoretical perspective that is currently absent from the Comprehensive System use of Rorschach responses. The COR scale, as discussed in this chapter, involves an integration of psychoanalytic, experiential-phenomenological, and cognitive-developmental theoretical concepts.

As we have therefore argued, the COR scale is one example of a family of post-Rapaportian approaches to the Rorschach (e.g., Leichtman, 1996; Lerner, 1998) that have emerged as part of the general movement in the psychoanalytic world since 1970 toward a more relational and experiential model of psychological functioning. But whereas the COR Scale was meant primarily to measure level of object relations, empirical research with this instrument has shown that object representation is in fact a multidimensional construct that cannot be reached through an atheoretical approach like that exemplified by the Comprehensive System, the MMPI, or many self-report measures. Thus, it is perhaps unsurprising that, as Blatt et al. (1976) showed in their initial study of the COR scale, object representations show increasing differentiation, articulation, and integration as testing participants grow from children to adults. One needs only a cognitive developmental theory like those of Piaget or Werner to account for this developmental progression. But this cognitive developmental model does not account for Blatt et al.'s finding, confirmed by Ritzler et al. (1980) and Lerner and St. Peter (1984), that accurately and inaccurately perceived human responses serve diverging psychological functions. Specifically, by differentiating between accurately and inaccurately perceived human responses on the Rorschach, Blatt et al. found that highly disturbed patients gave more differentiated, articulated, and integrated responses when their human percepts had poor form quality (i.e., were inaccurately perceived). To explain this seemingly paradoxical finding, Blatt et al., Ritzler et al., and Lerner and St. Peter turned to psychoanalytic object relations theory—specifically, to the idea that investment in unrealistic object relations was crucial to the psychological functioning of such individuals. For schizophrenic patients, this investment in unrealistic object relations reflects a withdrawal from a painful reality filled with malevolent objects into a world of idiosyncratic but benevolent fantasies. For borderline patients, the presence of inaccurate malevolent responses suggests this group of patients is unable to use unrealistic fantasies to contain negative object relations. Later research (e.g., Stuart et al., 1990) is also consistent with the observation that object representation is in fact multidimensional, and thus results from the COR scale, originally meant to be only a measure of a construct, object relations, have forced us to conclude that object representations are more complex and sophisticated than we had initially believed. In short, research with the COR scale, a measure derived from an integration of cognitive developmental theory with psychoanalytic object relations theory, has produced a more detailed view of psychoanalytic object relations theory and has elucidated aspects of psychopathology and the nature of therapeutic change.

Having described in some detail the consequences that research on the COR scale has had for object relations theory, we now turn, in closing, to the connections between the concepts of this measure and relational currents in psychology more generally. As we argued at the beginning of this chapter, psychoanalysis in the past 30 years has taken a relational turn, a shift from a one-person to a two-person psychology, and the COR scale was part of that shift within psychoanalysis and psychological assessment. The COR scale is important, however, not only because of the part it played in this paradigm shift in psychoanalysis, but also because it is congruent with a more general shift within psychology as a whole toward a relational understanding of human functioning. This development is particularly important because it reverses long-standing biases in Western thought toward autonomous individualism in our psychological theories. Perhaps most prominent in this shift is Bowlby's (1982) attachment theory (see Cassidy & Shaver, 1999) because Bowlby's ideas make the profound claims that the human desire for relatedness derives from Darwinian processes and that disturbances in attachment increase the likelihood for the development of psychopathology. Furthermore, although Bowlby's ideas on attachment are firmly rooted in psychoanalysis, he also formulated his theories in a manner that made them readily subject to empirical test. Indeed, a meta-analysis (Van IJzendoorn, 1995) showed that parents' attachment style can be used to predict the attachment styles of their children with a classification accuracy of approximately 75%, and a subsequent meta-analysis (Van IJzendoorn & Bakerman-Kranensburg, 1996) found that 55% of adults in the nonclinical population have secure attachments, as opposed to only 8% of participants from clinical samples. Because Bowlby's ideas, like those of Blatt, derive largely from psychoanalysis, it should come as little surprise that, although he has not updated the COR scale, Blatt and colleagues (e.g., Blatt, 1995b; Blatt, Auerbach, & Levy, 1997; Blatt & Levy, 2003; Diamond & Blatt, 1994; Levy & Blatt, 1999; Levy, Blatt, & Shaver, 1998) incorporated the findings of attachment theory and research into their current understanding of object representation. This was a surprisingly easy accomplishment because Blatt, like Bowlby, has long been interested in the psychological representation of emotionally significant relationships, as well as in the empirical test of psychoanalytic theories.

Attachment theory, however, is not the only perspective within psychology that reflects the field's recent relational turn. For example, two recent books published by the American Psychological Association (Horowitz, 2004; Joiner & Coyne, 1999) argued for the interpersonal or interactional nature of psychopathology, and in neither volume was there a specific link to psychoanalysis and its growing cadre of relational thinkers. Meanwhile, if we turn from the psychopathology literature to the literature on psychotherapy and treatment, we find a similar growth in relational thinking. For example, among radical behaviorists (e.g., Hayes, Strosahl, & Wilson, 1999; Kohlenberg, Hayes, & Tsai, 1993; Kohlenberg & Tsai, 1991), there is a new interest in the therapeutic relationship, conceptualized in terms of mutual operant processes, as a means of producing therapeutic change. Cognitive theorists (e.g., Migone & Liotti, 1998; Safran & Segal, 1990) are also writing about how cognitive change occurs in an interpersonal context, and in more recent writings, cognitive theorists like Safran and Muran (2000), increasingly influenced by relational currents within psychoanalysis, have begun to describe therapeutic change as an essentially relational process. Thus, in response to the movement for empirically validated treatments, psychotherapy researchers have martialed an impressive body of empirical evidence that factors like the therapeutic relationship and the therapeutic alliance are crucial to the process of therapeutic change (see Norcross, 2002; Wampold, 2001). For example, Klein et al. (2003) recently found, in a study of the cognitive behavioral analysis system of psychotherapy, that early therapeutic alliance predicted improvement in depressive symptoms but that symptomatic improvement did not predict the subsequent level or course of the alliance (see also Zurolf & Blatt, 2004). According to these results, the therapeutic relationship is a crucial factor in producing therapeutic change, not an artifact of symptomatic improvement. Meanwhile, in the psychoanalytic tradition, the process research of Jones and Price (1998) has pointed to the central role of what Jones (1997) termed *interaction structures* in psychoanalytic and psychodynamic treatments.

Indeed, the previous two paragraphs barely do justice to the many new relational currents within not only psychoanalysis but psychology as a whole, but it does bear reiteration that this relational turn began as a movement within psychoanalysis and that the COR scale was part of that movement, a part that has also insisted on the role of empirical scrutiny of the new movement's theoretical claims. Nearly three decades after this measure first appeared in the published literature, the COR scale remains surprisingly relevant, even in an age in which the Rorschach and other projective tests are under renewed criticism for their alleged empirical inadequacies (Dawes, 1994; Garb, 1998; Garb et al., 2002; Grove & Barden, 1999; Hunsley & Bailey, 1999;

Wood & Lilienfeld, 1999; Wood, Nezworski, Lilienfeld, & Garb, 2003). Sadly, space precludes a full discussion of the issues raised by recent Rorschach critics, although we note here that we are in agreement with many of their critiques of the Comprehensive System, perhaps most of all because we believe that the Rorschach is best regarded as a theoretical instrument with complex variables, rather than as the atheoretical, empirically driven test that Exner (2002) envisioned. We agree with many of the empirical critiques that these writers have leveled against the Comprehensive System as well. In this literature, concerns are raised about such topics as scoring reliability, test-retest reliability, validity, the extent and stability of the Comprehensive System's normative database, incremental validity, differential diagnosis, clinical utility, and accessibility of research results. In our opinion, the last of these issues is perhaps most important because it speaks to an essential issue in the process of scientific inquiry: the matter of review by one's academic peers. Unfortunately, many of the studies that Exner cited in support of his scoring system have never been peer reviewed and are published in his own private publication series, the Rorschach Workshops. A little over a decade ago, therefore, Sidney Blatt (personal communication, 1992) stated that, in his judgment, the Comprehensive System had initially saved the Rorschach because it appealed to the empirically oriented academic community but that Exner's atheoretical, non-peer-reviewed empiricism could eventually be responsible for the Rorschach's demise. It seems that Blatt's view of the Comprehensive System has proved to be prophetic.

Despite our concerns about the problems with the Comprehensive System (see Auerbach, 1999; Blatt, 1995a), we not surprisingly believe that there is significant evidence in support of the Rorschach as a method for assessing complex psychological processes and behaviors. Indeed, an important meta-analytic review (Hiller, Rosenthal, Bornstein, Berry, & Brunell-Neuleib, 1999) supports the validity of this means of personality assessment, and the volume in which this chapter appears stands as a testament to the creativity of Rorschach researchers in developing theoretically compelling, empirically validated means of using this assessment procedure. These approaches have demonstrated that the Rorschach is useful for what it discovers about psychological operations like object relations and cognitive processes like thought disorder and perhaps less so for its use in empirical prediction of behavior or diagnostic status, although there are several good examples available regarding the utility of Rorschach methods (e.g., the Thought Disorder index: Holzman, in press; Johnston & Holzman, 1979; the Rorschach Oral Dependency scale: Bornstein, 1996; Lilienfeld, Wood, & Garb, 2000; Masling, 1986; the Rorschach Prognostic Rating scale: Meyer & Handler, 1997) in psychodiagnosis and the prediction of objective behaviors.

As for the COR scale, its importance lies not only in its having garnered empirical support as a measure of object relations but also in its congruence with the relational turn within psychology. Indeed, two recent reviews of Blatt's contributions to the Rorschach and to projective testing in general conceptualize its contributions—theoretical, clinical, and empirical—in terms of these relational currents (Lerner, in press; Ritzler, in press). As a measure of object relations, the COR scale has helped to clarify the nature and function of object representations. Specifically, through its differentiation of realistic (*OR*+) and unrealistic (*OR*—) responses, the COR scale demonstrates that human representation is complex and multidimensional, and that a well-differentiated, articulated and integrated response may change dramatically in meaning, depending on whether it is accurately or inaccurately perceived. The original validation research for this measure also showed, in accordance with classic psychoanalytic thinking, that object relations and representations grow in sophistication—in differentiation, articulation, and integration—through the processes of normal development. Most of all, therefore, the value of the COR scale as a measure of psychological development and functioning, in both clinical and nonclinical contexts, speaks to the centrality and complexity of interpersonal relatedness in human affairs.

REFERENCES

Allison, J., Blatt, S. J., & Zimet, C. N. (1968). *The interpretation of psychological tests.* New York: Harper & Row.

Arlow, J. A., & Brenner, C. (1964). *Psychoanalytic concepts and the structural theory.* New York: International Universities Press.

Aron, L. (1996). *A meeting of minds: Mutuality in psychoanalysis.* Hillsdale, NJ: Analytic Press.

Atwood, G. E., & Stolorow, R. D. (1984). *Structures of subjectivity: Explorations in psychoanalytic phenomenology.* Hillsdale, NJ: Analytic Press.

Auerbach, J. S. (1999). Psychoanalysis and projective testing [Review of the book *The interpretation of psychological tests*]. *Journal of Personality Assessment, 72,* 147–163.

Bartholomew, K., & Shaver, P. R. (1998). Methods of assessing adult attachment: Do they converge? In J. A. Simpson & W. S. Rholes (Eds.), *Attachment theory and close relationships* (pp. 25–45). New York: Guilford Press.

Behrends, R. S., & Blatt, S. J. (1985). Internalization and psychological development throughout the life cycle. *Psychoanalytic Study of the Child, 40,* 11–39.

Benjamin, J. (1995). *Like subjects, love objects.* New Haven, CT: Yale University Press.

Blatt, S. J. (1974). Levels of object representation in anaclitic and introjective depression. *Psychoanalytic Study of the Child, 29,* 107–157.

Blatt, S. J. (1990). The Rorschach: A test of perception or an evaluation of representation. *Journal of Personality Assessment, 54,* 236–251.

Blatt, S. J. (1991). A cognitive morphology of psychopathology. *Journal of Nervous and Mental Disease, 179,* 449–458.
Blatt, S. J. (1992). The differential effect of psychotherapy and psychoanalysis with anaclitic and introjective patients: The Menninger Psychotherapy Research Project revisited. *Journal of the American Psychoanalytic Association, 40,* 691–724.
Blatt, S. J. (1995a, October 27). Blatt-Ford book. Message posted to SSCPnet, archived at http://www.sip.medizin.uni-ulm.de/abteilung/projekte/SSCP/SSCP7_95.html
Blatt, S. J. (1995b). Representational structures in psychopathology. In D. Cicchetti & S. Toth (Eds.), *Representation, emotion, and cognition in developmental psychopathology* (pp. 1–33). Rochester, NY: University of Rochester Press.
Blatt, S. J. (2000). Projective techniques. In A. E. Kazdin (Ed.), *Encyclopedia of psychology* (pp. 317–321). Washington, DC: American Psychological Association.
Blatt, S. J. (1999b, July). *The Rorschach in the 21st century.* Paper presented at the XVI International Congress of Rorschach and Projective Measures, Amsterdam, The Netherlands.
Blatt, S. J., Auerbach, J. S., & Levy, K. N. (1997). Mental representations in personality development, psychopathology, and the therapeutic process. *Review of General Psychology, 1,* 351–374.
Blatt, S. J., & Behrends, R. S. (1987). Internalization, separation-individuation, and the nature of therapeutic action. *International Journal of Psychoanalysis, 68,* 279–297.
Blatt, S. J., & Berman, W. H. (1990). Differentiation of personality types among opiate addicts. *Journal of Personality Assessment, 54,* 87–104.
Blatt, S. J., Berman, W., Bloom-Feshbach, S., Sugarman, A., Wilber, D., & Kleber, H. D. (1984). Psychological assessment of psychopathology in opiate addicts. *Journal of Nervous and Mental Disease, 172,* 156–165.
Blatt, S. J., Brenneis, B., Schimek, J., & Glick, M. (1976). Normal development and psychopathological impairment of the concept of the object on the Rorschach. *Journal of Abnormal Psychology, 85,* 364–373.
Blatt, S. J., & Ford, R. Q. (1994). *Therapeutic change: An object relations perspective.* New York: Plenum Press.
Blatt, S. J., Ford, R. Q., Berman, W., Cook, B., & Meyer, R. (1988). The assessment of change during the intensive treatment of borderline and schizophrenic young adults. *Psychoanalytic Psychology, 5,* 127–158.
Blatt, S. J., & Levy, K. N. (2003). Attachment theory, psychoanalysis, personality development, and psychopathology. *Psychoanalytic Inquiry, 23,* 104–152.
Blatt, S. J., & Shahar, G. (2004) Psychoanalysis: With whom? For what? And how?: An empirical attempt to identify differences between psychoanalysis and psychotherapy. *Journal of the American Psychoanalytic Association, 52,* 393–447.
Blatt, S. J., & Shichman, S. (1983). Two primary configurations of psychopathology. *Psychoanalysis and Contemporary Thought, 6,* 187–254.
Blatt, S. J., & Wild, C. M. (1976). *Schizophrenia: A developmental analysis.*
Blatt, S. J., Wild, C. M., & Ritzler, B. A. (1975). Disturbances of object representations in schizophrenia. *Psychoanalysis and Contemporary Science, 4,* 235–288.
Bornstein, R. F. (1996). Construct validity of the Rorschach Oral Dependency Scale: 1967–1995. *Psychological Assessment, 8,* 200–205.
Bornstein, R. F. (1999). Criterion validity of objective and projective dependency tests: A meta-analytic assessment of behavioral prediction. *Psychological Assessment, 11,* 48–57.

Bornstein, R. F. (2001). Clinical utility of the Rorschach Inkblot Method: Reframing the debate. *Journal of Personality Assessment, 77,* 39–47.
Bosson, J. K., Swann, W. B., Jr., & Pennebaker, J. W. (2000). Stalking the perfect measure of implicit self-esteem: The blind men and the elephant revisited? *Journal of Personality and Social Psychology, 79,* 631–643.
Bowlby, J. (1982). *Attachment and loss: Vol. 1. Attachment* (rev. ed.). New York: Basic Books.
Bromberg, P. M. (1998). *Standing in the spaces: Essays on clinical process, trauma, and dissociation.* Hillsdale, NJ: Analytic Press.
Cassidy, J., & Shaver, P. R. (1999). *Handbook of attachment: Theory, research, and clinical applications.* New York: Guilford Press.
Crowell, J. A., Fraley, R. C., & Shaver, P. R. (1999). Measurement of individual differences in adolescent and adult attachment. In J. Cassidy & P. R. Shaver (Eds.), *Handbook of attachment: Theory, research, and clinical applications* (pp. 434–465). New York: Guilford Press.
Dawes, R. M. (1994). *House of cards: Psychology and psychotherapy built on myth.* New York: Free Press.
Diamond, D., & Blatt, S. J. (1994). Internal working models of attachment and psychoanalytic theories of the representational world: A comparison and critique. In M. B. Sperling & W. H. Berman (Eds.), *Attachment in adults: Clinical and developmental perspectives* (pp. 72–97). New York: Guilford Press.
Exner, J. E., Jr. (2002). A new nonpatient sample for the Rorschach Comprehensive System: A progress report. *Journal of Personality Assessment, 78,* 391–404.
Fairbairn, W. R. D. (1952). *Psychoanalytic studies of the personality.* London: Routledge & Kegan Paul.
Farris, M. A. (1988). Differential diagnosis of borderline and narcissistic personality disorders. In H. D. Lerner & P. M. Lerner (Eds.), *Primitive mental states and the Rorschach* (pp. 299–337). Madison, CT: International Universities Press.
Fleiss, J. L. (1981). Balanced incomplete block designs for inter-rater reliability studies. *Applied Psychological Measurement, 5,* 105–112.
Fonagy, P., Gergely, G., Jurist, E., & Target, M. (2002). *Affect regulation, mentalization, and the development of the self.* New York: Other Books.
Fonagy, P., Target, M., Steele, H., & Steele, M. (1998). *Reflective functioning manual: Version 5.* Unpublished manuscript, University College, London.
Freud, A. (1965). *Normality and pathology in childhood: Assessments of development.* New York: International Universities Press.
Fritsch, R. C., & Holmstrom, R. W. (1990). Assessing object representations as a continuous variable: A modification of the Concept of the Object on the Rorschach scale. *Journal of Personality Assessment, 55,* 319–334.
Garb, H. N. (1998). *Studying the clinician: Judgment research and psychological assessment.* Washington, DC: American Psychological Association.
Garb, H. N., Wood, J. M., Lilienfeld, S. O., & Nezworski, M. T. (2002). Effective use of projective techniques in clinical practice: Let the data help with selection and interpretation. *Professional Psychology: Research and Practice, 33,* 454–463.
George, C., Kaplan, N., & Main, M. (1985). *The Berkeley adult attachment interview.* Unpublished manuscript, University of California, Berkeley.
Gill, M. M. (1983). The point of view of psychoanalysis: Energy discharge or person? *Psychoanalysis and Contemporary Thought, 6,* 523–551.
Gill, M. M., & Holzman, P. S. (Eds.). (1976). Psychology versus metapsychology: Psychoanalytic essays in memory of George S. Klein. *Psychological Issues Monographs, 9*(4, Serial No. 36).

Greco, C. M., & Cornell, D. G. (1992). Rorschach object relations of adolescents who committed homicide. *Journal of Personality Assessment, 59,* 574–583.

Greenberg, J. R., & Mitchell, S. A. (1983). *Object relations in psychoanalytic theory.* Cambridge, MA: Harvard University Press.

Grove, W. M., & Barden, R. C. (1999). Protecting the integrity of the legal system: The admissibility of testimony from mental health experts under Daubert/Kumho analyses. *Psychology, Public Policy, and Law, 5,* 224–242.

Gunderson, J. G., Kolb, J. E., & Austin, V. (1981). The diagnostic interview for borderlines. *American Journal of Psychiatry, 138,* 896–903.

Hathaway, S. R., & McKinley, J. (1983). *Manual for administration and scoring of the MMPI.* Minneapolis, MN: National Computer Systems.

Hayes, S. C., Strosahl, K. D., & Wilson, K. G. (1999). *Acceptance and commitment therapy: An experiential approach to behavior change.* New York: Guilford Press.

Hibbard, S., Hilsenroth, M. J., Hibbard, J. K., & Nash, M. R. (1995). A validity study of two projective object representations measures. *Psychological Assessment, 7,* 432–439.

Hiller, J. B., Rosenthal, R., Bornstein, R. F., Berry, T. R., & Brunell-Neuleib, S. (1999). A comparative meta-analysis of Rorschach and MMPI studies. *Psychological Assessment, 11,* 278–296.

Holt, R. R. (1989). *Freud reappraised: A fresh look at psychoanalytic theory.* New York: Guilford Press.

Holzman, P. S. (in press). The Rorschach method: A starting point for investigating formal thought disorder. In J. S. Auerbach, K. N. Levy, & C. E. Schaffer (Eds.), *Relatedness, self-definition, and mental representation: Essays in honor of Sidney J. Blatt.* London: Brunner-Routledge.

Horowitz, L. M. (2004). *Interpersonal foundations of psychopathology.* Washington, DC: American Psychological Association.

Hunsley, J., & Bailey, J. M. (1999). The clinical utility of the Rorschach: Unfulfilled promises and an uncertain future. *Psychological Assessment, 11,* 266–277.

Hymowitz, P., Hunt, H. F., Carr, A. C., Hurt, S. W., & Spear, W. E. (1983). The WAIS and Rorschach test in diagnosing borderline personality. *Journal of Personality Assessment, 47,* 588–596.

Jacobson, E. (1964). *The self and the object world.* New York: International Universities Press.

Johnson, D. R., & Quinlan, D. M. (1993). Can the mental representations of paranoid schizophrenics be differentiated from those of normals? *Journal of Personality Assessment, 60,* 588–601.

Johnston, M., & Holzman, P. S. (1979). *Assessing schizophrenic thinking.* San Francisco: Jossey-Bass.

Joiner, T. E., & Coyne, J. C. (Eds.). (1999). *The interactional nature of depression: Advances in interpersonal approaches.* Washington, DC: American Psychological Association.

Jones, E. E. (1997). Modes of therapeutic action. *International Journal of Psychoanalysis, 78,* 1135–1150.

Jones, E. E., & Price, P. B. (1998). Interaction structure and change in psychoanalytic therapy. In R. F. Bornstein & J. M. Masling (Eds.), *Empirical studies of psychoanalytic theories: Vol. 8. Empirical studies of the therapeutic hour* (pp. 27–62). Washington, DC: American Psychological Association.

Klein, D. N., Schwartz, J. E., Santiago, N. J., Vivian, D., Vocisano, C., Castonguay, L. G., et al. (2003). Therapeutic alliance in depression treatment: Controlling for prior change and patient characteristics. *Journal of Consulting and Clinical Psychology, 71,* 997–1006.

Klein, G. S. (1976). *Psychoanalytic theory: An exploration of essentials.* New York: International Universities Press.

Kohlenberg, R. J., Hayes, S. C., & Tsai, M. (1993). Radical behavioral psychotherapy: Two contemporary examples. *Clinical Psychology Review, 13,* 579–592.

Kohlenberg, R. J., & Tsai, M. (1991). *Functional analytic psychotherapy: Creating intense and curative relationships.* New York: Plenum Press.

Kohut, H. (1971). *The analysis of the self.* New York: International Universities Press.

Kohut, H. (1977). *The restoration of the self.* New York: International Universities Press.

Kohut, H. (1984). *How does analysis cure?* Chicago: University of Chicago Press.

Leichtman, M. (1996). *The Rorschach: A developmental perspective.* Hillsdale, NJ: Analytic Press.

Lerner, H. D. (in press). Object relations and the Rorschach. In J. S. Auerbach, K. N. Levy, & C. E. Schaffer (Eds.), *Relatedness, self-definition, and mental representation: Essays in honor of Sidney J. Blatt.* London: Brunner-Routledge.

Lerner, H. D., & St. Peter, S. (1984). Patterns of object relations in neurotic, borderline and schizophrenic patients. *Psychiatry, 47,* 77–92.

Lerner, P. M. (1998). *Psychoanalytic perspectives on the Rorschach.* Hillsdale, NJ: Analytic Press.

Levy, K. N., & Blatt, S. J. (1999). Psychoanalysis and attachment theory: Developmental levels of attachment. *Psychoanalytic Inquiry, 19,* 541–575.

Levy, K. N., Blatt, S. J., & Shaver, P. R. (1998). Attachment styles and parental representations. *Journal of Personality and Social Psychology, 74,* 407–419.

Lilienfeld, S. O., Wood, J. M., Garb, H. N. (2000). The scientific status of projective techniques. *Psychological Science in the Public Interest, 1,* 27–66.

Mahler, M. S. (1968). *On human symbiosis and the vicissitudes of individuation: Infantile psychosis.* New York: International Universities Press.

Mahler, M. S., Pine, F., & Bergman, A. (1975). *The psychological birth of the human infant: Symbiosis and individuation.* New York: Basic Books.

Masling, J. (1986). Orality, pathology, and interpersonal behavior. In J. Masling (Ed.), *Empirical studies of psychoanalytic theories* (Vol. 2, pp. 73–106). Hillsdale, NJ: Analytic Press.

McClelland, D. C., Koestner, R., & Weinberger, J. L. (1989). How do self-attributed and implicit motives differ? *Psychological Review, 96,* 690–702.

Meyer, G. J., & Handler, L. (1997). The ability of the Rorschach to predict subsequent outcome: A meta-analysis of the Rorschach Prognostic Rating scale. *Journal of Personality Assessment, 69,* 1–38.

Migone, P., & Liotti, G. (1998). Psychoanalysis and cognitive-evolutionary psychology: An attempt at integration. *International Journal of Psychoanalysis, 79,* 1071–1095.

Millon, T. (1983). *Millon Clinical Multiaxial Inventory manual* (3rd ed.). Minneapolis, MN: National Computer Systems.

Mitchell, S. A. (1988). *Relational concepts in psychoanalysis: An integration.* Cambridge, MA: Harvard University Press.

Mitchell, S. A., & Aron, L. (Eds.). (1999). *Relational psychoanalysis: The emergence of a tradition.* Hillsdale, NJ: Analytic Press.

Morgan, C., & Murray, H. A. (1935). A method for investigating fantasies: The Thematic Apperception Test. *Archives of Neurological Psychiatry, 34,* 289–306.

Norcross, J. C. (2002). *Psychotherapy relationships that work: Therapist contributions and responsiveness to patients.* London: Oxford University Press.

Ogden, T. H. (1997). *Subjects of analysis.* Northvale, NJ: Aronson.

Orange, D. M., Atwood, G. E., & Stolorow, R. D. (1999). *Working intersubjectively: Contextualism in psychoanalytic practice.* Hillsdale, NJ: Analytic Press.
Piaget, J. (1954). *The construction of reality in the child* (M. Cook, Trans.). New York: Basic Books. (Original work published 1937)
Piran, N. (1988). Borderline phenomena in anorexia nervosa and bulimia. In H. D. Lerner & P. M. Lerner (Eds.), *Primitive mental states and the Rorschach* (pp. 363–376). Madison, WI: International Universities Press.
Rapaport, D. (Ed.). (1951). *Organization and pathology of thought: Selected sources.* New York: Columbia University Press.
Rapaport, D. (1967). *The collected papers of David Rapaport* (M. M. Gill, Ed.). New York: Basic Books.
Rapaport, D, Gill, M. M., & Schafer, R. (1945). *Diagnostic psychological testing* (2 vols.). Chicago: Yearbook.
Rapaport, D., Gill, M. M., & Schafer, R. (1968). *Diagnostic psychological testing* (rev. ed.). New York: International Universities Press.
Ritzler, B. (in press). Sidney Blatt's contributions to the assessment of object representations. In J. S. Auerbach, K. N. Levy, & C. E. Schaffer (Eds.), *Relatedness, self-definition, and mental representation: Essays in honor of Sidney J. Blatt.* London: Brunner-Routledge.
Ritzler, B., Zambianco, D., Harder, D., & Kaskey, M. (1980). Psychotic patterns of the concept of the object on the Rorschach test. *Journal of Abnormal Psychology, 89,* 46–55.
Safran, J. D., & Muran, J. C. (2000). *Negotiating the therapeutic alliance: A relational treatment guide.* New York: Guilford Press.
Safran, J. D., & Segal, Z. V. (1990). *Interpersonal process in cognitive therapy.* Northvale, NJ: Aronson.
Sass, L. A. (1992). *Madness and modernism: Insanity in the light of modern art, literature, and thought.* New York: Basic Books.
Schafer, R. (1976). *A new language for psychoanalysis.* New Haven, CT: Yale University Press.
Shaver, P. R., Belsky, J., & Brennan, K. A. (2000). The adult attachment interview and self-reports of romantic attachment: Associations across domains and methods. *Personal Relationships, 7,* 25–43.
Skolnick, N. J., & Warshaw, S. C. (Eds.). (1992). *Relational perspectives in psychoanalysis.* Hillsdale, NJ: Analytic Press.
Spear, W. E., & Lapidus, L. B. (1981). Quantitative differences in manifest object representations: Implications for a multidimensional model of psychological functioning. *Journal of Abnormal Psychology, 90,* 157–167.
Stuart, J., Westen, D., Lohr, N. E., Benjamin, J., Becker, S., Vorus, N., et al. (1990). Object relations in borderlines, depressives, and normals: An examination of human responses on the Rorschach. *Journal of Personality Assessment, 55,* 296–318.
Sullivan, H. S. (1953). *The interpersonal theory of psychiatry* (H. S. Perry & M. L. Gawel, Eds.). New York: Norton.
Van IJzendoorn, M. H. (1995). Adult attachment representations, parental responsiveness, and infant attachment: A meta-analysis on the predictive validity of the Adult Attachment Interview. *Psychological Bulletin, 117,* 387–403.
Van IJzendoorn, M. H., & Bakerman-Kranenburg, M. J. (1996). Attachment representations in mothers, fathers, adolescents, and clinical groups: A meta-analytic search for normative data. *Journal of Consulting and Clinical Psychology, 64,* 8–21.
Wallerstein, R. S. (1986). *Forty-two lives in treatment: A study of psychoanalysis and psychotherapy.* New York: Guilford Press.

Wampold, B. E. (2001). *The great psychotherapy debate: Models, methods, and findings.* Mahwah, NJ: Lawrence Erlbaum Associates.
Werner, H. (1957). *Comparative psychology of mental development.* New York: International Universities Press. (Original work published 1948)
Werner, H., & Kaplan, B. (1963). *Symbol formation.* New York: Wiley.
Westen, D. (1989). *Object relations and social cognition TAT scoring manual.* Unpublished manuscript, University of Michigan, Ann Arbor.
Westen, D. (1990). Towards a revised theory of borderline object relations: Contributions from empirical research. *International Journal of Psychoanalysis, 71,* 661–693.
Winnicott, D. W. (1958). *Collected papers: From pediatrics to psychoanalysis.* New York: Basic Books.
Winnicott, D. W. (1965). *The maturational process and the facilitating environment.* New York: International Universities Press.
Wood, J. M., & Lilienfeld, S. O. (1999). The Rorschach Inkblot test: A case of overstatement? *Assessment, 6,* 341–351.
Wood J. M., Lilienfeld, S. O., Garb, H. N., & Nezworski, M. T. (2000). The Rorschach test in clinical diagnosis: A critical review, with a backward look at Garfield (1947). *Journal of Clinical Psychology, 56,* 395–430.
Wood, J. M., Nezworski, M. T., Lilienfeld, S. O., & Garb, H. N. (2003). *What's wrong with the Rorschach?: Science confronts the controversial inkblot test.* San Francisco: Jossey-Bass.
Zurolf, D. C., & Blatt, S. J. (2004). *Brief treatment of depression: Continuations of the therapeutic relationship in clinical improvement, reduced vulnerability, and enhanced resilience.* (In review)

Appendix
A Developmental Analysis of the Concept of the Object on the Rorschach

The importance of the human response on the Rorschach has been noted often in a variety of contexts, but generally with a minimum of theoretical elaboration. Aspects of these responses may have particular relevánce for the study of the development of the concept of the object and its impairment in psychopathology. This scoring system is an attempt to apply developmental principles of differentiation, articulation, and integration (Werner, 1948/1957; Werner & Kaplan, 1963) to the study of human responses given to the Rorschach.

Differentiation is defined as the nature of the response with human content; *articulation* is defined as the degree to which the response was elaborated; and *integration* is defined as the way the concept of the object is integrated in a context of action and interaction with other objects. Within each of these areas, categories are established along a continuum based on developmental levels. Within each category, ratings range from developmentally lower to developmentally higher levels.

CATEGORIES OF ANALYSIS AND SCORING PROCEDURES

I. Selection of Responses

A. Human and quasi-human responses

All human (*H*) and quasi-human ([*H*]) responses are scored. Human and quasi-human details are scored if they: (a) involve human activity (e g., talking, pointing, struggling), (b) involve a substantial portion of the card and not just small, rare, or edge details, and (c) contain some description of explicit human or humanoid characteristics. Thus, independent of their location, the following responses would be scored:

"the face ... of an old man with wisps of hair on the side"
"a man with sunglasses on"
"a girl's head"
"a baby's face"
"baby's hands with mittens on"
"face with a large hooked nose"
"faces of two angels"

B. Animal responses

In some rare instances, animal responses are classified as quasi-human if the animal is explicitly given qualities that only a human could have. The exceptional quality of this classification must be emphasized. It is not meant to include all responses scored as Animal Movement (*FM*). Though the following responses might be scored FM, they would not be included as a human or quasi-human response:

1. Humanlike actions that could be achieved as the result of special training and that might, therefore, be expected in the context of a circus act.
2. Activities that humans perform but that can also be performed by animals (e.g., rubbing noses). The human content must be explicit. If, for example, "Bugs Bunny" is given as a response, it is scored only if Bugs Bunny is engaged in a clearly human action. Thus, Bugs Bunny crying or talking would be scored as quasi-human ([*H*]) response.

Applying these criteria, the following animal responses would be scored as quasi-human:

"a hookah-smoking caterpillar ... from *Alice in Wonderland*"
"two drunken penguins leaning on a lamppost ... they're definitely sloshed"
"two lobsters coming out of a saloon ... and they kind of have their arms around one another"

"seagull ... laughing, making fun of somebody"
"two frogs ... tête-à-tête ... two angry frogs, their mouths are downcast"
"spiders (at an insect ball) eating spareribs"

II. Scoring Procedures

A. Accuracy of the response

Responses are classified as perceptually accurate or inaccurate (*F*+, *F*±, *F*–+, *F*–). *F*+ or *F*± responses are classified as accurate, and *F*– responses and *F*–+ responses are classified as inaccurate (Allison, Blatt, & Zimet, 1968); Rapaport, Gill, & Schafer, 1945).

B. Differentiation

Here responses are classified according to types of figures perceived–whether the figures or subjects of the action are quasi-human details, (*Hd*); human details, *Hd*; full quasi-human figures, (*H*); or full human figures, *H*.

1. Human responses: To be classified as a human response, the figure must be whole and clearly human. Examples are:
"people"
"men"
"baby"
"African slaves"
2. Quasi-human responses: Here the figures are whole but less than human or not definitely specified as human. Examples are:
"witches"
"dwarfs"
"two opposing forces, sticking out arms and hands. Opposing forces, pitted against each other ... looking at each other. With complicated ... of talons, appendages, arms raised in combat .... Person maybe ... standing there, being very offensive and attacking."
3. Human details: Here only parts of human figures are specified. Examples are:
"hands strangling"
"faces staring at each other"
4. Quasi-human details: Here only part of a quasi-human figures is specified. Examples are:
"angel's face"
"witch's head"
"devil face"

C. Articulation

Here responses are scored on the basis of types of attributes ascribed to the figures. A total of seven types of attributes are considered. These types of attributes were selected because they seem to provide information about human or quasi-human figures. The analyses are not concerned with the sheer detailing of features or with inappropriate articulation. The analyses are concerned only with articulations that enrich human or quasi-human responses, and that enlarge a listener's knowledge about qualities that are appropriate to the figures represented. For example, a response that states that a man has a head, hands, and feet does not enlarge the listeners' knowledge about the man. Possession of these features is presupposed by the initial response, "man." An articulation such as "a man with wings" is not scored as an articulation because it is an elaboration that does not add to the specifications of the human or quasi-human features of the figure.[4]

There are two general types of articulation: the articulation of perceptual and functional attributes.

1. Perceptual characteristics

a. Size or physical structure: For this aspect to be scored as articulated, descriptions of the figure must have adjective status. Thus, no credit is given in a response where an examinee only says that a man has feet or that a hand has fingers. Size or structure is scored as articulated only if there is a qualitative description of aspects of body parts of the whole body. Descriptions of bodies or body parts as "funny" or "strange" are not scored as indicating articulation of body structure.

Certain aspects of facial expression can be scored as articulations of size or structure. Included in this category are responses like "eyes closed" or "mouth open," in which the description of facial expression amounts to something more than just a description of physical appearance.

Applying these criteria, the following responses would be scored as articulations of size or physical structure:

"slim men"
"big feet"
"the top of the body is sort of heavy and her legs are real, real teeny"
"slanted eyes"
"chins protruding down from the face"
"eyes closed"
"mouths open"
"tongue was sticking out"

---

[4]Inappropriate articulations were not scored in the initial research with this manual (Blatt et al., 1976). In subsequent research it may prove useful to score both appropriate and inappropriate elaborations.

By contrast, the following responses are not scored as articulations of size or structure:
"women with breasts"
"they're shaped like people"
"eyes, nose, mouth"
"woman doesn't have a head"
"a pervert with bunny ears"
"person with wings instead of arms"

b. Clothing or hairstyle: For this aspect to be scored as articulated, there has to be a qualitative description of some aspect of either clothing or hairstyle. It must enrich the description of the figure. Simple mention of items of clothing implied by the response does not enrich one's understanding of the figures and is, therefore, not scored as an articulation. Using these criteria, the following responses are scorable as articulations of clothing or hairstyle:
"some kind of moustache ... right above its mouth"
"girls with ponytails"
"hair and the things sticking out of them, feathers"
"their pants would have to be skin tight and when they lean down, their jackets go pointing out, makes it look like a very tight jacket"
"a couple of witches with red hats"
"wearing a black coat and a homburg hat. Black coat is sort of billowing behind him ...."
"a full-tailed coat"
"two little girls all dressed up in their mother's things"
"Gay 90s type women ... both wearing a long bustle and feathers in hair"
"an American Indian in some ceremonial costume with wings and paraphernalia"
"a man ... with sunglasses on"

By contrast, the following responses would not be scored as articulations of clothing or hairstyle:
"two women with skirts on"
"shoes on"

c. Posture: Posture is scored if the response contains: (a) a description of body posture that is separate from the verb describing the activity of the figures or (b) a description of facial expression that goes beyond mere articulation of the physical appearance of features in that it contains a sense of movement or feeling. Posture is not scored if body posture is implied in the verb rather than being separately articulated or if it is simply a description of a figure's position in space (e.g., facing outward).

Thus, the following responses are scored as articulations of posture:

"arms flung wide"
"head tilted"
"standing with legs spread apart"
"leaning on a lamppost"
"shoulders hunched"
"somebody hanging ... dangling down, dropped, formless, shapeless"
"eyes look piercing"
"gritting teeth"
"smiling"

The following responses are not considered articulations of posture:

"sitting"
"standing"
"doing a high dive"
"back to back"
"facing outward"
"mouth closed"

2. Functional characteristics

a. Sex: For sex to be scored, there has to be either a specific mention of sex of the figure or an assignment to an occupational category that clearly implies a particular sexual identity. If the final sexual identity is not decided but alternatives are precisely considered, sex is scored as articulated. If, however, the indecision is based on a vague characterization of the figures with an emphasis on the sexual nature of the figure as a whole, sex is not considered articulated. In the following responses, sex is scored as articulated:

"man"
"girl"
"witch"
"mother"
"priest"
"either an old man or an ugly woman"
"two boys putting on a disguise kit or a girl with her makeup kit"

By contrast, sex is not scored as articulated in these responses:

"Well, these look like two human figures. I think when you look at the breasts there, they're girls. Then down here could look like phalluses. I don't know. It's rather ambiguous, confusing ... protrusions from the thorax, you know."

"Looks like two people. Could be a woman or a man. I debated this for a minutes. [sic, meaning?] Well, this form could be women or the costuming of man. [?] Well, I guess it would be tights and sort of loose shirt. I don't know exactly."

"Two people beating drums in a way like both might be women. In another way, like men. Doesn't seem to be any real indication whether they are male or female. The rather extended chests seem to represent breasts of women and protuberance on bottom seems to be leg. There is something barbaric about the figures. Seems to be something of a representation of gods or something like that. They seem to be wearing high-heel shoes. Both of figures seem to be very awkward and look as though they're doing some clumsy movements in beating the drums. The heads also don't look human—look as though they're some kind of bird's heads."

b. Age: For this aspect to be scored, specific reference must be made to some age category to which the figure belongs. Thus, age is assumed to be delineated in the following responses:
"child"
"baby"
"old woman"
"young girl"
"little boys"
"teenagers"

By contrast, although some indication of age is implied in the following responses, the references are not specific. Thus, age is not scored in these responses:
"man"
"girls"
"boys"
"priests"

c. Role: When figures are human, a clear reference to the work a figure does (occupation) is scored as an articulation of role. With regard to quasi-human figures, role is scored if the manner in which the figure is represented implies that it would engage in certain activities rather than others. Thus, role is assumed to be articulated in the following responses:[5]

[5]When sexual identity is clearly indicated in a role designation, both sex and role are scored as articulated. Such a situation exists in the following responses: "mother," "witch," and "priest."

"soldier"
"priest"
"Spanish dancer"
"ballet dancer"
"princess"
"mother"
"witch"
"devil"
"elves"

Role is not scored in the following responses because there is no clear indication that they refer to occupation rather than a momentary activity:
"dancer"
"singers"

d. Specific identity: Here a figure must be named as a specific character in history, literature, and so on.[6] Examples are:
"Charles DeGaulle"
"Theodore Roosevelt"

3. Degree of articulation: This is the simple enumeration of the total number of types of features articulated. In the preceding section, seven types of attribution were described (size, clothing or hairstyle, posture, sex, age, role, and specific identity). Thus, for any single Rorschach response, a total of seven types of features could be articulated. The average number of features taken into account in each human or quasi-human response constitutes the score for the degree of articulation of individual figures. If, for example, a subject gave four human responses and attributed a total of ten types of attributes to them, his score for degree of articulation would be 2.5.

D. Integration

Integration of the response was scored in three ways: (a) the degree of internality of the motivation of the action (unmotivated, reactive, and intentional); (b) the degree of integration of the object and its action (fused, incongruent, nonspecific, and congruent); and (c) the integration of the interaction with another object (malevolent-benevolent, active-passive, active-reactive, and active-active). These analyses can be applied only to figures engaged in human activity.

---

[6]To the degree that age, sex, and occupation are clearly indicated in the specific identity, these features are also scored as articulated. Thus, in the response "Charles DeGaulle," sex and occupation are specified. Such is not the case in the response "piglet."

1. Motivation of action: The articulation of action in terms of motive implies a developmentally advanced perception of action as differentiated from but related to the subject. Moreover, motive can be ascribed in two ways: as reactive or as intentional. Reactive explanations involve a focus on past events, and behavior is explained in terms of causal factors; one assumes that, for a certain prior reason, an individual had to do a certain thing. By contrast, intentionality is proactive and implies an orientation toward the present or future. The individual chooses to do something to attain a certain end or goal. The ability to choose between motives and to purposively undertake an activity implies a greater differentiation between subject and action than is the case when an individual is impelled to take an action because of past occurrences. For this reason, the analysis of action considers whether a motive was provided and whether the motivation was reactive (causal) or intentional.

a. Unmotivated activity: Here action is described with no explanation of why it occurs. Examples are:
"two people kissing each other"
"women looking at each other"
"men leaning against a hillside"

b. Reactive motivation: Here perceived activity is described as having been caused by a prior situation (internal or external), and the subject is seen as having little choice in his reaction. Examples are:
"A German soldier on guard duty. I think he sees something and points his gun at it."
"Arabs recoiling from an Israeli bomb"
"a person afraid of a snake, standing on a rocky cliff with arms upraised as if he's going to hit with something"
"two women struggling over ownership of a garment"

c. Intentional motivation: For motivation to be scored as intentional, the action must be directed toward some future moment and subjects must be seen as, in some sense, choosing their action rather than having to react. Examples are:
"Halloween witches, making incantations over the fire, in preparation for All Hallows Eve"
"an orchestra conductor, his arms raised, about ready to begin"

2. Object-action integration: In this analysis, four levels of integration of the object with its action are distinguished (fused, incongruent, nonspecific, and congruent).

a. Fusion of object and action: For a response to be included within this category, the object must be amorphous and only the activity articulated. In such situations, object and action are fused. The object possesses no separate qualities of its own. It is defined only in terms of its activity. This type of response is exemplified here. In both instances, nothing is known about the object except what it is doing:

"Two opposing forces, sticking out arms and hands. Opposing forces, pitted against each other ... looking at each other. With complicated ... of talons, appendages, arms raised in combat ... Person maybe ... standing there, being very offensive and attacking."

"figures there with hands, standing with legs spread apart, reaching out with hands as if trying to grab something"

b. Incongruent integration of object and action: For a response to be included within this category, there should be some separate articulation of object and action. Something must be known about the object apart from its activity. Nevertheless, the activity is incongruous, unrelated to the defined nature of the object. The articulation of action detracts from, rather than enriches, the articulation of the object. Examples are:

"a great big moth, dancing ballet"

"two figures, one half-human and one half-animal holding two sponges"

"a little baby throwing a bucket of water"

"a satyr-thing bowling"

"two sphinxes pulling a decapitated woman apart"

"two beetles playing a flute"

c. Nonspecific integration of object and action: Inclusion within this category also requires some separate articulation of object and action. However, the relationship between the two elements is nonspecific. The figures, as defined, can engage in the activity described, but there is no special fit between object and action. Many other kinds of objects could engage in the activity described. Thus, although the articulation of action does not detract from the articulation of the object, neither does it enrich it. Examples are:

"one big person standing with arms raised"

"a knight, standing ready to do his job"

"cavemen leaning against a hillside"

"two figures dancing"

"two older women trying to pull something away from each other"

"two men fighting"
"a man running away"
"a person, sort of a girl, standing on her toes"

d. Congruent integration of object and action: For a response to be assigned to this category, the nature of the object and the nature of the action must be articulated separately. In addition, the action must be particularly suited to the defined nature of the object. By way of contrast with the preceding category, the action not only must be something the object might do, it must be something that the object would be especially likely to do. There is an integrated and particularly well-suited relationship between the object and the specified action. Moreover, the articulation of the action enriches the image of the object.[7]

3. Integration of interaction with another object
   a. Content of interaction[8]
      i. Malevolent: The interaction is aggressive or destructive or the results of the activity imply destruction or harm or fear of harm.
      ii. Benevolent: The activity is not destructive, harmful, or aggressive. It may be neutral, or it may reflect a warm, positive relationship between the objects.

   b. Nature of interaction: This analysis applies to all responses involving at least two human or quasi-human figures. In addition, this analysis can pertain to situations where a second figure is not directly perceived, but its presence is necessarily implied by the nature of the action.
      i. Active-passive interaction: Two figures can involve a representation of one figure acting on another figure in an active-passive interaction. One figure is active and the other entirely passive, so, although acted on, it does not respond in any way.
      ii. Active-reactive interaction: In this type of interaction, the figures may be unequal. One figure is definitely the agent of the

[7]In situations where the role definition of the object amounts to nothing more than a literal restatement of the action, object and action are not considered integrated. Responses like "dancer 's dancing," or "singer's singing" are scored as nonspecific (Level 3) relationships. However, responses such as "ballerina dancing" or "character from a Rudolph Falls opera, singing" are classified as congruent (Level 4) relationships.

[8]Examples for scoring both the nature and the content of interaction are presented in Table 4.A1. Notations in the left-hand margin indicated scoring for the nature of the interaction (active-passive: *A-P*, active-reactive: *A-R*, active-active: *A-A*). Notations in the right-hand margin indicated the scoring for the content of the interaction (malevolent: *M*, and benevolent: *B*).

activity, acting on another figure. The second figure is reactive or responsive only to the action of the other.

iii. Active-active interaction: In this type of interaction, both figures contribute equally to the activity, and the interaction is mutual.

COMPOSITE SCORES FOR THE CONCEPT OF THE OBJECT ON THE RORSCHACH

The concept of the human object is assessed for all responses that have any humanoid feature. These responses are evaluated for the degree of differentiation (whether the figure is fully human, quasi-human, or a part feature of a human or quasi-human figure); articulation (the degree to which the figure is elaborated in terms of manifest physical or functional attributes); motivation of action (the degree to which the action of the figure is internally determined—unmotivated, reactive, or intentional action); integration of the action (the degree to which the action is a unique attribute of the figure, e.g., fused, incongruent, nonspecific, or congruent); the content of the action (the degree to which the action is malevolent or benevolent and constructive); and the nature of any interaction with another figure (the degree to which the interaction is active- passive, active-reactive, or active-active, in which mutual, reciprocal relationships are established). In each of these six categories (differentiation, articulation, motivation of action, integration of the object and its action, content of the action, and nature of the interaction), responses are scored on a developmental continuum. This developmental analysis should be made separately for those humanoid responses that are accurately perceived (*F*+) and for those that are inaccurately perceived (*F*–).

Differential weighting for scores within each of the six categories for assessing the concept of the object reflects a developmental progression, with higher scores indicating higher developmental levels. Score values are as follows:

Differentiation: (*Hd*) = 1, *Hd* = 2, (*H*) = 3, *H* = 4.

Articulation: Score 1 for each perceptual feature and 2 for each functional feature

Motivation: unmotivated = 1, reactive = 2, intentional = 3.

Integration of object and action: fused = 1, incongruent = 2, nonspecific = 3, congruent = 4.

Content of action: malevolent = 1, benevolent = 2.

Nature of interaction: active-passive = 1, active-reactive = 2, active-active = 3.

Reliability estimates for the scoring of these six categories in *F*+ and *F*– responses in both clinical and normal samples are quite high, ranging from .86 to .97.

To reduce the number of variables in the measurement of the concept of the object on the Rorschach, a factor analysis was conducted on the 12 object representation (*OR*) scores. A weighted sum for each of the six categories was obtained for *F*+ and *F*– responses separately. Each of these 12 weighted sums was corrected by covariance for total response productivity. The residualized scores for each of these 12 variables (six categories each for *F*+ and *F*– responses) were subjected to a common factors factor analysis with communalities less or equal to 1.00. Using the criteria of eigenvalues greater than 1.00, two factors were retained and rotated for an orthogonal varimax solution. These two factors accounted for 53.52% of the total variance. The factor analysis yielded two primary factors: the developmental level of accurately perceived responses (*OR*+; percent total variance = 27.19) and the developmental level of inaccurately perceived responses (*OR*–; percent total variance = 26.33). All six *OR*+ scoring categories had factor loadings on Factor I that exceeded .70, and all six *OR*– scoring categories had factor loadings on Factor I that were less than .20. All six *OR*– scoring categories had factor loadings on Factor II that exceeded .53, and the loadings of the *OR*+ categories did not exceed .20 on this factor.

All six residualized scores (that is, weighted sums covaried for total number of responses on the Rorschach) for *OR*+ scoring categories should be standardized and then summed to give a total residualized weighted sum score for accurately perceived responses. The same should be done for all six *OR*– scores. The residualized weighted sum of accurately perceived human responses (*OR*+) is viewed as indicating the capacity for investment in satisfying interpersonal relationships. The residualized weighted sum of inaccurately perceived human responses (*OR*–) is viewed as an indication of the tendency to become invested in autistic fantasies rather than realistic relationships.

In addition to the residualized weighted sum of *OR*+ and *OR*– scores, a mean developmental level should be obtained for each of the six categories for *F*+ and *F*– responses separately. The six mean developmental-level scores for *F*+ responses should be standardized and then combined into a total mean developmental-level score for *F*+ response. The same should be done for *F*– responses. The mean developmental level for accurately perceived responses (*F*+) is viewed as another measure of the capacity to become engaged in meaningful and realistic interpersonal relations. The mean developmental level of inaccurately perceived responses (*F*–) is viewed as another measure of the tendency to become involved in unrealistic, inappropriate, and possibly autistic types of relationships.

TABLE 4.A1
Integration of Interaction

Nature	*Example*	*Content*
A-P	A couple of undertakers lowering babies into the pit	M
A-P	A prostitute rolling drunk	M
A-P	Crucified man	M
A-P	A mother holding out her arm and telling her kid never to come back	M
A-P	Two sphinxes pulling a decapitated woman apart	M
A-P	Two people kneeling down with hands extended toward and touching other people	B
A-R	African natives beating a drum; martians applaud	B
A-R	Eve being tempted by a snake (snake seen on card)	M
A-R	Two people with hands up as if trying to ward off the two people coming to get them. Two guys with black capes ... coming in to get the other people	M
A-R	German soldier thinks he sees something and points gun at it	M
A-R	An orchestra conductor, arms raised, just about to begin	B
A-R	A woman crying out for something	M
A-R	A man trying to kill a little girl, who's running away	M
A-A	A woman with a child looking up at her	B
A-A	Someone having intercourse, a man child and a woman child, trying to make love but not knowing how	B
A-A	One person there is pointing and the other is listening	B
A-A	Two people and two martians fighting	M
A-A	Two gremlins ready to hit each other	M
A-A	People placing hands together—like victors, walking along like that	B

5

The Rorschach Oral Dependency Scale

Robert F. Bornstein
Gettysburg College

Joseph M. Masling
SUNY-Buffalo

Masling, Rabie, and Blondheim's (1967) Rorschach Oral Dependency (ROD) scale has been the most widely used projective measure of dependency during the past 35 years, appearing in about 80% of all published studies involving the projective assessment of dependent personality traits (Bornstein, 1996b, 1999). The ROD scale has been used in studies of psychiatric patients, medical patients, college students, and community members, successfully predicting dependency-related behavior in laboratory, classroom, and clinical settings (Bornstein, 1996b, 1999; Masling, 1986, 2002a). Few projective instruments—much less one constructed using psychoanalytic principles—have had such a sustained influence on contemporary clinical psychology.

This chapter reviews evidence regarding the construct validity of the ROD scale, and evaluates its utility as a research and clinical instrument. We begin by discussing the development and preliminary validation of the ROD scale, and go on to describe administration, scoring, and interpretation procedures. Next, we review research bearing on the reliability and validity of the scale, with particular attention to its psychometric properties. Finally, we discuss theoretical implications, clinical applications, and future directions in ROD research.

DEVELOPMENT AND PRELIMINARY VALIDATION OF THE ROD SCALE

In Freud's (1905/1953) classical psychoanalytic model, dependency is inextricably linked to events of the infantile, oral stage of development.

Frustration or overgratification during the oral stage is hypothesized to result in oral "fixation," and continued preoccupation with oral (i.e., food- and mouth-related) and dependent behaviors during adolescence and adulthood. Thus, classical psychoanalytic theory postulates that the orally fixated (or oral-dependent) person will: (a) be predisposed to rely on others for nurturance, guidance, protection, and support; and (b) continue to exhibit traits in adulthood that reflect the oral stage (e.g., preoccupation with activities of the mouth, reliance on food and eating as a means of coping with anxiety). Detailed discussions of the psychoanalytic model of oral dependence are provided by Bornstein (1996a, 2003), Masling (1986), and Masling and Schwartz (1979).

Although the concept of oral dependence is central to classical psychoanalytic theory, and plays an important role in other psychodynamic frameworks (e.g., object relations theory, self psychology), until the 1950s no valid and reliable measures were available for assessing dependency in psychiatric patients and nonclinical participants. This situation changed with the development of Navran's (1954) Minnesota Multiphasic Personality Inventory (MMPI) dependency (Dy) scale, the first widely used self-report measure of dependency (Bornstein, 2005). In the same year in which Navran published his initial MMPI Dy findings, Schafer (1954) outlined several psychoanalytic themes that could be inferred from Rorschach inkblots, laying the groundwork for projective assessment of dependency. Consistent with psychoanalytic thinking at that time, Schafer conceptualized two core psychodynamic themes—orality and dependency—as facets of the same underlying personality style.

The ROD scale, borrowed almost entirely from Schafer's (1954) speculations, was constructed by Masling et al. (1967), whose initial validation study focused on the link between oral dependency and obesity. Rorschach Inkblot Method (RIM) and Thematic Apperception Test (TAT) protocols were obtained from 18 obese outpatients and 16 matched normal-weight controls. Analyses revealed that: (a) RIM and TAT oral-dependency scores were positively intercorrelated (r = .58); and (b) obese patients obtained significantly higher scores than normal-weight controls on both scales. Thus, preliminary ROD validity data supported the convergent validity of the scale with respect to other projective dependency scores, as well as theoretically related "oral" behavior (i.e., pathological overeating).

ADMINISTRATION, SCORING, AND INTERPRETATION

A key strength of the ROD scale is the simplicity of its administration, scoring, and interpretation procedures, which have remained unchanged for more than 35 years. Because these procedures are highly standardized, clinicians and researchers can obtain useable ROD data with minimal training.

Administration and Scoring

ROD scores may be derived from existing (i.e., archival) RIM protocols, from individually administered RIM protocols collected in the standard manner, or from data collected using a group Rorschach administration (Masling, 1986, 2002b). In the group administration procedure, participants are shown slides of standard RIM inkblots projected onto a screen for 3 minutes each. They are asked to provide three written responses each to Cards I, II, III, VIII, and X, and two responses to each of the other five cards (25 responses total). There is no inquiry; only participants' initial free associations are scored.

Like group-derived ROD scores, ROD scores derived from archival or individually administered RIM protocols are based on the free association only. Regardless of which administration procedure is used, ROD scoring is based on a lexical strategy: Participants receive 1 point for each response that contains one or more percepts from the categories in Table 5.1. In individually collected RIM protocols, the number of responses containing at least one oral-dependent percept is divided by the total number of responses (i.e., *R*) to control for variations in response productivity. Although ROD scores collected using the group administration are typically reported as raw scores rather than percentages (because the number of responses is fixed at 25), researchers convert these raw scores to percentages when comparing individual and group ROD scores.

To date, most ROD investigations involving college students have used the group Rorschach administration, whereas most investigations involving clinical participants have used individually administered RIM protocols (Bornstein, 1996b). To ascertain that ROD data collected using these two methods yield comparable results, Bornstein, Bonner, Kildow, and McCall (1997) compared the means and distributions of ROD scores collected individually and in groups. In their first study, Bornstein et al. employed a between-participants design, with half the participants providing individual RIM protocols, and half providing protocols collected in a group setting. In their second study, Bornstein et al. used a within-participants design, with each participant providing ROD scores under both administration conditions (data were collected during two testing sessions separated by 14–28 weeks). In both studies, individual and group ROD administrations yielded comparable means and standard deviations. Moreover, skewness, kurtosis, and heteroscedasticity values indicated that the individual and group ROD score distributions did not differ from each other in either study.

TABLE 5.1
Categories of Scoreable Responses on the ROD Scale

Category	*Sample Responses*
Foods and drinks	Milk, whiskey, boiled lobster
Food sources	Restaurant, saloon, breast
Food objects	Kettle, silverware, drinking glass
Food providers	Waiter, cook, bartender
Passive food receivers	Bird in nest, fat or thin man
Begging and praying	Dog begging, person saying prayers
Food organs	Mouth, stomach, lips, teeth
Oral instruments	Lipstick, cigarette, tuba
Nurturers	Jesus, mother, father, doctor, God
Gifts and gift givers	Christmas tree, cornucopia
Good-luck objects	Wishbone, four-leaf clover
Oral activity	Eating, talking, singing, kissing
Passivity and helplessness	Confused person, lost person
Pregnancy and reproductive organs	Placenta, womb, ovaries, embryo
"Baby-talk" responses	Patty-cake, bunny rabbit, pussy cat
Negations of oral-dependent percepts	No mouth, woman with no breasts

Note. In Category 1, animals are scored only if they are invariably associated with eating (e.g., do not score *duck* or *turkey* unless food-descriptive phrases are used, such as *roast duck* or *turkey leg*). In Category 3, *pot* and *cauldron* are scored only if the act of cooking is implied. In Category 13, *baby* is scored only if there is some suggestion of passivity or frailness. In Category 14, *pelvis, penis, vagina,* and *sex organs* are not scored.

Interpretation

Following Masling et al.'s original (1967) strategy, researchers today use ROD scores for both categorical and dimensional analyses. Thus, in some studies ROD scores have been used to classify participants into discrete dependent and nondependent groups (e.g., Bornstein, Masling, & Poynton, 1987; Juni & LoCascio, 1985). In others, correlations between ROD scores and scores on theoretically related measures have been examined (e.g., Duberstein & Talbot, 1993; Masling, O'Neill, & Jayne, 1981).

Tables 5.2 and 5.3 summarize the mean ROD scores obtained in studies of college students (*N* of independent samples = 21) and psychiatric patients (*N* of independent samples = 11) during the past several de-

TABLE 5.2
Mean ROD Scores in Studies of College Students

Study	Participants	Mean ROD Score		
		Women	*Men*	*Combined*
Bornstein, Bonner, Kildow, and McCall (1997) (Study 1)	60 women, 60 men	—	—	.12
Bornstein et al. (1997) (Study 2)	40 women, 40 men	—	—	.12
Bornstein, Bowers, and Bonner (1996a)	36 women, 36 men	.13	.13	.13
Bornstein, Bowers, and Bonner (1996b)	47 women, 40 men	.12	.12	.12
Bornstein, Bowers, and Robinson (1995)	58 women, 25 men	.14	.16	.15
Bornstein, Galley, and Leone (1986)	193 men	—	.12	.12
Bornstein, Greenberg, Leone, and Galley (1990)	80 women, 74 men	.12	.11	.12
Bornstein, Leone, and Galley (1988)	77 women, 84 men	.14	.14	.14
Bornstein, Manning, Krukonis, Rossner, and Mastrosimone (1993)	60 women, 42 men	.15	.15	.15
Bornstein and Masling (1985)	304 men	—	.14	.14
Bornstein, Masling, and Poynton (1987)	60 men	—	.14	.14
Bornstein, O'Neill, Galley, Leone, and Castrianno (1988) (Study 1)	23 women, 25 men	.12	.12	.12
Bornstein, Poynton and Masling (1985)	417 men	—	.14	.14
Bornstein, Rossner, and Hill (1994)	54 women, 34 men	.13	.13	.13
Duberstein and Talbot (1993)	100 women, 98 men	.13	.13	.13
Juni (1981a)	39 women, 22 men	—	—	.13
Juni (1981b)	48 women, 46 men	.12	.12	.12
Juni, Nelson, and Brannon (1987)	61 women, 47 men	—	—	.12

(continued)

TABLE 5.2 (*continued*)

		Mean ROD Score		
Study	*Participants*	*Women*	*Men*	*Combined*
Masling, Bornstein, Poynton, Reed, and Katkin (1991)	84 men	—	.14	.14
Masling, O'Neill, and Jayne (1981)	65 men	—	.12	.12
Sprohge, Handler, Plant, and Wicker (2002)	25 women, 25 men	—	—	.16

Note. Only those studies reporting mean ROD scores (i.e., the mean proportion of oral-dependent Rorschach percepts) for college student participants are included in this table. Dashes indicate that: (a) participants of one gender took part in the study; or (b) only overall ROD means were reported, with data from women and men collapsed into a single score. Weighted averages were used to compute combined ROD means in column 3, so the gender that was more prevalent in a particular study had a larger influence on the combined ROD mean for that study.

cades. Scrutiny of these tables reveals a remarkable degree of consistency across different populations and settings. The mean proportion of oral-dependent imagery in studies of college students was .13, with women and men producing identical ROD means in these investigations. The mean proportion of oral-dependent responses produced by psychiatric patients was .11, with men (M = .12) producing slightly higher ROD scores than women (M = .10).[1]

No firm cutoffs for identifying dependent and nondependent participants have been delineated for use in clinical and research settings. Scores on the group ROD typically range from 0 to 8 (0–32%), and are somewhat positively skewed (Bornstein et al., 1997). When ROD scores are collected using the group administration, it is common to define nondependent participants as those scoring 2 or below, and dependent participants as those scoring 4 or above, which yields approximately equal numbers of dependent and nondependent participants (Masling, 1986). ROD scores in individually administered RIM protocols typically range from 0 to about 35%. Researchers have used various strategies to identify dependent and nondependent participants from individually administered RIM protocols (see, e.g., Masling, Weiss, & Rothschild, 1968; Sprohge, Handler, Plant, & Wicker, 2002). Some re-

[1]The number of studies in Tables 5.2 and 5.3 is smaller than the total number of published ROD studies because many researchers did not provide enough information to calculate mean ROD scores.

TABLE 5.3
Mean ROD Scores in Studies of Psychiatric Patients

		Mean ROD Score		
Study	*Participants*	*Women*	*Men*	*Combined*
Bertrand and Masling (1969)	40 male inpatients	—	.05	.05
Bornstein and Greenberg (1991)	51 female inpatients	.12	—	.12
Bornstein, Hilsenroth, Padawer, and Fowler (2000) (Inpatients)	40 female inpatients 20 male inpatients	—	—	.22
Bornstein et al. (2000) (Outpatients)	32 female outpatients 24 male outpatients	—	—	.14
Bornstein, O'Neill, Galley, Leone, and Castrianno (1988) (Study 2)	16 female inpatients 16 male inpatients	.09	.14	.11
Greenberg and Bornstein (1989)	46 female inpatients 29 male inpatients	.09	.12	.10
Masling, Rabie, and Blondheim (1967)	34 female outpatients 4 male outpatients	—	—	.06
Masling, Schiffner, and Shenfeld (1980)	14 female outpatients 7 male outpatients	—	—	.17
O'Neill and Bornstein (1990)	62 female inpatients 39 male inpatients	.10	.12	.11
O'Neill and Bornstein (1991)	20 female inpatients 20 male inpatients	.09	.16	.13
Sprohge, Handler, Plant, and Wicker (2002)	100 outpatients	—	—	.11
Weiss and Masling (1970)	42 female outpatients 106 male outpatients	—	—	.11

Note. Only those studies reporting mean ROD scores (i.e., the mean proportion of oral-dependent Rorschach percepts) for psychiatric inpatients or outpatients are included in this table. Dashes indicate that: (a) participants of one gender took part in the study; or (b) only overall ROD means were reported, with data from women and men collapsed into a single score. Weighted averages were used to compute combined ROD means in column 3, so the gender that was more prevalent in a particular study had a larger influence on the combined ROD mean for that study.

searchers use a simple mean or median split to select dependent and nondependent groups; others include only the extreme high and low scorers (e.g., the highest and lowest 20%).

In using ROD scores to identify dependent and nondependent participants, it is important to utilize separate gender-based mean or median scores. Although the sample sizes used in most studies are not sufficient to produce statistically significant gender differences in ROD scores, men do tend to obtain slightly higher ROD scores than women (see Table 5.3). Though these gender differences are small in magnitude, the mean difference across studies in Table 5.3 (.10 for women and .12 for men) actually represents a 20% shift in ROD scores across gender. Thus, when Bornstein (1995) used meta-analytic techniques to synthesize the available findings regarding gender differences in ROD scores (N of studies = 17), he found a modest but statistically significant effect size, with men obtaining higher ROD scores than women ($d = .17$, Combined $z = 2.08$, $p < .02$).

CONSTRUCT VALIDITY OF THE ROD SCALE

In the following sections we review evidence regarding the reliability and validity of ROD scores in clinical and nonclinical participants. Wherever possible, we have converted each investigation's validity or reliability outcome statistic (i.e., F, t, X^2, etc.) to a Pearson correlation coefficient (r), in order to facilitate comparison across studies.

Interrater Reliability

Interrater reliability in ROD scoring is uniformly excellent. When two raters, unaware of each other's judgments, independently scored a set of ROD protocols, they typically agreed on the scoring of 85 to 95% of percepts (Bornstein, Manning, Krukonis, Rossner, & Mastrosimone, 1993; Weiss & Masling, 1970). Pearson correlation coefficients between the two sets of ratings usually exceeded .90, regardless of whether data were collected from clinical or nonclinical participants (Gordon & Tegtemeyer, 1983; Juni, Masling, & Brannon, 1979). When researchers calculated ROD reliability using Spitzer, Cohen, Fliess, and Endicott's (1967) Kappa coefficient (which corrects for inflated reliability estimates that result from low-score base rates), reliabilities greater than .80 were usually obtained (Duberstein & Talbot, 1993; O'Neill & Bornstein, 1990). Kappa coefficients in this range are acceptable for any psychological test, and are particularly high for a projective rating scale (Nunnally & Bernstein, 1994).

Retest Reliability

Only one study has assessed the retest reliability of ROD scores. Bornstein, Rossner, and Hill (1994) collected ROD protocols from a mixed-sex sample of college students under identical conditions on two separate occasions, with one third of the participants retested after 16 weeks, one third retested after 28 weeks, and the rest retested after 60 weeks. Comparable retest reliability coefficients were obtained for women and men in this study, with retest reliability (r) being .67 at 16 weeks, .48 at 28 weeks, and .46 at 60 weeks.

Internal Reliability

Two approaches have been used to assess the internal reliability of ROD scores. Bornstein, Hill, Robinson, Calabrese, and Bowers (1996) calculated coefficient alpha (Cronbach, 1951) by collecting ROD scores from a large, mixed-sex sample of college students, then treating each Rorschach card as a single test item that could contribute to the total ROD score (Parker, 1983). Bornstein, Hill et al. (1996) obtained ROD coefficient alphas of .61 for women and .62 for men.

Other investigations assessed the relationship between the amount of oral (i.e., food- and mouth-related) and dependent imagery in participants' ROD protocols. These studies produced mixed results. One investigation (Bornstein et al., 1993) found significant, positive correlations between ROD dependency and orality scores in men ($r = .44$) and women ($r = .35$). However, two similar studies (Bornstein & Greenberg, 1991; Shilkret & Masling, 1981) found nonsignificant correlations between orality and dependency scores ($r = .01$ in the Bornstein & Greenberg study, and $r = -.06$ in the Shilkret & Masling study). When the correlation coefficients from these three investigations were combined using meta-analytic techniques, the overall correlation between ROD orality and dependency scores was modest ($r = .10$).

Convergent Validity

Evidence regarding the convergent validity of the ROD scale can be divided into three domains: orality, dependency, and other theoretically related variables.

Orality. Masling et al. (1967) and Weiss and Masling (1970) found that obese participants obtained significantly higher ROD scores than normal-weight participants matched on salient demographic and diagnostic criteria (rs were .51 and .33, respectively, in these investigations). These results are particularly compelling because: (a) ROD scores were calculated omitting food-related responses, to avoid obesity-food preoccupation confounds; and (b) similar patterns were obtained in separate samples of American psychiatric patients (Weiss & Masling) and Israeli metabolic patients (Masling et al.). In contrast to these earlier results, however, Bornstein and Greenberg (1991) found no relationship between obesity and ROD scores in an American sample of female psychiatric inpatients ($r = -.01$).

Although Bornstein and Greenberg (1991) found no relationship between ROD scores and obesity, they did find that anorexic and bulimic inpatients obtained significantly higher ROD scores than normal-weight inpatients matched on age, marital status, Wechsler Adult Intelligence Scale-Revised (WAIS-R) score, years of education, and number and type of Axis I and Axis II diagnoses ($r = .25$). Narduzzi and Jackson (2000, 2002) obtained similar results in samples of female college students ($r = .23$) and psychiatric outpatients ($r = .28$). Thus, ROD scores appear to be consistently linked with eating disorder symptomatology, and less consistently associated with obesity.

Along somewhat different lines, several investigations have assessed the relationship of ROD scores to alcoholism, obtaining highly consistent results. Bertrand and Masling (1969), Sprohge et al. (2002), Tognazzo (1970), and Weiss and Masling (1970) all reported that alcoholic psychiatric patients obtained significantly higher ROD scores than did nonalcoholic patients with similar demographic and diagnostic profiles (*r*s were .56, .18, .26, and .58, respectively, in these investigations). Because these researchers studied very different participant samples (Bertrand & Masling examined American Veterans Administration inpatients, Sprohge et al. assessed outpatients at a university counseling center, Tognazzo tested Italian psychiatric inpatients, and Weiss & Masling investigated outpatients at a mental health clinic), the ROD-alcoholism link appears robust and generalizable.[2]

Dependency. Numerous studies have assessed the relationship of ROD scores to dependency-related behavior. For example, Shilkret and Masling (1981) demonstrated that ROD scores predicted the frequency with which college students turned toward an experimenter (but did not ask for help directly) when solving difficult puzzles in the laboratory ($r = .85$). Masling et al. (1968) found that high scores on the ROD scale were associated with increased yielding in an Asch-type confor-

[2]As in the aforementioned orality-obesity studies, ROD scores in these investigations were calculated omitting percepts related to alcohol. In interpreting these results, however, it is important to note that ROD data were collected following alcoholism onset, and studies indicate that dependency levels increase as alcoholism worsens (Bornstein, 1993). Thus, ROD scores are associated with alcoholism, but do not predict it. It may be that the ROD score-alcoholism link is a product of the increase in dependent feelings and behaviors that occur as alcoholism progresses.

mity experiment (r = .32). Two investigations (Bornstein & Masling, 1985; Masling, O'Neill et al., 1981) showed that high ROD scores were associated with early completion of a required Introductory Psychology research participation requirement, presumably because students who score high on the ROD scale are concerned with pleasing their instructor by complying with course guidelines (rs were .12 and .29, respectively, in these studies).

In psychiatric inpatients, O'Neill and Bornstein (1990) found that ROD scores were positively correlated with an index of help-seeking response set (i.e., high F and low K scores) on the MMPI (r = .29).

Additional information regarding the ROD score-dependent behavior link came from Bornstein's (1999) meta-analysis, which compared the behaviorally referenced validity coefficients produced by an array of self-report and projective dependency tests. In this analysis, the ROD scale yielded an overall validity coefficient (r) of .37 (combined $Z = 8.49$, $p < .001$). This validity coefficient compared favorably with those produced by Navran's (1954) MMPI Dy scale (r = .20), Millon's (1987) Millon Clinical Multiaxial Inventory dependency subscale (r = .17), Hirschfeld et al.'s (1977) Interpersonal Dependency Inventory (r = .33), and Edwards' (1959) Personal Preference Scale succorance subscale (r = .35).[3]

Rather than assessing ROD-dependent behavior links, some researchers have examined relationships between ROD scores and scores on self-report measures of dependency. Table 5.4 summarizes the results of all published studies in this area. Although there was some variation in the magnitude of these intertest correlations, the overall ROD-self-report correlation (r) was .29. For those studies where intertest correlation data were calculated separately by gender, mean ROD-self-report correlations were .30 for women, and .24 for men (see Bornstein, 2002, for a detailed discussion of these results).

Other Theoretically Related Variables. Beyond these observed associations between ROD scores and behavioral and self-report indices of dependency, links between ROD scores and variables theoretically related to dependency have been reported repeatedly.[4] For example, several studies showed that high scorers on the ROD scale were sensitive to

---

[3]This behaviorally referenced ROD scale validity coefficient also compares favorably with those produced by other projective dependency tests such as the TAT dependency scale (Fisher, 1970; r = .34), the Blacky Test oral dependency scale (Blum, 1949; r = .50), and the Holtzman (1961) Inkblot Test dependency scale (r = .12). A complete list of self-report and projective dependency test validity coefficients was provided by Bornstein (1999).

[4]Although meta-analysts sometimes referred to such coefficients as indices of "unknown validity" (Parker, Hanson, & Hunsley, 1988), many of these variables are conceptually linked with dependency (see Bornstein, 1992, 1993). Thus, we view these validity data as representing links between ROD scores and variables that are indirectly related to dependency (i.e., a correlate of dependency-related thought, motivation, and emotional responding).

TABLE 5.4
Correlations of ROD Scores With Self-Report Dependency Scores

	Sample Size		*Test Score Intercorrelation*		
Study	*Women*	*Men*	*Women*	*Men*	*Overall*
Bornstein (1998a)	657	611	.26	.21	.24
Bornstein (1998b)	236	208	.30	.35	.32
Bornstein, Bowers, and Bonner (1996a)	72	72	.43	.35	.39
Bornstein, Bowers, and Bonner (1996b)	47	40	—	—	.54
Bornstein, Bowers, and Robinson (1995)	58	25	—	—	.42
Bornstein, Manning, Krukonis, Rossner, and Mastrosimone (1993)	60	42	.67	.48	.59
Bornstein and O'Neill (2000)	91	61	.04	.09	.06
Bornstein, Poynton, and Masling (1985)	0	417	—	.11	.11
Bornstein, Rossner, and Hill (1994)	54	34	—	—	.34
Bornstein, Rossner, Hill, and Stepanian (1994)	25	25	—	—	.46
Narduzzi and Jackson (2000)	114	0	.18	—	.18
Narduzzi and Jackson (2002)	286	0	.14	—	.14

Note. Test score intercorrelations are Pearson correlation coefficients (*r*s). All studies used the IDI and ROD scale, except for: (a) Bornstein (1998a), which used the PDQ-R to assess self-attributed dependency needs; (b) Bornstein and O'Neill (2000), which used the MMPI Dy scale to assess self-attributed dependency needs; and (c) Narduzzi and Jackson (2000, 2002), which used the PSI-II to assess self-attributed dependency needs.

subtle interpersonal cues (Juni & Semel, 1982; Masling, Johnson, & Saturansky, 1974; Masling, Schiffner, & Shenfeld, 1980). In these investigations, participants who scored high on the ROD scale were better able than low-scoring participants to infer the attitudes and personal beliefs of acquaintances, teachers, and therapists (the mean ROD—interpersonal sensitivity correlation in these studies was .32).

Masling, O'Neill, and Katkin (1982) further found that participants who scored high on the ROD scale showed increased autonomic arousal in response to perceived interpersonal rejection (r = .59); participants who scored low on the ROD scale showed significantly less autonomic arousal.

Similarly, Juni et al. (1979) found that college students who scored high on the ROD scale engaged in physical contact with a peer during a laboratory maze-solving task more readily than did students who obtained low scores on the scale ($r = .39$). Not surprisingly, Masling, Price, Goldband, and Katkin (1981) found that college students who obtained high ROD scores showed significantly higher levels of autonomic arousal than low-scoring students following a brief period of social isolation ($r = .12$). Juni (1981b) reported that high ROD scores predicted desire for test feedback in college students ($r = .36$), whereas Juni and LoCascio (1985) found that high ROD scores were associated with preference for forms of therapy with greater patient-therapist contact ($r = .25$).

Approaching this issue from a different perspective, Greenberg and Bornstein (1989) found that psychiatric inpatients who scored high on the ROD scale had greater difficulty terminating treatment than low scorers with similar diagnoses ($r = .46$). Consistent with these results, Duberstein and Talbot (1993) reported that high ROD scores were associated with self-reports of insecure attachment in college students ($r = .19$), whereas Levin and Masling (1995) obtained significant correlations between ROD scores and measures of state and trait anxiety (*r*s were .47 and .37, respectively, for state and trait scores). Juni and Fischer (1985) found that ROD scores were associated with self-reports of belief in a higher power in men ($r = .21$), but not in women ($r = .07$). Bornstein, Leone, and Galley (1988) reported that high scores on the ROD scale were associated with descriptions of the self as weak ($r = .21$) and unambitious ($r = .23$) in men.

Given these latter findings, it is not surprising that high ROD scores were also associated with the presence of internalizing disorders in children ($r = .30$; Gordon & Tegtemeyer, 1983), and with a defense style characterized by internally directed (rather than outwardly expressed) anger and aggression ($r = .34$; Bornstein, Greenberg, Leone, & Galley, 1990). High ROD scores were linked with depression ($r = .21$; O'Neill & Bornstein, 1991) and borderline personality disorder ($r = .19$; Bornstein, Hilsenroth, Padawer, & Fowler, 2000) in psychiatric inpatients. In college students, ROD scores were positively correlated with self-reports of depression ($r = .46$; Levin & Masling, 1995), and with reports of dependent personality disorder ($r = .33$) and histrionic personality disorder ($r = .27$) symptoms (Bornstein, 1998a).

Discriminant Validity

As is true for most psychological tests, researchers have devoted far more attention to convergent validity issues than to issues regarding the discriminant validity of the ROD scale (Bornstein, 1996b). However, several noteworthy findings have emerged in recent years. For example, Gordon and Tegtemeyer (1983), Kertzman (1980), and Bornstein and O'Neill (1997) found that ROD scores were unrelated to IQ scores in children and adults. Gordon and Tegtemeyer further found that ROD scores were unrelated to locus of control scores in children; Kertzman obtained no relationship between ROD scores and sociometric status in adults. Bornstein, Rossner, and Hill (1994) found that ROD scores were unaffected by number and severity of stressful life events experienced by participants during 16-, 28-, and 60-week intertest intervals. Finally, Bornstein, Bowers, and Bonner (1996b) reported that ROD scores were unrelated to masculinity and femininity scores on the Bem (1974) Sex Role Inventory.

EFFECTIVE USE OF THE ROD SCALE IN CLINICAL AND RESEARCH SETTINGS

Overall, findings regarding the construct validity of the ROD scale have been very positive. ROD scores show excellent interrater reliability, good internal reliability, and acceptable retest reliability up to 60 weeks. Convergent validity findings are supportive as well: ROD scores show moderate to strong correlations with scores on behavioral and self-report indices of orality and dependency, and with scores on measures of theoretically related traits (e.g., interpersonal sensitivity, insecure attachment). Finally, discriminant validity data confirm that ROD scores are not confounded by extraneous variables (e.g., intelligence, locus of control) that would raise questions regarding the specificity of the measure.

It is also worth noting that converging results have been obtained by researchers independent of those who developed and validated the ROD scale (e.g., Gordon & Tegtemeyer, 1983; Narduzzi & Jackson, 2000; Sproghe et al., 2002; Tognazzo, 1970). Given these encouraging findings, continued use of the ROD scale in clinical and research settings is clearly warranted. In the following sections, we discuss theoretical implications, clinical applications, and future directions in ROD research.

Theoretical Implications

Some researchers have argued that the modest correlations of ROD scores with questionnaire dependency scores represent a convergent validity problem for the ROD scale (Wood, Lilienfeld, Nezworski, & Garb, 2001). This view is incorrect. As McClelland, Koestner, and Weinberger (1989) pointed out, most self-report personality tests assess explicit (or self-attributed) needs—motives that people acknowledge as being characteristic of their day-to-day functioning and experience. In contrast, projective tests like the ROD scale assess implicit needs—motives that influence behavior automatically, and with little or no conscious awareness on respondents' part that their behavior is affected by these motives (see Weiner, 1999, 2003).

McClelland et al. (1989) went on to note that, because they assess different facets of a person's need states, projective and self-report tests should be only modestly intercorrelated, and would be expected to yield contrasting results in clinical and research settings. In this context, McClelland et al. (pp. 698–699) suggested that projective measures like the ROD scale:

> provide a more direct readout of motivational and emotional experiences than do self-reports that are filtered through analytic thought and various concepts of self and others, [because] implicit motives are more often built on early, prelinguistic affective experiences, whereas self-attributed motives are more often built on explicit teaching by parents and others as to what values or goals it is important for a child to pursue.

An important corollary of McClelland et al.'s (1989) framework is that implicit motive scores should be less susceptible than self-attributed motive scores to self-report and self-presentation biases. Consistent with this hypothesis, Bornstein, Rossner, Hill, and Stepanian (1994) found that Interpersonal Dependency Inventory (IDI) scores (Hirschfeld et al., 1977)—but not ROD scores—were significantly influenced by instructional manipulations designed to alter participants' self-presentation goals during the testing session. When participants were explicitly told to alter their test responses to appear highly dependent or independent (Study 1), their IDI scores changed significantly, but their ROD scores did not. When a subtler instructional manipulation was used to induce a positive or negative mind-set regarding dependency in a separate sample of participants (Study 2), highly similar results were obtained: IDI—but not ROD— scores changed significantly in response to the manipulation.

These results do not imply that ROD scores are unaffected by external variables and experimental manipulations. On the contrary, when Bornstein, Bowers, and Bonner (1996a) used laboratory mood-induction procedures to produce a positive, negative, or neutral affect state in participants who had been prescreened with the IDI and the ROD scale, they obtained results that contrasted sharply with those of Bornstein, Rossner, Hill et al. (1994). Bornstein, Bowers et al. found that induction of a negative mood produced a significant increase in ROD—but not IDI—scores in two separate samples of college students.

These results are consistent with Masling's (1960, 1966) conceptualization of projective testing as a dynamic social process, with test results influenced by the interpersonal milieu in which they are collected (see Masling, 2002b, for a detailed discussion of this perspective). As Bornstein (2002) noted, these findings also support McClelland et al.'s (1989) framework, and suggest that a process dissociation framework is a useful way of conceptualizing relationships between ROD scores and self-report dependency scores. Just as experimental psychologists disentangle implicit and explicit memory processes by introducing manipulations that affect one type of memory but not the other (e.g., Jacoby & Kelley, 1991), personality researchers can disentangle implicit and explicit motives and need states by introducing manipulations that influence scores on one type of test but not the other.

Clinical Applications

The contrasting patterns produced by the ROD scale and self-report measures of dependency suggest that, in clinical settings, it is useful to explore divergences as well as convergences between scores on projective and objective dependency tests. Figure 5.1 illustrates four outcomes that can be obtained when the ROD scale and one or more self-report dependency measures are administered to the same person. As shown in the upper left and lower right quadrants of Fig. 5.1, it is possible that a person will score high or low on both measures, which would indicate convergence between this person's self-attributed and implicit dependency scores. The other two cells in Fig. 5.1 illustrate discontinuities between implicit and explicit dependency needs. In one case (i.e., high ROD score coupled with low self-report dependency score), individuals with high levels of implicit dependency needs do not acknowledge them. These individuals may be described as having "unacknowledged dependency strivings." In the other case (i.e., low ROD score coupled with high self-report dependency score), individuals have low levels of implicit dependency needs, but describe themselves as being highly dependent. These individuals may be described as having a "dependent self-presentation."

Thus, by administering both types of scales to the same person, clinicians can obtain a more complete picture of that person's underlying and expressed dependency strivings. Exploration of these discontinuities may reveal important information regarding personality structure and interpersonal style (see Bornstein, 2002). These discontinuities may also have important diagnostic implications. For example, Bornstein (1998a) found that college students who met *Diagnostic and Statistical manual of Mental Disorders* (American Psychological Association, 1994) criteria for dependent personality disorder (PD) obtained high scores on the ROD scale and Hirschfeld et al.'s (1977) IDI. Students who met *DSM-IV* criteria for histrionic PD obtained high ROD scores and low IDI

SCORE ON OBJECTIVE DEPENDENCY TEST

		LOW	HIGH
SCORE ON PROJECTIVE DEPENDENCY TEST	LOW	Low Implicit Low Self-Attributed **Low Dependency**	Low Implicit High Self-Attributed **Dependent Self-Presentation**
	HIGH	High Implicit Low Self-Attributed **Unacknowledged Dependency**	High Implicit High Self-Attributed **High Dependency**

FIG. 5.1. Continuities and discontinuities between implicit and self-attributed dependency scores: A four-cell model. From "Implicit and Self-Attributed Dependency Strivings: Differential Relationships to Laboratory and Field Measures of Help Seeking," by R. F. Bornstein, 1998, *Journal of Personality and Social Psychology, 75,* p. 779. Copyright © 1998 by the American Psychological Association. Reprinted with permission.

scores. Apparently, dependent PD is associated with high levels of implicit and self-attributed dependency needs, whereas histrionic PD is associated high implicit dependency needs, but low self-attributed dependency needs.

Although dependency test score data by themselves cannot be used to derive *DSM-IV* diagnoses, they can—and should—be used to refine clinical decisions, and increase diagnostic accuracy (see Bornstein, 2001, in press, for discussions of this issue). Even for patients who do not show significant PD symptomatology, ROD scores and questionnaire dependency scores, used in combination, can clarify personality dynamics, insight, coping, and defense. In this respect, use of the ROD scale in addition to traditional self-report measures of personality and psychopathology can provide important clinical information, contributing incremental validity to a set of assessment data. Clinicians and researchers can make more precise predictions regarding individual differences and situational variations in dependent behavior by obtaining both types of motive scores from the same individual (Bornstein, 2001; Weiner, 2000).[5]

---

[5]A complementary perspective on this issue was described by Meyer (1996, 1997, 2000), who argued that in clinical settings, incremental validity can be conceptualized as an index of the cost effectiveness of objective and projective tests. According to this view, concurrent use of both types of measures is justified when the two tests used in combination make more accurate diagnostic or behavioral predictions than either measure alone (see also Finn, 1996). Thus, use of the ROD scale is warranted within Meyer's framework as well.

Although construct validity evidence for the ROD scale is quite strong, as with any psychological test, certain issues remain unresolved. For example, no researchers have explored changes in ROD score with age (e.g., from childhood through adolescence), or over the course of psychological or medical treatment. The ROD scale shows good retest reliability over 60 weeks, but evidence regarding long-term retest reliability in clinical and community samples would be useful. The only external or situational variable shown to moderate ROD scores thus far is mood; however, it is likely that other state variables affect ROD scores as well, and this possibility should be explored. Finally, few studies have compared the concurrent or predictive validities of the ROD oral and dependent subscales (cf. Bornstein et al., 2000; Bornstein & Greenberg, 1991; Masling et al., 1967, 1968). Further research in this area is needed.

In stark contrast to the results obtained with self-report measures of dependency (where women almost invariably obtained higher scores than men), meta-analyses suggest that men actually obtained slightly higher ROD scores than women (Bornstein, 1995). Paralleling these results, few ROD studies have obtained significantly different results for women and men (cf. Juni & Fischer, 1985; Masling et al., 1974; Shilkret & Masling, 1981); in most investigations, similar dependency-related behavior patterns emerged across gender. To date, most ROD studies have been conducted on men, or on mixed-sex samples, and future investigations should examine more closely gender differences in the predictive value of the ROD scale in various contexts and settings.

Also in contrast to findings obtained with self-report dependency tests, no studies have examined the impact of culture or ethnicity on ROD scores. Myriad findings have shown that individuals raised in sociocentric cultures (e.g., India, Japan) have higher levels of self-attributed dependency needs than do individuals raised in individualistic cultures (see Bornstein, 1993; Neki, 1976, for reviews). Whether similar cultural effects occur for implicit dependency needs is unknown.

It is noteworthy that scores on the ROD scale have predicted adaptive features of dependency (e.g., sensitivity to interpersonal cues, cooperativeness in academic settings), as well as dependency's maladaptive features (e.g., risk for depression and eating disorders). Continued research in this area is needed, along with closer examination of the variables that moderate the expression of underlying dependency needs, and that help determine whether dependency will lead to a positive or negative outcome in a given situation or setting.

Finally, given the usefulness of the process dissociation framework, it will be important to explore the range of variables that differentially affect ROD scores and scores on self-report measures of dependency.

Such findings not only have important theoretical implications, but may also lead to new uses of the ROD scale in clinical settings, and help resolve some lingering questions regarding projective test validity raised by RIM critics.

REFERENCES

American Psychiatric Association. (1994). *Diagnostic and statistical manual of mental disorders* (4th ed.). Washington, DC: Author.

Bem, S. (1974). The measurement of psychological androgeny. *Journal of Consulting and Clinical Psychology, 42,* 155–162.

Bertrand, S., & Masling, J. M. (1969). Oral imagery and alcoholism. *Journal of Abnormal Psychology, 74,* 50–53.

Blum, G. S. (1949). A study of the psychoanalytic theory of psychosexual development. *Genetic Psychology Monographs, 39,* 3–99.

Bornstein, R. F. (1992). The dependent personality: Developmental, social and clinical perspectives. *Psychological Bulletin, 112,* 3–23.

Bornstein, R. F. (1993). *The dependent personality.* New York: Guilford Press.

Bornstein, R. F. (1995). Sex differences in objective and projective dependency tests: A meta-analytic review. *Assessment, 2,* 319–331.

Bornstein, R. F. (1996a). Beyond orality: Toward an object relations/interactionist reconceptualization of the etiology and dynamics of dependency. *Psychoanalytic Psychology, 13,* 177–203.

Bornstein, R. F. (1996b). Construct validity of the Rorschach Oral Dependency scale: 1967–1995. *Psychological Assessment, 8,* 200–205.

Bornstein, R. F. (1998a). Implicit and self-attributed dependency needs in dependent and histrionic personality disorders. *Journal of Personality Assessment, 71,* 1–14.

Bornstein, R. F. (1998b). Implicit and self-attributed dependency strivings: Differential relationships to laboratory and field measures of help-seeking. *Journal of Personality and Social Psychology, 75,* 778–787.

Bornstein, R. F. (1999). Criterion validity of objective and projective dependency tests: A meta-analytic assessment of behavioral prediction. *Psychological Assessment, 11,* 48–57.

Bornstein, R. F. (2001). Clinical utility of the Rorschach Inkblot Method: Reframing the debate. *Journal of Personality Assessment, 77,* 39–47.

Bornstein, R. F. (2002). A process dissociation approach to objective-projective test score interrelationships. *Journal of Personality Assessment, 78,* 47–68.

Bornstein, R. F. (2003). Psychodynamic models of personality. In T. Millon & M. J. Lerner (Eds.), *Comprehensive handbook of psychology: Vol. 5. Personality and social psychology* (pp. 117–143. New York: Wiley.

Bornstein, R. F. (2005). *The dependent patient: A practitioner's guide.* Washington, DC: American Psychological Association.

Bornstein, R. F., Bonner, S., Kildow, A. M., & McCall, C. A. (1997). Effects of individual versus group test administration on Rorschach Oral Dependency scores. *Journal of Personality Assessment, 69,* 215–228.

Bornstein, R. F., Bowers, K. S., & Bonner, S. (1996a). Effects of induced mood state on objective and projective dependency scores. *Journal of Personality Assessment, 67,* 324–340.

Bornstein, R. F., Bowers, K. S., & Bonner, S. (1996b). Relationships of objective and projective dependency scores to sex role orientation in college student subjects. *Journal of Personality Assessment, 66,* 555–568.
Bornstein, R. F., Bowers, K. S., & Robinson, K. J. (1995). Differential relationships of objective and projective dependency scores to self-reports of interpersonal life events in college student subjects. *Journal of Personality Assessment, 65,* 255–269.
Bornstein, R. F., Galley, D. J., & Leone, D. R. (1986). Parental representations and orality. *Journal of Personality Assessment, 50,* 80–89.
Bornstein, R. F., & Greenberg, R. P. (1991). Dependency and eating disorders in female psychiatric inpatients. *Journal of Nervous and Mental Disease, 179,* 148–152.
Bornstein, R. F., Greenberg, R. P., Leone, D. R., & Galley, D. J. (1990). Defense mechanism correlates of orality. *Journal of the American Academy of Psychoanalysis, 18,* 654–666.
Bornstein, R. F., Hill, E. L., Robinson, K. J., Calabrese, C., & Bowers, K. S. (1996). Internal reliability of Rorschach Oral Dependency scale scores. *Educational and Psychological Measurement, 56,* 145–153.
Bornstein, R. F., Hilsenroth, M. J., Padawer, J. R., & Fowler, J. C. (2000). Interpersonal dependency and personality pathology: Variations in Rorschach Oral Dependency scores across Axis II diagnoses. *Journal of Personality Assessment, 75,* 478–491.
Bornstein, R. F., Leone, D. R., & Galley, D. J. (1988). Rorschach measures of oral dependence and the internalized self-representation in normal college students. *Journal of Personality Assessment, 52,* 648–657.
Bornstein, R. F., Manning, K. A., Krukonis, A. B., Rossner, S. C., & Mastrosimone, C. C. (1993). Sex differences in dependency: A comparison of objective and projective measures. *Journal of Personality Assessment, 61,* 169–181.
Bornstein, R. F., & Masling, J. M. (1985). Orality and latency of volunteering to serve as experimental subjects: A replication. *Journal of Personality Assessment, 49,* 306–310.
Bornstein, R. F., Masling, J. M., & Poynton, F. G. (1987). Orality as a factor in interpersonal yielding. *Psychoanalytic Psychology, 4,* 161–170.
Bornstein, R. F., & O'Neill, R. M. (1997). Construct validity of the Rorschach Oral Dependency (ROD) scale: Relationship of ROD scores to WAIS-R scores in a psychiatric inpatient sample. *Journal of Clinical Psychology, 53,* 99–105.
Bornstein, R. F., & O'Neill, R. M. (2000). Dependency and suicidality in psychiatric inpatients. *Journal of Clinical Psychology, 56,* 463–473.
Bornstein, R. F., O'Neill, R. M., Galley, D. J., Leone, D. R., & Castrianno, L. M. (1988). Body image aberration and orality. *Journal of Personality Disorders, 2,* 315–322.
Bornstein, R. F., Poynton, F. G., & Masling, J. M. (1985). Orality and depression: An empirical study. *Psychoanalytic Psychology, 2,* 241–249.
Bornstein, R. F., Rossner, S. C., & Hill, E. L. (1994). Retest reliability of scores on objective and projective measures of dependency: Relationship to life events and intertest interval. *Journal of Personality Assessment, 62,* 398–415.
Bornstein, R. F., Rossner, S. C., Hill, E. L., & Stepanian, M. L. (1994). Face validity and fakability of objective and projective measures of dependency. *Journal of Personality Assessment, 63,* 363–386.
Cronbach, L. J. (1951). Coefficient alpha and the internal structure of tests. *Psychometrika, 16,* 297–334.
Duberstein, P. R., & Talbot, N. L. (1993). Rorschach oral imagery, attachment style and interpersonal relatedness. *Journal of Personality Assessment, 61,* 294–310.
Edwards, A. L. (1959). *Manual for the Edwards Personal Preference Schedule.* New York: Psychological Corporation.

Finn, S. E. (1996). Assessment feedback integrating MMPI-2 and Rorschach findings. *Journal of Personality Assessment, 67,* 543–557.
Fisher, S. (1970). *Body experience in fantasy and behavior.* New York: Appleton-Century-Crofts.
Freud, S. (1953). Three essays on the theory of sexuality. In J. Strachey (Ed. & Trans.), *The standard edition of the complete psychological works of Sigmund Freud* (Vol. 7, pp. 125–245). London: Hogarth Press. (Original work published 1905)
Gordon, M., & Tegtemeyer, P. F. (1983). Oral dependent content in children's Rorschach protocols. *Perceptual and Motor Skills, 57,* 1163–1168.
Greenberg, R. P., & Bornstein, R. F. (1989). Length of psychiatric hospitalization and oral dependency. *Journal of Personality Disorders, 3,* 199–204.
Hirschfeld, R. M. A., Klerman, G. L., Gough, H. G., Barrett, J., Korchin, S. J., & Chodoff, P. (1977). A measure of interpersonal dependency. *Journal of Personality Assessment, 41,* 610–618.
Holtzman, W. H. (1961). *Guide to administration and scoring: Holtzman Inkblot Technique.* New York: Psychological Corporation.
Jacoby, L. L., & Kelley, C. M. (1991). Unconscious influences of memory: Dissociations and automaticity. In D. Milner & M. Rugg (Eds.), *The neuropsychology of consciousness* (pp. 201–233). London: Academic Press.
Juni, S. (1981a). Career choice and orality. *Journal of Vocational Behavior, 19,* 73–83.
Juni, S. (1981b). Maintaining anonymity versus requesting feedback as a function of oral dependency. *Perceptual and Motor Skills, 52,* 239–242.
Juni, S., & Fischer, R. E. (1985). Religiosity and preoedipal fixation. *Journal of Genetic Psychology, 146,* 27–35.
Juni, S., & LoCascio, R. (1985). Preference for counseling and psychotherapy as related to preoedipal fixation. *Psychological Reports, 56,* 431–438.
Juni, S., Masling, J. M., & Brannon, R. (1979). Interpersonal touching and orality. *Journal of Personality Assessment, 43,* 235–237.
Juni, S., Nelson, S. P., & Brannon, R. (1987). Minor tonality music preference and oral dependency. *Journal of Psychology, 121,* 229–236.
Juni, S., & Semel, S. R. (1982). Person perception as a function of orality and anality. *Journal of Social Psychology, 118,* 99–103.
Kertzman, D. (1980). *Dependency, frustration tolerance, and impulse control in child abusers.* Saratoga, CA: Century Twenty-One.
Levin, R., & Masling, J. M. (1995). Relations of oral imagery to thought disorder in subjects with frequent nightmares. *Perceptual and Motor Skills, 80,* 1115–1120.
Masling, J. M. (1960). The influence of situational and interpersonal variables in projective testing. *Psychological Bulletin, 57,* 65–85.
Masling, J. M. (1966). Role-related behavior of the subject and psychologist and its effects upon psychological data. In D. Levine (Ed.), *Nebraska symposium on motivation* (pp. 67–104). Lincoln: University of Nebraska Press.
Masling, J. M. (1986). Orality, pathology, and interpersonal behavior. In J. M. Masling (Ed.), *Empirical studies of psychoanalytic theories* (Vol. 2, pp. 73–106). Hillsdale, NJ: Lawrence Erlbaum Associates.
Masling, J. M. (2002a). How do I score thee? Let me count the ways. (Or some methods of categorizing Rorschach responses). *Journal of Personality Assessment, 79,* 399–421.
Masling, J. M. (2002b). Speak, memory, or goodbye Columbus. *Journal of Personality Assessment, 78,* 4–30.

Masling, J. M., Bornstein, R. F., Poynton, F. G., Reed, S. D., & Katkin, E. S. (1991). Perception without awareness and electrodermal responding. *Journal of Mind and Behavior, 12,* 33–48.

Masling, J. M., Johnson, C., & Saturansky, C. (1974). Oral imagery, accuracy of perceiving others, and performance in Peace Corps training. *Journal of Personality and Social Psychology, 30,* 414–419.

Masling, J. M., O'Neill, R. M., & Jayne, C. (1981). Orality and latency of volunteering to serve as experimental subjects. *Journal of Personality Assessment, 45,* 20–22.

Masling, J. M., O'Neill, R. M., & Katkin, E. S. (1982). Autonomic arousal, interpersonal climate, and orality. *Journal of Personality and Social Psychology, 42,* 529–534.

Masling, J. M., Price, J., Goldband, S., & Katkin, E. S. (1981). Oral imagery and autonomic arousal in social isolation. *Journal of Personality and Social Psychology, 40,* 395–400.

Masling, J. M., Rabie, L., & Blondheim, S. H. (1967). Obesity, level of aspiration, and Rorschach and TAT measures of oral dependence. *Journal of Consulting Psychology, 31,* 233–239.

Masling, J. M., Schiffner, J., & Shenfeld, M. (1980). Client perception of the therapist, orality, and sex of client and therapist. *Journal of Counseling Psychology, 27,* 294–298.

Masling, J. M., & Schwartz, M. A. (1979). A critique of research in psychoanalytic theory. *Genetic Psychology Monographs, 100,* 257–307.

Masling, J. M., Weiss, L., & Rothschild, B. (1968). Relationships of oral imagery to yielding behavior and birth order. *Journal of Consulting and Clinical Psychology, 32,* 89–91.

McClelland, D. C., Koestner, R., & Weinberger, J. (1989). How do implicit and self-attributed motives differ? *Psychological Review, 96,* 690–702.

Meyer, G. J. (1996). The Rorschach and MMPI: Toward a more scientific understanding of cross-method assessment. *Journal of Personality Assessment, 67,* 558–578.

Meyer, G. J. (1997). On the integration of personality assessment methods: The Rorschach and MMPI. *Journal of Personality Assessment, 68,* 297–330.

Meyer, G. J. (2000). Incremental validity of the Rorschach Prognostic Rating Scale over the MMPI Ego Strength Scale and IQ. *Journal of Personality Assessment, 74,* 356–370.

Millon, T. (1987). *Millon Clinical Multiaxial Inventory-II manual.* Minneapolis, MN: National Computer Systems.

Narduzzi, K. J., & Jackson, T. (2000). Personality differences between eating-disordered women and a nonclinical comparison sample: A discriminant classification analysis. *Journal of Clinical Psychology, 56,* 699–710.

Narduzzi, K. J., & Jackson, T. (2002). Sociotropy-dependency and autonomy as predictors of eating disturbance among Canadian female college students. *Journal of Genetic Psychology, 163,* 389–401.

Navran, L. (1954). A rationally derived MMPI scale to measure dependence. *Journal of Consulting Psychology, 18,* 192.

Neki, J. S. (1976). An examination of the cultural relativism of dependence as a dynamic of social and therapeutic relationships. *British Journal of Medical Psychology, 49,* 1–10.

Nunnally, J. C., & Bernstein, I. H. (1994). *Psychometric theory.* New York: McGraw-Hill.

O'Neill, R. M., & Bornstein, R. F. (1990). Oral dependence and gender: Factors in help-seeking response set and self-reported psychopathology in psychiatric inpatients. *Journal of Personality Assessment, 55,* 28–40.

O'Neill, R. M., & Bornstein, R. F. (1991). Orality and depression in psychiatric inpatients. *Journal of Personality Disorders, 5,* 1–17.

Parker, K. C. H. (1983). A meta-analysis of the reliability and validity of the Rorschach. *Journal of Personality Assessment, 47,* 227–231.

Parker, K. C. H., Hanson, R. K., & Hunsley, J. (1988). MMPI, Rorschach, and WAIS: A meta-analytic comparison of reliability, stability, and validity. *Psychological Bulletin, 103,* 367–373.

Schafer, R. (1954). *Psychoanalytic interpretation in Rorschach testing.* New York: Grune & Stratton.

Shilkret, C. J., & Masling, J. M. (1981). Oral dependence and dependent behavior. *Journal of Personality Assessment, 45,* 125–129.

Spitzer, R. L., Cohen, J., Fliess, J. L., & Endicott, J. (1967). Quantification of agreement in psychiatric diagnosis. *Archives of General Psychiatry, 17,* 83–87.

Sprohge, E., Handler, L., Plant, D. D., & Wicker, D. (2002). A Rorschach study of oral dependence in alcoholics and depressives. *Journal of Personality Assessment, 79,* 142–160.

Tognazzo, D. (1970). Sui contenuti orali del Rorchach in un gruppo di alcoolisti [On the oral contents of the Rorschach in a group of alcoholics]. *Psychiatria Generale e Dell'eta Evolutiva, 8,* 323–325.

Weiner, I. B. (1999). What the Rorschach can do for you: Incremental validity in clinical applications. *Assessment, 6,* 327–339.

Weiner, I. B. (2000). Using the Rorschach properly in practice and research. *Journal of Clinical Psychology, 56,* 435–438.

Weiner, I. B. (2003). *Principles of Rorschach interpretation* (2nd ed.). Mahwah, NJ: Lawrence Erlbaum Associates.

Weiss, L. R., & Masling, J. M. (1970). Further validation of a Rorschach measure of oral imagery: A study of six clinical groups. *Journal of Abnormal Psychology, 76,* 83–87.

Wood, J. M., Lilienfeld, S. O., Nezworski, M. T., & Garb, H. N. (2001). Coming to grips with negative evidence for the Comprehensive System for the Rorschach: A comment on Gacano, Loving and Bodholt, Ganellen, and Bornstein. *Journal of Personality Assessment, 77,* 48–70.

6

Body Image, Body Boundary, and the Barrier and Penetration Rorschach Scoring System

Richard M. O'Neill
SUNY Upstate Medical University

In 1923, Freud, building theory from clinical observations, made his famous, pithy statement, "The ego is first and foremost a body ego" (Freud, 1923/1953, p. 26). Less well known and more obtuse is the immediate continuation of this definition of the ego, "It is not merely a surface entity but it is itself the projection of a surface" (p. 26). Freud's translator, Joan Riviere, clarified Freud's meaning with the following note: "That is, the ego is ultimately derived from bodily sensations, chiefly from those springing from the surface of the body. It may thus be regarded as a mental projection of the surface of the body" (p. 26). Thus, for Freud the theoretician and clinician, the psychological agency that represents the person's ability to deal with the environment throughout life comes into being and has its particular character determined by transactions with the environment at the body's own boundary or surface. Fenichel (1945) elaborated on this process:

> In the development of reality the conception of one's own body plays a very special role. At first there is only the perception of tension, that is, of an "inside something." Later, with the awareness that an object exists to quiet this tension, we have an "outside something." ... One's own body becomes something apart from the rest of the world and thus the discerning of self from nonself is made possible. The sum of the mental representations of the body and its organs, the so-called body image, constitutes the idea of I and is of basic importance for the further formation of the ego. (pp. 35–36)

Thereafter, the strength of the ego largely determines the quality of a person's life.

In the decades following Freud's (1923/1953) statements, numerous clinicians, theoreticians, and researchers attempted to connect the body and the mind in psychological theory of personality and behavior. In 1958, Fisher and Cleveland published their pioneering work on body image. As they conceptualized it:

> [Body image] refers to the body as a psychological experience, and focuses on the individual's feelings and attitudes toward his own body. It is concerned with the individual's subjective experiences with his body and the manner in which he has organized these experiences .... The body image is literally an image of his own body which the individual has evolved through experience .... Body image may in certain respects overlap the various usages of concepts like ego, self, and self-concept. (pp. x–xi)

Like Freud, Fisher and Cleveland conceptualized the body image as a psychological representation with a functional boundary differentiating the inner world of the self from the rest of the world. And although their body image concepts may be somewhat similar to Freud's notions of the ego, Fisher and Cleveland's work was unique in how they operationalized, tested, and developed their theory.

DATA, DISCOVERY, AND DEVELOPMENT OF THE BARRIER AND PENETRATION RORSCHACH SCORING SYSTEM

Early in the development of their body image theory, Cleveland and Fisher (1954) evaluated 25 male patients diagnosed with rheumatoid arthritis. Using interviews, the Rorschach, the Thematic Apperception Test (TAT), and figure drawings, they searched for unique behavior or fantasy patterns that characterized these patients from the "body-image frame of reference" (Fisher & Cleveland, 1968, p. 54) and eventually differentiated them from other patient and nonpatient groups. Perhaps not surprisingly, they found that the arthritic was intensely focused on his body, and the assessment protocols were permeated with body-related responses.

Then they made an important discovery; they found that arthritics gave unusual Rorschach responses, body focused and otherwise, in which "either the hardness or protective insulation value of the *periphery* is prominent" (Fisher & Cleveland, 1968, p. 55, emphasis added). This emphasis was reportedly echoed in a similar concern with the "periphery of percepts" (p. 55) and boundary-defining phenomena in these patients' TAT responses. Fisher and Cleveland put these findings in the context of the clinical observations and theoretical constructions of

Freud (1923/1953), Reich (1949), Jung (1944), and others concerned with body image and body boundary phenomenon, and theorized, "a fundamental aspect of the body image is the manner in which the individual experiences the limits of his body" (Fisher, 1970, p. 155). Next, they made an integrative theoretical and empirical leap. They hypothesized that the boundary-defining characteristics of these individuals' Rorschach and TAT responses reflected qualities of their own body images, that "the way in which an individual depicts the boundaries of his ink blot responses mirrors how he feels about his own body boundaries" (Fisher, p. 157). They began operationalizing these observations and hypotheses:

> Perhaps people show wide differences in the degree to which they experience their body boundaries as definite and firm versus indefinite and vague. One could conceive of each individual as equating his body with a "base of operations," a segment of the world that is specially his. His body would encompass his private domain and be the cumulative site for all of his past integrated experiences. It could be regarded as bounding and containing a complex system which has developed to deal with the world. It would encompass a structure which the individual has built up in his attempts to make life satisfying for himself. Therefore, would one not expect that the sort of boundaries which the individual attributes to his body would tell a good deal about his overall life-building operations? Would one not assume that the person who sees his body as an area highly differentiated from the rest of the world and girded by definite boundaries had constructed a different type of "base of operations" from that of the person who regards his body as an area with indefinite boundaries? (Fisher & Cleveland, 1968, p. 56)

Fisher and Cleveland (1968) recognized that to test these and related body image and body boundary hypotheses they needed a reliable, objective method to measure the relevant qualities of an individual's body boundary. Reviewing the arthritic sample's interview and test data, they concluded that people have little conscious awareness of body boundary representations and thus interview data would be of little use. In addition, they "noted that the Rorschach elicited considerably more information that was pertinent and subject to quantification" (p. 57) than either the TAT or the Draw-A-Person. As a consequence of these observations and their underlying assumptions, Fisher and Cleveland (1958) decided to develop such a boundary definiteness assessment method using only the content (not structural) aspects of the inkblot responses as the raw data.

To develop the boundary scoring system, they studied intensively the Rorschach records of the arthritics, with special attention to references to the qualities of the surface, periphery, or boundary of percepts. They discovered that these references fell into two general categories: those with an emphasis on the definite structure, substance, and surface qualities of boundaries; and those emphasizing their "weakness, lack of substance, and penetrability" (Fisher & Cleveland, 1968, p. 58; see Table 6.1). The former were labeled "Barrier" responses; the latter were termed "Penetration of Boundary" responses. For example, responses containing definite boundaries such as: "cave with rocky walls," "flower pot," "knight in armor," "something with a wall around it," "cocoon," "turtle with a shell," and "mummy wrapped up" (p. 55), are classified as Barrier responses. Three general categories of Rorschach responses comprised the Penetration of Boundary scoring criteria: (a) "images that involve the penetration, disruption, or wearing away of the outer surfaces of things"; (b) "modes or channels for getting into the interior of things or for passing from the interior outward to the exterior"; and (c) "images that involve the surfaces of things as being easily permeable or fragile" (pp. 59–60). Respective examples include: (a) "bullet penetrating flesh," "shell of a turtle that has been broken open"; (b) "vagina," "an entrance"; and (c) "soft ball of cotton candy," "fleecy fluffy cloud" (pp. 59–60). Together these came to be known as the Barrier and Penetration (BP) scoring system for the Rorschach[1] (see Appendix A for complete BP scoring criteria; see Appendix B for illustrative Rorschach protocols).

Administration and Scoring

To obtain protocols for scoring, the inkblots can be presented either to an individual or to a group with the inkblot images projected on a screen. The BP and Rorschach Oral Dependency (ROD; Masling, 1986) are the only two Rorschach indices administered individually or in groups. Fisher and Cleveland (1968, p. 65) recognized that response total might influence the BP scores; they developed several methods for managing this potential problem, including requiring new research subjects to produce 25 total responses, or, with archival Rorschach protocols, "eliminating all Rorschach records with less than 15 responses and reducing all records with more than 25 responses to 25" (p. 65), using their specific method for such reductions.

Scoring a protocol for Barrier involves assigning a maximum value of 1 to each response containing one or more elements matching the Barrier criteria; responses containing one or more elements matching the Penetration criteria receive a value of 1 for Penetration. A single re-

[1]Numerous researchers, including Fisher and Cleveland (1968), applied the BP scoring system to Holtzman Inkblot Test (HIT) protocols. Fisher and Cleveland viewed the HIT results as so consistent theoretically with the Rorschach-based results that they made almost no distinction in citing them in building their body image theory. We report a number of these studies later to demonstrate the robustness and validity of the BP scoring system.

sponse may contain elements of both Barrier and Penetration and thus simultaneously receive a separate score on each dimension (e.g., "volcano erupting," "broken vase"; Fisher, 1970, p. 609). A simple tally of Barrier scores equals the total Barrier score, and the total number of Penetration credits is the final Penetration score (see Table 6.1).

Reliability

Fisher and Cleveland (1958, 1968) conducted a series of studies of interrater reliability. Fisher (1986) summarized scoring objectivity results, showing typical interrater reliability coefficients for the Barrier score ranging from .82 to .99 and for the Penetration score from .86 to .99 (see Table 11.1, p. 332). In 1996, Zennaro and Lis found interscorer reliability "above .90" (p. 534).

Fisher (1970, see Table 6.2, p. 159) summarized BP test-retest reliability coefficients from six samples showing good reliability over periods ranging from 30 minutes to 60 days.[2] Those for the Barrier score ranged

TABLE 6.1
BP Scoring Criteria

Response Type	*References*
Barrier	Clothing, jewelry and body adornment; body protection; camouflage, mechanical attachments to the body
	Buildings or other enclosing structures
	Vehicles with containing or holding qualities
	That which contains, covers, or conceals living things (except human) described as having special surface qualities; creatures with shells or similar protective structures
	Geographic or natural formations with delimiting or container-like qualities
Penetration	The fact of disruption, penetration, damage, or destruction of any object or living thing
	Body openings or acts involving body openings
	Perceptions involving a perspective of bypassing or evading the usual boundaries of the body or other objects
	The process of entering or leaving structures and the means for doing so
	Natural contexts that involve intake or explusion
	Images that are insubstantial or vague in their delimitation

[2]The Rorschach Inkblots were administered in three of these studies, the HIT in the other four; results were comparable. In contrast, Holtzman, Thorpe, Swartz, and Herron's (1961) evaluation of the test-retest reliability of the Barrier score alone, using the HIT, were lower; several samples over intervals ranging from 3 weeks to 1 year produced coefficients in the .40s.

(*continued*)

from .65 to .89, with five of six being .78 to .89. Those for the Penetration score ranged from .63 to .89, with five of six being .80 to .89.[3]

Normative Sex and Age Differences

Several early studies demonstrated small sex differences for both Barrier and Penetration scores in adults (Fisher, 1970; Hartley, 1964; Jacobson, 1966) and children (Colvin, 1977; Swartz, 1965). In an attempt to provide definitive data regarding sex differences in adults, Fisher (1970) undertook a large-scale study of male ($n = 274$) and female ($n = 290$) college students. Using the group administration of the Rorschach with responses limited to 25, he found median scores of 6 Barrier and 3 Penetration responses for men, whereas women produced medians of 7 Barrier and 2 Penetration responses. These differences were highly significant: Barrier chi-square = 11.5, $df = 1$, $p < .001$; Penetration chi-square = 13.6, $df = 1$, $p < .001$. In 1986, Fisher reviewed all of the sex difference data up to that point and concluded, "Females tend to a small degree to have more definite body image boundaries than do males" (p. 337). He pointed out that this contradicts the commonly held stereotype that men are more secure and comfortable with their bodies than women and speculated that "it may indeed be the importance of the body as a container for the creation of new life that is primarily responsible for the female's apparently greater sense of having a bounded body" (p. 337). Of seven BP studies published since 1986, three examined the relationship of gender and BP scores: Spigelman and Spigelman (1991) found no sex difference in the Rorschach protocols of a sample of 90 children (46 girls, 44 boys) between the ages of 10 and 12; Zennaro and Lis (1996) found that men scored significantly higher on Rorschach Penetration $F = 7.67$, $df = 1, 263$, $p = .006$, but not on Barrier; Hayslip, Cooper, Dougherty, and Cook (1997), using the HIT, found women scored higher than men on Barrier, $F = 8.78$, $df = 1, 177$, $p < .01$, with no significant difference on Penetration. These results seem con-

---

[2](*continued*) It was not clear what accounted for the difference between Holtzman et al.'s Barrier score results and those of the other investigators. Dorsey (1965; cited in Fisher, 1970) examined only Barrier score spilt-half reliability in two college student samples, and reported reliabilities of .67 and .43. Using samples of normal adults, Holtzman et al. reported odd-even reliability coefficients around .70 for the Barrier score, and between .65 and .70 for the Penetration score. Using samples of schizophrenic patients, Holtzman et al. reported slightly higher odd-even reliabilities for both scores, from the .70s into the lower .80s.

[3]Fisher (1970) noted that one researcher (Koschene, 1965) found a .18 "test-retest" correlation for the Penetration score, however, this was obtained in a pre- and postexperiment in which the score was expected to be responsive in the situational variables. As surgery should alter these scores, this correlation may more correctly be thought of as evidence for the validity of the score.

sistent with Fisher's (1986) conclusion that women have slightly more definite boundaries than men.

In 1986, Fisher examined all the research findings regarding developmental trends in Barrier and Penetration scores. He concluded that although there was some inconsistency in the data, broadly speaking, boundary definiteness as measured by the Barrier score increased from about age 5 or 6 to age 20. To examine the relationship of age and Barrier score in adults, Fisher (1959) compared the scores of a group of older persons (median age = 67) to matching, younger, immediate family members (median age = 36). He found no significant difference and concluded, perhaps prematurely, that the boundary scores were unaffected by aging. More recent evidence from Hayslip et al. (1997) demonstrated "that younger persons were higher on both Barrier ($F = 8.10$, $df = 2, 177$, $p < .01$), and Penetration ($F = 12.04$, $df = 2, 177$, $p < .01$), than middle-aged and older individuals" (p. 635). They suggested that BP scores reflect aging, intrapsychic, and interpersonal factors in the context of culturally based messages transmitted through various mass media.

Validity

The development of the BP scoring system inspired over 100 research studies and 25 doctoral dissertations in the first 15 years or so after its introduction (and hundreds more in the next 20 years). In reviewing that first 15 years of work, Fisher and Cleveland (1968) were surprised to find that results with the Barrier score were much more predictable and consistent than those with the Penetration score. Although they had initially assumed the two scores would be highly negatively correlated, the accumulated data failed to support this hypothesis (see, in contrast, Jupp, 1989a). They concluded that the Penetration score was valid only with "abnormal or extreme" (p. 92) groups. Many researchers had been scoring only for the Barrier score and Fisher and Cleveland themselves decided to use only the Barrier score with normal adults. As a result, in the selective review that follows, research employing the Barrier score is emphasized; only a few studies regarding Penetration scores are mentioned, if they seem particularly pertinent or compelling or have been replicated repeatedly. Overall, the intent is not to be comprehensive, but rather to highlight the breadth of studies and to present work that represents areas of research in which the overall sum of findings examines the utility of the Barrier or Penetration score.

DISCRIMINANT VALIDITY

Before reviewing convergent validity studies, it should be noted that Fisher and Cleveland (1958, 1968) carefully investigated whether their results were simply an artifact of the relationship of the BP scores to other known factors. For instance, as previously mentioned, when early work demonstrated that the scores were related to overall Rorschach response productivity, Fisher and Cleveland (1968) developed protocol-limiting procedures to deal with that problem. When other research seemed to indicate a correlation with verbal productivity, their series of studies (Fisher, 1970) demonstrated that this finding, if not totally spurious, had little practical significance. Furthermore, considerable research failed to show any consistent significant relationship between the scores and the other main Rorschach determinants (e.g., Holtzman et al., 1961; Shipman, Oken, Grinker, Goldstein, & Heath, 1964; see Fisher for a review). These researchers found a sole exception: a repeatedly replicated significant positive correlation between Human Movement and Barrier scores (more recently confirmed by Jupp, 1989a). These correlations have typically been in the .30 to .45 range. Fisher understood that this occurred because both scores are related to "the individual's habitual degree of muscular activation and kinesthetic awareness [and] the impact of the kinesthetic experience upon the perceptual-imaginative process involved in the production of ink blot responses" (p. 164).

In addition, BP scores have little or no consistent significant relationship to intelligence (Appleby, 1956; Fisher & Cleveland, 1958; Ware, Fisher, & Cleveland, 1957; see Fisher, 1970, for review). Nor are they related in anything other than a sporadic fashion to "an infinite number of paper and pencil, self-report questionnaire measures" (Fisher, 1986, p. 507) tapping dimensions such as extraversion-introversion, defense mechanisms, masculinity-femininity, anxiety, locus of control, or psychopathology. This is consistent with the general finding that self-report and projective test data are not related in many, perhaps most, situations (Bornstein, 2002). Of note, Fisher (1986) pointed out that the BP scores have not, except in isolated instances, been related to other measures of body image, including the Witkin et al. (1954) measure related to field independence-dependence and boundary differentiation.

CONVERGENT VALIDITY

Boundary Definiteness and Body Phenomena

Continuing their work with the arthritic sample, Fisher and Cleveland (1958) hypothesized that patients with psychosomatic symptoms in the exterior of the body would have more definite body boundary images than patients with such symptoms in the body interior. They defined the body exterior as "all the tissue (viz., skin and musculature) which constitutes the sheath of the body and its appendages" (1958, p. 74). They selected three groups of exterior symptom psychosomatic patients at a Veterans Administration hospital: 25 rheumatoid arthritics, 25 with neurodermatitis not related to any known external irritant, and 20 conversion disorder patients with prominent muscular paralysis, tics, or muscle spasms. They compared these patients' BP scores to those of two groups with psychosomatic symptoms in the interior of the body: 18 patients with stomach difficulties including ulcers, pain, or vomiting (from the same VA hospital), and 20 female patients with ulcerative colitis at a private hospital. Results showed that all of the body-exterior groups had significantly higher Barrier score means than the body-interior groups, with the combined exterior group mean versus combined interior group mean also significantly higher, chi-square = 36.5, $df = 1$, $p = .001$. Whereas all the interior body Penetration score means were higher that the exterior body Penetration score means, only two of the six comparisons were significantly different, with a third at borderline $p < .10$ significance. The combined interior body Penetration score mean was also significantly higher than the combined exterior body Penetration score mean, chi-square = 5.3, $df = 1$, $p = .02$.

To test whether the physical symptoms at the respective interior or exterior body sites generated reflective BP score differences, or whether the symptoms were somehow a result of body image differences, Fisher and Cleveland (1955, 1958) created two additional control groups with subjectively comparable physical symptoms. The first group was from the same VA hospital, 20 patients with trauma-related muscle pain and stiffness, chosen to match the rheumatoid arthritic sample demographically, with only a slightly shorter duration of symptoms; the second was from an industrial plant, 22 patients with similar skin problems except with an identifiable external cause such as burns or chemical exposure. This group had similar demographics to the psychosomatic neurodermatitis sample except for having a much shorter duration of symptoms. As predicted, the psychosomatic groups had significantly higher Barrier score means than each respective comparison group. Several additional analyses suggested these results were not related to symptom duration. Fisher and Cleveland (1955, 1958) concluded that the body image boundary concept had predictive significance with respect to the body-interior or exterior site of psychosomatic symptoms. Fisher and Cleveland (1960) and Cleveland, Snyder, and Williams (1965) replicated these findings with three separate samples of adult arthritics and stomach ulcer patients. Cleveland, Reitman, and Brewer (1965) also compared juvenile arthritics to asthmatic children. They found that the juvenile arthritics gave significantly more Barrier responses than the asthmatics; no differences were found with respect to the Penetration score.

Subsequently, a number of related studies (primarily of the Barrier score) were conducted with normal subjects (e.g., Fisher & Cleveland,

1968; Osofsky & Fisher, 1967) reporting exterior and interior body complaints and symptoms. Fisher (1986, see Table 12.1, p. 458) reviewed all of the pertinent studies up to that time and concluded that, although there were occasional mixed results (e.g., Hirt, Ross, & Kurtz, 1967), the overall weight of the evidence supported the positive relationship between the Barrier score and the presence of or report of body-exterior symptoms.

Physiological Reactivity and Exterior Versus Interior

Speculation about the physiological mechanism linking body image to localized physical complaints and symptoms centered on unconscious channeling of excitation during stress; for high-Barrier persons the activation would be via the striate musculature, for low-Barrier persons it would be through the autonomic nervous system into internal organs such as the heart and stomach (Fisher, 1970, 1986; Fisher & Cleveland, 1968). Fisher (1959) tested this hypothesis in a group of 30 normal girls, ages 9 to 15. Barrier scores were determined from individually administered Rorschachs. The physiological measures were Galvanic Skin Reactivity (GSR) and heart rate, measured during a stress condition in which a gong was sounded and a chair kicked over, and during an ensuing rest condition. During the stress condition, GSR frequency was positively correlated with Barrier score, $r = .46$, $p = .01$, whereas heart rate was negatively correlated, $r = .–51$, $p < .01$. During the rest condition, the correlations were in the same direction but failed to reach significance.

Using the Rorschach, Armstrong (1968) selected a group of high- and low-Barrier male college students and investigated "differential ease of acquisition of autonomic conditioned responses" (p. 696). As predicted, he demonstrated that high-Barrier subjects were more easily conditioned to GSR, whereas low-Barrier subjects were more easily conditioned to heart rate.

Cloete (1978) used the HIT to select a sample of 19 high-Barrier and 19 low-Barrier males. He then measured skin conductance and heart rate during a reaction time experimental protocol; a 10-minute habituation was followed by a 5-second warning signal and then 5 seconds of preparation before the stimulus was presented. During the warning period, the low-Barrier subjects' heart rate accelerated significantly from baseline whereas that of the high-Barrier group rose but not significantly. Average heart rates were not significantly different between the two groups during this period. Significantly greater deceleration in average heart rate was shown during the preparation period for the high-Barrier group than for the low-Barrier group. In addition, skin conductance had greater amplitude for the high-Barrier subjects but did not reach significance. Skin conductance recovery for high-Barrier subjects was significantly more rapid than for the low-Barrier group.

Cloete (1979) extended these findings with a second sample of 15 high-Barrier and 15 low-Barrier males selected using the HIT. Again, he measured heart rate and skin conductance. The design involved a 10-minute habituation period followed by a loud, sudden-onset, white-noise stimulus for 90 seconds. The low-Barrier subjects' heart rate accelerated significantly from baseline by 1 second after stimulus onset and reached significantly different averaged and peak rates in the first 10 seconds. The high-Barrier group's heart rate peaked after 2 seconds but not significantly, and this group's averaged and peak rates never achieved significant difference from baseline. Furthermore, the peak rate increase was significantly greater in the initial 10 seconds of noise for the low-Barrier subjects than for the high-Barrier group. Habituation to the stimulus also took significantly longer for the low-Barrier than high-Barrier subjects. As in the Cloete (1978) study, skin conductance amplitude did not significantly differentiate high-Barrier from low-Barrier subjects; however, the high-Barrier subjects again showed significantly faster skin conductance recovery time compared to the low-Barrier group.

Farmer and Wright (1971) investigated high-Barrier and low-Barrier subjects' response to behavior therapy interventions involving voluntary muscle relaxation and activation as anxiety inhibitors. Rorschach protocols were collected from 28 female college students with relatively high anxiety about snakes. Three sets of high-Barrier and low-Barrier subjects were assigned to the different experimental conditions: (a) the no-treatment control, (b) the relaxation training condition with two sessions of relaxation training and ten subsequent standard desensitization sessions, and (c) the relaxation training condition with two sessions of relaxation training and ten subsequent desensitization sessions with an alternative anxiety-inhibition method of muscle activation. The latter sessions involved reviewing elements of a desensitization hierarchy while repeatedly hitting a pillow.

As predicted, posttreatment anxiety ratings showed muscle relaxation was significantly better as an anxiety inhibitor than muscle activation for high-Barrier subjects; there was no difference between muscle relaxation and activation for low-Barrier subjects alone. However, when comparing the responses of high-Barrier versus low-Barrier subjects to muscle activation as the anxiety inhibitor, low-Barrier subjects had significantly better outcomes. Furthermore, the muscle activation method resulted in significantly lower anxiety in the low-Barrier group as compared to the controls, whereas the muscle activation method resulted in no difference when comparing outcomes of the high-Barrier experimental group and the high-Barrier control group.

Managing Stress

Fisher and Cleveland (1958, 1968) initially conceived of people with definite boundaries as having an enhanced ability to cope with threat, change, and stress when compared to people with less definite boundaries. A series of studies tested and supported this hypothesis with respect to adaptation to bodily change and threat in such forms as paralysis (Ware et al., 1957), amputation (Fisher & Cleveland, 1958), pregnancy (McConnell & Daston, 1961), pain (Nichols & Tursky, 1967), invasive physical examination (Fisher & Bialos, 1970), and others (see Fisher, 1986, for review). Indeed, the Barrier score seems to be a powerful measure for predicting adaptation to physical change and disablement.

As an illustration, Ware et al. (1957) individually collected Rorschach protocols and determined Barrier scores on 59 patients hospitalized with poliomyelitis. Assessment showed no relationship between Barrier score and duration or degree of disability from the disease. Staff members familiar with their patients' progress over several months rated the patients on their level of adjustment to their disability. Patients with higher Barrier scores were significantly more likely to be judged as adapting well.

Blumetti and Modesti (1976) determined Barrier scores from the individually collected Rorschach protocols of a group of chronic low-back pain patients scheduled for related surgery. The Minnesota Multiphasic Personality Inventory (MMPI) was also administered. These patients had a mean duration of symptoms of 2.5 years and all but two had a history of prior back surgery. The sample consisted of 34 men and 8 women. At least 6 months after surgery, patient improvement for back pain was assessed. Higher Barrier scores (as well as lower MMPI Hypochondriasis and Hysteria scores) predicted significantly more improvement in pain.

Several months into a 3-year prospective study of adaptation to hemophilia, Mattsson, Gross, and Hall (1971) used the HIT to determine BP scores of 10 severely hemophiliac boys, ages 6 to 14 years. Adaptation level was rated by nurses during a hospital admission for research procedures, and during a 3-year follow-up by two independent physicians who rated the boys on several dimensions that were totaled into an average adaptation score. Results showed that Barrier score, but not Penetration score, correlated positively and significantly with the physicians' average adaptation score, $r = .71$, $p < .05$. There was no significant relationship between the BP scores and the nurses' ratings.

McConnell and Daston (1961) obtained BP scores from Rorschach protocols of 28 pregnant women tested in their last trimester and again a few days postpartum. The women's favorableness of attitude toward their pregnancy was positively and significantly correlated with Barrier but not Penetration score. In addition, there was no change in Barrier score pre- to postpartum, but there was a significant decline in Penetration score.

Taylor, Altman, Wheeler, and Kushner (1969) examined the effect of 8 days of stressful social isolation on a group of 160 male subjects. BP scores were obtained from administration of the HIT prior to and following the confinement, as were MMPI scale scores. The men were confined to a small room either alone or in pairs with no recreational material and given only water, liquid food, and crackers for sustenance. During the experiment, some subjects became uncooperative and disruptive. Although the design and results are too complicated for complete discussion, the major finding of interest here is that the initial Barrier score was significantly higher for the men who successfully coped with the stress without discharging their emotions into the environment by acting out. Barrier score did not change over the experiment, whereas the Penetration score showed a significant decline.

This evidence supports Fisher's (1986) conclusion that "people with well-articulated body image boundaries fare better in threatening situations than do those with poorly defined boundaries" (p. 425).

Psychopathology, Life Adjustment, and Self-Steering Behavior

Schizophrenia has frequently been conceptualized as a failure to maintain adequate boundaries between oneself and the world outside (e.g., Fenichel, 1945). Similarly, but to a lesser degree, delinquent behavior involving inappropriate acting out has been hypothesized to be a failure to contain impulses inside personal boundaries (Fisher, 1970). Numerous studies of schizophrenic persons have utilized the BP scoring system. Interestingly, results generally did not confirm a lack of boundary definiteness (Fisher, 1986).

In contrast, numerous studies did confirm relatively low Barrier scores in male, but not in female, delinquents (see Fisher, 1986, for review). For example, Fisher (1966) used the Rorschach blots to ascertain Barrier scores on 45 normal boys and 46 boys in an educational program for those who had failed to adjust to standard classrooms. Failure to adjust was defined by aggressive and impulsive acting out and significant related academic difficulty. The boys in the special educational program had significantly lower Barrier scores ($p < .01$) than the normal boys.

Similarly, Megargee (1965) used the Holtzman blots to determine Barrier scores from 75 male juvenile delinquents (mean age = 15) in detention. These boys' mean Barrier score was significantly lower than the mean score of two samples ($ns = 197, 72$) of boys from Holtzman et al.'s (1961) norms, $ts = 4.10, 3.44$, respectively, both $p < .001$. The delinquent sample was differentiated into those judged most likely ($n = 28$) and less likely ($n = 44$) to be a serious threat to the community. Barrier scores of the former were significantly lower, $F = 4.72, p < .001$. In addition, counselor ratings of aggressiveness while in custody were correlated with boundary definiteness. Higher Barrier score significantly predicted lower ratings of aggressiveness, $r = .23, p < .05$.

Liebetrau and Pienaar (1974) administered the Rorschach to South African children of four different ages: 6, 8, 10, and 12. There were 10 boys and 10 girls at each age level. BP scores were compared to teacher ratings of good versus poor adjustment. There was no relationship between Barrier score and adjustment at age 6. However, for ages 8, 10, and 12, higher Barrier score was significantly and positively related to better adjustment (penetration scores showed a significant and nonlinear relationship with adjustment ratings). Fisher (1986), consistent with his psychoanalytic theory framework, speculated that this may have been due to the physical and psychological changes related to latency and impending sexual maturation. Today, in an era in psychology with significantly less emphasis on unconscious processes and related assessment methods such as the Rorschach, and an era in psychoanalysis itself in which less emphasis is placed on psychosexual development and much more on object relations, this interpretation may seem distinctly, perhaps surprisingly, Freudian. Of course, in hindsight, other interpretations of these results are possible (see further discussion in the concluding section).

Self-Steering Behavior

Fisher and Cleveland (1968) hypothesized the following:

> Definiteness of boundaries is linked with the ability to be an independent person who has definite standards, definite goals, and forceful, striving ways of approaching tasks. We visualized the person with definite boundaries as one who sought special success in life and as one who could not easily be diverted by stress or obstacles from goal attainment. We pictured boundary definiteness as carrying with it a facility for expressing tension by attacking and shaping the environment to make it conform to the individual's internalized standards. (p. 117)

They termed this stance toward life a "self-steering" orientation, and tested these ideas in a series of studies. Although the term *self-steering* may overlap significantly with descriptors such as "confident" and "assertive," it is distinguished in the context of Fisher and Cleveland's body image theory, and it was the unifying concept leading to a series of empirical studies using the similarly theoretically derived BP Rorschach scoring system. In general, their research (and that of others) confirmed the hypothesis that high-Barrier individuals would be more self-steering. Specifically, they found that individuals with more definite boundaries had higher achievement motivation, set more ambitious goals for themselves, had a greater desire for task completion, were less suggestible, made fewer errors on stressful tasks, and more realistically adjusted to task-performance failure. Interpersonally, they were more likely to communicate with others, and were more interested in careers involving people rather than things (e.g., psychology vs. physics; see Jupp, 1989b). Fisher (1986) summarized the findings to date stating, "These traits, attitudes, and skills turned out to be aspects of even broader organizing configurations that were represented also at the physiological and sensory levels" (p. 338).

One final study and its replication illustrate the predictive power of the body image and body boundary concept as operationalized with the Rorschach Barrier score. Fisher (1970, 1986) conceived of the body boundary as a psychological medium through which stimuli from the environment passed, as a boundary for "modulating contact with the world" (1986, p. vii). Individuals with a highly differentiated boundary were thought to be acutely receptive to stimuli from the environment, and to perceive input more vividly than individuals with indefinite boundaries.

Fisher (1970) employed the Ames Thereness and Thatness Table (T-T; Kilpatrick, 1952) to assess how vivid a picture appeared to the subjects. The T-T apparatus has two side-by-side viewing tunnels. It allows subjects to regulate the apparent distance of a projected image inside one tunnel of the apparatus in relationship to selected sites in the other tunnel. The tunnel with the projected image contains no cues for size or distance and subjects are actually and unwittingly manipulating the size of the projected image as they apparently move it back and forth in space. Previous work by Hastorf (1950) "demonstrated that a picture presented in the T-T apparatus which is more vivid than another requires a smaller or 'further away' setting in order to be lined up with a spatial reference point. The less vivid a picture the greater the 'magnification' it requires in order to match the standard of how one would expect it to look at a given distance" (Fisher, 1970, p. 237).

In his first study, Fisher (1970) had 70 male college students as subjects (mean age = 20). In the second study, he had 39 female college students (mean age = 20). The Rorschach inkblots were used to collect protocols for generating Barrier scores. The experimental procedures were identical except that different pictures were used as stimuli. Fisher hypothesized that "the more definite an individual's boundaries the more intense the picture would appear to him and therefore the greater the likelihood he would place it so as to reduce its apparent size" (p. 237).

Results were as predicted. In the first sample, there was a significant relationship between boundary definiteness and picture size. The same results were obtained with the second sample. Fisher (1970) concluded:

> Apparently, the stimulus does "pass through" the boundary and is affected by the process .... With increasing boundary delineation, there is a demonstrated greater interest in communication and readiness to invest energy in perceptual receptivity. This orientation imparts increased subjective intensity to experience .... Perhaps degree of perceptual vividness contributes to how lively, stimulating, and interesting the "outer world" appears. (p. 239)

Like Freud (1923/1953), Fisher and Cleveland (1968) were fascinated with the relationships among the individual's body, psychology, and "life building operations" (p. 56). Again like Freud, they used clinical observations of patients as the foundation for a body-based theory of human functioning. Indeed, they used the empirical tools psychologists had developed to take psychodynamic, body-based hypotheses from the couch and armchair of the consulting room into the laboratory. Their central resources were intelligent curiosity about people, a commitment to scientific methodology, and a set of ten cards with various inkblots, the Rorschach Inkblot Technique.

With determination and remarkable creativity, Fisher and Cleveland (1958, 1968) and Fisher (1970, 1986) took their awareness of the significance of differences in Rorschach percepts, translated those differences into a unique method for scoring the Rorschach, and invested a significant portion of their lives in exploring their meaning. As a result, they demonstrated the utility of their BP Rorschach scoring system in contributing a more differentiated and integrated understanding of human psychological functioning and its relationship to quantified experience at the body boundary.

Along the way, they showed that the BP Rorschach scoring system was reliable. They showed that the BP scoring system produced essentially equivalent results with the Rorschach and HIT, independently supportive of the validity of the BP scale. Specifically, they demonstrated that their body image theory, as operationalized with the BP scoring system and the Rorschach (as well as the HIT), could be uniquely useful in predicting across a broad array of areas of human functioning, including pregnancy reactions, psychosomatic symptoms, physiological reactivity and awareness, delinquent behavior, ambition, suggestibility, response to stress and failure, response to career choice, interest in communication, and perceptual vividness (see Fisher, 1986, for review).

Obviously, Fisher and Cleveland (1958, 1968) and Fisher and colleagues (see, e. g., Fisher & Greenberg, 1996) used a psychoanalytic framework to conceptualize much BP (and other) research. Developments in other areas of psychology in the period since Fisher's (1986) review might form the basis for equally, and perhaps even more plausible, explanations of some BP results. For example, some BP findings may reflect differences in cognitive style between two groups, or they might reflect psychopathology differences unrelated (or tangentially related) to psychodynamics. In this same vein, a renewed look at the Penetration score may prove fruitful; examination of the BP scoring criteria related to damage and destruction (see Appendix A) shows considerable overlap with Exner's (1993) criteria for a "Morbid" designation, which forms part of his index for depressive experience and his suicide constellation. More recently available statistical techniques may help in differentiating those aspects of the BP score consistent with Fisher and Cleveland's (1968) body image theory and those more related to depression and other factors (see, e.g., Jupp, 1989a, 1989b).

Similarly, a combination of the BP scoring system with structural aspects of Rorschach scoring may be useful. For example, this might help in differentiating Penetration responses indicative of poorly differentiated boundaries from those indicating a boundary that is appropriately permeable to exchanging information with the environment. In this regard, a reformulation and integration of BP results in the context of recent systems theory may be useful. For example, Agazarian's (1997, 2001) theory of living human systems conceptualizes the survival, development, and transformation of human systems, and system capacity to master the environment, from the perspective of transactions across more or less appropriately permeable boundaries. Reconceptualizing BP results from this perspective may afford theoreticians and researchers new avenues for understanding and investigation that could take BP and the Rorschach from an emphasis on the individual, to a theory placing the individual more in the context of a hierarchy of mutually influencing systems. An intriguing example is Armstrong and Tan's (1978) Barrier score research using individually collected Rorschach protocols on the Senoi Aboriginal people living among the Malaysian population. Armstrong and Tan found the Senoi had, as predicted by Fisher and Cleveland (1968), relatively high Barrier scores (in comparison with other cultures with less warm, caring, and physically affirming childrearing practices). The researchers also determined mean Barrier scores on their three subgroups of the Senoi aborigines composed of individuals from villages classified as: " 'roadside,' 'fringe,' 'deep jungle' " (Armstrong & Tan, p. 167) by the Malaysian government. The researchers used these subgroup classifications as "a convenient, if rough, index of 'assimilation' or degree of exposure to the heterogenous value system existing in the larger Malaysian cultured milieu" (Armstrong & Tan, p. 167). The deep jungle subgroup was very isolated geographically and had almost no communication with the more urban Malaysian culture; the fringe group was closer and had limited contact; and the roadside subgroup lived closer still. Armstrong and Tan found that Barrier score was significantly context dependent, that is, the Barrier score for the most isolated group was the highest, the limited contact group had a somewhat lower Barrier score, and the third group with the most communication with the urbanized environment had the lowest Barrier score. Fisher and Cleveland found similar results with Japanese men living in Japan and in America. Putting such results in a systems theory context might help further determine how Rorschach responses reflect the state of individuals' environmental context (Masling, 1960), as well as their more enduring individual psychodynamics and other psychological structures. Perhaps psychological functioning reflects the quality of communication transactions across the boundaries of mutually influencing systems, and the degree of difference between the two systems, more than the initial state of the systems within their respective boundaries. Schizophrenia research demonstrating that the emergence of schizophrenic behavior from genetically susceptible children is less dependent on genetics than on the presence of parental "communication deviance" (Wahlberg et al., 1997, p. 355), as measured by the Rorschach, supports this notion. So does their finding (Singer, Wynne, & Toohey, 1978; Wahlberg et al.) that a healthy adoptive-parent communication pattern results in less thought disorder in the genetically at-risk children than in comparison control subjects living in a family context of deviant communication. Spigelman and Spigelman's (1991) BP research with children of divorced versus intact families is also relevant here. They demonstrated that children of intact families had higher Barrier scores and lower Penetration scores than children of divorced families. In addition, in divorced families, Barrier scores were related to the quality of boys' (but not girls') relationship with their noncustodial father. Perhaps systems theory (e.g., Agazarian, 1997), as recently integrated with object relations and attachment theory (McCluskey, 2002), could help determine ways to generate familial and cultural environments that would facilitate the development of highly differentiated, appropriately permeable boundaries, as assessed by BP and otherwise.

Of course, as with all psychological research, there are limitations to the accumulated BP Rorschach scoring system data. For example, some BP studies cited by Fisher (1986), primarily doctoral dissertations, were not published in refereed journals; statistical analyses were sometimes relatively unsophisticated by today's standards; the extant research contains limited behavioral validity data; researchers often used different systems (e.g., using Rorschach protocols obtained with standardized research administration and specified response total vs. archival Rorschach protocols with a post hoc response total limit; Exner's administration procedure vs. others; individual vs. group administration; Rorschach vs. HIT) for determining BP scores, thus making it difficult to compare results with certainty. However, hopefully this chapter, although presenting a selective rather than comprehensive examination of the BP research, is sufficient to stimulate further interest in an area of Rorschach and body image research that still has great untapped potential.

REFERENCES

Agazarian, Y. M. (1997). *Systems-centered therapy for groups.* New York: Guilford Press.

Agazarian, Y. M. (2001). *A systems-centered approach to inpatient group psychotherapy.* London: Kingsley.

Appleby, L. (1956). *The relationship of a Rorschach barrier typology to other behavioral measures.* Unpublished doctoral dissertation, University of Houston, TX.

Armstrong, H. E., Jr. (1968). Relationship between a dimension of body image and two measures of conditioning. *Journal of Consulting and Clinical Psychology, 32,* 696–700.

Armstrong, H. E., Jr., & Tan, E. K. (1978). Body-image Barrier perception as a function of assimilation within the Malaysian Aborigines. *Journal of Social Psychology, 105,* 165–173.

Blumetti, A. E., & Modesti, L. M. (1976). Psychological predictors of success or failure of surgical intervention for intractable back pain. In J. J. Bonica & D. Albe-Fessard (Eds.), *Advances in Pain Research and Therapy* (Vol. 1, pp. 323–325). New York: Raven Press.

Bornstein, R. F. (2002). A process dissociation approach to objective-projective test score interrelationships. *Journal of Personality Assessment, 78,* 47–68.

Cleveland, S. E., & Fisher, S. (1954). Behavior and unconscious fantasies of patients with rheumatoid arthritis. *Psychosomatic Medicine, 16,* 327–333.

Cleveland, S. E., Reitman, E. E., & Brewer, E. J., Jr. (1965). Psychological factors in juvenile rheumatoid arthritis. *Arthritis and Rheumatism, 8,* 1152–1158.

Cleveland, S. E., Snyder, R., & Williams, R. L. (1965). Body image and site of psychosomatic symptoms. *Psychological Reports, 16,* 851–852.

Cloete, N. (1978). Autonomic responsivity of high and low body boundary subjects during a reaction time task. *Journal of Behavioral Science, 2,* 319–325.

Cloete, N. (1979). Autonomic responsivity of subjects with body boundary differences: White noise stimulation. *ACTA Psychological, 43,* 177–183.

Colvin, C. (1977). *Barrier-Penetration scores in latency aged individuals.* Unpublished master's thesis, California School of Professional Psychology, San Francisco.

Dorsey, D. S. (1965). *A study of the relationship between independence of group pressure and selected measures of body image.* Unpublished doctoral dissertation, University of California, Los Angeles.

Exner, J. E., Jr. (1993). *The Rorschach: A comprehensive system: Vol. 1. Basic foundations* (3rd ed.). New York: Wiley.

Farmer, R. G., & Wright, J. M. C. (1971). Muscular reactivity and systematic desensitization. *Behavior Therapy, 2,* 1–10.

Fenichel, O. (1945). *The psychoanalytic theory of neurosis.* New York: Norton.

Fisher, R. L. (1966). Failure of the Conceptual Styles Test to discriminate normal and highly impulsive children. *Journal of Abnormal Psychology, 71,* 429–431.

Fisher, S. (1959). Body image boundaries in the aged. *Journal of Psychology, 48,* 315–318.

Fisher, S. (1970). *Body experience in fantasy and behavior.* New York: Appleton-Century-Crofts.

Fisher, S. (1986). *Development and structure of the body image* (2 vols.). Hillsdale, NJ: Lawrence Erlbaum Associates.

Fisher, S., & Bialos, D. (1970). Barrier score gynecological examination. Unpublished raw data.

Fisher, S., & Cleveland, S. (1955). The role of body image in psychosomatic symptom choice. *Psychological Monographs, 68,* No. 17.

Fisher, S., & Cleveland, S. (1958). *Body image and personality.* New York: Van Nostrand.

Fisher, S., & Cleveland, S. (1960). A comparison of psychological characteristics and physiological reactivity in ulcer and rheumatoid arthritis groups II. Difference in physiological reactivity. *Psychosomatic Medicine, 22,* 290–293.

Fisher, S., & Cleveland, S. (1968). *Body image and personality* (2nd ed.). New York: Dover.

Fisher, S., & Greenberg, R. P. (1996). *Freud scientifically reappraised: Testing the theories and therapy.* New York: Wiley.

Freud, S. (1953). The ego and the id. In J. Strachey (Ed. & Trans.), *The standard edition of the complete psychological works of Sigmund Freud* (Vol. 19, pp. 3–66). London: Hogarth Press. (Original work published 1923)

Hartley, R. B. (1964). *A homonym word association measure of the barrier variable and its comparison with the inkblot barrier measure.* Unpublished dissertation, University of Washington, Seattle.

Hastorf, A. H. (1950). The influence of suggestion on the relationship between stimulus size and perceived distance. *Journal of Psychology, 29,* 195–217.

Hayslip, B., Cooper, C., Dougherty, L., & Cook, D. (1997). Body image in adulthood: A projective approach. *Journal of Personality Assessment, 68,* 628–649.

Hirt, M., Ross, W. D., & Kurtz, R. (1967). Construct validity of body-boundary perception. In E. Mallinoff (Ed.), *Proceedings of the 75th Annual Convention of the American Psychological Association* (pp. 187–188). Washington, DC: American Psychological Association.

Holtzman, W. H., Thorpe, J. S., Swartz, J. D., & Herron, E. W. (1961). *Inkblot perception and personality.* Austin: University of Texas Press.

Jacobson, G. R. (1966). Effect of brief sensory deprivation on field dependence. *Journal of Abnormal Psychology, 71,* 115–118.

Jung, C. J. (1944). *Psychology and alchemy.* New York: Pantheon Books.

Jupp, J. J. (1989a). Fisher and Cleveland barrier and penetration scores: Correlations with Rorschach category scores (Pt. 1). *Perceptual and Motor Skills, 69,* 1011–1018.

Jupp, J. J. (1989b). Fisher and Cleveland barrier and penetration body-image scores, self-steering style, and academic achievement (Pt. 2). *Psychological Reports, 64,* 1075–1081.

Kilpatrick, F. P. (Ed.). (1952). *Human behavior from the transactional point of view.* Hanover, NH: Institute for Associated Research.

Koschene, R. L. (1965). *Body image and boundary constancy in kidney transplant patients: A test of the Fisher-Cleveland hypotheses.* Unpublished master's thesis, University of Colorado, Boulder.

Liebetrau, C. E., & Pienaar, W. D. (1974). The relation between adjustment and body image at various age levels. *Journal of Personality Assessment, 38,* 230–233.

Masling, J. M. (1960). The influence of situational and interpersonal variables in projective testing. *Psychological Bulletin, 57,* 65–85.

Masling, J. M. (1986). Orality, pathology, and interpersonal behavior. In J. M. Masling (Ed.), *Empirical studies of psychoanalytic theories* (Vol. 2, pp. 73–106). Hillsdale, NJ: Lawrence Erlbaum Associates.

Mattsson, A., Gross, S., & Hall, T. W. (1971). Psychoendocrine study of adaptation in young hemophiliacs. *Psychosomatic Medicine, 33,* 215–225.

McCluskey, U. (2002). The dynamics of attachment and systems-centered group psychotherapy. *Group Dynamics: Theory, Research, and Practice, 6,* 131–142.

McConnell, O. L., & Daston, P. G. (1961). Body image changes in pregnancy. *Journal of Projective Techniques, 25,* 451–456.

Megargee, E. I. (1965). Relation between Barrier scores and aggressive behavior. *Journal of Abnormal Psychology, 70,* 307–311.

Nichols, D. C., & Tursky, B. (1967). Body image, anxiety, and tolerance for experimental pain. *Psychosomatic Medicine, 29,* 103–110.

Osofsky, H., & Fisher, S. (1967). Psychological correlates of the development of amenorrhea in a stress situation. *Psychosomatic Medicine, 29,* 15–23.

Reich, W. (1949). *Character analysis.* New York: Orgone Institute.

Shipman, W. G. , Oken, D., Grinker, R. R., Goldstein, I. B., & Heath, H. A. (1964). A study in the psychophysiology of muscle tension: II. Emotional factors. *Archives of General Psychiatry, 11,* 330–345.

Singer, M. T., Wynne, L. C., & Toohey, M. L. (1978). Communication disorders and the families of schizophrenics. In L. C. Wynne, R. Cromwell, & S. Matthysse (Eds.), *The nature of schizophrenia: New approaches to research and treatment* (pp. 499–511). New York: Wiley.

Spigelman, A., & Spigelman, G. (1991). The relationship between parental divorce and the child's body boundary definiteness. *Journal of Personality Assessment, 56,* 96–105.

Swartz, J. D. (1965). Performance of high- and low-anxious children on the Holtzman Inkblot Technique. *Child Development, 36,* 569–575.

Taylor, D. A., Altman, I., Wheeler, L., & Kushner, E. N. (1969). Personality factors related to response to social isolation and confinement. *Journal of Consulting and Clinical Psychology, 33,* 411–419.

Wahlberg, K. E., Wynne, L. C., Oja, H., Keskitalo, P., Pykäläinen, L., Lahti, I., et al. (1997). Gene-environment interaction in vulnerability to schizophrenia: Findings from the Finnish adoptive family study of schizophrenia. *American Journal of Psychiatry, 154,* 355–361.

Ware, K., Fisher, S., & Cleveland, S. (1957). Body image boundaries and adjustment to poliomyelitis. *Journal of Abnormal and Social Psychology, 55,* 88–93.

Witkin, H. A., Lewis, H. B., Hertzman, M., Machover, K., Meissner, P. B., & Wapner, S. (1954). *Personality through perception.* New York: Harper.

Zennaro, A., & Lis, A. (1996). Fisher and Cleveland Barrier and Penetration scores: Analysis of some psychometric aspects for a normal Italian adult sample. *Perceptual and Motor Skills, 82,* 531–543.

Appendix A[4]
Barrier and Penetration Scoring[5]

CRITERIA FOR BARRIER SCORING

1. All references to clothing, whether mentioned as separate articles (e.g., dress, girdle, sweater); described as worn by a person (e.g., He has a tie on); or indirectly referred to (e.g., There are pleats; It has a pocket).

This category embraces all forms of jewelry and body adornment (e.g., earrings, bracelet, comb in her hair, ring, wig, false eyelashes). It does not include special hairdos, beards, or long hair.

It pertains to all forms of body protection and camouflage, for example, gas mask, armor, helmet, umbrella, shield, mask, halo, catcher's mask, disguise, false nose, cast, arm sling, bandage, sheet (wrapped around), veil.

It includes all mechanical attachments to the body (e.g., glasses, hearing aid, wax wings, scuba tank, flippers, skates, skis, badge).

2. All references to buildings and similar enclosing structures. Examples are:

arch	closet	merry-go-round	store
barracks	cottage	mine	subway
basement	fence (also hedges)	mineshaft	tent
bomb shelter	hall	monument	tower
bridge	house	porch	tunnel
catwalk	hut	shelter	warehouse
church	kitchen	skyscraper	

It embraces images that indirectly connote the existence of such structures (e.g., city, metropolis, village, town, colony, airport).

Also, it includes parts of buildings and structures (e.g., chimney, roof, stairway, walls, ceiling) and adornments within or on them (e.g., gargoyles, door knockers, wallpaper).

Furthermore, it involves structures that delimit or organize an area (e.g., road, sidewalk, street, curb, alley, playground, backyard, football field).

---

[4]From *Body Experience in Fantasy and Behavior* (pp. 605–609), by S. Fisher, 1970, New York: Appleton-Century-Crofts. Copyright © 1970 by Ardent Media. Reprinted with permission.

[5]This scoring scheme differs from that first published in Fisher and Cleveland (1958) insofar as it includes all references to clothing, buildings, and vehicles instead of selected instances of such classes. It also includes popular responses previously omitted. In addition, it includes all masks. These changes have been made to simplify scoring by reducing the number of exceptions. Correlations between scores based on the old and the new, more simplified criteria are on the order of .98.

3. All references to vehicles with some containing or "holding" qualities. Examples are:

airplane	boat	motorcycle	ski lift	wagon
automobile	elevator	rocket ship	sled	
bicycle	magic carpet	scooter	train	

4. All references to that which contains, covers, or conceals. This may be subdivided into the following categories:

Container (or container-like shapes); examples are:

anthill	box	freezer	pouch
bag	bubble	glass	radio
bagpipes	cage	globe	sheath
ball	candleholder	hammock	spoon
balloon	chair	lamp	stove
bed	couch	nest	tank
beehive	cup	net	throne
bell	dish	oil well	toaster
billfold	drawer	pillow	trap
book	envelope	pipe	TV set
bookends	flask	pocketbook	vat
bottle	folder	pot	well

Includes living things with special container qualities (e.g., pregnant woman, kangaroo, camel).

Coverings; examples are:

bear rug	mountain with snow on it
blanket	moss on a log
rug	bowl overgrown by a plant
tablecloth	donkey with load covering his back

Concealment; includes references to hiding or being in a concealed position. Also includes references to objects with concealing functions. Examples are:

behind a rock	peeking out	shutters
behind a tree	screen	smoke screen
curtains	shades	

5. All living things (except human) described as having special surface qualities (e.g., fuzzy, rough, hard, smooth, striped, spotted, bristly, feathered, long-haired). Does not include references to the surface being light, dark, or possessed of specific hues (e.g., red, yellow).

This category also embraces a series of animals, in the following list, considered to possess distinctive or unusual skins.

alligator	goat	mountain goat	Siamese cat
badger	hippo	peacock	skunk
beaver	hyena	penguin	tiger
bobcat	leopard	porcupine	walrus
buffalo	lion	prairie dog	weasel
chameleon	lizard	rhinoceros	wildcat
coyote	lynx	sea lion	wolverine
crocodile	mink	seal	zebra
fox	mole	sheep	lamb

(These animals are scored Barrier only if more than the head is seen.)

6. All creatures possessed of shells or similar protective structures (e.g., snail, lobster, shrimp, clam, oyster, mussel, bug with shell, crab, cactus, scorpion, turtle).

7. All references to geographic or natural formations with delimiting or container-like qualities. Examples are:

abyss	harbor	river
banks of river	island	spring
canal	lake	valley
cave	pathway in woods	volcano
	ravine	

When scoring a record, give credit of 1 to each response that contains any of the previous images, but no more than 1 credit can be assigned to any given response, no matter how many Barrier images it contains.

CRITERIA FOR PENETRATION SCORING[6]

Score the following for Penetration:

1. All references to the fact of disruption, penetration, damage, or destruction of any object or living thing. Examples are:

amputated arm	man being shot
autopsy	man sick
body cut open	man wasted away

[6]This scoring scheme is a revised version of that published in Fisher and Cleveland (1958). The intent was to simplify scoring by eliminating a few instances in which special exceptions were made to general categories. Scores derived from the old criteria correlate on the order of .98 with scores based on the new simplified criteria.

bombed building
bullet entering flesh
cancer
deteriorated old house
diseased flesh
diseased flower
dog run over
hurt
house burning
killed
killing woman
operating on patient
saw cutting wood
scar
squashed bug
stabbing a person
tooth pulled
torn muscle
ulcer
wilted flower
worn out shirt
wound bleeding
wounded

(Includes instances of body distortion exemplified by responses like cripple, hunchback, paralyzed, cross-eyed, midget, blind, and deaf.)

2. All references to body openings or to acts involving body openings. Examples are:

anus
being born
bite
chew
chicken pecking
defecating
drink
eat
looking down someone's throat
mouth (separately)
nostril (separately)
spitting
stick tongue out
vagina
vomiting
yawn

(Do not score references to singing, talking, or making sounds.)

3. All references to perceptions that involve a perspective of bypassing or evading the usual boundaries of the body or other objects. Examples are:

can see through it
cross-section of an organ
fluoroscope of chest
inside of body
transparent gown
x-ray

("Inside of body" does not include references to the inside of objects that can ordinarily be entered without disrupting the boundaries, e.g., inside of house, inside of flower.)

4. All references to the process of entering or leaving structures and also the means for doing so. Examples are:

came out the window
climbed out the chimney
exit
jet exhaust

door	rocket exhaust
doorway	smoke coming out of a pipe
entrance	walked through the door
	window

5. All references to natural contexts that involve intake or expulsion. Examples are:

geyser
oil spurting out of ground
volcano erupting

6. All images that are insubstantial or vague in their delimitation. Examples are:

ghost shadow spirit

Each response that contains one or more Penetration images is given a value of 1. No more than a credit of 1 can be assigned by any response, no matter how many Penetration images it contains.

Appendix B[7]
Normal College Student

A 23 year old, single college student who was in his junior year and majoring in economics. This is a Rorschach record obtained in a group setting and with the number of responses per card specified by the examiner in order to result in a consistent total of 24 responses. No formal inquiry is conducted, but each subject is asked to describe each response as fully and in as much detail as he can. It will be noted that this record furnishes fantasies which are as rich, complex, and varied as those obtained in individual records.

Responses	Scoring
I.	
1. A decaying moth.	1. Penetration, because of the degeneration of the object.
2. A winged horse walking beside a reflection pool.	2. Score "pool" for Barrier as an enclosed space.
3. Skull bone of a prehistoric animal.	3.

[7]From *Body Image and Personality* (pp. 395–397, 409–411), by S. Fisher and S. E. Cleveland, 1968, New York: Dover. Copyright © 1968 by Dover. Reprinted with permission.

II.

4. Two red-haired girls playing patty-cake.	4.
5. Two bloody animal skins.	5. Score for Penetration the "bloody skins" which indicate damage to the body wall.
6. A Douglas skyray about to fly into a cloud.	6. Not scored for Barrier as the object is not seen as covered or hidden, but only potentially so.

III.

7. Two gnomes stirring a kettle.	7. A Barrier response as a container.
8. Design on a Grecian vase.	8. Could be scored Barrier both for the decorative design as well as for container. But only one score given for any one response.
9. Fluoroscope of a whirlpool.	9. Score for Penetration, as all X- rays are so scored. The "whirlpool" would not be scored as Barrier because it does not clearly refer to an enclosed "pool" area.

IV.

10. A worm's-eye view of a gorilla.	10.
11. Two women leaning back to back against a post.	11.

V.

12. Two snails.	12. Score for Barrier hard-shell animal.
13. Two bearded men's heads leaning against each other.	13. Beards are not scored for Barrier.

VI.

14. A modernistic Christmas tree.	14. Not scored for Barrier as there is not enough detail. If the tree were described as decorated, then a Barrier score would be assigned.
15. A bear rug attached to a totem pole.	15.

VII.

16. Two women in 18-century costumes back to back, looking over their shoulders at each other.	16. Score all costumes for Barrier.
17. Bust of Napoleon.	17.

VIII.

18. Form of some kind of shellfish.	18. Score all reference to shell for Barrier.
19. Portion of human breastbone.	19.
20. Two seahorses back to back and upside down.	20. Not included in the list of animals to be scored Barrier.

IX.

21. Two pot-bellied gnomes or witches facing each other and laughing, shaking their fingers.	21. The incidental reference to "pot-bellied" is not scored as Barrier, despite the pot connotation of the reference.
22. An A-bomb test.	22. Simply explosions, or A-bomb, are not scored Penetration. If reference is made to something being broken or burst by the explosion, a scoring for Penetration would be indicated.

X.

23. Eiffel Tower.	23. Towers are not scored as Barrier.[8]
24. A cowboy wearing chaps.	24. Score "chaps" for Barrier as protective and decorative covering.

Total Barrier Score = 7

Total Penetration Score = 3

[8]Since 1958 all references to buildings and related structures are scored Barrier.

Duodenal Ulcer

A 25-year-old, single, white male college student, who had had ulcers of five years' duration. Persistent nausea and vomiting were present as secondary symptoms.

Free Association	Inquiry	Scoring
I.		
1. Form of a woman.	1. Hips down.	1.
2. Head of a man.	2. Profile, has a hat on his head, a grass hat like Chinese coolies wear.	2. Score for Barrier an unusual article of clothing ("a grass hat").
3. Someone standing near the windows of a building.	3. Like a picture frame, a window.	3. Double scoring: A frame is an enclosed space and is scored for Barrier. A window is an opening and is scored for Penetration.
II.		
4. Two roosters fighting.	4. Red is feathers falling off.	4. Score for penetration because part of the body wall is falling apart.
5. Vagina.	5. See the lips and opening.	5. Penetration response, a body orifice.
6. Two people lying down, one a woman on one side, a man on the other.	6. Both asleep or dead.	6.

III.		
7. Two people trying to pull aside a chest of a person.	7. Pulling apart a chest.	7. Penetration, because part of the body is being split open.
8. Lungs.	8. They pulled the chest apart and there are the lungs.	8.
IV.		
9. Hideous-looking thing, a booger man, a nightmare.	9. Grotesque head.	9.
10. Face, funny face, big mouth open	10. Porky Pig.	10. Penetration: body opening.
V.		
12. A bat.	12. Shape of one.	12.
13. Face of the devil.	13. Horns.	13.
VI.		
14. A stream of water.	14. A river, a deep stream.	14. Score for Barrier: an enclosed space.
15. Beak of a reptile with open mouth.	15. Just the head.	15. Penetration: a body opening
VII.		
16. Vagina again.	16. See the slit.	16. Penetration: a body opening.
17. Another picture of the devil.	17. Horns.	17.
VIII.		
18. Face of a Buddha.	18. Profile.	18.
19. Vertebra of a person.	19. Ribs.	19.

IX.

20. Ugly old face.	20. Deformed, crooked nose. Something dangles from his nose. Maybe he swallowed something.	20. Score for Penetration, because of the use of the term "deformed" and because there is a reference to something which is penetrating into the body via the nose.
21. Another man, no eyes, all sunk in where eyes should be.	21. A devil with no horns. The eyes are gone or sunk in.	21. Score for Penetration, surface of the body is broken and degenerated ("eyes gone").

X.

22. A grasshopper.	22. Green.	22.
23. Insects and two bees.	23. Yellow bees.	23.

Total Barrier Score = 3
Total Penetration Score = 10

7

The Pripro Scoring System

Robert R. Holt
New York University

When David Rapaport taught me how to use the Rorschach, as part of a set of tests used in psychodiagnosis, he stressed from the beginning the need to form interpretations on a theory-based psychological understanding of how the responses come into being. It was simple enough: All behavior is caused by many aspects of the behaving person's personality, from biology to life situation and cultural embeddedness. Reading the implied equations backwards therefore yielded interpretation.

Therefore, when Bruno Klopfer asked me to contribute a chapter on theory to the revision of his first book (Klopfer & Kelley, 1942), I naturally approached it by asking not "What do various theories of personality imply about the meaning of M responses?" (or of W, etc.), but "How do the available theories help us understand the process of responding to inkblots?" One of the first fruits of that inquiry was my discovery that various psychoanalytic propositions and concepts directly suggested ways they could be seen in Rorschach responses. The end result was my starting down a 50-year road of deepened understanding of theoretical psychoanalysis, especially Freud's (1900/1953) theory of thinking, and translating what he said about the primary process into a scoring system. The most important advance began when I grasped the practical significance of the distinction between pathological emergence of primary process thinking and its appearance in playful, humorous, and creative thought. Shortening Kris's (1952) term "regression in the service of the ego" to adaptive (vs. maladaptive) regression, I found scorable indications of controlling and defensive operations that made the difference.

Another of Rapaport's teachings had a profound and lasting effect on me. He pointed out the ways in which diagnostic testing, rigorously done, was like the scientific method. You get a hunch on the basis of some observation, perhaps the way a person verbalizes what he or she sees in an inkblot: that is merely a hypothesis, which must be tested, and supported or refuted by new, independent data. In large part, he told us (his students), the content of responses is independent of their location and determinants; but better yet, one can and should test hypotheses from the Rorschach on the other tests in the battery, and finally on the independent clinical observations of other members of a mental health team (if you are lucky enough to be working with one, as we were in Topeka).

Nothing happened in the subsequent decades to shake my conviction that being a sensitive, intuitive clinician is *not* incompatible with being a rigorous scientist. Indeed, I continue to believe that one of the great things about the profession of clinical psychology is that you can use many facets of your own personality and abilities. Accordingly, I have devoted most of my career to the project of analyzing and understanding how good clinicians work, to find ways of teaching and of improving such work. The hypotheses suggested by this kind of work directly suggest propositions testable by research, an undertaking that has occupied most of my subsequent working time.

One more bit of personal history is relevant. Before becoming a clinical psychologist, for several years I worked in public opinion research with such masters of *content analysis* as Rensis Likert and Dorwin Cartwright. In the government agency where we tried to find out how to make federal policies work better by interviewing the people they directly impacted, I learned the art and science of working with verbatim texts of free interviews: devising scoring categories, training technicians to code them to a satisfactory level of reliability, and working with quantitative analyses of these qualitative data. Moreover, the interviewees were carefully chosen to be stratified random samples of populations about which we wanted to generalize. I have rarely been able to work with such samples of people since, but it gave me a healthy respect for the limitations on generalizations that can be drawn from results with available subjects.

The primary process scoring scheme, then, is a kind of content analysis in that sense, not in the more limited meaning it has in the Rorschach literature. Much as I dislike jargon, it is so much more convenient to use a neologism (a sort of condensation of primary and process), *pripro*, for my system that I will use it here, with apologies. The scoring scheme is regrettably too long and complex to present here in full (see Holt, 2005), but in order to talk about its claims to your interest I begin with a brief summary of what it is and how it is used, followed by a brief sample of the full text.

OVERVIEW OF PRIPRO SCORING

Content Scores

In several places, Freud (1900/1953, 1911/1958, 1915/1957) implied that the kind of thinking he called "primary process" is *wishful* or "drive-dominated," for example, by saying (though never explicitly) that it is organized by the pleasure principle. Following the classical Freudian theory of motivation (or dual instinct theory), I made this assumption: Whenever a person looks at a meaningless inkblot and sees in it images of temptation, engagement, or consequences of libidinal or aggressive types, that can be taken as indicating an emergence of primary process into conscious cognition, even though Freud usually spoke as if it were mainly unconscious. It was a simple matter to look for signs of the various subdivisions of the libidinal (sometimes called "partial drives"): oral, anal, exhibitionistic-voyeuristic, and phallic-genital. Not being able to differentiate the last into the less and more mature types, I combined them as "sexual." It seemed easy and interesting to distinguish clearly homosexual responses from the others. There remained a group of minor and less frequent, more or libidinally tinged interests, combined as miscellaneous. Guided by the seemingly natural divisions in the data rather than theory, which gave little guidance in the realm of aggression, I distinguished among responses featuring aggressors, victims, and the aftermath or results of aggression. There remained one obvious group of images involving both orality and aggression, which I originally lumped with oral-receptive types in a general Oral category. As time went on, I began to realize that both the behavior of these responses and their implications argued for listing them among the types of aggression. (A list of all scores is given in Fig. 7.1.)

I soon noticed that within any of the just-mentioned realms could be found a range of subtypes differing in blatancy, directness of implied gratification, focus on the most involved part of the anatomy, or degree of social acceptability in ordinary discourse. At first I merely split each type into a more and a less primary (blatant, uncontrolled, primitive, etc.), which I called Levels 1 and 2, the former being assumedly closer to primary, the latter to secondary process.

To make this condensed description more intelligible, an unabridged excerpt from the manual (Holt, 2004), dealing with four types of oral material is provided in the Appendix.

Formal Scores

Most of the time, when Freud (1900/1953) talked about the primary process, he emphasized its strangeness, its deviation from acceptable

Content

Libidinal

L 1 O (oral)
L 1 A (anal)
L 1 S (sexual)
L 1 E-V (exhibitionistic-voyeuristic)
L 1 H (homosexual)
L 1 M (miscellaneous libidinal)
L 2 O (oral)
L 2 A (anal)
L 2 S (sexual)
L 2 E-V (exhibitionistic-voyeuristic)
L 2 H (homosexual)
L 2 M (miscellaneous)

Aggressive

Ag 1 A (attack)
Ag 1 O (oral aggression)
Ag 1 V (victim)
Ag 1 R (results)
Ag 2 A (attack)
Ag 2 O (oral aggression)
Ag 2 V (victim)
Ag 2 R (results)

Formal Variables

Condensation

C-ctm 1 (contamination)
C-ctgn 1 (contagion)
C-int 1 (interpenetration)
C-co 1 (composition, idiosyncratic)
C-co 2 (composition, socially accepted)
C-a-c 2 (arbitrary combination)
C-arb 1 (arbitrary color)
C-arb 2 (inappropriate color)

Displacement

D-chain 1 (chain association)
D-dist 1 (distant association)
D-clang 1 (clang association)
D-clang 2 (puns etc.)
D-fig 2 (figures of speech)
D-time 2 (anachronism)
D S 2 (slips)

Symbolism

Sym-C 1 (color symbolism, idiosyncratic)
Sym-C 2 (conventional)
Sym-S 1 (spatial)
Sym-I 1 (image, idiosyncratic)
Sym-I 2 (image, conventional)

Contradiction

Ctr A 1 (affective)
Ctr L 1 (logical)
Ctr R 1 (of reality)
Ctr R 2 (impossible/inappropriate activities/attributes)

Distortions (*miscellaneous*)

Au Lg 1 (autistic logic)
Hal 1 (hallucination)
M L 1 (memory loosening)
Intr 1 (irrelevant intrusions)
Impr 2 (impressionistic response)
Do 2 (fragmentation)
Un Rel 1 (unreal relationship)
Trans 1 (fluid transformation)
S-R 1 (self-reference)
Au El 1 (autistic elaboration)
Au El 2 (fabulation)
F-msc 1 (perseveration; literalism; physiognomic)
F-msc 2 (other)

Verbalizations

V I 1 (incoherence)
V C 1 (condensation)
V Q 1 (queerness)
V P 2 (peculiarity)

Controls and Defenses

Remoteness

R-min (minimal)
R-eth (ethnic)
R-an (animals, most)
R-(an) (animals, ego-alien)
R-pl (plants)
R-ia (inanimate)
R-dep+ (depictions)
R-geo+ (geographic)
R-time+ (in time)
R-time (less appropriate)
R-char (character)
R-fic s+ (fictional, specific, appropropriate)
R-fic s; s– (fictional, indifferent; bad)
R-fic n+ (nonspecific, good)
R-fic n; n– (nonspecific; indifferent/bad)

R-rel+ (religious, good)
R-rel; – (indifferent; bad)
R-fan+ (fantasy, good)
R-fan; – (indifferent; bad)
R-fig+ (figurative, good)
R-fig; – (figurative, indifferent; bad)
R-cond (conditional)

Contexts
Cx C+ (cultural, good)
Cx C; – (cultural, indifferent; unsuccessful)
Cx E+ (esthetic, successful)
Cx E; – (esthetic, indifferent; unsuccessful)
Cx I+ (intellectual, successful)
Cx I (intellectual, indifferent)
Cx I– (intellectual, unsuccessful)
Cx H+ (humorous, successful)
Cx H; – (humor, indifferent; unsuccessful

Other Controls
Vulg– (vulgarity)
Refl+ (reflection, good)
Refl (reflection, less successful)
Del (delay)
Inh (inhibition)
Blkg– (blocking)
Eu (euphemism)
Impl (implication)
Mod+ (modification)
Ratn+ (rationalization, successful)
Ratn (rationalization, less good)
Neg+ (negation, successful)
Discl (disclaimed responsibility)
Minz (minimization)

Defenses (pathological)
Cphb– (counterphobic)
Self-D– (self-deprecation)
Rep– (repudiation)
Va– (vagueness)
Prj– (projection)
Obs– (obsessiveness)
Iso– (isolation)
Eva– (evasiveness)
Imp– (impotence)

Sequence
S C 1-0 (change, Level 1 to unscored)
S C 2-0 (change, Level 2 to unscored)
S C 1-2 (change from Level 1 to 2)

Overtness
O-beh (behavioral)
O-vbl (verbal)
O-exp (experiential)
O-pot (potential)

FIG. 7.1. Contents of scoring manual. Modified from Holt (2005, Vol. 2, pp. 35–36).

standards of logic and realism, and the presence of condensation and displacement—the qualities that separate dreams, neurotic symptoms, and psychotic language from their normal counterparts. In his rich clinical description of the dream work and the joke work, he clearly distinguished types of condensation, displacement, contradiction, and symbolism, which I converted into specific scores, again splitting them into Levels 1 and 2 when the data called for it.

Some of these were familiar Rorschach categories, like contamination (which has no Level 2 variety), but many of them were familiar to me as Rapaport's "verbalization scores" (Rapaport, Gill, & Schafer, 1968). Those in turn presented some kinds of formally deviant thinking not explicitly described by Freud, but arguably also manifestations of primary process, which made up a number of other formal scores.

Controls and Defenses

Early in my work with the emerging scoring system, I was struck by the fact that many of the signs of primary process occurred in the Rorschachs of normal college students and psychiatric residents, despite their origin in work with psychotic patients. It soon became evident that the well-adjusted people were taking the sting or the social shock from their sexual or aggressive, condensed or illogical responses by using a variety of controls: in several ways, putting disturbing ideas at a distance from themselves, supplying humorous, esthetic, intellectual, and other contexts that made them interesting rather than embarrassing, amusing instead of shocking. The more pathological the person who supplied the responses, the more likely it was that responses earning the same kinds of Content or Formal scores showed, instead, signs of many classical maladaptive Defenses, such as Projection, Isolation, Evasiveness, or Counterphobic defense.

Overall Ratings: Form Level

Another, more familiar kind of difference between adaptive and maladaptive responses not unexpectedly showed up: the level of perceptual accuracy, traditionally measured more or less dichotomously as *F+* or *F–*. Rapaport had introduced a more clinically sensitive, differentiated scheme for scoring form level, which our mutual friend Martin Mayman (1970) carefully extended and developed into a scoring manual 25 years later. With his permission, I incorporated Mayman's system into mine. I am happy to be able to make this clinically sensitive and broadly useful scheme widely available by publishing it as a chapter in the full presentation of my own system (Holt, 2005), because Mayman unfortunately died before he was able to include it in a planned Rorschach book of his own.

Creativity

A second overall rating (applied, like Form Level, to all responses) also originated in a dichotomy, or a pair of dichotomies that implicitly produced a 3-point scale: popular, (ordinary), and original. I expanded that into a 6-point rating scale.

Defensive Demand (DD)

Every response containing scorable Content or Formal signs of primary process is rated on this and the next variable. Again, a two-valued distinction (between Level 1 and Level 2) proved after awhile to be reliably expandable into a 6-point scale of the degree of a response's shockingness or implicit demand for some kind of defense or control.

Defensive Effectiveness (DE)

The natural complement to *DD* is a judgment of how effectively the responder succeeds in meeting the demand—another 6-point scale. All of these categories and scales are presented, in the scoring manual, with full definitions, examples, and advice on solving difficult problems of scoring. As it grew from a couple of pages to over 100, the manual went through ten revisions, not formally published, but duplicated and distributed to interested persons. A semifinal version was published in an Italian translation (Holt, 1983), but the final, further enlarged revision only recently appeared (Holt, 2005), with a full discussion of the psychoanalytic theory of thinking and a review of the large body of research that has used it.

THE PROCEDURE OF SCORING EXEMPLIFIED

Defining the Response

This issue—more complicated than may appear at first—is taken up in some detail in chapter 3 of the manual (Holt, 2005, Vol. 2). The main point of difference from Exner's (1993) rules about the matter is that sometimes when scorable material appears in a remark or in inquiry it is counted as a separate response. The following excerpt from a well-administered Rorschach begins with one of those remarks that some examiners do not even write down. Annie, a college student aged 18 years, was participating in a research project in Bethesda several decades ago when she took the test. (The text has been slightly abridged, leaving out only filler words like "well," "uh," "just," and "like," and a good deal of repetition.)

> I. (11") 1. I don't know how good I'll do it. It's imagination; I don't have too much .... Can I turn it any way I want to? It looks kinda like a statue, you know? And they're kind of, there's two figures and I don't know what they are. But they've got wings. Keep going? [Yes.] .... And that's about all I see.

The self-criticism in the opening remarks looks relevant, but should it be considered a separate response? It should not; self-derogation has to go beyond this quite ordinary defensiveness to warrant an *Aggression 2 Victim* score. Our compromise is to consider it part of the first response, where it enters as a mild form of the self-deprecation defense.

Annie continued:

2. There's two other little creatures here with their mouths open. And that's all I see. [usual "mittens"] Inquiry [1. (Two figures: two separate things or the statue?)] Yeah, this whole thing is the statue, the thing in the middle and they're some kind of creatures, clinging onto this thing and the head is up here and here's the legs and the wings. [Question about determinants] Uh, it reminds me of those, on the [local] bridge, on either side, there are, identical statues. It just looks symmetrical ... just the way the figures are, holding on to the post in the middle. [Tell me about the figures.] ... First thing I noticed was the wings. [?] The shape of the wings, two figures and then, it just follows that there's a body and the legs. [Affect inquiry] I don't know, I think it's nice for bridges, but, otherwise I wouldn't care for this ... [Pleasant, unpleasant, neutral?] It would be neutral, but, slanting toward the unpleasant side, because they do look like creatures that, uh, would do harm, rather than good.

[Location?] That's part of the statue. [Point out?] That and that. It's just the heads. [Question about determinants] Well, they're kinda like sea serpents; they're not actual, they're not real, could be fictional, but when you think of sea serpents, you usually think of something like that, with their mouths open. [Shape?] Yes, it has the shape. [Affect inquiry] The same as the others. That they would do more harm rather than good.

Compound responses pose a similar problem; in a combinatory *W*, for example, some *D* areas may call forth pripro material that must be scored, whereas others stimulate secondary process material and are listed as unscored (except for Form Level and Creativity, ratings are given to *every* response in a record). In our sample record, what is scored as the second response on Card I might be considered just an elaboration of the first, *W* response; Annie said, "That's part of the statue." Both components of her combinatory W get pripro scores, but different ones.

Compare Card II, second response:

II. (10") 1. When I first looked at it, it reminded me of, two, storybook characters. Uh, little elves, like. [Location] Well, it was just the general—not this part down here, but all the rest of it. [Determinants] You know the story of Rip van Winkle? Not him, but just the kind of little people that you associate with that, and, I don't know what they're called, but the kind of hats they wore were tall and this made me think of that. And they look like they're dancing. [Affect] Well, I'd say pleasant.

2. But then, uh, then it looked like they were two bears dancing, except that I don't know what kinda heads they had. [Location?] This black part, all of the black. [Determinants?] Well, because they're large and fuzzy. [Fuzzy?] just the texture and the irregularity of the outline. [Affect?] I'd

say it would be more pleasant but it doesn't represent reality, but it's still pleasant to think of two bears dancing.

3. Kinda like, uh, birds' heads. [Birds' heads where the bears' heads were?] The bears didn't have heads. In the place, there were birds' heads. [?] All of this red on the top here. I didn't mean that they necessarily had to be connected. [Different part of blot?] It's just that the bears don't have heads, but there are birds' heads there. [When bears were dancing, they didn't have heads?] That's right. [Determinants?] Well the shape resembles the birds' heads and these resemble beaks. [Affect?] Mm, I don't, I'd say neutral.

Here she tried in the inquiry to abandon her first interpretation of an impossible hybrid creature and make the bears and the birds' heads into separate responses. But we take her literally, and her undoing of the first, composite image—a normal but still disturbing cousin of the pathological Contamination response—is achieved by making it an awkward, unexplained Arbitrary Combination of two incomplete creatures. Hence, we treat it as two separate responses with different scores.

After dividing the responses, the next step (omitted here) is usually to score the Rorschach protocol according to the all-purpose system to which you are accustomed, for the pripro system does not aspire to replace, only to supplement, such scoring as the Comprehensive System.

Scoring Forms

Figure 7.2 presents pripro scores for Annie's responses, entered on a portion of a scoring sheet. Notice that a separate line is used for each response; for very rich protocols with extended responses that may incur many scores, you may spill over into the next line.

Ratings: Form Level and Creativity

Whether there are any signs of primary process thinking or not, we first score all responses for their perceptual adequacy and for creativity, as noted earlier. In doing so, the experienced scorer notices any scorable content or formal manifestations of primary process. If not, go on to the next response.

Content Scoring

Looking at the first response to Card I, we see that Annie at first gives no hint of any motivational themes, but in the affect inquiry tells us that the unspecified animals in the sculpture she envisages look dangerous.

S No. 070 Date 4/19/63 RORSCHACH PRIPRO SCORING SHEET Scored by RRH Page # 1

R No.	Form Level	Cr	Content	Formal Aspects	Control & Defense	DD	DE	DDXDE
I								
1	$Fw+_I$	2	Ag 2 A wk	C-co 1 wk	R-(an), R-dep+, Cx E+, Del, Self-Dep wk, Va– tend, O-pot	3	0	0
2	Fw+	3	Ag 2 O	C-a-c.2	Del, R-(an), R-dep+, R-fic n+, Cx E+, Minz, O-pot	3	0	0
II								
1	Fo_c	2						
2	Fo_c	1	Ag 2 A wk, Ag 2 R	C-co 1 wk, Ctr R 2	Neg, R-an, Mod+, Rep– tend, O-pot	3	+.5	+1.5
3	Fw–	2	Ag 2 O tend	C-a-c 2	X	3	0a	0
4	F+	3	Ag 2 A wk	C-co 2	R-an, R-fic n+, Cx C+, Del, O-pot	2	+2	+4

FIG. 7.2. Pripro scoring sheet.

Anything that "would do harm" is treated as a manifestation of Attack, safe though this one appears (because of the controls; see later discussion). The scorer's trick is to undo the efforts the respondent makes to make everything all right and consider the basic idea unalloyed, so to speak. Under the scores for Aggression, the manual says that a potentially harmful, unspecified animal is scored *Ag 2 A* (*Aggression, Level 2, Attack*).

Parenthetically, she continued to find fearsome, hostile animals on most of the cards, or partly destroyed objects, and only once did she produce a pleasant image of oral gratification—her single Libidinal response. The impression given by her self-deprecation and her dependent relation to the tester, that this is an insecure person, is much reinforced by these scores: She seems to live in a frightening world without much feeling of an inner ability to cope with danger. Such a preponderance of Aggressive over Libidinal content is quite unusual in female college freshmen.

Scoring Formal Aspects

Having recorded the Content score (or scores; there may be quite a few in one response), the scorer moves on to consider Formal possibilities. Here (Card I, 1) is something unrealistic right away: scary winged creatures that are neither birds nor bats. They are in an area often seen as some kind of quadruped, so she is passively accepting what the blot gives her, reporting some impossible fused creature: like the kind of dream image Freud (1900/1953) called a "composition" achieved by condensation. That is symbolized by *C-co 1: C* for condensation, *co* for composition, and *1* for Level 1—a relatively extreme deviation from the prosaic and conventional. As compared to most such responses, however, it is *weak*, because she never quite acknowledges that she sees such an imaginary or unrealistic creature. Compare it to the next response, the snakes' heads that are also part of the same sculpture. That too is an arbitrary combination of things that do not go together in reality, which Freud also considered a work of condensation, but less extreme. In a Composition, the natural boundaries of organisms are invaded, whereas in Arbitrary Combinations (Level 2, closer to secondary process) they are respected.

Scoring Controls and Defenses

We now consider the ways in which the response has been made as presentable and socially acceptable as the test taker can make it. Being tested is a social situation, typically one in which the respondents convey what they see verbally, implicitly following a complex if unspoken set of rules (be coherent; speak the other person's language—here, clearly not that of the street; don't act nasty, seductive, or shocking; try to perform the task given you; etc.). An easy and natural way to cope with ideas that have disturbing motivational implications is to put them at a distance. Adopting an idea suggested by Tomkins (1947) for the Thematic Apperception Test (TAT), I distinguished several kinds of Remoteness, two of which our subject Annie used. She attributed the aggressive threat to an imaginary animal, seen moreover in the safer guise of a sculptural depiction. That constitutes appropriately invoking the safety of an Esthetic Context. Moreover, she achieved control to some degree by reporting the disturbing material only in the Inquiry, in response to questioning (scored as *Delay*). And the harm the creature might do remains safely Potential (scored *O-pot;* every Content theme is scored for its Overtness). We have already noticed that she makes some use of less adaptive Defenses, notably Self-Deprecation. Her wording is also noticeably Vague, not enough for a full-fledged score but worth noting as a *tendency*—a form of something that does not quite meet the manual's standards for even the *weak* form of a category.

Final Ratings

Finally, the scorer rates the response's implicit shock value as its Demand for Defense. The manual gives a suggested rating (*DD*) on a 6-point scale for each Content or Formal manifestation, summarized in the next column on the scoring sheet. It tells us that a *C-co 1 wk* deserves a 3 on the scale; a full score would get 4. Because the aggression score is only worth 2, the final rating stands at 3.

Defensive Effectiveness (*DE*) is, obviously, a rating of how well the job of smoothing over and "making nice" has been done. It is a more complicated process, following rules set down in the manual. One takes into account the form level, the Control and Defense scores given, the expression of accompanying emotion (here the affect inquiry played an important part), and finally clinical judgment, matching the response to a set of model responses for each point on a scale from +2 (most adequate control) to –3 (most pathogenic defense). This particular uneasily given, apologized for, but basically sound response ends up squarely in the middle with a *DE* of 0. Its net effect is not to tip the balance toward either end of the scale.

Last Step of Scoring: Tallying

When you have scored the entire protocol, you must reduce the array to something more manageable. The manual presents a tally sheet, listing every score and rating so that everything on the scoring sheet can be entered as a mark of some kind and then totaled. That is still too fine-grained a summary for most purposes, so scores have to be integrated somehow into indices: groupings, means of ratings, and ratios. Specific ones will be introduced later, as we investigate reliability and validity.

RELIABILITY

Obviously, both clinicians and researchers want to work with well-behaved numbers. If you get a certain result on one occasion, you need to know that it can be counted on to measure something lasting about the person, not a passing whim or mood. Moreover, if the number has been produced by the intervention of someone's judgment, not directly by the participant's responses, we need assurance that the judgments are securely reproducible by others with comparable credentials. Those rather different matters eventuate in measures of stability (repeat reliability) and of the agreement between scorers (judge reliability). Happily, the years of work developing the scoring manual have produced a system that gets comfortably over both of these hurdles.

Detailed summaries of results to back up that statement from scores of independent studies occupy many pages in the published manual (Holt, 2005, chap. 11). Naturally, indices based on the largest number of responses are inherently the most reliable. Overall measures of primary process (like Total Percent Pripro: the proportion of all responses containing any Content or Formal indication of primary process; or the simple number of such responses) are as stable over time as indices from conventional scores (r = about .85), for periods from a week to a month. The same overall indices hold up well over long periods: Douglas Heath (personal communication, 1976) found that indices of Total Percent Pripro from 68 college men were correlated at .51 with indices obtained 12 or 13 years later. Lavoie, Michaud, Elie, and Amar (1987) reported a repeat correlation of .57 with 27 hospitalized psychotics retested after 10 to 17 years, using the total number of pripro responses.

Observer reliability of these summary scores is usually excellent. The median reliability for indices of total pripro reported in twenty-two independent studies is .92. But any measure of the simple total amount of pripro in a Rorschach unfortunately does not yield very interesting results. For example, it rarely differentiates significantly among psychodiagnostic groups or those separated on many other useful criteria.

An immediate reaction might be to conclude that either the concept of primary process or the method of assessing it is not worth further attention. That would be too hasty a reaction, I hope to demonstrate. Rather, primary process, as Freud (1900/1953) defined it, occurs universally in human cognition, and even though he believed that most of it went on unconsciously, mild manifestations make their way into most people's conscious, communicated thought as well. We must look, instead, at individual differences in somewhat more specific or complicated ways.

Let us look at the second level of generality or pooling. The median judge agreement coefficient for Percent Content, across eleven studies, is r = .94 (kappa = .89 in another)—impressive by any psychometric standard. The comparable measures of formal aspects yield slightly poorer agreement between judges, the median of ten reported coefficients being r = .85. That is generally considered satisfactory for a projective technique, however. One reliability (Langan, 1984) was .96, which shows that excellent agreement can be had with sufficient effort and enough variance within the sample.

A second way to split total pripro and make it a bit more meaningful is into the two levels. Sum or Percent Level 1 has a median judge reliability of .89, and Level 2 is just slightly better, at .91. Content is often usefully split into libidinal and aggressive, with median rater reliabilities of .93 and .88, respectively. Clearly, it is not necessary to lump everything together.

It is worth noting that our shared psychometric standards are based on work with traditional psychological tests like self-administering inventories. In them, it is pretty obvious that reliability is a prerequisite to good validity. Most psychologists, therefore, are puzzled by the proposition, which I strongly support, that some of the very procedures we have traditionally been urged to adopt to maximize reliability tend to undermine the validity of the Rorschach. A number of people, for example, have tried the obvious expedient of replacing the free response format with forced choice of prefixed alternatives (with predetermined scoring, thus eliminating judgment), with one response to each blot and plenty of them. The result is even better reliability, but no useful validity.

Here we confront a dilemma familiar to anyone who has done research in clinical psychology. To achieve something like the insightful, individualized portraits of a skilled and experienced clinician, one needs variables that combine several aspects of Rorschach responses, for example, the kind and intensity of both content and formal pripro when they are found in the same response, combined with indicators of how well or poorly controlled it is. But such variables are bound to have regrettable psychometric properties: They occur rarely, and it is difficult for scorers to agree satisfactorily on them. To get comfortable frequencies and scorer reliabilities, you need to sacrifice the very richness of clinical meaning that attracts most of us to the Rorschach in the first place! Or so it seems. In any event, that is the struggle I have been caught up in throughout.

In his doctoral dissertation, done under my supervision, Leo Goldberger (1961) was the first to propose a useful way to combine the frequency and intensity of pripro material in a Rorschach with an evaluation of its control, to obtain an approximation of the concept of "regression in the service of the ego" versus pathological regression (Kris, 1952). Besides being too complicated to describe briefly, it resulted in the ranking of a group of subjects instead of a better distributed variable. Therefore, I converted it into what became known as the Adaptive Regression Index (*ARI*). For each response, one multiplies its overall ratings of *DD* and *DE*, recording the product in the final column on the scoring sheet. The algebraic sum of those numbers (some of which are positive, some negative, and some zeroes) divided by their count yields the *ARI*. High positive numbers represent Rorschachs containing relatively strong stuff, calling for vigorous controls and defenses that have been effectively applied. Numbers close to zero indicate records with little pripro material or those in which the controlling efforts are, on average, neither very good nor very bad. High negative numbers are obtained with Rorschachs with strong expressions of pripro and a lot of it, accompanied by poor control and the use of pathogenic defenses.

Hence, according to Kris's (1952) elaboration of Freud's (1900/1953) brief remarks on the subject, if the *ARI* is a good measure of his concept, positive scores should characterize creative people who have ready access to ordinarily unconscious material well enough controlled so they use it productively. Conversely, negative *ARI*s should be given by schizophrenics, conceived of as people whose uncontrolled unconscious ideation breaks through their maladaptive defenses and takes over cognition in a distressing way.

Because the Adaptive Regression Index is based on the products of two rated variables, let us first see how good the agreement is on those. First, *DD*: I have collected reports of 25 scorer reliabilities. The median coefficient is .89, with two studies (Allison, 1967; Blatt & Berman, 1984) reporting agreement of .99. *DE* fares less well, being based on the combination of several judged aspects: in 27 studies, the median is .83, and only seven correlations are .90 or higher. Surprisingly, *ARI* was not more difficult to score reliably: The median of the 19 available results is .85, 5 being.90 or higher, to which might be added 8 other studies in which the method of computing the index was slightly idiosyncratic, but the median judge reliability was .83.

It is difficult to emphasize sufficiently that no scoring system has intrinsic rater reliability. It should be evident that, the more two people are alike in their level of training, clinical sensitivity, general intelligence, and culture, the more they tend to agree on many things. And if they go through the same course of training in making judgments, that will improve their agreement. Having trained a good many students in my method, I have seen that demonstrated many times. Some of the research that yielded the data just presented came from the Research Center for Mental Health, where such training was available; but any advantage conveyed thereby seems to have been small. The median of the 87 judge reliabilities (including many other indices) when I had trained one or both raters was .88; the median of the 109 reported by investigators who had learned from the manual or from someone else not trained at NYU was .84![1] That speaks well for the adequacy of the manual itself, I believe.

Yet the point remains, that one should not begin any research until those who are to score the Rorschachs have attained a minimal level of agreement *on the scores and indices to be actually computed and used.* It does not matter if your scorers have not learned to make closely matching ratings on the manual's Creativity scale if you are not going to use it. By the same token, in a detailed study of oral issues you might find it worth the extra trouble to focus scorers' attention on the subcategories found in the manual (e.g., *L 1 O.a*). With practice, raters can learn to make these fine distinctions, which may happen to separate different types of, let us say, anorectic patients. I suspect that many failures to confirm plausible clinical hypotheses with pripro scores may have resulted from a failure to examine the data in just that way.

I am also convinced, however, that many disappointing results could have been avoided if researchers had been willing to put in the extra time and effort to apply the complete pripro system instead of settling for a quick and easy expedient like scoring content only. Some early work on schizophrenics made that mistake, thus discarding the very parts of the manual that might have worked best.

VALIDITY

Again, the standard psychometric model against which Rorschach researchers tend to be judged assumes an unrealistically simple approach to validating a test score: simply correlate it with a criterion measure of what it is supposed to measure. People still ask meaningless questions like "What is the validity of the Rorschach?" Even to limit the query to a specific scoring system makes little sense if one expects it to measure some particular trait or quality, as the pripro system does not. And when that requirement is met, where is the face-valid criterion measure? None exists even for that hoary veteran of the psychometric tradition, intelligence tests.

Two initial points must be made: We must look for evidence concerning the validity of *specific scores or indices*, and we must follow the general approach of *construct validity.* As the late Sam Messick (1995)

[1]These numbers omit reliabilities reported as percentages. To be conservative, kappa coefficients were treated as if they were correlations.

cogently argued, however, the latter is a complex matter. He identified six aspects, to the discussion of four of which—the content, substantive, structural, and generalizability aspects—my monograph (Holt, 2005, Vol. 2) devotes 30 pages. In doing so, I found it relevant to cite data from several studies (e.g., Eagle, 1964) indicating that pripro scores applied to Rorschach responses, TAT stories, and dreams are not usually intercorrelated very highly. Because this book is concerned only with the Rorschach, that result is not particularly important, as long as the Rorschach scores themselves prove useful. That same chapter 12 also presents findings from five factor analyses, using strikingly different samples and somewhat different pripro variables in each. Nevertheless, two similar factors could be discerned, either the only or the strongest factors in each study: one usually featuring *DD* and Percent Level 1, and some measure of formal aspects; the other loaded with *DE*, and measures of form level and intellectual competence. That evidence was broadly supportive if not definitive.

The usual interpretation of construct validity, called by Messick (1995) its "external aspect," asks how highly any given test measure is correlated with independent measures with which it shares theoretical meaning. In available research reports, that often comes down to a slightly different question: Among the obtained external correlates of a pripro variable (score or index), is there a consistent pattern across studies? Some of the time, of course, specific hypotheses derived from theory have been tested. Five chapters of Holt (2005, Vol. 2), together comprising several hundred pages, present evidence of these kinds.

Empirical Tests of Psychoanalytic Theory

Let us first review the work that has used the pripro method's main feature: that it provides quantitative, operational measures of important concepts in psychoanalytic theory.

A preliminary word about that theory is in order. During the five decades since I began the work summarized in my monograph (Holt, 2005), I have spent much time closely examining Freud's theories. In part that was necessitated by the work on the manual, and in part by its place in the announced aim of the Research Center for Mental Health, of which I was director and codirector for 20 years. That aim was to subject the psychoanalytic theory of thinking to empirical test, using both of Cronbach's (1975) "two disciplines of scientific psychology."

One early result of that theoretical immersion was the finding that the theory is too sprawling and loosely organized to lend itself to anything like rigorous derivation of testable hypotheses directly from Freud's writings. Instead, we had to proceed more informally, as will be evident in what follows.

Another result, however, was that I discovered so many flaws and fallacies in Freud's metapsychology, an effort more abstract and ambitious than his clinical theory, that I reluctantly concluded it was beyond revitalization and needed complete replacement. Because his most prominent statements about primary and secondary processes were couched in metapsychological language, it might seem that I had succeeded in destroying the foundations or relevance of my own scoring system.

The pripro system was conceived during the era when ego psychology dominated American psychoanalysis, and when I was working within that frame of reference. In the decades since then, ego psychology has fallen out of favor not only with me, but also more generally. Is the pripro system therefore mired in an anachronistic type of psychoanalytic theory? Do scholars who undertake the job of learning and applying it commit themselves to an outmoded approach to clinical or personological matters?

I strongly believe that the answer to these questions is "No!" Just as Freud created in the primary process a concept that has outlived the death of his metapsychology in terms of which he defined it, I believe that the pripro scoring system has a demonstrated robustness and value that makes it useful no matter what the user's own theoretical commitments are. In this way, it is similar to the Minnesota Multiphasic Personality Inventory (MMPI): You do not have to be a Kraepelinian or believe that mania or psychasthenia are "mental diseases" to find that test's clinical scales useful. Their meaning is carried in large part by their empirical correlates. People use those scales, in clinical contexts as well as in research, as measures of the somewhat vaguely defined but meaningful clusters of correlated variables.

Just so, I present the pripro system with the evidence that many of its indices and scores have a similar kind of rich meaning. It seems unlikely that many psychologists will want to have a measure of condensation solely because of anything Freud said about that hypothetical mental process. But knowing that various indices made from the several scores under the heading, Condensation, have the correlates listed in my chapters 13–17 (Holt, 2005), we can get an idea of the kind of person who will give more than the usual one or two of those responses. He (and perhaps to a lesser extent, she) will have an unconventional and unstereotyped enough mind, for example, to be better than average in endeavors requiring originality, the capacity to break accustomed sets in solving problems, or creative production.

Thus, the scoring method does not require fealty to any particular theoretical point of view. It may be used equally well by those who still believe in metapsychology, as the only detailed, textually based, operational realization of some of Freud's concepts; by adherents of any modern school of psychoanalysis; and by those who have no interest in psychoanalytic theory as such but merely want a way to distinguish empirically demonstrable types of thinking, which have been proved to be of practical interest.

Let us begin with a brief summary of the evidence concerning the construct validity of measures of adaptive regression. As mentioned earlier, Goldberger (1961) was the first to construct an index of adaptive versus maladaptive regression. His procedure involved ranking his subjects on total pripro and on a measure of control, based on the *DE* scores. The result, another ranking, put at one extreme subjects who were high on both the amount of pripro expressed in their Rorschachs and on the effectiveness with which it was controlled; in the middle were subjects who produced least; and at the other end were those who expressed a great deal but ranked low on control (indicating maladaptive or pathological regression).

Goldberger (1961) used his index to test a prediction that persons who had little tolerance for primary process modes of thought (in the Rorschach) would be disturbed when they were deprived of perceptual contact with the structure of external reality, which would allow deviant thought processes to become conscious. On the contrary, those who were on good terms with their own primary processes should withstand being perceptually isolated with less upset, even positive enjoyment. Briefly, in an experiment in which student volunteers lay on a bed in a soundproof room with halved ping pong balls fastened over their eyes, which gave only patternless visual stimulation for 8 hours, the results significantly validated this prediction.

In a first attempt to replicate these encouraging findings (Holt & Goldberger, 1961), despite the use of similar conditions and measures, none of the original results was reproduced. The only significant finding involving pripro scoring was a correlation of .49 between *mean DD* and the amount of time spent sleeping. Retrospectively, we decided that the key difference between the two studies was probably the nature of the subjects. The first study used undergraduate students in the New York University School of Education, the most disturbed among them showing a pattern of defensive machismo. All were males seeking to enter teaching, a profession popularly stereotyped as feminine; many of them seemed to react with a kind of masculine protest. The chronologically much older second sample was made of actors, predominantly unemployed, few of whom gave signs of being uncomfortable with their feminine sides. Most of them thought of themselves as artists; the maladjusted minority among them were promiscuous homosexuals.

In other centers of research on sensory deprivation, however, Goldberger's (1961) measure of adaptive regression, or approximations to it, did reliably predict good response versus emotional disturbance or quitting in three studies using subjects more like the population from which potential astronauts might be drawn (Myers, 1972; Wright & Abbey, 1965; Wright & Zubek, 1969). Indeed, it has been called the best-replicated finding on individual differences in reaction to perceptual isolation or sensory deprivation.

Virtually all of the remaining work to be summarized has used the Adaptive Regression Index.

A second body of research tested the following hypothesis: The more fully alert and conscious a person's state, the more nearly will thinking approach the ideal of the secondary process or, conversely, as the state in which cognitive processes go on approaches full unconsciousness, those processes should ever more closely approximate the primary process. That is an attempt to translate into researchable terms Freud's statements that in the System Ucs. the primary process holds sway, and in the System Cs. the secondary process does (Freud, 1915/1957, p. 186).

Several investigators have developed techniques of measuring a capacity or tendency to enter special or unusual states of consciousness. Four researchers have tested the hypothesis that persons who are capable of adaptive regression should be the most likely to enter such states, or the related hypothesis that persons who experience such altered states would be more open to admitting primary process into their Rorschach protocols. All studies reported some positive results, but with only slightly overlapping sets of pripro indices. Allison (1967) approached the hypothesis by dividing 20 students of theology into three groups, based on how often they had experienced exalted states of religious conversion. The amount of that experience was significantly correlated with *Mean DD*, Formal pripro, and the *ARI*. Reports by runners of attaining a special state of consciousness called "runner's high" stimulated Ewing and collaborators to carry out several pieces of research. In the first, they found an increase in Rorschach pripro among college students after physical exercise. A first replication with a mixed group of patients found positive results only with neurotic depressives, whereas another replication with a group of normal adults (but a different kind of exercise) failed entirely (Ewing, Gillis, Ebert, & Matthews, 1975; Ewing, Gillis, Scott, & Patzig, 1982).

Freud (1923/1961) asserted that: "Thinking in pictures ... stands nearer to unconscious processes than does thinking in words, and it is unquestionably older than the latter both ontogenetically and phylogenetically" (p. 21). If, then, visual imaging partakes of the primary process, a number of investigators have argued that persons who tend to experience sensory, nonverbal imagery more easily and frequently than others should have a capacity for adaptive regression.

Seven studies have addressed this topic, with mixed results. Only one reported entirely negative results, and none unambiguously supported the hypothesis. Bergan (1965) found that the amount of (predominantly visual) sensory imagery in the dreams of male subjects was strongly correlated with their *ARI*'s, whereas the excellence of women's auditory imagery (as measured by a pitch discrimination task) was related to the same index of adaptive regression. In my own data (Holt, 2005), unfortunately with an all-male sample, there was no generality across types of imagery, even within the visual modality, a finding that if replicated, could explain much of the disagreement among research findings. Moreover, in my data, the frequency of visual imagery during sensory deprivation and under the influence of LSD, besides being unrelated to each other, were both strongly correlated with various specific types of pripro scores but in a completely different pattern. For example, the only pripro variables to be significantly related to both types of imagery, the number of Level 1 condensations plus the closely related frequency of all composition responses, were negative predictors of imagery in isolation, but positive predictors of similar phenomena experienced under LSD! Here is an example of one way in which laboratory findings, if replicated, can improve psychoanalytic theory by making its variables more sharply focused and responsive to unexpected realities.

Because the effects of psychedelic drugs are often reported to be phantasmagoric and dream-like, it is simple to predict that drugged states should increase the amount of pripro in verbal productions along with poorer controls. Only two projects have used the scoring manual to investigate such effects, both with positive findings. Bennett (1973) studied alcohol, finding different effects on men and on women and according to the situation. Philip (1959) administered LSD in a double-blind study, the overall results verifying his predictions. Even more interesting findings showed how congruent the specific kinds of changes in pripro were to the personalities and types of drug effects of individual subjects (Barr, Langs, Holt, Goldberger, & Klein, 1972).

The largest single body of pripro research on altered states is a series of investigations either seeking a relationship between adaptive regression and hypnotizability, or testing the hypothesis that ideation in the hypnotic state is more subject to primary-process intrusion than it is in the normal. Eight studies addressed the former question, correlating standard measures of susceptibility to hypnosis with the *ARI* (two positive results, one negative, all unpublished studies), or with various other indices of primary process. Not surprisingly, one investigator who looked only at the percentage of total pripro found no relationship to hypnotizability in a college population; another (Rosegrant, 1980) obtained positive results for mean *DD* but only with women. Lavoie and his collaborators and students worked with hospitalized psychotic subjects, reporting a wealth of striking and replicated findings: mainly, that aspects of pripro in the Rorschach that measure thought disorder were negatively related to hypnotic susceptibility (e.g., Lavoie & Elie, 1985; Lavoie et al., 1987; Lavoie, Sabourin, Ally, & Langlois, 1976).

Four investigators (or teams) tested the hypothesis that the altered state of consciousness produced by hypnosis allows the emergence of more primary process thinking (Ackman, 1960; Fromm, Oberlander, & Gruenewald, 1970; Levin & Harrison, 1976; Wiseman & Reyher, 1973). All four obtained some positive evidence, notably with the mean *DD* index, though two used the Rorschach, and two scored dreams about Rorschach cards. Two of these investigators predicted an increase in the *ARI* under hypnosis but did not find it; it is not obvious to me that psychoanalytic theory implies such a prediction.

Perhaps the most interesting research using the *ARI* tested a proposition closely associated with Kris (1952), though he made it clear that he got it from some remarks by Freud: that in creative work, people use the primary process in a controlled way. By contrast, uncontrolled primary process characterizes the thought not of creative persons but of psychotics.

Two principal approaches to a *criterion measure* of creativity have been used in research that attempts to test the former hypothesis. The first, the method of extreme groups, is to select as subjects people who are in other respects as well matched as possible, but who differ in their creative behavior, usually as judged by expert evaluation of their creative products. The second is to administer tests of creativity to an unselected group of available subjects, that is, to ask them to be creatively productive in certain specified ways and then to evaluate their products according to explicit criteria.

In ten studies, the method of extreme groups has yielded strong and consistent evidence that creative artists (in the graphic arts, musical performance, and to some extent literature) have ready access to the primary process. In four studies, they outperformed comparison groups on the *ARI*, as well as on various measures of the amount of pripro (Dudek & Chamberland-Bouhadana, 1982; Hoechstetter, 1981; Huard, 1985; Vezina, 1981). Also, in one group of adolescent schizophrenic art students (Borofsky, 1971), the most creative subgroup produced higher scores on both *ARI* and *DE* but not on any measure of the quantity of pripro in their Rorschachs. As to the other five studies, the *ARI* failed to discriminate the most and least creative third-grade students in one (Rogolsky, 1968), and it was not used in four others: twice because it was not yet available (Dudek, 1968; Freed, 1961), and two more times because only content manifestations of pripro were scored (Caldwell, 1993; Gagnon, 1977). Positive findings were limited to adults and adolescents, and were best replicated in painters and in all-male groups. In the four researches on adults in which *ARI* was not used, the most creative subjects' Rorschachs contained more pripro, especially of the more obvious and blatant sort.

The remaining eleven studies used the second type of criterion, tests of creativity: principally those of Guilford (1950, 1967) and his group, but also the somewhat similar tests developed by Torrance (1966). These were generally administered to unselected samples of adults or children and the results were correlated with Rorschach indices of pripro. Thus, this criterion has less face validity than the method of extreme groups, especially when the highly creative subjects had won national or international acclaim for their art (in seven studies). The creativity test method is useful, however, in asking a more difficult question: Are smaller degrees of creativeness over a more restricted range still significantly associated with independent assessments of capacity for adaptive regression?

The results are complicated, and do not strongly support Kris's hypothesis: There were positive results in three researches, negative in four, and mixed in three—that is, positive for males and negative for females. (In one, no measure of adaptive regression was used.) Let us, however, look more closely at these results, breaking them down by the gender of subjects. Three experiments' samples contained one sex only: Newmeyer (1972) obtained strong positive results with adult male soldiers, whereas Pine (1962) got negative results with 50 male actors; Lazar (1975), whose findings were negative, used females only. In three of the others, the data of the sexes were not separately analyzed; two had positive findings, one negative. The samples in four other studies contained both sexes; in three of them (Murray & Russ, 1981; Pine & Holt, 1960; Russ, 1988a), the correlations of creativity and *ARI* were significantly different for the sexes, positive only for the male subjects and in one, for neither men nor women.

To summarize: Significant positive correlations between creativity and *ARI* in two mixed samples, positive findings with males in five studies; there were clear negative results with males in two, and the other three negative results came from samples composed entirely or preponderantly of female subjects. Positive results with women or girls occurred only when they were mixed with approximately equal numbers of males; their data, when separately analyzed, failed to support the Kris hypothesis. Despite two unambiguously negative findings with male samples, the results for men and boys were otherwise positive (four samples). Also, in one study with a mixed sample, Langan (1984) did not present data analyzed by sex, but remarked that the findings were stronger for the males.

In short, the weight of the evidence seems to me impressively positive—for males, at least—despite the many limitations of individual researches. True, the Rorschach pripro scores that have shown statistically significant relationships to measures of creativity have varied from study to study, but then so have the populations sampled and the kinds of creative functions considered as criteria. With so much error variance on both sides of the equation, it is remarkable that so many positive findings have come through: Not only is there something to Kris's hypothesis, but the phenomenon seems to be rather strong to show up so persistently. Despite the confusions, we are left with a theoretically interesting message: that more creative persons—predominantly, males—have more controlled access to primary process modes of thought than less creative ones. Sometimes, if they are in general well-controlled, secure, and healthy persons taking the Rorschach test, this access is *without* indications of control and defense targeted on the specific manifestations of pripro.

These research findings seem to be congruent with the idea, which is probably not controversial, that in the arts and sciences alike, a man we call "original" or "creative" must find a way to break apart the usual, received ways of thinking and working and recombine them in fresh ways. Not just any novelty will do; the new product must meet standards of esthetic value (e.g., beauty) or scientific usefulness. Thus, it must be produced less in an ecstatic frenzy than with disciplined craft coupled with inspiration. Despite several studies aimed at helping us understand why the formula, or the specific indices used, do not work with females, the role of gender remains an unsolved mystery.

Maladaptive Regression and Schizophrenia. The psychoanalytic conceptualization of schizophrenia emphasizes the emergence—indeed, it is sometimes said, the eruption—of primary-process thinking from the *Ucs.* into conscious thought and language. Let us then look briefly at research on this issue, for more evidence about the validity of the *ARI*.

Fourteen studies addressed the usefulness of pripro scoring in the diagnosis of schizophrenia. Of these, four asked whether schizophrenics' Rorschachs contain more pripro than nonschizophrenics' (normals or neurotics, usually); the answer was positive in all but one Japanese study (Inoue, 1965), in which the patients produced *fewer* Level 2 pripro responses than normals. Seven more provide mixed results: that is, no positive findings with Total Pripro indices, but other indices did differentiate as expected. A study of Italian schizophrenics (Caprara et al., 1977) found that they produced less total pripro than normals in both Rorschach and TAT, but with higher mean *DD*. In other research reports, schizophrenics had the highest mean scores of four hospitalized diagnostic groups, but differed significantly only from the depressives; or were described qualitatively as having given more "extreme and blatant" responses than others; or as differing only on the scored *Level 1 %* (Harrow & Quinlan, 1985; Quinlan, Harrow, Tucker, & Carlson, 1972).

In two (unpublished) studies, special indices of the Formal indications of pripro made the differential diagnosis; in one of those (Lavoie, 1964), the subjects were mothers of schizophrenic children, compared to mothers of neurotic or normal children. In a project wherein only content was scored, process schizophrenics had significantly more Level 1, and reactive schizophrenics produced more of the Level 2 variety (Zimet & Fine, 1965).

Two research reports (Borofsky, 1971; Chapman, 1968) focused on the *ARI* as a measure of maladaptive regression. Both found schizophrenics to have significantly lower (i.e., more pathological) scores than normals. Another obtained similar results, using Goldberger's index of maladaptive regression to compare groups of college students who were diagnosed as "ambulatory schizophrenics" or normals, on the basis of the MMPI (Derman, 1967). Using his own variant of the *ARI*, which he calls *Rego*, Lavoie (1964) found that mothers of schizophrenic children had significantly lower scores than mothers of normals, and similarly differentiated chronic male adult schizophrenics from matched normals (Hébert, Lavoie, & Ally, 1973). Where neither index was computed, the combination of scores suggests that the *ARI* might have worked: Schizophrenic adolescents surpassed patients with other diagnoses on a combination of many Formal scores plus poor *DE* scores (Silverman, Lapkin, & Rosenbaum, 1962). Chronic schizophrenic adults differed from medical patients on a combination of Formal pripro with negative *DE* ratings and high *DD* (Silverman, 1963). Where relevant data are reported, there are no studies with contradictory findings.

Supportive findings emerge from two projects on the treatment of schizophrenics with chlorpromazine or similar drugs: In one, as patients improved, *Mean DE*—measuring the control of pripro—increased, as well as several types of positive control scores (Saretsky, 1966); in the other (Ebert, Ewing, Rogers, & Reynolds, 1977), *DE* was not used but there were progressive decreases in total and especially Formal pripro scores. Finally, a follow-up study of schizophrenic children after about 5 years during which all improved (mostly with psychotherapy) showed a decrease in the index of total pripro and in the percentage of pripro responses accompanied by poor form level (Nass, 1963).

On the whole, then, these scattered data from research on schizophrenia support the psychoanalytic expectation that that illness is accompanied by the disruptive emergence of primary process thinking into conscious thought, and provide further construct validation of pripro scoring.

Psychotherapy. The finding of improved *DE* after successful treatment has been replicated in some nonpsychotic patients, too. There are a few indications that pripro does not yield useful findings in research using patients whose symptoms are predominantly of the acting-out (alloplastic) type.[2] Rabkin (1967) got positive findings with *DE* and *ARI*, both increasing after psychotherapy, for patients presenting classical neurotic and other ideational symptoms, but not with Menninger Clinic patients diagnosed as character disordered. In Fishman's (1973b) research, 6 months into psychotherapy the therapist's rating, Inner versus Outer perceived cause of problems, was correlated at +.43 with *mean DE*, and later *DE* was significantly correlated with therapists' ratings and other criteria of success.

Findings Not Predicted From Theory

There follows a group of research results indicating potentially valuable uses for pripro indices in assessment and diagnostic work.

There is good evidence that appropriate measures, notably *% Formal* and *% Level 1*, are sensitive to degrees of maladjustment in normal populations. Not coincidentally, those indices have the highest loadings on the pripro factor in several factor analyses.

In his intensive studies of Haverford college students, Heath (1965) found that both of those indices were correlated with one or more independent measures of maladjustment in two independent samples. In addition, when he followed up on his subjects 10 years after graduation (Heath, 1976a, 1976b), he found *% Level 1* negatively correlated with measures of vocational and sexual adjustment. Similarly, Ducey (1975) reported that several measures of marital adjustment in a sample of Harvard University graduates were significantly correlated with both *Σ Lib 1* and *Σ Ag 1*, but especially the latter, from Rorschachs administered 14 years earlier. A similar finding with Canadian children, was obtained by Matalon (1975): Free anxiety as rated by a psychiatrist was correlated .47 with *Σ Formal 1*.

If we turn to the somewhat related concept of maturity, we find similar patterns of relationships to pripro indices. Heath (1965) reported that *% Level 1* strongly predicted maturity in one sample, weakly replicated in another, and Benfari and Calogeras (1968) found it correlated with their measure of moral maturity, especially *% Level 1 Aggression*, which was related to a different measure of maturity by Ducey (1975). Maturity was measured in different ways by Heath and by Loevinger (1976), but both Heath (1965) and Langan (1984) reported that it was correlated with *Mean DE*, and the latter also found *ARI* a good predictor

[2]Von Wiederhold (1995) found that people who engage in multiple body piercings—arguably a form of acting out—produce less pripro than those who had only pierced ears. This finding is consistent with the finding that men who reacted to LSD primarily by experiencing bodily symptoms rather than with perceptual and ideational changes showed little alteration in their Rorschach pripro (Barr et al., 1972). See my Vol. 2, chapters 13 and 15 for details.

of Loevinger's index. In addition, Heath found % *Formal* to be significantly related to immaturity in two samples.

SOME DIRECTIONS FOR FUTURE RESEARCH [3]

Creativity

Despite the many studies done in this area using pripro scoring, considerable room remains in which to build on, extend, and improve what exists. I devoutly hope that scholars will extend the work to types of creative artists not yet tested (e.g., composers of both classical and popular music; performers of several arts including music, such as dancers, actors, and performance artists; writers of novels, plays, poetry, short stories, etc.; ceramicists; photographers, film makers, and other visual artists besides painters; choreographers). Someone will surely rise to the challenge of exploring the differences between male and female creative artists, investigating the possibility of finding Rorschach indicators other than the Adaptive Regression Index that will identify creative talent in women, and of improving and extending the selective efficiency of the *ARI*.

I strongly recommend the investigative model I used in the first place: taking two well-chosen criterion groups representing extremes of the variable under study but similar in other important respects, administering Rorschachs (ideally, by well-trained examiners who are blind to the criterion status of the participants), and having them transcribed and scored (again, blindly). Then use available indices like *ARI* to predict group membership, and select for particular study false positives and false negatives. Examine not only all the pripro variables singly and in various configurations, but look also for unscored aspects of the protocols that seem differentiating. Apply any new categories or scales to the entire sample and refine, if necessary, to optimize the differentiation. Finally, **very important**, cross-validate! No matter how "significant" findings may seem in terms of conventional statistical criteria, in our realm nothing is secure until it has been found repeatedly, ideally by different hands in different loci.

This model can be used with either of the two types of criteria: (a) outstanding creative artists as judged by prominent critics versus representative journeymen in the same art who are well matched on basic demographic variables; or (b) tests like those of Guilford and Torrence given to a relatively unselected group of persons, like college students, who might plausibly become future members of either of the two

[3]More extended advice of this kind may be found in Holt (2005, Vol. 2, chap. 18).

groups just described. In addition, giving a sample of the first type a set of carefully selected Guilford tests would provide a kind of Rosetta stone to help clarify the relevance of the two approaches to one another.

Another striking lack in the pripro research done so far is the failure to study *scientific* creativity. Surely it would not be difficult to find face-valid criteria (e.g., Nobel laureates) and to use the method of extreme groups. There might be important social value if a good predictive measure usable at the college level could be found, especially if it could add to the value of available predictors like intelligence tests and academic record. Thus, it would be most desirable to compare the outstandingly creative scientists with colleagues who looked, on those traditional predictors, equally promising but who failed to become creative. A well-done study of persons in one science would doubtless stimulate similar work in the others. It should not be automatically presumed that the same predictors would work equally well with both sexes, though that might turn out to be the case. Thus, any initial work needs sufficiently large samples of both sexes to permit analysis by sex.

In any work on creativity, I believe that we shall not learn as much by efforts to get one all-purpose measure of adaptive regression as by a more microscopic analysis of specific impulse-defense configurations, or specific kinds of formal properties of pripro and controls thereof. Moreover, researchers should remember the advice of such sage elders as Cronbach (1975) to look for somewhat different patterns of relationship in various demographically and personologically diverse segments of the population, not sweeping, universal correlations. That may be especially important in the hard sciences that today see so many outstanding contributors from Asian cultures.

Psychopathology

Much of the work in this area has followed clinically useless or at least unpromising models: attempting to find scores (or even patterns of scores) that differentiate significantly between a diagnostic group and "normals." Even when a clinically more promising comparison is made (between, e.g., psychotic depressives and superficially similar schizophrenics), the working clinician would be much more interested in hearing about effective cutting scores and the numbers of false positives and false negatives entailed in using them than in regression coefficients or correlations. Diagnostic testers would be well served by research that found Rorschach indicia of good versus poor prognosis within a diagnostic grouping. The control and defense scores might prove particularly useful in such work, along with such little-explored aspects of pripro scoring as combinations and integrations or the creativity ratings.

Finally, as I have argued at greater length elsewhere (Holt, 2003), remember that *most of our theoretical propositions as well as our empirical generalizations are, and must be, probabilistic in form*. We soft psychologists must therefore abandon the dream of the crucial experiment, in which theory is put to empirical test so aseptically and inescapably that one disconfirmation requires us to abandon the theory, at least in that form. Once we accept this fundamental probabilism, does it imply that all we can do about any particular hypothesis is to find out how often it tends to be true? By no means. Much more interestingly and fruitfully, we can try to learn when, where, and in whom it is true or false—in short, to discover its parameters. Freud (1900/1953) observed the oedipus complex in some patients (and himself) and concluded that it was universal. How much more useful it would have been, and still can be, to discover in what kinds of people (demographically, diagnostically, in terms of sociological and cultural anthropological settings, in the context of what genetic predispositions, what kind of family system, etc.) the oedipal pattern holds true, in what milieux it breaks down, in what ways, etc. Once one starts to think about it, the possibilities seem endless and the information to be gained much more useful than just a *p* value attached to the basic statement. The value for the working clinician of this kind of information, laden with some of the juice of real life, should be evident.

REFERENCES[4]

*Ackerman, S. J., Hilsenroth, M. J., Clemence, A. J., Weatherill, R., & Fowler, J. C. (2000). The effects of social cognition and object representation on psychotherapy continuation. *Bulletin of the Menninger Clinic, 64,* 386–408.

Ackman, P. (1960). The effects of induced regression on thinking processes (Doctoral dissertation, University of Michigan, 1960). *Dissertation Abstracts International, 21,* 365–366.

Allison, J. (1967). Adaptive regression and intense religious experiences. *Journal of Nervous and Mental Disease, 145,* 452–463.

*Alston, L. (1970). Ego functioning and memory style. *Journal of Consulting and Clinical Psychology, 34,* 348–354.

*Bachrach, H. (1968). Adaptive regression, empathy, and psychotherapy: Theory and research study. *Psychotherapy, 5,* 203–209.

*Baity, M. R., & Hilsenroth, M. J. (1999). Rorschach aggression variables: A study of reliability and validity. *Journal of Personality Assessment, 72,* 93–110.

Barr, H. B., Langs, R. J., Holt, R. R., Goldberger, L., & Klein, G. S. (1972). *LSD: Personality and experience.* New York: Wiley.

*Bellak, L., & Rosenberg, S. (1966). Effects of anti-depressant drugs on psychodynamics. *Psychosomatics, 7,* 106–114.

[4]Includes all works cited, plus other published reports of pripro research marked with an asterisk.

Benfari, R. C., & Calogeras, R. C. (1968). Levels of cognition and conscience typologies. *Journal of Projective Techniques and Personality Assessment, 32,* 466–474.
Bennett, R. M. (1973). The effects of alcohol on primary process thinking (Doctoral dissertation, Rutgers University, 1973). *Dissertation Abstracts International, 34*(1-B), 404.
Bergan, J. R. (1965). Pitch perception, imagery, and regression in the service of the ego. *Journal of Research in Music Education, 13,* 15–32.
*Berman, A. L. (1972). Videotape self-confrontation of schizophrenic ego and thought processes. *Journal of Consulting and Clinical Psychology, 39,* 78–85.
*Blais, M. A., Hilsenroth, M. J., Castlebury, F., Fowler, J. C., & Baity, M. R. (2001). Predicting *DSM-IV* Cluster B personality disorder criteria from MMPI-2 and Rorschach data: A test of incremental validity. *Journal of Personality Assessment, 76,* 150–168.
*Blais, M. A., Hilsenroth, M. J., Fowler, J. C., & Conboy, C. A. (1999). A Rorschach exploration of the *DSM-IV* borderline personality disorder. *Journal of Clinical Psychology, 55,* 563–572.
*Blatt, S. J., Allison, J., & Feirstein, A. (1969). The capacity to cope with cognitive complexity. *Journal of Personality, 37,* 269–288.
Blatt, S. J., & Berman, W. H., Jr. (1984). A methodology for the use of the Rorschach in clinical research. *Journal of Personality Assessment, 48,* 226–239.
*Blatt, S. J., & Feirstein, A. (1977). Cardiac response and personality organization. *Journal of Consulting and Clinical Psychology, 45,* 115–123.
*Blomquist, K., & Sakki, M. L. (1991). Children with dermatological disease and their mothers. *Acta Dermato-Venereologica, 156*(Suppl.), 28–36.
Borofsky, G. L. (1971). Regression and ego functioning in creative normals and psychotics (Doctoral dissertation, Michigan State University, 1971). *Dissertation Abstracts International, 32*(12-B), 7301.
Caldwell, E. (1993). A longitudinal study of self-image and regression in aging architects of varying degrees of creativity (Doctoral dissertation, University of Montreal, 1993). *Dissertation Abstracts International, 55*(7-B), 3007.
*Caprara, G. V. (1984) Aggressive content and related defenses in Rorschach responses of children ages 6 to 14. *Aggressive Behavior, 10,* 213–220.
Caprara, G. V., e altri. (1977). *Studi sulla personalità: Quattro richerche con il metodo di R. Holt [Studies in personality: Four researches with the method of R. Holt].* Torino, Italy: Boringhiere.
*Caprara, G. V., D'Innocenti, A., Giannotti, A., Pazielli, M. F., & Sicuro, L. (1983). Manifestationi e trasformazione del processo primario in eta evolutiva: Contributo di ricerca [Primary process in childhood and preadolescence: A research on its features and its evolution]. *Neuropsichiatria Infantile, 258–259,* 17–24.
*Caprara, G. V., Giannotti, A., & Pazielli, M. F. (1982). L'analisi del processo primario in eta evolutiva (contributo preliminare di recerca con il reattivo di Rorschach siglato secondo il metodo di Holt) [The analysis of the primary process according to the developmental perspective through the use of Rorschach test according to the Holt method. Preliminary report.]. *Neuropsichiatria Infantile, 248,* 145–158.
*Caprara, G. V., Holt, R. R., Pazielli, M. F., & Giannotti, A. (1986). The development of primary process in children's Rorschachs. *Journal of Personality Assessment, 50,* 149–170.
Chapman, M. V. (1968). Measuring thought process as an ego function in schizophrenic, mentally retarded, and normal adolescents by means of the Rorschach

(Doctoral dissertation, University of Southern California, 1968). *Dissertation Abstracts International, 29*(4-B), 1504.

*Coursey, R. D. (1984). The dynamics of obsessive-compulsive disorder. In T. R. Insel (Ed.), *New findings in obsessive-compulsive disorder* (pp. 104–121). Washington, DC: American Psychiatric Press.

Cronbach, L. J. (1975). Beyond the two disciplines of scientific psychology. *American Psychologist, 30,* 116–127.

Derman, B. I. (1967). Adaptive vs. pathological regression in relation to psychological adjustment. (Doctoral dissertation, University of Georgia, 1967). *Dissertation Abstracts International, 1968, 28*(11-B), 4754–4755.

*Dittborn, J. (1984). Precisiones en torno as diagnostico de la psicosis a traves del test de Rorschach [Diagnostic accuracy in psychotic states with the Rorschach test]. *Terapia Psicologica, 3*(4), 55–61.

*Dittborn, J. (1986). Las organizaciones limitrofes de personalidad en el test de Rorschach: Indices y diagnostico diferencial [Borderline personality organization on the Rorschach test: Indices and differential diagnosis]. *Terapia Psicologica, 5*(8), 11–18.

Ducey, C. P. (1975). *Rorschach experiential and representational dimensions of object relations: A longitudinal study.* Unpublished doctoral dissertation, Harvard University, Cambridge, MA.

Dudek, S. Z. (1968). Regression and creativity. *Journal of Nervous and Mental Disease, 147,* 535–546.

*Dudek, S., & Chamberland-Bouhadana, G. (1982). Primary process in creative persons. *Journal of Personality Assessment, 46,* 239–247.

*Dudek, S., & Verreault, R. (1989). The creative thinking and ego functioning of children. *Creativity Research Journal, 2,* 64–86.

Eagle, C. J. (1964). An investigation of individual consistencies in the manifestations of primary process (Doctoral dissertation, New York University, 1964). *Dissertation Abstracts International, 1965, 25*(3), 2045.

*Ebert, J. N., Ewing, J. H., Prost, M. A., & Enoch, A. L. (1977). Verbal productivity and expression of primary process. *Perceptual and Motor Skills, 44,* 671–675.

Ebert, J. N., Ewing, J. H., Rogers, M. H., & Reynolds, D. J. (1977). Changes in primary process expression in hospitalized schizophrenics treated with phenothiazines: Two projective tasks compared. *Journal of Genetic Psychology, 130,* 83–94.

*Ewing, J. H., Gillis, C. A., Ebert, J. H., & Mathews, H. M. (1975). Profile of perceptual-cognitive traits and personality style of possible relevance to creative productivity. *Perceptual and Motor Skills, 40,* 711–718.

Ewing, J. H., Gillis, C. A., Scott, D. G., & Patzig, W. J. (1982). Fantasy processes and mild physical activity. *Perceptual and Motor Skills, 54,* 363–368.

Ewing, J. H., Scott, D. G., Mendez, A. A., & McBride, T. J. (1984). Effects of aerobic exercise upon affect and cognition. *Perceptual and Motor Skills, 59,* 407–414.

Exner, J. E., Jr. (1993). *The Rorschach, a comprehensive system. Vol. 1: Basic foundations* (3rd ed.). New York: Wiley.

*Feirstein, A. (1967). Personality correlates of tolerance for unrealistic experiences. *Journal of Consulting Psychology, 31,* 387–395.

*Fishman, D. B. (1973a). Holt's Rorschach measure of adaptive regression, mathematical artifact, and prediction of psychotherapy outcome. *Journal of Personality Assessment, 37,* 328–333.

Fishman, D. B. (1973b). Rorschach adaptive regression and change in psychotherapy. *Journal of Personality Assessment, 37,* 218–224.

*Fowler, J. C., Brunnschweiler, B., & Brock, J. (2002). Exploring the inner world of eating disordered patients: An empirical investigation of psychoanalytic concepts. In J. M. Masling & R. F. Bornstein (Eds.), *The psychodynamics of gender and gender roles* (pp. 129–153). Washington, DC: APA Books.

*Fowler, C., Hilsenroth, M. J., & Handler, L. (1995). Early memories: An exploration of theoretically derived queries and their clinical utility. *Bulletin of the Menninger Clinic, 59,* 79–98.

*Fowler, C., Hilsenroth, M. J., & Handler, L. (1996). A multimethod approach to assessing dependency: The early memory dependency probe. *Journal of Personality Assessment, 67,* 399–413.

*Fowler, C., Hilsenroth, M. J., & Nolan, E. (2000). Exploring the inner world of self-mutilating borderline patients: A Rorschach investigation. *Bulletin of the Menninger Clinic, 64,* 365–385.

*Frank, M. A., Tuber, S. B., Slade, A., & Garrod, E. (1994). Mothers' fantasy representations and infant security attachment: A Rorschach study of first pregnancy. *Psychoanalytic Psychology, 11,* 475–490.

Freed, G. O. (1961). *A projective test study of creativity in college students in visual arts.* Unpublished doctoral dissertation, University of Michigan, Ann Arbor.

Freud, S. (1953). The interpretation of dreams. In J. Strachey (Ed. & Trans.), *The standard edition of the complete psychological works of Sigmund Freud* (Vols. 4–5). London: Hogarth Press. (Original work published 1900)

Freud, S. (1957). The unconscious. In J. Strachey (Ed. & Trans.), *The standard edition of the complete psychological works of Sigmund Freud* (Vol. 14, pp. 166–215). London: Hogarth Press. (Original work published 1915)

Freud. S. (1958). Formulations on the two principles of mental functioning. In J. Strachey (Ed. & Trans.), *The standard edition of the complete psychological works of Sigmund Freud* (Vol. 12, pp. 218–226). London: Hogarth Press. (Original work published 1911)

Freud, S. (1961). The ego and the id. In J. Strachey (Ed. & Trans.), *The standard edition of the complete psychological works of Sigmund Freud* (Vol. 19, pp. 12–66). London: Hogarth Press. (Original work published 1923)

*Fromm, E., Oberlander, M. I., & Gruenewald, D. (1970). Perceptual and cognitive processes in different states of consciousness: The waking state and hypnosis. *Journal of Projective Techniques and Personality Assessment, 34,* 375–387.

Gagnon, P. E. (1977). *Sublimation de l'agressivité chez les artistes-peintres* [Sublimation of aggressiveness in artist-painters]. Unpublished doctoral dissertation, Université de Montréal, Canada.

*Gamble, K., & Kellner, H. (1968). Creative functioning and cognitive regression. *Journal of Personality and Social Psychology, 9,* 166–271.

Goldberger, L. (1961). Reactions to perceptual isolation and Rorschach manifestations of the primary process. *Journal of Projective Techniques, 25,* 287–302.

*Goldberger, L., & Holt, R. R. (1961a). A comparison of isolation effects and their personality correlates in two divergent samples (ASD Tech. Rep. No. 61-417). Wright-Patterson Air Force Base, OH: U.S. Air Force.

*Goldberger, L., & Holt, R. R. (1961b). Experimental interference with reality contact: Individual differences. In P. Solomon et al. (Eds.), *Sensory deprivation* (pp. 130–142). Cambridge, MA: Harvard University Press.

*Gray, J. J. (1969). The effect of productivity on primary process and creativity. *Journal of Projective Techniques and Personality Assessment, 34,* 213–218.

*Greenberg, N. (1977). The effects of subliminal neutral and aggressive stimuli on the thought processes of schizophrenics. *Canadian Journal of Behavioural Science, 9,* 187–196.

*Grisso, J. T. (1971). The action-thought dimension, social competence, and defense effectiveness. *Journal of Consulting and Clinical Psychology, 36,* 448.

*Gruenewald, D., Fromm, E., & Oberlander, M. I. (1972). Hypnosis and adaptive regression: An ego-psychological inquiry. In E. Fromm & R. E. Shor (Eds.), *Hypnosis: Research developments and perspectives* (pp. 495–509). Chicago: Aldine-Atherton.

Guilford, J. P. (1950). Creativity. *American Psychologist, 14,* 469–479.

Guilford, J. P. (1967). *The nature of human intelligence.* New York: McGraw-Hill.

*Harrow, M., & Quinlan, D. M. (1985). *Disordered thinking and schizophrenic psychopathology.* New York: Gardner Press.

*Harrow, M., Bromet, E., & Quinlan, D. M. (1974). Predictors of post-hospital adjustment in schizophrenia: Thought disorders and schizophrenic diagnosis. *Journal of Nervous and Mental Disease, 158,* 25–36.

*Harrow, M., Quinlan, D., Wallington, S., & Pickett, L., Jr. (1976). Primitive drive-dominated thinking: Relationship to acute schizophrenia and sociopathy. *Journal of Personality Assessment, 40,* 31–40.

Heath, D. H. (1965). *Explorations of maturity.* New York: Appleton-Century-Crofts.

*Heath, D. H. (1968). *Growing up in college: Liberal education and maturity.* San Francisco: Jossey-Bass.

*Heath, D. H. (1976a). Adolescent and adult predictors of vocational adaptation. *Journal of Vocational Behavior, 9,* 1–10.

*Heath, D. H. (1976b). Competent fathers: Their personalities and marriages. *Human Development, 19,* 26–39.

*Heath, D. H. (1978). Personality correlates of the marital sexual compatibility of professional men. *Journal of Sex and Marital Therapy, 4,* 67–82.

Hébert, A., Lavoie, G., & Ally, G. (1973, August). *Primary process manifestations at three age levels, in chronic schizophrenics and normal controls, monks and laymen.* Paper presented at the 81st Annual Convention of the American Psychological Association, Montréal.

*Hilsenroth, M. J., Hibbard, S. R., Nash, M. R., & Handler, L. (1993). A Rorschach study of narcissism, defense, and aggression in borderline, narcissistic, and Cluster C personality disorders. *Journal of Personality Assessment, 60,* 346–361.

Hoechstetter, F. (1981). *Dynamique pulsionnelle et travail de la fonction synthétique dans le Rorschach de l'artiste créateur* [Drive dynamics and the work of the synthetic function in the Rorschach of the creative artist]. Unpublished doctoral dissertation, Université de Montréal, Canada.

*Holt, R. R. (1960). Cognitive controls and primary processes. *Journal of Psychological Researches, 4,* 105–112.

*Holt, R. R. (1966). Measuring libidinal and aggressive motives and their controls by means of the Rorschach test. In D. Levine (Ed.), *Nebraska symposium on motivation, 1966* (pp. 1–47). Lincoln: University of Nebraska Press.

*Holt, R. R. (1970). Artistic creativity and Rorschach measures of adaptive regression. In B. Klopfer, M. M. Meyer, & F. B. Brawer (Eds.), *Developments in the Rorschach technique: Vol. 3. Aspects of personality structure* (pp. 263–320). New York: Harcourt Brace Jovanovich.

Holt, R. R. (1983). *Il processo primario nel Rorschach e nel materiale tematico* [The primary process in the Rorschach and in thematic materials]. (A. De Coro, Trans., G. V. Caprara & N. Dazzi, Eds.). Rome: Borla.

Holt, R. R. (2003). New directions for basic psychoanalytic research: Implications from the work of Benjamin Rubinstein. *Psychoanalytic Psychology, 20,* 195–213.

Holt, R. R. (2005). Primary process thinking: Theory, assessment, and empirical research (2 vols.). *Psychological Issues Monograph No. 65/66.*

Holt, R. R., & Goldberger, L. (1961). Assessment of individual resistance to sensory alteration. In B. E. Flaherty (Ed.), *Psychophysiological aspects of space flight* (pp. 248–262). New York: Columbia University Press.

*Huard, M. (1985). Les processus primaires et secondaires de pensée chez les musiciens de jazz professionnels: Une étude sur la créativité. [Primary and secondary thought processes in professional jazz musicians: A study of creativity]. *Revue Québécoise de Psychologie, 6,* 109–118.

Inoue, K. (1965). Resiliency of psychic functioning—A study by means of the Rorschach test. *Rorschachiana Japonica, 8,* 57–69.

*Irizarry, R. (1971). Anxiety, repression, and varieties of antisocial behavior in psychopaths. *Journal of Personality Assessment, 35,* 56–61.

*Kahn, M. H. (1965). A factor-analytic study of personality, intelligence, and history characteristics of murderers. *Proceedings of the 73rd Annual Convention of the American Psychological Association, 1965.* Washington, DC: American Psychological Association.

*Kahn, M. H. (1971). Murderers who plead insanity: A descriptive factor-analytic study of personality, social, and history variables. *Genetic Psychology Monographs, 84,* 275–360.

*Kleinman, M. J., & Russ, S. W. (1988). Primary process thinking and anxiety in children. *Journal of Personality Assessment, 52,* 254–262.

Klopfer, B., & Kelley, D. M. (1942). *The Rorschach technique.* New York: World.

Kris, E. (1952). *Psychoanalytic explorations in art.* New York: International Univ. Press.

Langan, R. (1984). Progressive regressions: Ego development and primary process thinking (Doctoral dissertation, New York University, 1984). *Dissertation Abstracts International, 46*(1-B), 305.

*Lapkin, B. (1962). The relation of primary process thinking to the recovery of subliminal material. *Journal of Nervous and Mental Disease, 135,* 10–25.

Lavoie, G. (1964). *Les processus primaires et secondaires chez les mères d'enfants schizophrènes.* [Primary and secondary processes in the mothers of schizophrenic children]. Unpublished doctoral dissertation, Université de Montréal, Canada.

*Lavoie, G., & Elie, R. (1985). The clinical relevance of hypnotizability in psychosis: With reference to thinking processes and sample variances. In D. Waxman, P. Misra, M. Gibson, & M. A. Basker (Eds.), *Modern trends in hypnosis* (pp. 41–64). New York: Plenum Press.

*Lavoie, G., Lieberman, J., Sabourin, M., & Brisson, A. (1978). Individual and group assessment of hypnotic responsivity in coerced volunteer chronic schizophrenics. In F. H. Frankel & H. S. Zamansky (Eds.), *Hypnosis at its bicentennial* (pp. 109–124). New York: Plenum Press.

Lavoie, G., Michaud, M., Elie, R., & Amar, V. (1987). Hypnotizability as a prognostic index in schizophrenia. II: The functional relationship between increasing mastery over autistic thinking disorders and improvement in hypnotic response over a 10–17 years period [Abstract]. *International Journal of Clinical and Experimental Hypnosis, 35,* 179.

*Lavoie, G., Sabourin, M., Ally, G., & Langlois, J. (1976). Hypnotizability as a function of adaptive regression among chronic psychotic patients. *International Journal of Clinical and Experimental Hypnosis, 24,* 238–257.

Lazar, B. (1975). Creativity, primary process manifestations and ego activity and passivity (Doctoral dissertation, University of Chicago, 1975). *Dissertation Abstracts International, 36*(4-B), 1922.

*Lazar, B. S., & Harrow, M. (1985). Paranoid and nonparanoid schizophrenia: Drive dominated thinking and thought pathology at two phases of disorder. *Journal of Clinical Psychology, 41,* 145–151.

*Lehtinen, S. (1981). Developmental changes in primary process manifestations in thought: A follow-up study of girls from four to seventeen. *Psychiatria Fennica, 12,* 131–152.

*Lehtinen-Railo, S. (1983). Consolidation of primary process thought and its integration. II. A longitudinal study of girls from four to seventeen. *Psychiatria Fennica, 14,* 107–117.

*Leichsenring, F. (1991). Primary process thinking, primitive defensive operations and object relationships in borderline and neurotic patients. *Psychopathology, 24,* 39–44.

*Leiderman, P. (1962). Imagery and sensory deprivation, an experimental study (Tech. Rep. No. MRL-TDR-62-28). Wright-Patterson Air Force Base, OH: U.S. Air Force.

Levin, L. A., & Harrison, R. H. (1976). Hypnosis and regression in the service of the ego. *International Journal of Clinical and Experimental Hypnosis, 24,* 400–418.

Loevinger, J. (1976). *Ego development.* San Francisco: Jossey-Bass.

Matalon, E. (1975). *Primary process thought and its relation to some areas of functioning in ten-year-old children.* Unpublished doctoral dissertation, Université de Montréal.

*Maupin, E. W. (1965). Individual differences in response to a Zen meditation exercise. *Journal of Consulting Psychology, 29,* 139–145.

Mayman, M. (1970). Reality contact, defense effectiveness, and psychopathology in Rorschach Form-Level scores. In B. Klopfer, M. M. Meyer, F. B. Brawer, & W. G. Klopfer (Eds.), *Developments in the Rorschach technique: Vol. 3. Aspects of personality structure* (pp. 11–46). New York: Harcourt-Brace-Jovanovich.

*Meloy, J. R. (1984). Thought organization and primary process in the parents of schizophrenics. *British Journal of Medical Psychology, 57,* 279–281.

Messick, S. (1995). Validity of psychological assessment: Validation of inferences from persons' responses and performances as scientific inquiry into score meaning. *American Psychologist, 50,* 741–749.

*Mezei, A., & Erdely, E. (1965). As alkoholista szemelyisegszerkezet megmutatkozasaa a Rorschach-probaban [Personality structure of the alcoholic as reflected in the Rorschach test]. *Pszichologiai Tanulmanyok* (Budapest), 639–658. (English summary.)

*Michaud, M., Lavoie, G., Elie, R., & Amar, V. (1987). Hypnotizability as a prognostic index in schizophrenia. I: Prediction of personality improvement and discharge rate over a 10–17 years period. *International Journal of Clinical and Experimental Hypnosis, 35,* 179 (abstract).

*Murray, J. F. (1985). Borderline manifestations in the Rorschachs of male transsexuals. *Journal of Personality Assessment, 49,* 454–466.

Murray, J. F., & Russ, S. (1981). Adaptive regression and types of cognitive flexibility. *Journal of Personality Assessment, 45,* 59–65.

Myers, T. (1972). *Psychobiological factors associated with monotony tolerance* (Report No. R-72-1). Washington, DC: American Institute for Research.

Nass, M. (1963). *Report on clinic follow-up study of schizophrenic children.* Unpublished manuscript. Brooklyn College, New York: Educational Clinic.

Newmeyer, J. A. (1972). Creativity and non-verbal communication in pre-adolescent white and black children (Doctoral dissertation, Harvard University, 1972). *Dissertation Abstracts International, 33*(1-B), 426–427.

*Oberlander, M. I., Gruenewald, D., & Fromm, E. (1970). Content and structural characteristics of thought processes during hypnosis. *Proceedings of the Annual Convention of the American Psychological Association, 5*(pt. 2), 843–844.

*Patrick, J., & Wolfe, B. (1983). Rorschach presentation of borderline personality disorder: Primary process manifestations. *Journal of Clinical Psychology, 39,* 442–447.

Philip, A. F. (1959). The effect of lysergic acid diethylamide (LSD-25) on primary process thought manifestations (Doctoral dissertation, New York University, 1959). *Dissertation Abstracts International, 24*(4), 961.

Pine, F. (1962). Creativity and primary process: Sample variations. *Journal of Nervous and Mental Disease, 134,* 506–511.

Pine, F., & Holt, R. R. (1960). Creativity and primary process: A study of adaptive regression. *Journal of Abnormal and Social Psychology, 61,* 370–379.

*Pryor, D. B. (1967). A comparison of the occurrence of oral and anal content on the Rorschach. *Journal of Projective Techniques and Personality Assessment, 31*(5), 26–28.

*Quinlan, D., & Harrow, M. (1974). Boundary disturbances in schizophrenia. *Journal of Abnormal Psychology, 83,* 533–541.

*Quinlan, D., Harrow, M., Tucker, G., & Carlson, K. (1972). Varieties of "disordered" thinking on the Rorschach: Findings in schizophrenic and nonschizophrenic patients. *Journal of Abnormal Psychology, 79,* 47–53.

Rabkin, J. (1967). Psychoanalytic assessment of change in organization of thought after psychotherapy (Doctoral dissertation, New York University, 1967). *Dissertation Abstracts International 1968, 28*(11-B), 4763.

Rapaport, D., Gill, M. M., & Schafer, R. (1968). *Diagnostic psychological testing* (rev. ed., R. R. Holt, Ed.). New York: International Universities Press.

*Ribiero da Silva, A. (1962). Atrizes, atores e diretores do Brasil através do teste de Rorschach [Actresses, actors, and directors of Brazil via the Rorschach test]. *Arquivos Brasileiros de Psicotécnica, 14,* 5–30.

*Rivard, E., & Dudek, S. Z. (1977). Primary process thinking in the same children at two developmental levels. *Journal of Personality Assessment, 41,* 120–130.

*Rogolsky, M. M. (1968). Artistic creativity and adaptive regression in third grade children. *Journal of Projective Techniques and Personality Assessment, 32*(1), 53–62.

Rosegrant, J. (1980). Adaptive regression of two types. *Journal of Personality Assessment, 44,* 592–599.

Rosegrant, J. (1982). Primary process patterning in college students' Rorschach responses. *Journal of Personality Assessment, 46,* 578–581.

*Rosina, P. L. (1965). Componenti istintuali e motivazionali nel processo creativo [Instinctual and motivational components in the creative process]. *Contributi dell'Instituto di Psicologia, 27,* 197–244.

*Russ, S. W. (1980). Primary process integration on the Rorschach and achievement in children. *Journal of Personality Assessment, 44,* 338–344.

*Russ, S. W. (1981). Primary process integration on the Rorschach and achievement in children: A follow-up study. *Journal of Personality Assessment, 45,* 473–477.

*Russ, S. W. (1982). Sex differences in primary process thinking and flexibility in children. *Journal of Personality Assessment, 46,* 569–577.

Russ, S. W. (1988a). Primary process thinking on the Rorschach, divergent thinking, and coping in children. *Journal of Personality Assessment, 52,* 539–548.

*Russ, S. W. (1988b). The role of primary process thinking in child development. In H. O. Lerner & P. M. Lerner (Eds.), *Primitive mental states and the Rorschach* (pp. 601–618). Madison, CT: International Universities Press.
*Russ, S. W., & Grossman-McKee, A. (1990). Affective expression in children's fantasy play, primary process thinking on the Rorschach, and divergent thinking. *Journal of Personality Assessment, 54,* 756–771.
Saretsky, T. (1966). Effects of chlorpromazine on primary-process thought manifestations. *Journal of Abnormal Psychology, 71,* 247–252.
*Saunders, E. A. (1991). Rorschach indicators of chronic childhood sexual abuse in female borderline inpatients. *Bulletin of the Menninger Clinic, 55,* 48–71.
*Schimek, J. G. (1974). Some developmental aspects of primary process manifestations in the Rorschach. *Journal of Personality Assessment, 38,* 226–229.
*Scott, D. G., Ewing, J. H., Miller, W. S., & Gillis, C. A. (1984). Physical activity and responses to projective stimuli in neurotic vs. psychotic depression. *Journal of Personality, 48,* 240–244.
*Seguin, M.-H., & Bouchard, M.-A. (1996). Adaptive regression and countertransference mental activity. *Psychoanalytic Psychology, 13,* 457–474.
*Silver, M. J. (1974). Hypnotizability as a function of repression, adaptive regression, and mood. *Journal of Consulting and Clinical Psychology, 42,* 41–46.
Silverman, L. H. (1963). On the relationship between aggressive imagery and thought disturbance in Rorschach responses. *Journal of Projective Techniques and Personality Assessment, 27,* 336–344.
*Silverman, L. H. (1965). A study of the effects of subliminally presented aggressive stimuli on the production of pathological thinking in a non-psychiatric population. *Journal of Nervous and Mental Disease, 141,* 443–455.
*Silverman, L. H. (1966). A technique for the study of psycho-dynamic relationships: The effects of subliminally presented aggressive stimuli on the production of pathological thinking in a schizophrenic population. *Journal of Consulting Psychology, 30,* 103–111.
*Silverman, L. H. (1967). An experimental approach to the study of dynamic propositions in psychoanalysis: The relationship between the aggressive drive and ego regression. *Journal of the American Psychoanalytic Association, 15,* 376–403.
*Silverman, L. H., & Candell, P. (1970). On the relationship between aggressive activation, symbiotic merging, intactness of body boundaries and manifest pathology in schizophrenics. *Journal of Nervous and Mental Disease, 150,* 387–399.
*Silverman, L. H., & Goldweber, A. M. (1966). A further study of the effects of subliminal aggressive stimulation on thinking. *Journal of Nervous and Mental Disease, 143,* 463–472.
Silverman, L. H., Lapkin, B., & Rosenbaum, I. S. (1962). Manifestations of primary-process thinking in schizophrenia. *Journal of Projective Techniques, 26,* 117–127.
Tomkins, S. S. (1947). *The Thematic Apperception Test: The theory and technique of interpretation.* New York: Grune & Stratton.
Torrance, E. P. (1966). *Torrance Tests of Creative Thinking: Norms, technical manual.* Princeton, NJ: Personnel Press.
*Verrault, R. (1986). La créativité et la régression au service du Moi chez l'enfant [Creativity and regression in the service of the ego in children]. *Revue Québécoise de Psychologie, 7*(1–2), 26–43.
Vezina, V. (1981). *Étude comparative de la personalité de l'artiste et du psychothérapeute à travers le test de Rorschach* [Comparative study of the personalities of artists and

psychotherapists by means of the Rorschach test]. Unpublished doctoral dissertation, Université de Montréal, Canada.
*von Holt, H. W., Jr., Sengstake, C. B., Sonoda, B. C., & Draper, W. A. (1960). Orality, image fusions and concept formation. *Journal of Projective Techniques, 24,* 194–198.
von Wiederhold, M. W. (1995). Piercing the body: A symbolic voice. A psychoanalytic view of contemporary body modification (Doctoral dissertation, Wright Institute, 1995). *Dissertation Abstracts International, 56*(5-B), 2890.
Warner, M. (1998). *No go the bogeyman: Scaring, lulling, and making mock.* London: Chatto & Windus.
Wiseman, R. J., & Reyher, J. (1973). Hypnotically induced dreams using the Rorschach inkblots as stimuli: A test of Freud's theory of dreams. *Journal of Personality and Social Psychology, 27,* 329–336.
Wright, N. A., & Abbey, D. S. (1965). Perceptual deprivation tolerance and adequacy of defenses. *Perceptual and Motor Skills, 20,* 35–38.
Wright, N. A., & Zubek, J. P. (1969). Relationship between perceptual deprivation tolerance and adequacy of defenses as measured by the Rorschach. *Journal of Abnormal Psychology, 74,* 615–617.
*Wulach, J. S. (1977). Piagetian cognitive development and primary process thinking in children. *Journal of Personality Assessment, 41,* 230–237.
*Zarcone, V., Zukowsky, E., Gulevich, G., Dement, W., & Hodges, E. (1974). Rorschach responses subsequent to REM deprivation in schizophrenic and nonschizophrenic patients. *Journal of Clinical Psychology, 30,* 248–250.
*Zimet, C. H., & Fine, J. J. (1965). Primary and secondary process thinking in two types of schizophrenia. *Journal of Projective Techniques and Personality Assessment, 29,* 93–99.

Appendix A
Excerpt From Scoring Manual

L 1 O. ORAL: Images and themes from the early, oral-sucking/oral-receptive period of life; but also crude oral material that has no further qualitative specification. Distinguish carefully from *Ag 1 O,* however.

(2)[5] a. *Sucking; nursing.*

'Animal sucking from this red part.'

(3) b. *Breasts, nipples.* Score when seen in isolation or unclothed; score also *L 2 S.*

'Two women dancing, topless go-go girls.' (Score also *L 1 E-V, Impl.,* and *Eu.*)

(2) c. *Mouth; lips; tongue.* Score when seen in isolation (i.e., not just as one part pointed out in a face). (See also *Ag 1 O.d.*)

Do NOT score: 'Jaws of a crocodile'; 'shark's mouth'—these are all scored *Ag 1 O*; or 'bird's bill'—*Ag 1 O wk.*

(3) d. *Famine; drought; starving.* (Score also *Neg.*)

'He was dying of thirst'; 'a scene in one of those African countries where they had devastating crop failures.'

Do NOT score: 'smothering,' 'choking'—though these activities often involve the mouth, they refer to respiratory need, only rarely treated as related to orality in the Freudian literature. Just score the Aggression.

(3) e. *Nausea; vomit.* (Score also *Neg.*)

L 2 O. ORAL content of the receptive (or nonspecific) kind, milder than *L 1 O.*

(3) a. *Breasts* when seen as part of a person *and* emphasized either by description or by manner of presentation. Mention among several other body parts earns only *L 2 O tend.* Score also *L 2 S.*

---

[5]Parenthetical numbers are the *DD* ratings for the examples.

'Large, motherly figure because of the large bosom'; 'lack of hair makes them look like men, "buz-ooms" make them look like women' (for the latter response, score also *L 2 H, C-co 1.b, Cx H–*); 'buxom woman'; 'well-endowed woman.' (For last two, score also *Eu.*)

Do NOT score: breasts when bare or seen in isolation (as a separate body part); score *L 1 O* and *L 1 E-V.*

(1) b. *Mouth; lips; tongue; throat; gullet.* Score when seen as part of a person or animal *and* unduly emphasized (either by description, by size, by activity, e.g., open, or by bad form level). If in doubt, do not score (or *tend* only).

'Mask—grinning mouth, maybe a tongue; it *is* a tongue'; 'animals holding a bridge in their mouths, big wide open mouth'; 'fish's face, big lips.' (In each of these responses, note the attention and concern given the mouth; in the last, the description is unusual when applied to a fish.) 'People ... mouths wide open'; faces of two boys with something sticking out of their mouths'; 'lip-print'; 'head of some prehistoric animal' (upper side D of Card IV; in the inquiry, S said that the *white space* was the mouth. The blot offers little perceptual support for this notion and the mouth dominates the percept though not mentioned in the original verbalization: *Del;* also *R-an, R-time.*)

Do NOT score: 'A face—eyes, nose, mouth'; 'a fish, this would be the mouth.' Even though 'mouth' is the only part mentioned (hence, *tend*), it is not emphasized; form level was OK).

(1) c. *Stomach, belly,* when seen in isolation or unduly emphasized, either external as in 'fat bellies' or as internal anatomy.

'Stomach and esophagus' (Card III, upper red D; also, *Cx I*); 'clowns with enormous, ridiculous fat bellies and holding something.' (But if merely 'clowns with fat bellies' score *wk.*)

Do NOT score: 'A person—the head, arms, stomach, legs' (*tend* only); 'a fat woman' (no mention of belly). Any reference to obesity should be scored only *L 2 O tend.*

(2) d. *Kissing,* attributed to either people or animals; score also *L 2 S* except when clearly nonsexual.

'Animals rubbing noses' (score *wk,* also *R-an* and *L 2 S tend*).

Do NOT score: 'Mother kissing her baby'; 'two dogs, nose to nose' (description of position only).

(1) e. *Intoxicated people; drug taking:* any reference to addictive or intoxicating substances or their use. N.B.: Includes 'shooting up' (with *Ag 2 A*, also *R-fig*).

'Drunks'; 'two people, stoned'; 'men a little drunk over a punch bowl'; 'opium pipe'; 'people turning on'; 'joint of grass.'

Do NOT score: 'pink elephants'—*tend* only (stereotype of delirium tremens).

(1) f. *Pig; hog.*

(1) g. *Smoking, smoking materials.*

'Face, eyes, nose, has a cigarette in his mouth'; 'cigar'; 'nicotine stain'—score *wk.*

Do NOT score: 'ash tray'—*tend* only.

(1) h. *Eating, drinking.* Score when described as activities of either people or animals; also score chewing gum, and active attempts to get food or drink. If the emphasis is on the destructive aspect (as, biting or tearing) or on stalking or looking for prey, score *Ag 2 O* instead. In general, food-seeking by aggressive, predatory animals is scored *Ag O.* The mention of food or drink is not separately scorable (as j.) if h. has been scored.

'Bears celebrating, having a toast' (also *C-a-c 2*); 'animals drinking water'; 'fish swimming for their dinner'; 'chickens pecking on the ground—greed.'

(1) i. *Cooking, preparation or serving of food.* (See also n., below.)

'Two women, stirring up something in a couple of pots' (of course, if S does not specify, it could be something inedible like dye, but here we make the normative assumption since there was no inquiry); 'ducks cooking something in two pots' (score also *C-a-c* 2).

Do NOT score: 'witches stirring something in a cauldron.'

(1) j. *Food, drink* (non-alcoholic). Score whether seen in isolation or as part of larger response. A response that describes eating, drink-

ing, or cooking and also depicts a food substance is, however, scored only once (under the appropriate category above).

'Couple of carrots'; 'orange and strawberry icing'; 'chicken legs' (do not score if clear that this is seen not as food but just as part of a bird); 'meat hanging in a butcher shop'; 'wishbone' (weak).

Do NOT score: 'Crab' or 'lobster' (*tend* only) unless it is specified or implied that it is food (e.g., by having the red color given by cooking). If lobster is seen as red but edibility is implied in no other way, score *L 2 O wk*.

(1) k. *Containers for food or drink; utensils for cooking or eating.* Do not give more than one *L 2 O* score to a response even if it includes reference to activity, object, and substance; but you may increase the *DD*.

'Wine glass'; 'bottle opener'; 'tureen'; 'frying pan'; 'silverware'; 'decanter.'

BUT: Score as *wk* 'tea-kettle' and 'dish pan'; these have a more remote association with eating. Also, score 'pot' or 'cauldron' on Card 3 only if the act of cooking is implied; otherwise, *tend.*

'Empty cupboard': score *wk,* with Neg.

(1) l. *Hunger, appetite.* (Usually expressed in thematic elaboration.)

'Boy in Campbell's soup ads—I don't know why his tongue is sticking out; maybe in anticipation'; 'hungry birds waiting for mother to bring something to eat'; 'he was terribly hungry and did not know where to go' (*DD*=2).

(1) m. *Persons with oral identity or social role:* glutton, gormandizer, tea-taster, waiter, cook, gourmet.

(1) n. *Places where food or drink is available:* restaurant, picnic, birthday party; bar, saloon.

Ag 1 O. PRIMITIVE ORAL AGGRESSION. Material that Freudians call drive-derivatives from the late, oral-biting stage. The work of Lavoie (see Chapter 15) suggests that poorly controlled oral aggression is strongly associated with schizophrenia and schizotypy. For an illuminating discussion of its roots and manifestations in mythology, art, and culture since ancient times, see Warner (1998).

Exner score: AG (for any movement response with active aggression).

(4) a. *Cannibalism; eating of human beings* (if done by animals, score *wk* and *R-an*).

'Two men cutting up the body of a third to eat him'; 'frightened figure, going to be eaten up by these four chattering figures.' (Note that the latter is also scored *L 2 O* for 'chattering.') 'Other bugs will eat him [spider] up'—*wk*.

BUT: Cannibals seen on Card III (popular response) are scored *Ag 1 O wk* (also *Cx C*), with *DD*=3, because in that context they are typically seen in a kind of cultural stereotype, often as portrayed in cartoons (in which case *R-dep* and *Cx H* apply), unless elaborated in a way that justifies a full *Ag 1 O*. If they are seen as cooking, score *L 2 O* as well.

(4) b. *Sadistic or castrative biting.*

'Grasping mouth—it's going to bite off this part' (of another person); 'mouth, fangs; I can't tell whether it's pain or desire to harm in that mouth.'

(3) c. *Parasitic animals.*

'Tapeworm'; 'liver fluke.'

(2) d. *Teeth; jaws* when seen in isolation.

'Jaws of a crocodile'; 'shark's mouth'—score even when teeth are not explicitly mentioned; 'bird's bill'—score *wk*. In a response that qualifies for *L 1 O.c* when teeth are also mentioned, score *both L 1 O* and *Ag 1 O*. Note that if gruesomely elaborated, the *DD* should be raised.

Ag 2 O. ORAL AGGRESSION. Formerly scored as *L 2 O-Ag*, this score may be included in the totals for Oral and Libidinal as well as for Aggression, depending on one's needs and purposes.

Exner score: AG (for any movement response with active aggression) b., some d., e. g.

(3) a. *Poison:* poisonous foods and plants, poisonous snakes or spiders.

'Deadly nightshade flower'; 'bottle of poison'; 'poisonous toadstool'; 'cobra'; 'black widow.' Since all spiders are popularly feared as poisonous, they should be scored, even without mention of poisonousness: 'big scary spider.'

(2) BUT: The popular 'spider ' on Card X is scored *wk* unless appropriately elaborated. N.B.: 'A spider, not poisonous, one of the friendly kind'—score *wk* and *Neg+*.

Do NOT score: if danger or poison is not mentioned, score 'toadstool' *Ag 2 O tend.*

b. *Biting, chewing.* Even sucking may be scored if done aggressively, as in four of the examples below:

(3) 'Something with snapping jaws; there's his hot breath coming out to get you'; ''worms sucking the eyes out of this poor rabbit'; 'vampire sucking blood.'

(2) 'An animal rending his prey'; 'figures sucking—weird! Look more like dragons than people'; 'rats ... symbolic of the nibbling away of the good green earth; here it looks like it's dying' (also *Ag 2 R*).

BUT score *wk:* 'Devastated chicken; looks the way a chicken does after you get through eating it.' The initial statement suggests that the emphasis is on the destructive aspects of eating; the response thus gets a full *Ag 2 R* and *L 2 O* plus *Ag 2 O wk.*

(2) c. *Teeth, jaws, beak,* also 'mouth' of a prototypically aggressive animal: when seen as part of a face or organism *and* unduly emphasized, according to the same principles as in *L 2 O* (above).

'An animal's head; the eyes, nose, fangs' (here the use of the word 'fangs' is considered enough emphasis to justify the score); 'these people have very strange jaws, as if their teeth are too big' (part of a longer description of complete human figures); 'old man with missing teeth, his mouth collapsed' (also *Ag 2 R* and *Neg* as control); 'claws of a crab' (the big claw of a crab or lobster *bites* as hurtfully as many another animal's jaws).

(2) d. ***Big, biting animals: shark, alligator, crocodile, tiger, lion; also vampire bat.*** All animals (mostly ferocious carnivores) that are feared because of their biting are scored if teeth, beak, jaws, open mouth, or food-seeking are mentioned. If simply named without elaboration of the threat or biting parts, score *wk.* (See g., below.)

'Sabre-toothed tigers'; 'wolverine, stalking prey'; 'mad dog chasing somebody'; 'bat, one of those blood-suckers'; 'two lions, not exactly as if ready to leap' (also score *Neg* for the negation of hostile intent, which *is* verbalized and so is scored);

Do NOT score: 'bat' (not specified as vampire, biting, etc.); 'buzzard', 'vulture'—score *Ag 2 O tend* but full *Ag 2 R* because carrion-eaters are associated primarily with death.

(2) e. *Verbal aggression:* Arguing, cursing, bawling out, tirade, etc.

'Ladies saying nasty things to each other'; 'people arguing, swearing at each other'; 'motherly figure who is telling them not to do something, threatening'; 'women having an argument.' (Score the control *O-vbl* for all of these.)

Do NOT score: 'Two dogs barking at each other, fighting over meat': *Ag 2 A* for the fighting plus *L 2 O* for the meat, but only *Ag 2 O tend* for the barking.

(2) f. *Spitting; spit.*

'A glob of mucous someone just coughed up'—*wk* because aggressive spitting is not explicit.

(1) g. *Prey-taking by animals* not specified as in d., above.

'Animals stalking'; 'some kind of animal looking down at its prey.'

BUT: 'raccoon, stalking'—score *wk* because this animal is not usually thought of as fierce or menacing.

8

Defense and Its Assessment: The Lerner Defense Scale

Paul M. Lerner
Private Practice, Camden, Maine

Rapaport envisioned the relationship between psychoanalytic theory and the Rorschach as a two-way street. In one direction, he saw the theory as offering the Rorschach assessor a vast array of clinical concepts and formulations that could serve to enliven, broaden, and deepen test-derived inferences remarkably. In the other direction, he saw the Rorschach as providing the psychoanalytic theorist and researcher a means for operationalizing concepts, often elusive and overly abstract, and saw further how this process could allow the empirical investigation of important but untested formulations, adding to the evolving scope of psychoanalytic theory. This chapter is based upon and exemplifies the latter aspect of Rapaport's vision.

The concept of defense has been a cornerstone of psychoanalytic theory and, correspondingly, a major subject of Rorschach investigation (Holt, 1970; Lerner & Lerner, 1986; Schafer, 1954). Until the 1980s, however, the concept remained relatively immune to theoretical shifts taking place in psychoanalytic theory, especially those emerging from object relations theory and self theory. As Stolorow and Lachmann (1980) noted, "An examination of the history of the concept of defense indicates that while ideas about what a defense wards off have evolved, the concept of defense itself has remained static" (p. 89). As a consequence, applications of the Rorschach, for assessing defense both clinically (Schafer) and in research (Holt; Levine, & Spivak, 1964), were exclusively and limitedly wedded to older theoretical models.

In contrast with this earlier period, the past 20 years have witnessed a virtual explosion of new ways of understanding defense and the mechanisms of defense. Most significant of these newer conceptualizations are the following: theories of complex motivational properties of the ego (Kris, 1984; Schafer, 1968), a functional theory of defense (Brenner, 1982), an object representational theory of defense (Kernberg, 1976), a "two-person" theory of defense (Modell, 1984), and a self-psychological theory of defense (Kohut, 1984). These newer formulations differ from each other and from older theories of defense in several ways, including the referent of the defense (e.g., impulse, affect, environmental failure, self-fragmentation) and the assumed relationship between internal homeostasis and the external world. In parallel with these changing models of defense have also come novel and innovative Rorschach approaches for assessing defense.

In this chapter I report on the development and current status of one of these innovative Rorschach measures—the Lerner Defense scale. Because the scale is theoretically based, I first review several psychoanalytic conceptualizations of defense, emphasizing the contributions of Freud, Klein, and Kernberg. I then present the scale itself, including studies involving its reliability and validity. Finally, I review another innovative measure of defense and compare it with the Lerner Defense scale.

CONCEPTIONS OF DEFENSE

Freud's various and changing views of defense have been reviewed by several authors (Hoffer, 1968; Leeuw, 1971; Madison, 1961; Rapaport, 1958). In his earliest writings, prior to 1900, Freud used the term *defense* to describe the ego's struggles against painful ideas and affects. In these early papers he outlined the processes of conversion, displacement of affects, withdrawal from reality, repression, and projection. Freud presented his initial concept of defense within the concept of an incomplete conceptualization of the ego; nonetheless, as Rapaport noted, the implicit notions within this early view—that drives are dammed up and displaced and that the defense, by preventing the recall or reencountering of a reality experience, prevents or delays the experience of a painful affect—remained foundations upon which most later psychoanalytic conceptions of defense were built.

Following a period in which his concern with defense waned, Freud's (1923/1961) interest rekindled with his publication of *The Ego and the Id*. In that work he made explicit his tripartite model of the personality and accorded the concept of defense a central role. Freud conceived of defense as an ego function and regarded the defense mechanisms as executive methods of this ego capacity (Leeuw, 1971). Whereas in his earlier view he conceptualized repression as responsible for the creation of anxiety, herein he posited that it was anxiety that prompted the need for repression. Freud further suggested that the ego had a range of defenses at its disposal. He outlined isolation, undoing, denial, and splitting of the ego, and reconsidered repression.

Building on the structural model as outlined in *The Ego and The Id* (Freud, 1923/1961), authors subsequent to Freud drew attention to the chronology and genesis of the defense mechanisms, as well as to their relation to levels of ego and drive organization. Anna Freud (1936) systematized the concepts of the specific defense mechanisms, clarified the relationship between defense and reality relations, and studied the role of affects (Rapaport, 1958). Reich (1933) investigated and described the defensive aspects of character formation. He conceived of character as bolstering the primary repression of instincts.

While anchoring her views in several of Freud's specific formulations, Klein (1935, 1946) fundamentally reconceptualized defense by suggesting that such mechanisms not only regulate affects and drives, but are also related to the effects on intimacy and cognition of the experience, organization, and internalization of object relations. For Klein, defenses not only protect the ego from overwhelming sensations, but are also nondefensive organizing principles of infantile mental life.

Two organizing principles stand out in Klein's (1935) portrait of infantile mentation: splitting and projection. Klein's understanding of splitting derives from Freud's (1915/1957) use of the concept in *Instincts and Their Vicissitudes*. In that work, he proposed the idea of an early developmental distinction between a purified pleasure ego and a collection of excessively negative object impressions (Grala, 1980). Whereas the former represents an internalization of gratifying object relations, the latter results from a projection of feelings associated with nongratifying, frustrating object relations.

A special form of projection detailed by Klein (1935) was projective identification. In this instance, unwanted parts of the self and internal object are split off and placed into an external object. Because the object is not experienced as distinct and separate, but rather is identified with the projected parts, the process allows possession of and control over the object. Bion (1967) extended the concept of projective identification using the metaphor of the container and the contained. He suggested that projective identification not only afforded the disavowal and projection of unwanted parts of the self, but also permitted the containment of such parts within the object. For a fuller discussion of this concept, including the contributions of Winnicott (1960) and Ogden (1983) and its extension to the treatment situation, see Lerner (1988).

An attempt to integrate the two streams of psychoanalytic formulations of defense—the ego psychological and that evolving from Klein and the British school of object relations—is represented by the work of Kernberg (1975), particularly by his structural concept of levels of defensive organization. Kernberg proposed a hierarchical organization of levels of character pathology linked to type of defensive functioning and developmental level of internalized object relations. For Kernberg, internalized object relations are organized on the basis of specific defensive operations. As part of this model, he systematically defined and coordinated the more primitive defenses described by Klein and clarified the distinction between splitting and repression. Accordingly, although splitting is a developmental precursor of repression, it continues to function pathologically in those patients who are preoedipally fixated, as indicated by an inability to form whole object relations and by a disturbance in object constancy.

Overall, Kernberg (1975) identified two major levels of defensive organization of the ego, one associated with preoedipal and the other with oedipal pathology. At the lower level, splitting or primitive dissociation is the basic defensive operation, with a concomitant impairment of the ego's synthetic function. Splitting is bolstered through the related defenses of low-level denial, primitive idealization, primitive devaluation, and projective identification. At a higher developmental level, associated with oedipal pathology, repression supplants splitting as the major defense and is accompanied by the related defensive operations of intellectualization, rationalization, undoing, and high-level forms of denial and projection.

Although not as directly pertinent to the focus of this chapter as the work of Kernberg (1975), two other recent conceptualizations of defense merit inclusion in this review. In suggesting that defenses directly mediate affect between objects, Modell (1984) relocated defensive activity from the intrapsychic to the interpersonal, or what he referred to as a "two-person context." He contended that "affects are the mediums through which defenses against objects occur" (p. 41). Once affects are linked to objects, "the process of instinct-defense becomes a defense against objects" (p. 41). The individual, as it were, masters affects by controlling the object carriers (Brierly, 1937, p. 51).

On the assumption that the communication of affects is "object-seeking," Modell (1975, 1984) described a tendency among certain borderline and narcissistic patients to withdraw into a cocoon of self-sufficiency and nonrelatedness, to defend against a painful piece of reality rather than a wish or a drive. Modell's work is closely linked to Winnicott's (1961) concept of the "false self," and represents an extension of the view of LaPlanche and Pontalis (1973), who defined defense as "a group of operations aimed at the reduction and elimination of any change liable to threaten the integrity and stability of the biopsychological individual" (p. 103).

Concerned that classical formulations of defense tended to obscure considerations of the individual's self-experience, Kohut (1984) reconceptualized defense as referring to any attempt by a person to minimize painful affect associated with the exposure of structural deficits, or what Newman (1980) described as "experiential deficiencies." According to Cooper (1989), "Kohut speaks of particular defensive structures almost exclusively in the context of maintaining remnants of the self that will preserve the vigor of the self" (p. 882).

Kohut's (1984) formulations are close to those of Modell's (1975), in that both emphasized the notion of a vulnerable self needing to be safeguarded. Modell's concept of the self's "cocoon state," like Guntrip's (1969) earlier designation of the "schizoid citadel," are terms describing defensive steps mobilized to protect equivalents of Kohut's "enfeebled self."

LERNER DEFENSE SCALE

On the basis of Kernberg's (1975) theoretical model of defense and the clinical test work of Mayman (1967), Pruitt and Spilka (1964), Holt (1970), and Peebles (1975), Lerner and Lerner (1980) devised a Rorschach scoring manual designed to evaluate the specific defensive operations presumed to characterize the developmentally lower level of defensive functioning.

The scoring manual sections are based on the specific defenses of splitting, devaluation, idealization, projective identification, and denial. Within each section the defense is defined, Rorschach indices of the defense are presented, and clinical illustrations are offered. The sections on devaluation, idealization, and denial call for an identification of the defense and a ranking of the defense on a continuum of high versus low order. The system involves a systematic appraisal of the human figure response. This is based on the core assumption from object relations theory that, as part of normal development, defenses and the internal object world are intimately related, as well as from the empirical relationship Blatt and Lerner (1983) found between human figures on the Rorschach and quality of object relations. In assessing the human percept, attention is given to the precise figure (e.g., clowns, warriors, magicians), the way it is described, and the action ascribed to it.

SCORING SYSTEM

Rationale

The emphasis on the structural concept of defense was prompted by several considerations. These defenses are considered intrinsic to the nature and quality of the borderline patient's object relations. In addition, because these structures have been well described and illustrated in a clinical context, they lend themselves to operationalization and, eventually, quantification. Finally, if these defenses can be reliably and validly assessed, then not only the clinical researcher, but also the clinical practitioner, would be furnished a tool of much explanatory and predictive worth.

General Scoring Consideration

1. In general, the basic unit to be scored is the response containing an entire human figure.
2. Before applying the system, all responses should be scored for form level using a system devised by Mayman (1970).
3. The sections on devaluation, idealization, and denial call for an identification of these defenses, as well as a ranking of the defense on a continuum of high versus low order.
4. Any response may receive more than one score.
5. In assessing the human percept, attention should be paid to the following aspects of the response: the action ascribed to the figure, the way it is described, and the exact figure seen.

SPECIFIC DEFENSES AND THEIR SCORING

Splitting

Splitting involves an admixture of separations of drives, affects, internal object representations, external object relations, and introjective mechanisms (Robbins, 1976). With regard to object relations, splitting refers to what individuals do to and with their inner and outer objects. Specifically, it involves a division of internal and external into: (a) parts, as distinct from wholes, and (b) good and bad part-objects (Pruyser, 1975). Behaviorally, splitting is manifest in a tendency to perceive and describe others in terms of overruling polarities (Pruyser). Although these polarities convey the division of good versus bad, they may take several forms, including frustrating versus satisfying, dangerous versus benign, and friendly versus hostile. The tendency to polarize affective descriptions of objects underlies the indices considered indicative of splitting.

To denote splitting, use the letter *S*, and score splitting in the following cases:

1. In a sequence of responses, a human percept described using a specific, nonambivalent, nonambiguous affective dimension is immediately followed by another human response in which the affective description is opposite that used to describe the preceding responses, for example, "looks like an ugly criminal with a

gun" immediately followed by "couples sitting together cheek to cheek."

2. In the description of one total human figure, a clear distinction of parts is made, so that one part of the figure is seen as opposite to another part, for example, "A giant. His lower part here conveys danger, but his top half looks benign."
3. Included in one response are two clearly distinguished figures, and these figures are described in opposite ways, for example, "Two figures, a man and a woman. He is mean and shouting at her. Being rather angelic, she's standing there and taking it."
4. An implicitly idealized figure is tarnished or spoiled by the addition of one or more features, or an implicitly devalued figure is enhanced by the addition of one or more features, for example, "a headless angel."

Devaluation

Devaluation refers to a tendency to depreciate, tarnish, and lessen the importance of one's inner and outer objects. It is considered a muted form of spoiling and, as such, is closely linked to envy. Specifically, devaluation is conceptualized as an aim of envy as well as a defense against it. Envy aims at being as good as the object; when this seems unattainable, however, it then seeks to spoil that goodness in the object and thus remove the source of the envious feelings (Segal, 1973). In addition to identifying the defense, devaluation is also rated on a 5-point continuum. Underlying the continuum are three dimensions. The first dimension involves the degree to which the humanness of the figure is retained. For example, such percepts as waiters or clowns are accorded a higher score than are more distorted forms, such as monsters and mythological objects. A temporal-spatial consideration determines the second dimension. Contemporary human percepts set in a current and close locale are scored higher than are those percepts from either the past or future and placed in a distant setting. The final dimension involves the severity of depreciation as conveyed in the affective description. Figures described in more primitive, blatant, socially unacceptable ways are scored lower than those described in negatively tinged but more civilized and socially acceptable ways. To denote devaluation, use the letters *DV*. Add to this score the number that corresponds to the appropriate level of devaluation. For example, "an angry man" is scored "*DV*1":

1. The humanness dimension is retained, there is no distancing of the figure in time or space, and the figure is described in negatively

tinged but socially acceptable terms, for example, "two people fighting," "a girl in a funny costume."

2. The humanness dimension is retained, there may be distancing of the figure in time or space, and the figure is described in blatantly negative and socially unacceptable negative terms. This score would also include human figures with parts missing, for example, "a diseased African child," "a woman defecating," "sinister-looking male figure," "a disjointed figure with the head missing."

3. The humanness dimension is retained, but involved in the percept is a distortion of human form; there may be distancing of the figure in time or space; and if the figure is described negatively, it is in socially acceptable terms. This rating includes such figures as clowns, elves, savages, witches, devils, and figures of the occult, for example, "sad looking clowns," "cannibal standing over a pot," "the bad witch."

4. The humanness dimension is retained, but implied in the percept is a distortion of human form. There may be distancing of the figure in time or space, and the figure is described in blatantly negative and socially unacceptable terms. This rating involves the same types of figures as in (3); however, the negative description is more severe, for example, "a couple of evil witches," "two people from Mars who look very scary," "a sinister Ku Klux Klansman."

5. The humanness dimension is lost, there may be distancing of the distorted form in time or space, and the figure is described in either neutral or negative terms. This rating includes puppets, mannequins, robots, creatures with some human characteristics, part-human, part-animal responses, and human responses with one or more animal features, for example, "mannequins with dresses but missing a head," "two people but half-male and half-animal from outer space," "a woman with breasts, high-heeled shoes, and bird's beak for a mouth."

Idealization

Idealization involves a denial of unwanted characteristics of an object and then an enhancing of the object by projecting one's own libido or omnipotence onto it. It aims at keeping an object completely separate from persecutory objects, which preserves the object from harm and destruction. This defensive aspect of idealization—that is, its aim is to protect the object from inner harm—is precarious, for the more ideal the object becomes, the more likely it is to arouse envy. As in the case of devaluation, idealization is also rated on a 5-point continuum. Underlying the continuum are the same three dimensions. For scoring, denote idealization with the letter I. Add to this score the number that corresponds with the appropriate level of idealization. Thus, "a person with a big smile" is scored "I1":

1. The humanness dimension is retained, there is no distancing of the figure in time or space, and the figure is described in a positive but not excessively flattering way, for example, "two nice people looking over a fence," "a person with a happy smile."

2. The humanness dimension is retained, there may or may not be distancing of the person in time or space, and the figure is described in blatantly and excessively positive terms, for example, "two handsome, muscular Russians doing that famous dance," "what an angelic figure; long hair, a flowing gown, and a look of complete serenity."

3. The humanness dimension is retained, but implied in the percept is a distortion of human form. There may be distancing of the figure in time or space, and if the figure is described positively, it is in moderate terms. This rating includes such objects of fame, adoration, or strength as civic leaders, officials, and famous people, for example, "Charles de Gaulle," "an astronaut, one of those fellows who landed on the moon."

4. The humanness dimension is retained, but implied in the percept is a distortion of human form. There may be distancing of the figure in time or space, and the figure is described in blatantly and excessively positive terms. This rating includes the same types of figures as in (3); however, the positive description is more excessive, for example, "a warrior; not just any warrior but the tallest, strongest, and bravest," "Attila the Hun, but with the largest genitals I have ever seen."

5. The humanness dimension is lost, but implied in the distortion is an enhancement of identity. There may be distancing of the distorted form in time or space, and the figure is described in either neutral or positive terms. This rating includes statues of famous figures, giants, supermen or superwomen, space figures with supernatural powers, angels, and idols. Also included are half-humans in which the nonhuman aspect nonetheless adds to the figure's appearance or power, for example, "a bust of Queen Victoria," "powerful beings from another planet ruling over these softer creatures."

Projective Identification

This refers to a process in which parts of the self are split off and projected onto an external object or part-object. It differs from projection proper in that what is projected onto the object is not experienced as ego alien. Rather, the self "empathizes" (Kernberg, 1975) with the object and tries to control the object by means of the projection. A close examination of the concept of projective identification suggests the operation of at least three subprocesses: an externalization of parts of the self with a disregard of real characteristics of the external object, a capacity to blur boundaries between self and other, and an overriding need to control the other. The two indices of projective identification represent an attempt to assess these subprocesses. To denote this score, use the letters PI. Score projective identification in the following cases:

1. Confabulatory responses involving human figures in which the form level[1] is *Fw–* or *F–* and the percept is overly embellished with associative elaboration to the point that real properties of the blot are disregarded and replaced by fantasies and affects. Typically, the associative elaboration involves material with aggressive or sexual meaning, as in the following example: "A huge man coming to get me. I can see his huge teeth. He's staring straight at me. His hands are up as if he will strike me."
2. Those human or detail responses in which the location is *Dr*, the determinant is *Fc*, and the figure is described as either aggressive or having been aggressed against,[2] for example, "an ugly face" (with forehead and features seen in reference to the inner portion of Card IV), "an injured man" (Card VI upper, center area).

Denial

Denial in this system refers to a broad group of defenses arranged on a continuum based on the degree of reality distortion involved in the response. Higher level forms of denial involve a minimum of reality distortion, whereas middle and lower level manifestations of denial include increasingly greater degrees of reality distortion. Examples of denial at the highest level include several defensive processes observed by Holt (1970) and presented in his manual for the scoring of manifestations of primary process thinking. Middle-level denial includes responses in which there is major contradiction between the human figure perceived and the actions or characteristics ascribed to that figure. Lower level

---

[1]These scores are taken from Mayman's (1970) manual for form level scoring. The *Fw*-score is assigned to unconvincing, weak form responses in which only one blot detail is accurately perceived. The *F*-score refers to arbitrary form responses in which there is little resemblance between the percept and the area of the blot being responded to.

[2]*Dr* is a location score used when the area chosen is small, rarely used, and arbitrarily delimited; *Fc* is a determinant used when the subject makes out forms within a heavily shaded area without using shading or uses the nuances of shading within a colored area (Rapaport, Gill, & Schafer, 1945–1946).

manifestations of denial involve significant distortions of reality, to the point that a segment of subjective experience or of the external world is not integrated with the rest of the experience. There is a striking loss of reality testing, and individuals act as if they were unaware of an urgent, pressing aspect of reality. To score denial, use the letters *DN*. Add to this score the number that corresponds to the level of denial. Thus, the response "I know they are not fighting" would be scored "*DN*1."

1. Higher level denial: Denial at this level consists of several subsidiary defenses manifested in responses in which the form level of the percept is *F+*, *Fo*, or *Fw+*.

   (a) Negation: Negation involves a disavowal of impulse. The disavowal may be manifested in two ways. In one, the disavowal is smoothly blended into the response itself, whereas in the other, the response, or aspects of the response, are couched in negative terms, for example, "virgin," "angel," "these figures are not angry."

   (b) Intellectualization: In this process, the response is stripped of its drive and affective charge by being presented in an overly technical, scientific, literate, or intellectual way, for example, "two Homo sapiens," "two Kafkaesque figures."

   (c) Minimization: With minimization, drive-laden material is included in the response, but in a reduced and nonthreatening way. This includes changing a human figure into a caricature or cartoon figure, for example, "a shadow cast by an evil person," "a child with his hand clenched in a fist," "a funny man, more like a caricature."

   (d) Repudiation: With repudiation, a response is retracted or the individual denies having even given the response.

2. Middle-level denial: Denial at this level involves responses in which the form level is *F+*, or *Fw+*, and involved in the response is a basic contradiction. The contradiction may be on affective, logical, or reality grounds, for example, "a sexy Santa Claus," "two nuns fighting," "a man reading while asleep."

3. Lower level denial: At this level, reality adherence is abrogated, but in a particular way. Specifically, an acceptable response is rendered unacceptable either by adding something that is not there or by failing to consider an aspect of the blot that is clearly seen.

This corresponds to Mayman's (1970) "form spoil" (*Fs*) response.[3] In addition, this level also includes responses in which incompatible descrip-

[3]The *Fs* response differs from the *F*– response in that a basically acceptable response is spoiled by a perceptual oversight or distortion. In the *F*– response, the percept is totally unacceptable.

tions are given to the percept, for example, "two people, but their top half is the female and bottom half male; each has breasts and a penis," "a person, but instead of a mouth there is a bird's beak," "a person sitting on its huge tail."

RELIABILITY STUDIES

The reliability of the scoring system has been reported in several studies. As dictated by the scale, independently trained judges rate a series of Rorschach protocols and then the level of agreement among the judges for each of the defenses is determined.

In the initial investigation (Lerner & Lerner, 1980), 10 Rorschach records including 5 borderline and 5 neurotic patients were randomly selected and scored independently by two well-trained raters. The percentage of perfect agreement between the raters for the major defense categories was as follows: splitting, 100%; devaluation, 91%; idealization, 87%; projective identification, 100%; and denial, 83%. For the subcategories, percentages of perfect agreement ranged from 76% to 95%.

A second study (Lerner, Sugarman, & Gaughran, 1981) that included borderline and schizophrenic groups obtained comparably high levels of interrater reliability. Correlation coefficients ranging from .94 to .99 were found for the major defense categories, and coefficients between .74 and .95 were found for the continuum variables. Collapsing the continuum variables into composite scores yielded reliability coefficients ranging from .94 to .96.

Subsequent authors also reported high levels of interrater agreement. Van-Der Keshet (1988), in a study involving anorexic subjects, reported Cronbach alpha coefficients ranging from 1.00 to .80. An investigation of several subgroups of psychopaths (Gacono, 1988) obtained the following percentages of agreement between raters: projective identification, 100%; idealization, 100%; denial, 100%; and devaluation, 88%. Among the protocols selected for determining reliability, Gacono found no scoreable responses for splitting.

In summary, findings from various studies indicate that the reliability of the scoring system, as judged by level of interrater agreement, is more than adequate and especially high for an inkblot measure.

VALIDITY AND FINDINGS

Kernberg (1975, 1977, 1979) has repeatedly asserted that the constellation of lower level primitive defenses distinguishes borderline and psychotic patients from neurotic patients. His assertion is based on his own diagnostic scheme, a scheme that differs in important ways from the *Di-*

agnostic and Statistical Manual of Mental Disorders (American Psychiatric Association, 1980) system (Lerner, 1998). Whereas the *DSM*-schema calls for assessing patients along one dimension, basically a descriptive dimension, Kernberg's (1975) schema involves assessing patients along two relatively independent dimensions. The first axis consists of a descriptive characterological diagnosis in terms of character structure. The second dimension, however, involves an evaluation of the underlying level of personality organization. This second axis involves a systematic appraisal of less visible, structural personality variables, including level of instinctual development, manifestations of ego weakness, quality of internalized object relations, level of superego development, attainment of ego identity, and level of defense organization. The designations *borderline*, *psychotic*, and *neurotic* lie along the second axis and, although they have diagnostic import, they refer to different levels of personality organization and not to specific diagnoses. To evaluate the construct validity of the scoring system, as well as the efficacy of Kernberg's proposals, the initial validating studies involved comparing the Rorschach records of borderline patients (as defined by Kernberg, 1976) with the protocols of other clinical groups with respect to manifestations of primitive defenses.

The first study (Lerner & Lerner, 1980) compared the Rorschach protocols of 15 outpatients organized at a borderline level with 15 outpatients organized at a neurotic level with regard to indices of primitive defenses. The 30 Rorschach records were selected from the private files of one of the authors and scored using the proposed system. Because the testing had initially been conducted for research purposes, the protocols had not been used in formulating the final diagnoses on which the selections were based. In this way, the selection procedures were not confounded by psychological test data. The full assessments included independently obtained mental status examinations and social developmental histories. Each of the patients subsequently entered either psychotherapy or psychoanalysis. Therefore, the initial diagnosis could and was confirmed in discussions with the patients' therapists or analysts.

The two groups (borderlines and neurotics) were matched on the variables of age, sex, and socioeconomic status. The Rorschachs obtained from the two groups did not differ significantly with regard to the total number of responses. Because the Rorschachs of borderline patients often include dramatic and distinguishing features, it is possible this influenced the scoring. However, a careful look at the scoring system indicates that many of these characteristics (e.g., confabulations) are accounted for in the scoring.

Several significant findings emerged from this study. The borderline patients manifested scale indices of splitting, low-level devaluation, projective identification, and low-level denial significantly more often than did the neurotic patients. The measures of splitting and projective identification not only proved especially discriminatory, but also were observed exclusively in the borderline group. By contrast, indices of high-level devaluation and high-level denial were found more often in the neurotic group. In general, and irrespective of level of severity, measures of idealization occurred more frequently in the records of the neurotic group. With devaluation, the opposite was found, that is, borderline patients depreciated their human figures significantly more often than did the neurotic patients. A review of the individual Rorschach records highlighted the importance of high-level denial. When neurotic patients used low-level devaluation or low-level idealization, it was usually accompanied by manifestations of high-level denial. This was not the case with the borderline patients. Their expressions of severe depreciation and excessive idealization were not mitigated by forms of higher level denial.

The results of the study supported Kernberg's (1975) theoretical propositions and matched clinical experience. Those of us who work with borderline patients are familiar with these patients' intense rage, seeming imperviousness to their impact on others, and tendency to fluctuate rapidly between overvaluing their therapist and regarding and treating their therapist with disdain and contempt. More so than with other patients, therapists pay close attention to how they are treated by these individuals. The obtained research findings, from the perspective of defense, help to explain these clinical events. It appears that defensive structures available to better organized patients—in this case, high-level denial and idealization—are not available to the borderline patient. That is, these patients not only make use of lower level defenses, but also do not have higher level defenses at their disposal. From a therapeutic vantage point, this suggests that, because such modulating structures cannot be used for containing affects and urges, regulation needs to be provided by the environment. Winnicott (1956) similarly noted that the aggressive and destructive actions of certain patients may be understood as unconscious attempts to evoke specific responses from their environment.

A second study (Lerner et al., 1981) compared the Rorschach records of a group of hospitalized borderline patients with those of a group of hospitalized schizophrenic patients. Rorschach protocols were drawn from patient files at a university teaching hospital, where patients were routinely psychologically tested within the first several weeks of their admission. The sample of borderline patients ($N = 21$) was selected according to criteria set out in the *DSM-III* (1980). The criteria were applied to a preadmission report that included a history of the present illness, past history, a mental status examination, and a tentative diagnostic formulation. The sample of schizophrenic patients ($N = 19$) was selected using the Research Diagnostic Criteria (RDC) developed by Spitzer, Endicott, and Robbins (1975). The RDC was applied to the preadmission report in the same way as *DSM-III* was used for the borderline sample. In this study as well, the groups were matched for demographic variables. Their Rorschachs did not differ with regard to total number of responses.

Here, too, several significant and interesting findings emerged when the Rorschach defense scores of the borderline and schizophrenic patients were compared. Indices of splitting appeared significantly more frequently in the protocols of the borderline patients than in the records of the schizophrenic patients. Four of the five scale measures of devaluation were also observed significantly more often in the borderline group, and indices of projective identification appeared exclusively in the borderline group. With respect to denial, the borderline patients gave significantly more responses at the middle and low levels. Denial, especially when treated as a composite score, distinguished the two groups.

Results from both studies were especially interesting when viewed from the perspective of Kernberg's (1975) theory of defense. Whereas findings from the Lerner and Lerner (1980) study confirmed Kernberg's contention of two overall levels of defense organization that differentiate borderline and neurotic patients, findings from the Lerner et al. (1981) investigation questioned his formulation that borderline and schizophrenic patients share a primitive defensive constellation. In counterdistinction to Kernberg, Lerner and Lerner (1982) interpreted their findings as indicating that the defensive organization of schizophrenic patients differs along several developmental and structural parameters from that of borderline patients. Splitting, projective identification, denial, and various levels of devaluation discriminated significantly between the two groups. Because the Rorschach measures of defense were based on an appraisal of the full human response, Lerner and Lerner (1982) concluded that "differences in the level of object representation underlying the specific defenses" (p. 99) accounted for the group differences. In keeping with this inference, the authors further found that the schizophrenic patients provided far fewer human responses than did the borderline patients.

Although the Lerner et al. (1981) study was designed to investigate the efficacy of the Lerner Defense scale by comparing defensive structure between groups differing in severity of psychopathology, the study also produced findings relevant to schizophrenia. Specifically, the study found differences between the groups with regard to their capacity to represent objects internally. Here, the findings suggested that, whereas the internal world of the borderline patient is populated with highly charged—either highly depreciated or highly idealized—representations, the inner world of the schizophrenic patient is devoid of representations. If inner representations develop from the internalization of invested external objects, then one might conjecture that schizophrenics never invested in external relations, accounting for their empty and barren inner object world. This suggestion is consistent with those theorists (Fromm-Reichmann, 1950; Sullivan, 1962; Searles, 1965) who considered schizophrenia as essentially a form of attachment disorder.

Further support for the validity of the defense scale and cross-validation for several of the findings from these studies came from an investigation by Collins (1983). Using Gunderson's (1986) Diagnostic Interview for Borderlines and *DSM-III* (1980) criteria, Collins administered the Rorschach to 15 adult subjects from each of three samples (neurotic, borderline, and schizophrenic). Subjects were drawn from several inpatient and outpatient facilities. The 45 Rorschachs were scored using the Lerner Defense scale. The differences among all three groups were highly significant, confirming the general hypothesis that patients organized at a borderline level present a defensive structure distinctly different from that of schizophrenics and neurotics. The borderline patients differed from the schizophrenics in producing significantly more scale indices of splitting, projective identification, low-level idealization, and mid-level devaluation. Although not statistically significant because the scores are relatively rare, the records of the borderlines as compared with those of the neurotics included more splitting scores and more instances of projective identification.

Using the *DSM-III* (1980) classification scheme, Farris (1988) applied the Lerner Defense scale to the Rorschach records of nine matched pairs of borderline personality disorders and narcissistic personality disorders. He hypothesized that the borderline patients would manifest greater disturbances in defensive organization than would the narcissistic patients. In support of his hypothesis, he did find that the borderline patients produced a significantly greater number of responses indicative of the use of primitive defenses. Specifically, applying chi-square analysis to each of the defense categories, he found significant differences with regard to splitting and projective identification.

In each of these studies, the Lerner Defense scale was applied to the Rorschachs of groups differing in severity of psychopathology; however, one of the comparative groups inevitably included patients diagnosed as borderline. In the following studies, the defense scale was used to study the defensive structure of specific clinical populations who did not bear the formal diagnosis of borderline, yet, in keeping with Kernberg's (1975) diagnostic model, were assumed to have a borderline personality organization. The groups studied included anorexic patients (Brouillette, 1987; Piran & Lerner, 1988; Van-Der Keshet, 1988), antisocial offenders (Gacono, 1988, 1990), and gender-disturbed children (Kolers, 1986).

Anorexic Patients

Van-Der Keshet (1988) applied the defense scale to the Rorschachs of clinical anorexics, anorectic ballet students, nonanorectic ballet students, and a normal control group. The clinical anorectic group was further subdivided into those patients who manifested solely restrictive characteristics (i.e., restricting food intake) and those who exhibited bulimic symptoms (i.e., binging and purging). A comparison of the different groups on the defense scale yielded several interesting findings. As hypothesized, the two clinical anorectic groups (restrictive and bulimic) and the anorectic ballet students used splitting and devaluation significantly more often than did the nonanorectic ballet students and the controls. The restricting anorexics used denial significantly more frequently than any of the other groups. The normal control group employed idealization significantly more often than any of the other groups. And, although the anorectic ballet students did not differ from the nonanorectic ballet students on idealization, both groups used defense significantly more often than the bulimic anorexics.

Van-Der Keshet's (1988) finding regarding differences in the use of denial between the restrictive anorexics and the bulimic anorexics has important treatment implications. Those treating restrictive anorexics have often employed more extreme types of interventions such as forcing patients to look at themselves in a mirror. This is understood as a way of directly confronting the patient's distorted body image. Findings from this study suggest that such a practice not only addresses the patient's distorted body image, but also addresses the patient's major reliance on denial.

In a series of studies (Piran & Lerner, 1987; Piran, Lerner, Garfinkle, Kennedy, & Brouillette, 1988) using nonprojective instruments, Piran and colleagues found that, although restrictive anorexic and bulimic anorexic patients both manifested a personality organized at a borderline level, the two groups differed with respect to quality of impulse control. Whereas bulimics discharged impulses and affects directly and with limited regulation through action, restrictive anorexics appeared as overcontrolled, massively inhibited, and highly restricted. This consistent finding led Piran and Lerner (1988) to investigate the defensive structure of both groups through the use of the Lerner Defense scale.

Piran and Lerner's (1988) sample consisted of 65 eating-disordered patients (bulimic, n = 34; restricters, n = 31) admitted or placed on a waiting list for admission to two large general hospitals with special units for treating eating disorders. All subjects were female, ranging in age from 16 to 35, who fulfilled *DSM-III* (1980) criteria for anorexia nervosa. As predicted, and consistent with the respective nature of their presenting symptoms, the bulimic anorexics tended to use test indices of projective identification and low-level devaluation, whereas restrictive anorexics relied more often on denial and high-level idealization.

Thus, although restrictive and bulimic anorexics both used primitive defenses, the respective patterning of defenses differed. Furthermore, not only were differences in defenses found, but, and importantly, the specific defenses seemed directly related to symptoms. For example, by definition, bulimia involves a forceful expulsion of something that has been taken in. In a parallel fashion, projective identification involves the expulsion of parts of the self. In other words, both the symptom and the defense share in common "a getting rid of."

Brouillette (1987), in a novel and important study, assessed the personality organization, including defensive structure, of women suffering from eating disorders and also their mothers. The three groups of daughters, between 18 and 40 years of age, included 11 women with anorexia nervosa, 10 women with bulimia, and 10 normal control women. Rorschach records were obtained from all daughters and their mothers and assessed using scales devised to measure level of object representation, level of boundary disturbance, quality of reality testing, and nature of defenses. Comparison of mothers and daughters produced intriguing results. First, no significant differences were found between daughters and mothers in all three groups on any measure of psychological functioning. Second, significant differences were found between the two eating disorder groups when compared to the normal control group for both the mothers and daughters on all of the measures. Finally, neither the mothers nor the daughters in the restrictive anorexia group differed significantly on any measure from the mothers and daughters in the bulimic group. With respect to the defense scale, evidence of splitting, low-level devaluation, projective identification, and low-level denial occurred with significantly greater frequency in the protocols of restrictive patients and their mothers and bulimic patients and their mothers than in the records of the normal controls and their mothers. Although not statistically significant, there was a tendency within the bulimic pairing (daughter and mother) to use splitting more often than the restrictive pairing.

Antisocial Offenders

The Lerner Defense scale was also administered to a second clinical group: antisocial personality. Making use of Kernberg's (1975) formulation that severe character disorders, including antisocial personality, are organized at a borderline level of personality organization, Gacono (1988) compared a group of highly psychopathic males with a group of low to moderately psychopathic males for their use of borderline object relations and borderline defenses.

Thirty-three subjects who met the *DSM-III-R* (1987) criteria for antisocial personality disorder participated in a semistructured interview and completed the Rorschach. From a review of their records and information obtained in the interview, each subject was rated on the Hare Psychopathy Checklist. Using a score of 30 as a cutoff, 14 subjects were assigned to the high-psychopathy group and 19 placed in the low-to-moderate-psychopathy group.

A between-group comparison indicated that none of the individual defense categories significantly distinguished the two groups. In fact, and quite unexpectedly, the low-to-moderate-psychopathy group produced almost twice as many defense scores (40) as did the high-psychopathy group (24). A closer look at the individual categories revealed that the high-psychopathy group, as compared to the low-to-moderate group, tended to use devaluation, whereas the low-to-moderate group made more frequent use of projective identification and higher level denial. The Rorschach records of both groups showed a predominant use of lower levels of denial, with all levels of devaluation found.

Gacono's (1988) results were a function, in part, of his research design. He did not include a control group. Had a control group been included, it would have been possible to determine whether the psychopathy sample as a whole employed primitive defenses more often than the controls.

In any event, Gacono (1988) interpreted his findings as demonstrating limitations in the scoring system. In accordance with Hammond (1984), Gacono concluded:

> First, borderline individuals often have difficulty experiencing objects as wholes and many respond to the Rorschach by producing the kind of part human response not scoreable by the system; secondly, human movement responses (M) symbolize an advanced human percept in motion. Children and some developmentally immature individuals may express movement responses in terms of animal content (FM), considered to be developmentally less mature. Lerner and Lerner's (1980) system prohibits the scoring of animal movement, thereby eliminating important data that reveal a subject's defensive functioning. (pp. 120–121)

Collins (1983) expressed similar concerns. The issue involved here is the tug between methodological strategy on the one hand and conceptual integrity on the other. This will be discussed more fully later.

Gender-Disturbed Children

The defense scale has also been extended to gender-disturbed children. Using the Rorschach, Kolers (1986) assessed and compared various ego functions, including defense, of a group of feminine boys, their siblings, and a group of normal controls. The subjects, ages 5 to 12 years, included 37 feminine boys diagnosed as having cross-gender disturbance, 19 siblings with no history of cross-gender behavior, and 23 normal controls. Kolers found that, although the normal controls offered significantly more human figure responses and more potentially scoreable responses, the gender-disturbed children and their siblings produced significantly more projective identification scores. With respect to the other defenses, higher level devaluation was found significantly more frequently in the records of the controls.

Of note in Kolers' (1986) study was the finding that the projective identification indices, though differentiating the normal controls from both the feminine boys and their siblings, failed to discriminate between the latter two groups. A companion study by Ipp (1986) helped to explain this finding. Ipp studied the object relations and object representations of this same sample by scoring their Rorschachs for several other measures, including Blatt, Brenneis, Schimek, and Glick's (1976) scale for assessing object representations, Blatt and Ritzler's (1974) scale for evaluating boundary disturbances, and Ipp's own measure for scoring developmental object relations (DORS). Based on her own findings, specifically those related to severity of boundary disturbance, and Lerner's (1985) formulation of various levels of projective identification depending on the aim (i.e., defense, control, or communication) and the degree to which self-boundaries are blurred, Ipp concluded that projective identification works somewhat differently in the two groups.

From the Boundary Disturbance scale, Ipp (1986) found that the confabulation score appeared significantly more often in the records of the feminine boys than in those of their siblings. She related this finding to projective identification and concluded that, in feminine boys, projective identification is at a lower level. Because they tend to blur self-other boundaries, the defense serves the aim of control. By contrast, because the siblings did not blur self-other boundaries, their projective identification was at a higher level. Here, it served to empathize with potential sources of danger and to communicate through preverbal modalities.

ANOTHER RORSCHACH MEASURE OF PRIMITIVE DEFENSES

A second Rorschach scale designed to assess primitive defenses (Cooper & Arnow, 1986; Cooper, Perry, & Arnow, 1988) is broader in scope than the Lerner Defense scale and is based on a different theoretical perspective. Cooper's system is an attempt to evaluate defense in general, rather than borderline defenses in particular. Nonetheless, Cooper and his coworkers identified the following five defenses, which they considered borderline defenses: splitting, devaluation, idealization, projective identification, and omnipotence (Lerner, Albert, & Walsh, 1987).

Based on the theoretical formulations of Winnicott (1953), Kohut (1977), and Stolorow and Lachmann (1980), Cooper's scale attempted to integrate object relations theory, Kohut's theory of narcissism, and Stolorow and Lachmann's concepts of developmental arrest and structural deficiency. Consistent with a position of developmental arrest, the scale incorporates Ames' (1966) empirical finding that growth and development is accompanied by an increased frequency of the human figure response on the Rorschach and that this parallels and eventually supplants animal responses. This reasoning, begun by Ames and conceptually expanded to include defensive functioning by Stolorow and Lachmann, leads to the formulation of "prestages" of defense. Prestages are those initial precursors to a defense occurring prior to the consolidation of self and object representation, whereas a defense proper is the end point in a series of developmental achievements" (p. 338).

Consistent with the concept of defense precursors, Cooper and Arnow (1986), in contrast to Lerner and Lerner (1980), did not restrict their scores to the human figure response:

> Lerner and Lerner (1980) ... restrict their analysis to percepts that include human figures, static or in motion. In agreement with Smith (1980), we find this circumscription unduly limiting for interpreting protocols in which there is a relative or absolute absence of human figures. More important, however, borderline defenses are more profitably examined with a broader data base regardless of the number of human responses. (Cooper & Arnow, p. 144)

The two scoring systems differ in another way as well. Whereas Cooper's scale includes scoring for omnipotence, defined as an idealization of the self in which there is the conviction that one is entitled to admiration and privileged treatment, the Lerner and Lerner scale provides for the scoring of denial on a graded continuum.

Cooper et al. (1988) investigated the relationship between defenses and specific dimensions of psychopathology in borderline, antisocial, and bipolar Type II adults. The authors reported that borderline psychopathology was positively associated with the defenses of devaluation, projection, splitting, and hypomanic denial. By contrast, it was negatively related to intellectualization and isolation. Furthermore, indices of splitting on the Rorschach correlated significantly with clinical ratings of splitting from independently obtained diagnostic interviews.

Cooper, Perry, and O'Connell (1991) investigated the effectiveness of the Cooper defense scale in longitudinally predicting global functioning. The authors found that two defenses—devaluation and projection—especially predicted impaired global functioning. Intellectualization and isolation of affect, by contrast, were significantly related to higher levels of global functioning.

Gacono (1988, 1990) and Gacono, Meloy, and Berg (1992) employed Cooper's scale to assess preferred defenses among subgroups of antisocial offenders, narcissistic personality disorders, and borderline personality disorders. Although not statistically significant, a high-psychopathy group had more responses indicating prestage splitting, total splitting, omnipotence, and devaluation as compared with a group of low to moderate psychopaths. The low-to-moderate group had more responses reflective of projective identification and idealization. The narcissistic personality disorder group, not unexpectedly, produced more primitive idealization responses than did any of the other groups.

In a study designed to study ego functions in borderline and narcissistic patients, Berg (1990) used Cooper's scale to compare the defensive structure of each group. As predicted, whereas the borderline sample produced more responses indicating splitting, the narcissistic sample produced more responses reflective of omnipotence.

A comprehensive comparison of the two defense scales was conducted by Lerner et al. (1987). Rorschach protocols obtained and used in two previous studies (Lerner & Lerner, 1980; Lerner et al., 1981) and scored according to Lerner and Lerner's system, were recoded and scored according to Cooper's criteria. Statistical analysis of differences between the four psychiatric groups (neurotics, outpatient borderlines, inpatient borderlines, schizophrenics) were completed separately to assess the power of each scale to discriminate between diagnostic groups and to evaluate the discriminatory capacity of specific defenses within each scale to differentiate among groups.

A profile analysis was conducted to assess the relative capacity of each scale to distinguish among groups. A parallelism of profiles test was run; the results indicated that the two scales were not parallel. That is, subjects from the four clinical groups were responding somewhat differently to the two scales.

To assess statistical differences between scales in predicting group membership, a discriminant function was conducted. A review of this analysis indicated the following: (a) The Cooper scale significantly differentiated neurotics from inpatient borderlines ($p < .01$), outpatient from inpatient borderlines ($p < .05$), and inpatient borderlines from schizophrenics ($p < .002$); (b) the Cooper scale failed to statistically discriminate neurotics from outpatient borderlines, neurotics from schizophrenics, and outpatient borderlines from schizophrenics; (c) the Lerner Defense scale significantly differentiated neurotics from inpatient borderlines ($p < .001$), neurotics from schizophrenics ($p < .001$), outpatient borderlines from schizophrenics ($p < .001$), and inpatient borderlines from schizophrenics ($p < .001$); (d) the Lerner Defense scale was unable to distinguish statistically between the two outpatient samples and the two borderline groups. Although both scales validly discriminated between groups, overall these results suggest that whereas the Cooper scale more effectively distinguishes between higher functioning outpatients, the Lerner Defense scale better discriminates more seriously disturbed inpatients.

To evaluate the discriminatory power of the specific defenses, an analysis of differences among the four experimental groups was conducted separately for each scale. With regard to the Cooper scale, three specific defense scores distinguished among groups. Splitting distinguished inpatient borderlines from both neurotics and schizophrenics; devaluation differentiated both borderline groups from schizophrenics and neurotics from outpatient borderlines; and omnipotence separated the outpatient borderlines from neurotics and schizophrenics. Subscale measures of idealization and projective identification failed to differentiate significantly among groups.

For the Lerner Defense scale, all five defenses distinguished among groups to a statistically significant degree. Splitting, devaluation, and idealization all differentiated both borderline groups from the neurotics and the schizophrenics. Projective identification appeared exclusively within the two borderline groups. Although it differentiated these groups from the neurotics and schizophrenics, it did not separate the two borderline groups from each other. Finally, denial, like projective identification, distinguished the borderline groups from the other two, but not from each other.

One purpose of Lerner et al.'s (1987) study was to assess the relative discriminatory power of omnipotence, a score exclusive to Cooper's scale, and denial, a defense exclusive to the Lerners' scale. Both indices were effective but in somewhat different ways. Whereas omnipotence distinguished both outpatient groups (borderline and neurotic) from inpatient borderlines, denial distinguished neurotics from both inpatient groups and inpatient borderlines from schizophrenics. These particular findings are consistent with the overall pattern of results indicating the Cooper scale's greater sensitivity in distinguishing outpatient groups and the Lerner Defense scale's greater sensitivity in distinguishing inpatient groups.

Finally, to assess the overlap and distinctive features of each scoring system, the two scales were intercorrelated. Significant correlations were obtained between the subscales measuring splitting (.49) and devaluation (.64). Little relationship was found between the measures of idealization (.13) and projective identification (.30). A review of the within-scale correlations indicated differences in the structure of each defense system. For the Lerner Defense scale, subscale measures of splitting, devaluation, denial, and projective identification were all intercorrelated. However, for the Cooper scale, the specific defense measures correlated substantially less. As such, the findings regarding the Lerner Defense scale are consistent with Kernberg's (1975) theoretical formulations related to defense. On the other hand, the Cooper scale has superior psychometric properties.

DISCUSSIONS AND IMPLICATIONS FOR PSYCHOANALYTIC THEORY

Based on the intimate relationship Rapaport envisioned among research, theory, and method, I reviewed in this chapter the development and validation of an innovative Rorschach scale designed to assess primitive defenses. Because the scale was conceptually rooted in Kernberg's (1975) theory of defense, the accompanying studies not only served to assess the scale's reliability and validity, but also permitted an examination of several of Kernberg's theoretical formulations.

With respect to the defense scale, given its specific theoretical foundation, initial studies involved an evaluation of the scoring system's efficacy in distinguishing groups of borderline patients from groups of other diagnostic entities. The combined results from the first two studies (Lerner & Lerner, 1980; Lerner et al., 1981) convincingly supported the proposition that borderline patients present an identifiable constellation of defenses, different from that of neurotic and schizophrenic patients, and that the defense scale is a reliable and valid means of identifying these defenses.

Further studies extended the use of the scale to clinical groups differing in their symptomatic presentation, but presumed by Kernberg's theory to have a common underlying borderline personality structure. Here, the scale was effective in identifying the importance of devaluation and low-level denial in the defensive structure of antisocial individuals and the role of projective identification in discriminating gender-disturbed children and their siblings from a group of normal controls. Furthermore, in a series of studies (Brouillette, 1987; Piran & Lerner, 1988; Van-Der Keshet, 1988), scale scores consistently distinguished eating-disordered patients from normal controls.

Van-Der Keshet's (1988) study was important because it helped explain the inconsistent findings repeatedly obtained regarding idealization. In several studies regarding the defense scale, the results related to idealization were strikingly discrepant from the results reported for the other defenses. Indices of idealization, regardless of level, rarely appeared in the protocols of individuals with a borderline personality organization, and typically appeared more often in the records of less disturbed groups and normal controls (Kolers, 1986; Lerner & Lerner, 1980; Van-Der Keshet), and were found to be independent of measures of the other defenses (Lerner et al., 1987). Collectively, these findings suggest that the Idealization subscale is measuring something other than idealization as conceptualized as a primitive defense.

The most comprehensive discussion of idealization, in both its defensive and adaptive (nondefensive) aspects, was provided by Kernberg (1980), who advanced the notion of idealization falling on a developmental line ranging from pathological to normal. Kernberg proposed the following three levels of idealization:

> (1) A primitive level of ego states that reflect a predominance of splitting mechanisms; this is found in the borderline personality organization ... (2) An idealization linked to the establishment of the capacity for mourning and concern (the depressive position), with a more realistic awareness of and empathy for the object, but still devoid of genital features. This level is characteristic of states of falling in love of the usual neurotic patient ... (3) A normal idealization achieved toward the end of adolescence or in young adulthood, which is based upon a stable sexual identity and a realistic awareness of the love object. (p. 221)

According to Kernberg (1980), at the lower, more primitive pole, idealization supports splitting. At this lower level, idealization is associated with borderline pathology. Toward the upper, more normal end on the continuum, the adaptive, nondefensive aspects of idealization are emphasized, including its role as a necessary condition for mature love. At this higher level, idealization is associated with the absence of psychopathology.

Van-Der Keshet (1988), as part of her study, examined the specific idealization scores in her protocols. Her up-close look at the individual records revealed that the normal controls had a marked tendency to provide idealization responses at the upper end of the Idealization scale (scale points 1 and 2). From the perspective of Kernberg's (1980) model, the data suggest that the upper end of this scale is more sensitive to the adaptive aspects of idealization than to the defensive ones.

Van-Der Keshet's (1988) findings are more suggestive than conclusive; however, there is a separate set of Rorschach studies relevant here. Exner (1991) developed a special score, designated as COP, for assessing cooperative movement. The score is assigned to any movement response (*M*, *FM*, or *m*) involving two or more objects engaged in an interaction that is unequivocally positive or cooperative. Despite differences in the basic unit of analysis (human response vs. all movement responses), to judge from Exner's definitions and the examples he offered ("two people leaning toward each other, sharing a secret," pp. 18–19), there appear to be points of overlap between his cooperative movement response and scale points 1 and 2 on the Idealization scale. In both cases, there is undiluted positive affect.

Exner (1991) reported that COP responses appeared at least once in 80% of the Rorschachs from a sample of 700 adult nonpatients. He further found that third-year high school students and college freshmen who had more than two COP responses on their Rorschach protocols were identified by peers, at a rate five times greater than other subjects, as being the one who "is easiest to be with."

Several studies (Gacono, Meloy, & Berg, 1992; Lerner & Lerner, 1980), including Van-Der Keshet's (1988), found a relative absence of any idealization score in the more severely disturbed groups. Although it is not clear what to make of this consistent finding, it seems likely, based on theoretical and clinical considerations, that such individuals (i.e., borderline patients, antisocial males, bulimic anorexics), given their specific histories, have not developed the structures that allow for high levels of idealization.

Additional findings in Exner (1991) support this impression. In contrast with his sample of adult nonpatients, Exner found that COP responses appeared at least once in only 65% of the test records of an outpatient sample, 50% of the protocols of inpatient depressive and schizophrenic patients, and 40% of the Rorschachs of patients diagnosed with character disorders.

From these results, and in the context of Kernberg's (1980) model, it seems likely that the upper scale ratings (points 1 and 2) on the Idealization scale reflect idealization as an adaptive capacity rather than idealization as a defense. The meaning of the lower three ratings, those in which there is a progressive distortion of the humanness of the human figure, is unclear. A second model for understanding idealization, one somewhat different from Kernberg's, is represented in the work of Kohut (1971, 1977). According to Kohut (1971), children have "two chances" in their development of self-cohesion and self-consolidation. The initial opportunity to establish a cohesive grandiose-exhibitionistic self involves the child's early relationship with an empathically responsive, merging-mirroring-approving self-object, usually the mother. If the mother frustrates or in any way does not meet this need for merging and mirroring, the child still has a second chance for self-cohesion. This second chance is provided by the father and his capacity to empathize with and accept the child's need, first to idealize him and then to merge with him as an idealized object. If this idealizing process is successful, self-cohesion is advanced, and the structure that emerges is referred to as a "compensatory structure."

Kohut (1977) described it this way: "A failure experienced at the first way station can be remedied by a success at the second one" (p. 180). If, however the success of one of these opportunities is insufficient to compensate for the failure of the other, then the compensatory structure does not function reliably and self-cohesion is compromised. For Kohut, then, idealization, or more directly, the capacity to idealize, is indispensable to the development of compensatory structures toward self-consolidation.

When viewed from this Kohutian perspective, Van-Der Keshet's (1988) finding that the symptomatic ballet students employed idealization significantly more often than the bulimic anorexics takes on a possible meaning. In reviewing the individual protocols of these students, Van-Der Keshet found that they tended to use higher levels of idealization than the controls but to a lower degree. One might speculate that the presence of higher level idealization among these ballet students indicates that, despite their being symptomatic, they have been able to develop compensatory structures, structures that have enabled them to function more effectively and adaptively than the bulimic patient group.

From one vantage point, the reviewed studies helped clarify the defense scale's psychometric properties. From a different vantage point, the articles yielded findings related to several of Kernberg's specific propositions. For example, and as noted previously, Lerner et al.'s (1981) results did not support Kernberg's contention that borderline and schizophrenic patients have a similar defensive organization. Lerner et al. found significant differences between the two groups on virtually all of the defenses. Because the schizophrenic patients offered far fewer human responses on their Rorschachs than did the borderline patients, Lerner and Lerner (1982) concluded that, because of differences in their levels of object representations, their defenses are different as well.

Kernberg's two-tier model of defense was part of his attempt to develop a diagnostic scheme that went above and beyond the *DSM* (1980) diagnostic system. Like other clinicians and psychoanalysts, Kernberg recognized the limitations presented by a classification system that placed almost total emphasis on that which is observable and describable, with little attention paid to underlying and more invisible structures, dynamics, and meanings. One consequence of such an approach is an inability to conceptualize similarities among individuals who differ in their overt presentation.

To overcome this limitation, Kernberg, as noted previously, proposed a diagnostic scheme that involved assessing patients along two relatively independent dimensions. The first dimension is similar to the

DSM (1980) system in that it is essentially descriptive. It consists of establishing a characterological diagnosis in terms of character structure. The second dimension is altogether different. It involves an evaluation of the underlying level of personality organization.

As noted, basic to the second dimension is the contention that individuals who differ in their presenting symptoms and complaints may share a common underlying personality structure. Although several of the reviewed studies were based on this contention, at the same time and quite unintendedly, the combined results support the proposition itself. Specifically, as judged by a Rorschach assessment of defense, groups as diverse as eating disorder patients, antisocial personalities, and gender-disturbed children all share important structural features.

The defense scale presented here, together with the accompanying research, is consistent with a broad shift in psychoanalysis, namely, a decreasing interest in drives, drive-defense interplay, and conflict, and increased interest in structures and structure formation. With an emphasis on the process of structure formation has come a reexamination of the complex interactions among early object relations, the development and level of psychological structures including defensive functioning and the internal representational world, and ongoing object relations and the ways these units of experience are internalized and become part of the personality.

Part of this major shift in psychoanalytic theory involves changes in psychoanalytic conceptualizations of psychopathology and treatment. Concepts of psychopathology based on the more traditional foundations of psychic conflict and unconscious strivings drew attention to the drives and their vicissitudes, the prevailing mode of defense, and the interaction of the two as expressed in character traits and symptoms. Concepts of psychopathology based on impairments in psychic structure formation, by contrast, draw attention to the nature and level of the structures themselves (i.e., self system, internalized object relations, level of defense, etc.), the degree to which they have been internalized, and their genetic roots.

These newer models of psychopathology have important treatment implications. Michaels (1983) summarized these implications in this way:

> Concepts of pathology as the product of psychic conflict and unconscious wishes and fears invite models of treatment that emphasize interpretation and insight, with therapy being seen as a special kind of education, and the therapeutic relationship as a unique laboratory for exploring and demonstrating the critical dynamic configurations as they emerge in the transference. Concepts of pathology as the product of developmental arrest and deviance with the resulting formation of abnormal psychic structures invite models of treatment that emphasize the psychological

> substrate and nutriments necessary for growth and development, with therapy being seen as a second chance for development with a special kind of parenting, the interpretive process as a model of growth promoting interaction, and the therapeutic relationship as a substitute for the nuclear family as a matrix for individuation and growth. (p. 5)

Finally, the Lerner Defense scale was developed at a time when, owing to the work of Kernberg (1975), the borderline concept held sway. For instance, at that time Pruyser (1975) referred to the term *borderline* as a "star word," meaning that, like a shooting star, it held the promise of illuminating a great deal. Subsequently, however, especially in descriptive psychiatry, both the concept and diagnosis have declined in popularity and, in my judgment, have been replaced with other concepts and diagnoses, including multiple personality disorder, dissociative identity disorder, and bipolar disorder. Unfortunately, with this shift in emphasis has come a lessening of interest in underlying, less observable and invisible personality structures. To redress this imbalance, it would be interesting and informative to apply the defense scale to these diagnostic entities to determine whether, from a Kernbergian perspective, they too present an underlying borderline organization.

In this chapter, I have reviewed and discussed a scale developed by Lerner and Lerner to assess primitive defenses. Consistent with its theoretical underpinnings, early studies employing the scale demonstrated its validity in distinguishing borderline patients from neurotic and schizophrenic patients. Subsequent studies used the scale to evaluate the defensive structure among other types of clinical groups assumed to have a borderline personality structure. The combined findings supported the scale's reliability and validity. More indirectly, the results supported Kernberg's contention that patients who present different symptoms and complaints, nonetheless, may share a common underlying personality structure.

Because defense represents a structural and not simply a descriptive variable, focusing on it allows one, in Kernberg's (1975) terms, to move beyond descriptive considerations. Unfortunately, defense has typically been studied in isolation and not in terms of its relationship with other structural factors (e.g., reality testing, thought processes, ego identity, etc.). One exception, the work of Lerner and Lerner (1982), related defense to level of object representation. With the development of several Rorschach scales designed to assess other structural variables, such as developmental object relations (Coonerty, 1986; Ipp, 1986; Kwawer, 1980), boundary disturbances (Blatt & Ritzler, 1974), and object representations (Mayman, 1967), we can now examine the dynamic interplay among structural factors and approximate more closely the richness of Kernberg's and others' psychoanalytic theories. Doing this would be keeping alive Rapaport's dream regarding the place of the Rorschach in psychoanalytic theory.

REFERENCES

American Psychiatric Association. (1980). *Diagnostic and statistical manual of mental disorders* (3rd ed.). Washington, DC: Author.

American Psychiatric Association. (1987). *Diagnostic and statistical manual of mental disorders* (3rd ed. rev.). Washington, DC: Author.

Ames, L. (1966). Longitudinal survey of child Rorschach responses: Older subjects aged 10 to 16 years. *Genetic Psychological Monographs, 62,* 185–229.

Berg, J. (1990). Differentiating ego functions of borderline and narcissistic personalities. *Journal of Personality Assessment, 55,* 537–548.

Bion, W. (1967). *Second thoughts: Selected papers on psychoanalysis.* London: Heinemann.

Blatt, S., Brenneis, C., Schimek, J., & Glick, M. (1976). *A developmental analysis of the concept of the object on the Rorschach.* Unpublished manuscript, Yale University, New Haven, CT.

Blatt, S., & Lerner, H. (1983). The psychological assessment of object representation. *Journal of Personality Assessment, 47,* 7–28.

Blatt, S., & Ritzler, B. (1974). Thought disorder and boundary disturbances in psychosis. *Journal of Consulting and Clinical Psychology, 42,* 370–381.

Brenner, C. (1982). *The mind in conflict.* Madison, CT: International Universities Press.

Brierly, M. (1937). Affects in theory and practice. *Trends in psychoanalysis* (pp. 43–56). London: Hogarth Press.

Brouillette, C. (1987). *A Rorschach assessment of the character structure of anorexia nervosa and bulimia patients and of their mothers.* Unpublished doctoral dissertation, University of Toronto, Canada.

Collins, R. (1983). *Rorschach correlates of borderline personality.* Unpublished doctoral dissertation, University of Toronto, Canada.

Coonerty, S. (1986). An exploration of separation: Individuation themes in the borderline personality disorder. *Journal of Personality Assessment, 50,* 501–511.

Cooper, S. (1989). Recent contributions to the theory of defense mechanisms. *Journal of the American Psychoanalytic Association, 37,* 865–891.

Cooper, S., & Arnow, D. (1986). An object relations view of the borderline defenses: A review. In M. Kisson (Ed.), *Assessing object relations phenomena* (pp. 143–171). New York: International Universities Press.

Cooper, S., Perry, J., & Arnow, D. (1988). An empirical approach to the study of defense mechanisms: I. Reliability and preliminary validity of the Rorschach defense scale. *Journal of Personality Assessment, 52,* 187–203.

Cooper, S., Perry, J., & O'Connell, M. (1991). The Rorschach Defense scales: II. Longitudinal perspectives. *Journal of Personality Assessment, 56,* 191–201.

Exner, J. (1991). *The Rorschach: A comprehensive system* (Vol. 2, 2nd ed.). New York: Wiley.

Farris, M. (1988). Differential diagnosis of borderline and narcissistic personality disorders. In H. Lerner & P. Lerner (Eds.), *Primitive mental states and the Rorschach* (pp. 299–338). Madison, CT: International Universities Press.

Freud, A. (1936). *The ego and the mechanisms of defense.* New York: International Universities Press.

Freud, S. (1957). Instincts and the vicissitudes. In J. Strachey (Ed. & Trans.), *The standard edition of the complete psychological works of Sigmund Freud* (Vol. 14, 109–140). London: Hogarth Press. (Original work published 1915)

Freud, S. (1961). The ego and the id. In J. Strachey (Ed. & Trans.), *The standard edition of the complete psychological works of Sigmund Freud* (Vol. 19, 12–59). London: Hogarth Press. (Original work published 1923)

Fromm-Reichmann, F. (1950). *Principles of intensive psychotherapy.* Chicago: University of Chicago Press.

Gacono, C. (1988). *A Rorschach analysis of object relations and defensive structure and their relationship to narcissism and psychopathy in a group of antisocial offenders.* Unpublished doctoral dissertation, United States International University, San Diego, CA.

Gacono, C. (1990). An empirical study of object relations and defensive operations in antisocial personality. *Journal of Personality Assessment, 54,* 589–600.

Gacono, C., Meloy, J. R., & Berg, J. (1992). Object relations, defensive operations, and affective states in narcissistic, borderline, and antisocial personality. *Journal of Personality Assessment, 59,* 32–49.

Grala, C. (1980). The concept of splitting and its manifestations on the Rorschach. *Bulletin of the Menninger Clinic, 44,* 253–271.

Gunderson, J. (1986). Pharmacotherapy for patients with borderline personality disorders. *Archives of General Psychiatry, 43,* 698–700.

Guntrip, H. (1969). *Schizoid phenomena, object relations and the self.* New York: International Universities Press.

Hammond, J. (1984). *Object relations and defensive operations in gender identity disordered males.* Unpublished doctoral dissertation, United States International University, San Diego, CA.

Hoffer, W. (1968). Notes on the theory of defense. *The Psychoanalytic Study of the Child, 23,* 178–188.

Holt, R. (1970). *Manual for the scoring of primary process manifestations and their controls in Rorschach responses.* New York: Research Center for Mental Health.

Ipp, H. (1986). *Object relations of feminine boys: A Rorschach assessment.* Unpublished doctoral dissertation, York University, Toronto, Ontario, Canada.

Kernberg, O. (1975). *Borderline conditions and pathological narcissism.* New York: Aronson.

Kernberg, O. (1976). *Object relations theory and clinical psychoanalysis.* New York: Aronson.

Kernberg, O. (1977). The structural diagnosis of borderline personality organization. In P. Hartocollis (Ed.), *Borderline personality disorders* (pp. 57–121). New York: International Universities Press.

Kernberg, O. (1979). Two reviews of the literature on borderlines: An assessment. *Schizophrenia Bulletin, 5,* 53–58.

Kernberg, O. (1980). *Internal world external reality.* New York: Aronson.

Klein, M. (1935). A contribution to the psychogenesis of manic-depressive states. In *Contributions to psycho-analysis, 1921–1945* (pp. 282–310). London: Hogarth Press.

Klein, M. (1946). Notes on some schizoid mechanisms. In *Envy and gratitude and other works, 1946–1963* (pp. 1–12). New York: Delacorte Press/Seymore Lawrence.

Kohut, H. (1971). *The analysis of the self.* New York: International Universities Press.

Kohut, H. (1977). *The restoration of the self.* New York: International Universities Press.

Kohut, H. (1984). *How does analysis cure?* Chicago: University of Chicago Press.

Kolers, N. (1986). *Some ego functions in boys with gender identity disturbance.* Unpublished doctoral dissertation, York University, Toronto, Ontario, Canada.
Kris, A. (1984). The conflict of ambivalence. *The Psychoanalytic Study of the Child, 38,* 439–458.
Kris, A. (1984). *Free association: Method and process.* New Haven, CT: Yale University Press.
Kwawer, J. (1980). Primitive interpersonal modes, borderline phenomena, and Rorschach content. In J. Kwawer, H. Lerner, P. Lerner, & A. Sugarman (Eds.), *Borderline phenomena and the Rorschach test* (pp. 89–106). New York: International Universities Press.
LaPlanche, J., & Pontalis, J. (1973). *The language of psychoanalysis.* New York: Norton.
Leeuw, P. (1971). On the development of the concept of defense. *International Journal of Psychoanalysis, 52,* 51–58.
Lerner, H., Albert, C., & Walsh, M. (1987). The Rorschach assessment of borderline defenses. *Journal of Personality Assessment, 51,* 344–354.
Lerner, H., & Lerner, P. (1982). A comparative study of defensive structure in neurotic, borderline, and schizophrenic patients. *Psychoanalysis and Contemporary Thought, 5,* 77–113.
Lerner, H., & Lerner, P. (1986). Contributions of object relations theory towards a general psychoanalytic theory of thinking. *Psychoanalysis and Contemporary Thought, 9,* 469–513.
Lerner, H., Sugarman, A., & Gaughran, J. (1981). Borderline and schizophrenic patients: A comparative study of defensive structure. *Journal of Nervous and Mental Disease, 169,* 705–711.
Lerner, P. (1985). Current psychoanalytic perspectives on the borderline and narcissistic concepts. *Clinical Psychology Revue, 5,* 99–114.
Lerner, P. (1988). Rorschach measures of depression, the false self, and projective identification with narcissistic personality disorders. In H. Lerner & P. Lerner (Eds.), *Primitive mental states and the Rorschach* (pp. 71–94). Madison, CT: International Universities Press.
Lerner, P., & Lerner, H. (1980). Rorschach assessment of primitive defenses in borderline personality structure. In J. Kwawer, H. Lerner, P. Lerner, & A. Sugarman (Eds.), *Borderline phenomena and the Rorschach test* (pp. 257–274). New York: International Universities Press.
Levine, M., & Spivak, C. (1964). *The Rorschach index of repressive style.* Springfield, IL: Thomas.
Madison, P. (1961). *Freud's concept of repression and defense: Its theoretical and observational language.* Minneapolis: University of Minnesota Press.
Mayman, M. (1967). Object representations and object relationships in Rorschach responses. *Journal of Projective Techniques and Personality Assessment, 31,* 17–24.
Mayman, M. (1970). Reality contact, defense effectiveness, and psychopathology in Rorschach form level scores. In B. Klopfer, M. Meyer, & F. Brawer (Eds.), *Developments in Rorschach technique* (Vol. 3, pp. 11–44). New York: Harcourt-Brace-Jovanich.
Michaels, R. (1983, April). *Plenary address.* Paper presented at the Distortions of Personality Development and Their Management Symposium, Toronto, Canada.
Modell, A. (1975). A narcissistic defense against affects and the illusion of self-sufficiency. *International Journal of Psychoanalysis, 44,* 282–292.
Modell, A. (1984). *Psychoanalysis in a new context.* Madison, CT: International Universities Press.

Newman, K. (1980). Defense analysis in self psychology. In A. Goldberg (Ed.), *Advances in self psychology* (pp. 263–278). New York: International Universities Press.
Ogden, T. (1983). The concept of internal object relations. *International Journal of Psychoanalysis, 64,* 227–243.
Peebles, R. (1975). Rorschach as self-system in the telophasic theory of personality development. In P. Lerner (Ed.), *Handbook of Rorschach scales* (pp. 71–136). New York: International Universities Press.
Piran, N., & Lerner, P. (1987). *Piagetian cognitive development and ego development: A study of anorexic patients.* Unpublished manuscript, Toronto General Hospital, Canada.
Piran, N., & Lerner, P. (1988). Rorschach assessment of anorexia nervosa and bulimia. *Advances in Personality Assessment, 7,* 77–102.
Piran, N., Lerner, P., Garfinkle, P., Kennedy, S., & Brouillette, C. (1988). Personality disorders in anorexic patients. *International Journal of Eating Disorders, 7,* 589–600.
Pruitt, W., & Spilka, B. (1964). Rorschach empathy object relationship scale. In P. Lerner (Ed.), *Handbook of Rorschach scales* (pp. 315–323). New York: International Universities Press.
Pruyser, P. (1975). What splits in splitting. *Bulletin of the Menninger Clinic, 39,* 1–46.
Rapaport, D. (1958). An historical review of psychoanalytic ego psychology. In M. Gill (Ed.), *The collected papers of David Rapaport* (pp. 745–757). New York: Basic Books.
Rapaport, D., Gill, M., & Schafer, R. (1945–1946). *Diagnostic psychological testing* (2 vols.). Chicago: Year Book.
Reich, W. (1933). *Character analysis.* New York: Farrar, Straus, and Giroux.
Robbins, M. (1976). Borderline personality organization: The need for a new theory. *Journal of the American Psychoanalytic Association, 24,* 831–854.
Schafer, R. (1954). *Psychoanalytic interpretation in Rorschach testing.* New York: Grune and Stratton.
Schafer, R. (1968). The mechanisms of defense. *International Journal of Psychoanalysis, 49,* 49–62.
Searles, H. (1965). *Collected papers on schizophrenia and related subjects.* New York: International Universities Press.
Segal, H. (1973). *Introduction to the work of Melanie Klein.* London: Hogarth Press.
Spitzer, R., Endicott, J., & Robbins, E. (1975). Research Diagnostic Criteria (RDC). *Psychopharmacological Bulletin, 11,* 22–24.
Stolorow, R., & Lachmann, F. (1980). *Psychoanalysis of developmental arrest.* New York: International Universities Press.
Sullivan, H. (1962). *Schizophrenia as a human process.* New York: Norton.
Van-Der Keshet, J. (1988). *Anorexic patients and ballet students: A Rorschach analysis.* Unpublished doctoral dissertation, University of Toronto, Canada.
Winnicott, D. (1953). Transitional objects and transitional phenomena. *International Journal of Psychoanalysis, 34,* 89–97.
Winnicott, D. (1956). The antisocial tendency. In *Through paediatrics to psycho-analysis* (pp. 306–315). London: Hogarth Press.
Winnicott, D. (1961). Ego distortion in terms of true and false self. In *The maturational processes and the facilitating environment* (pp. 140–152). London: Hogarth Press.

Author Index

H

T

U

V

Subject Index

Note: Page numbers in *italics* refer to figures; those in **boldface** refer to tables.

A

B

Q

R

S